CONTENTS

We would both like to extend our sincere gratitude and appreciation to all the wonderful people who helped us out along the way, especially: Rich Rollman for keeping us up to date and for his mentoring efforts; David Turner for arranging things for us at Microsoft; Kathryn Malm for all the edits and for making sure we finished on time; and Cary Sullivan, Christina Berry, and the folks at Wiley for all their help and for trusting two brand new authors.

Alex would also like to thank: Ian Graham, Scott Isaacs, Adam Denning and Peter Weiss for sharing their writing experiences; my friends and my housemates for being patient while I typed away at the manuscript; my family for their love and support; my friends at IDRC and at Microsoft, and Faraz for teaching me the ways of the industry; and I wouldn't want to forget to thank all the 1s and 0s, for without them, we wouldn't get too far with these things called computers.

Faraz would also like to thank: My parents, Samir and Khatoon, and my brother, Umair, for their love and tireless support; my Aunt Naseem, Uncle Iftikhar, and cousins, Azhar and Mahnaz, for their continual encouragement; my advisor, Professor Tom Willemain, for helping me see the "big picture" and keeping me on track; my friend and co-author, Alex, for being the best partner a guy could ask for; and my good buddies, Sabahat, Awais, Masoud, Maroof, and Adil who taught me that when the going gets tough, the tough take coffee breaks. Finally, to the late Dr. Eqbal Ahmad, thank you for having been a part of my life and for showing me and so many thousands more, "the right path" by walking there first.

Technology is a funny business. One day everyone's screaming "object-oriented!" the next it's "push!" and today it's "XML!" How does one separate the wheat from the chaff?

That's not something we try to tackle in this book.

Our objective in this book is to show you how to apply XML to real world scenarios. Yes, we spend some time covering the conceptual details of XML—but that's the easy stuff. What we chose to write about are things that most books couldn't cover before: *how to use XML while creating real world applications.*

About XML

That XML is big is something you already know or you wouldn't be picking out books from this shelf.

If you're asking yourself what XML is and why on earth everyone's making so much noise about it, XML is the eXtensible Markup Language. It is a universal method for representing information that is especially well suited to distribution over the Internet. It is a technology that, aside from having a lot of hype, has the real potential to change the way we compute today and a technology that has the backing of virtually every major industry player.

From a lifecycle perspective, XML today is where HTML was in 1992. Between then and 1995, if you knew anything about HTML, you were in for the ride of your life. While it is dangerous to draw parallels in the technology business, we're confident saying that *now* is a good time to know how to use XML.

About "Applied XML"

We wrote this book to provide what most other XML books do not: the nitty-gritty, how-to details about working with XML.

To be fair, most other authors simply could not write about these things before because the industry just wasn't at that point where enough tools were available for one to do any serious work. Sure, you could make some toy applications that looked pretty or proved a point, but the support just wasn't out there for you to create "real applications." Thus, the vast majority of books written on XML so far have focused more on the concepts of XML and on more abstract models, or focused on presenting scenarios based on the promise of XML.

Even now, the industry isn't where we'd like it to be, but it has progressed hugely over the past year—so much so that there is currently enough support out there for developers to begin creating "real" applications that actually *do* something.

As developers, we've spent *a lot* of time pounding our heads against the wall wishing that the details surrounding XML were more lucid, especially those surrounding the DOM and XSL. We've read tomes upon tomes of information while working on XML and, honestly (and not meaning to be self-serving), we *wish* we had a book like this when we started out writing XML applications!

See, we believe very firmly in the induction model of learning; that it is easier to learn by looking at working examples than by pure concepts alone. For the longest time, those examples just weren't out there. By and large, they still aren't. So we learned the hard way: by making them ourselves. That's not necessarily the best thing to do in today's day and age.

Thus, our aim in this book is to change all that by giving you the tools you need to begin creating meaningful solutions using XML. That's why we titled this book *Applied XML*. We wrote this book in the hope that you won't have to go through those frustrating periods of "how do I do that?" Well okay, this book won't solve *all* your problems, but it will help alleviate a lot of them.

How This Book Is Organized

This book is organized in three major parts, and while it helps to read all of them, we've tried to keep each independent and self-contained.

Part One—XML—A Panoramic View

In Part One we start from simple concepts that you are familiar with and provide you with a scaffolding of strut-like information so you can climb to the top and see XML in its entirety. We begin with a very general approach to XML and then move into more of an industry-specific overview of where XML is and what is happening. We then jump straight into describing the W3C XML 1.0 standard and provide you with the details you need to begin creating XML documents.

- *Chapter 1, XML FAQ.* If you've never heard of XML, this is the place to start. In this chapter we present an overview of XML in a very broad and general context. It is laid out as a Frequently Asked Questions list, similar to those you find while browsing the Web.

- *Chapter 2, Pioneering the Electronic Frontier.* This chapter provides a more industry-specific overview of XML. It is presented from the perspective of a chief technology officer or a chief information officer interested in understanding the impact that XML will have on the industry as a whole and how it can provide both strategic and tactical benefits to your organization. In it we talk about XML from a systems architecture perspective and discuss several examples of real applications of XML. We close the chapter with a roundup of the technical support available for XML today.

- *Chapter 3, Details, Details.* In this chapter we delve straight into the fundamental details of creating XML documents. This chapter includes an overview of the official W3C XML 1.0 specification and covers the basic building blocks of XML documents and includes many examples. It also includes a primer on creating Document Type Definitions (DTDs) to help you define a formal structure to your documents and a discussion on namespaces in XML.

Part Two—XML Document Object Model

Part Two describes the Document Object Model (DOM) specification as outlined in the W3C Recommended specification. The DOM is the critical link that exposes XML to programmers. It is a layer of abstraction in the form of objects that isolates the programmer from the nitty-gritty details of working with text documents. Even more importantly, this layer of abstraction can be implemented on top of existing databases (for example, SQL or Oracle databases) and make the data appear to be XML.

- *Chapter 4, Introduction to Document Object Model (DOM).* In this chapter, we explain what the DOM is, why you would use it and give a high level rundown of how it is used.

- *Chapter 5, DOM Reference.* Here we jump straight into the internals of the DOM. There are various methods and properties that exist to help write applications. We present these details with several script-based examples. The majority of our examples are written in JavaScript and run under Microsoft Internet Explorer 5. If you don't know the details of JavaScript, don't worry, because we briefly go over what you need to know to understand the examples. A few VBScript examples are also included for programmers who deal only with VBScript.

- *Chapter 6, Using the DOM in Different Environments.* In this chapter we show how the DOM can be used from different languages and platforms. We cover several examples involving the two most predominant script-based languages, JavaScript and VBScript. In recognition that Java and XML are forecasted as the next great Web duo, we show how to use the DOM from Java by presenting working examples with three Java-based XML parsers (Datachannel XML parser, IBM XML parser for Java, and the SUN XML parser.) In addition, we talk about how to use the DOM from Java Servlets and Active Server Pages, two popular server-side platforms. Lastly, we introduce how to use the DOM from Visual Basic.

- *Chapter 7, XML Support in Internet Explorer 5*. In this chapter, we cover the specifics of the XML support that is provided with Internet Explorer 5 is outlined. The topics we cover include data types, namespaces, querying XML, XSL stylesheets, threading models, and asynchronous downloading.

After covering Chapters 4 through 7, you will have a firm understanding of the DOM. Knowing the details gives us all opportunity to be creative and apply our knowledge to real world scenarios. We dedicate the remaining three chapters in the DOM part to Scenarios.

- *Chapter 8, Internet Explorer 5 and Server-Side Scenario: Online Shopping Demo*. In this chapter we design and implement an online shopping site that uses Internet Explorer 5 as the client. This chapter covers important design issues by explaining how to use XML with the server. Active Server Pages are used to implement the server side processing for delivering catalogs and processing orders.

- *Chapter 9, Java Scenario: Online Shopping Demo Continued*. In this chapter, we extend the Online Shopping scenario by implementing a Java-based client.

- *Chapter 10, Visual Basic Scenario: DOMifier*. XML is not just limited to browsers; in this chapter, we explain how to build standalone desktop applications using the XML DOM. In it we build a Visual Basic application called the DOMifier. We've used this application throughout the book to assist you with learning and using the DOM.

Part Three—Presenting XSL—The XML Stylesheet Language

Perhaps the most visible application of XML will be through XSL, the XML Stylesheet Language. While XML provides a universal way of describing data, XSL provides a way for manipulating, transforming and displaying the data contained in XML documents. XSL is currently a W3C work in progress, however, partial implementations of it do exist.

- *Chapter 11, XSL Overview*. In this chapter, we provide a high level rundown of XSL. We present our arguments on why XSL is our method of choice for displaying XML by comparing it with other stylesheet formats. We also provide several scenarios of how XSL can be used in an organizational context and describe scenarios of deployment from a systems architecture perspective

- *Chapter 12, XSL Syntax*. Here we introduce you to the syntax of XSL. In it we go over the basic vocabulary of XSL and provide several examples of how to use XSL to display information stored in XML documents in your browser. This chapter includes a reference of XSL elements.

- *Chapter 13, Querying XML with XSL*. In this chapter we go into greater details of the XSL syntax and focus on XSL patterns, a way for identifying information stored in XML documents. Topics include pattern matching, filters, Boolean operators, set operators, comparison operators, and pattern methods.

- *Chapter 14, XSL Formatting Model*. In this chapter we spend some time discussing the second portion of the W3C working draft on XSL devoted to formatting. This chapter will help you see where XSL is going and help you decide if now is the time for you to start implementing XSL solutions.

- *Chapter 15, Putting It All Together*. This chapter is devoted to showing you how to use XSL in your site solution. In a nutshell, XSL is used to convert your XML to some presentation medium. In this chapter we present how to use XSL with varying degrees of complexity depending on your situation. We present various site designs that use XSL and explain when each one would be used. We close the chapter out by developing working scenarios to show all the details of designing a site that uses XSL.

Who Should Read This Book

We've written this book so that it can benefit a wide array of readers, from novices to experts; our intention is to bring all readers to the latter stage, regardless of where you start.

That being said, we should qualify that by saying that this is book is primarily for people who are in the business of creating solutions and have been working with information technology for some time. We neither expect nor presume you to have any prior knowledge of XML but we do assume that you understand programming concepts and are familiar with the basic terminology of the information technology business.

Here are some generalized reader-roadmaps that may help you decide if this book is for you:

- **If you're a Web developer** looking for models and solutions on how to create XML solutions, then we suggest skimming over Part One and jumping straight into Parts Two and Three.
- **If you're new to XML** and are looking to see XML in its entirety (top down and bottom up), then you should start with Part One and move on from there to Part Three and then to Part Two.
- **If you're a hard core applications developer** looking for specific information on how to leverage XML into your applications then you will love Part Two.
- **If you're a technical writer** or someone responsible for maintaining and writing organizational documentation and want to see how you can leverage XML, Parts One and Three are for you.
- **If you're a CIO,** CTO, or responsible for determining the strategic and/or tactical adoption of technology in your organization, then Part One is a must for you.
- **If you've never heard of computers,** the Internet or Information Technology, then this book is not for you.

Tools You Will Need

To get the most out of this book, we expect that you will have access to a personal computer or workstation. We make no pretensions that you will learn everything by reading alone—we expect you to get your hands dirty working with XML. If you are looking for web-based solutions, you will find that most of our solutions are tailored for Internet Explorer 5, though as other browsers become XML compliant, most of our examples should work with little or no modifications. From a software tools perspective, we've tried to include everything that you will need (and more!) on the CD-ROM.

What's on the CD-ROM

Our CD-ROM may well be worth the price of the book itself! We've packed it chock full of utilities that you will find very handy for working with XML, no matter what you intend to do with XML. Here's some of the tools we include:

- Copies of all our code examples
- Microsoft Internet Explorer 5
- IBM XML parser for Java
- Link to the Sun Java parser
- DataChannel Java parser
- XML Spy (an XML editor)
- Link to Netscape's Gecko
- Links to W3C XML 1.0 Recommendations and supplemental documentation

Concluding Thoughts

To be honest, we wrote this book for ourselves as college students; we like books that avoid fluff and get right to the point. We only buy books that help us get things done, not books that look pretty on a bookshelf. And we expect you probably feel the same way (why would you bother framing a book that is going to be obsolete in less than two years anyway?) That XML is big is obvious. That you can use XML in a variety of situations is equally obvious. We see no point in flogging those dead horses. *How to use* XML is not as obvious. That's what we've focused on throughout this book.

Hopefully, this is the kind of information you are looking for. If it is, then welcome aboard and let's get on to making XML work for you!

PART ONE

XML—A Panoramic View

CHAPTER 1

XML FAQ

This chapter tries to squeeze the essence of XML into a few pages. It is intended for readers who are looking for an executive summary of XML—the more technical aspects are discussed in subsequent chapters. This chapter is for people who don't have a lot of time and yet want to understand what XML is and how it fits in the grand scheme of things.

An Executive Summary of XML

XML is hot. You've heard the hype, you've read the reports, and now you want to understand for yourself what it is all about. Great! This book's for you! We're skeptics by nature—most engineers are—and words like "killer app" inspire us to come out with guns blazing to shoot down the idea. So it is with a little embarrassment that we have to admit that XML is the real deal.

In this chapter, we argue our case in the form of a FAQ (frequently asked question) list, answering questions that we've been asked and that we asked when we first started. By the time you've read this chapter, you should have a pretty good idea of the big picture and have enough information to hold your own at the next informal discussion about hot technologies with your friends and colleagues, bosses and underlings, and maybe even—though this may be stretching it a bit— mom and dad.

What Is XML?

XML is an acronym that stands for eXtensible Markup Language. It is a method for describing information so that every computer, and most humans, can understand it. Think of it as the "Esperanto" of the computer world but with one fundamental difference: Everyone can understand it.

What Is "Markup" and Why Do We Use It?

When we were younger, our English teachers used a lot of red ink on our essays to clearly delineate where we had made spelling and grammatical mistakes. *Markup* refers to the instructions written on top of our essay by the teacher, including things such as "you'll never be a writer." Actually the term was first used in the paper printing industry when copy editors would write in the margin of paper telling the printer where to use a particular typeface (for example, "use bold print" or "drop cap here"). The word processing industry has largely been a spin-off of the paper printing industry and so the instructions for telling a computer when to use bold or underline styles were also called markup.

Today we've extended the concept of markup to encode instructions that can tell an application what to do with information chunks. Think of markup as street signs on a road. You see a stop sign, and you stop. You see a detour, and you take a detour. The road is your raw information, and the street signs are the markup you need to navigate your way around.

Keeping this analogy in mind, XML is a standard method of putting up road signs that help you navigate your way through the sheer magnitude of information on the Web.

Is XML Like HTML?

XML is sort of like HTML, but not quite. Both HTML (HyperText Markup Language) and XML come from the same parent technology: SGML (Standard Generalized Markup Language). SGML is an older technology that was heavily deployed across mainframes and so-called "legacy systems" for financial institutions, defense systems, government information systems, to name a few. SGML remains a very powerful technology, but it is not for everyone—in its purest form, it's like swatting a fly with a bazooka.

In deference to those of us who wanted to do only some of the things that SGML could do, such as displaying formatted text without having to learn the entire complicated language, HTML was invented. HTML had to be simple and easy so that everyone could use it on a variety of computer platforms (for example, PCs, Unix machines, and mainframes). Tough order, but HTML delivered and today is ubiquitous over the Web.

As great as it is for displaying information, HTML is not the best way to represent information. Enter XML: a universal method for representing information. XML is a *complementary technology* to HTML, not a replacement of it.

For Example...

Let's take, for example, a clip of HTML that's being used to represent information from an address book. To keep it simple, let's say this address book only contains information about names, phone numbers, and addresses. Our address book clip could look like this:

```
<p><strong><u>Contact Information:</u></strong></p>
<p>Name: Alley Gator</p>
<p>Phone: 515-5551235</p>
<p>Street Address: 112 Main Street</p>
<p>City: Muddy Waters</p>
<p>State: FL</p>
<p>ZIP: 55544</p>
```

From a computer's perspective, there is no indication of the inherent structure of the information. You might think that, "anything with a colon in front of it is a field name," but there's an underlying structure to this data that you cannot pick out from this clip. To show you what we mean, look at a snippet of XML that could be used to represent the preceding information:

```
<Contact_Information>
  <Name>Alley Gator</Name>
```

```
<Phone_Number>515-5551235</Phone_Number>
<Address>
    <Street_Address>112, Main Street</Street_Address>
    <City>Muddy Waters</City>
    <State>FL</State>
    <ZIP>55544</ZIP>
</Address>
</Contact_Information>
```

See what we mean by the "structure of the information?" Visual inspection of the above code tells us something about how the information is organized. By looking at it, we can tell that Contact_Information consists of a Name, a Phone_Number, and an Address field. Furthermore, the Address section can be broken into subfields. Armed with the knowledge of the structure, we can then perform more interesting tasks, such as displaying only the information contained in the Name and Phone_Number tags. We could also perform more intelligent searches based on information contained within certain tags as opposed to information contained within entire documents.

So XML Has Its Own Set of Tags Such as <Name> and <Address>?

No, as the name implies, the set of tags is *extensible* so you can create them as you go along. Although a few tag names are reserved in XML, you can pretty much create your own tags to represent your data as descriptively as you'd like.

Why Don't They Just Add More Descriptive Tags to HTML?

More descriptive tags aren't added to HTML mainly because it's too hard to think of a set of tags that would describe every type of data in existence. It is easier to create a *standard method* of creating tags to describe your data so that you can richly represent your data.

What's the Fundamental Concept Here?

The fundamental concept is that XML allows you to separate data from display, and once you know the structure of a data set, you can do more things with it. To draw an analogy, think of a picture of a building versus its blueprint. With a picture, you can only see the building from one angle. Feed a picture into a computer, and it won't do very much beyond displaying it as is. Feed a blueprint into a computer, and you can generate 3-D views, change the layout, and try different arrangements. The view of the building from the angle in the picture is, therefore, just one of many of the results that can be achieved by manipulating the blueprint. Analogy: Information stored in an XML format is a blueprint, whereas information represented in HTML is just a picture (see Figure 1.1).

Is HTML Obsolete?

HTML is a great technology. For many of us, it has changed the way we live and even think by assisting what Vanevar Bush in 1945 called our *associative indexing* thought processes. HTML is one with the Web. Are we really going to get rid of it altogether? Is no technology holy?

First off, no technology is holy. We create technologies so that we can break them down and replace them with something better. That being said, we still have a need to display information, and we humans want visually appealing sites. XML is not going to change our fundamental desires as humans. So, no, HTML is not doomed or obsolete. It will still be around for some time. XML is not out to replace HTML; it's there to complement it and to perform a function that HTML was never designed for in the first place.

Is XML an Application? What Does It Do?

XML is not an application. It is not something like Microsoft Word or Netscape Navigator that you can double-click and run. It is a form of expression that's been standardized, just as any language is characterized and standardized by rules of grammar. Because it is a language, it is only as good as the person or persons who speak it, write in it, and use it.

Vanevar Bush

In the article "As We May Think" (*The Atlantic Monthly,* July 1945), Vanevar Bush introduced the concept of *associative indexing,* the belief that human beings do not think linearly, but that our thoughts are constantly bouncing around and certain sensory input results in thought processes in a nonlinear fashion. For example, when you look at the word *tree,* your next thought could be of a natural tree, a branched diagram, a memory associated with a tree, or anything else. The process of "thinking the next thought" based on stimuli is what Bush called *associative indexing.*

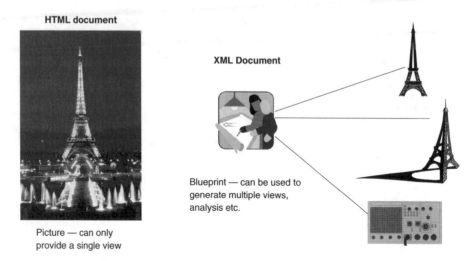

HTML document

Picture — can only
provide a single view

XML Document

Blueprint — can be used to
generate multiple views,
analysis etc.

Figure 1.1 XML is to HTML what a blueprint is to a picture.

Why Isn't XML Called "EML" Instead?

Engineers and computer scientists always have a good reason. In this case, it's because XML sounds cooler. We geeks and nerds like things that sound cool. *X* has a particularly enigmatic aura about it (for example, The X-Files, X-Men, and *X* marks the spot). XML is cool. Besides, EML sounds like it's for weenies.

What Can You Do with XML?

We're tempted to say just about anything, but that's too abstract. Here are some more tangible examples of what you can do with XML:

Electronic commerce. Far and away the most hyped application of XML is electronic commerce. Because XML gives you a rich way of describing information, you can create more intelligent transport mechanisms to conduct business over the Web. Chapter 2 explores this application area in more detail.

Creating other markup languages. XML is not just another markup language. You could say it is trying to be the mother of all languages by creating a standard method for describing your information. That being true, nothing is stopping you from creating information to further describe more information (that is, a language). If you think about it, one day HTML could be an application of XML! Other examples of markup languages that are XML applications include CML

(Chemical Markup Language, which is used by members of the scientific community), CDF (Channel Definition Format, used in push technology applications), and OFX (Open Financial Exchange, an initiative launched by several companies to standardize information exchange in the financial sector).

Online banking.   Most banks are moving in this direction. Although the security protocols and requirements are more stringent than other applications, XML is flexible enough to be used to enable these applications.

Push technology.   This is one of those buzzwords from not too long ago. It is also known as *webcasting*. Push technology refers to the idea of the user indicating general areas of interest that he or she would like information about from a particular server. The server then detects the request and sends the user periodic (or on demand) updates to any related information. This information is then downloaded to the user's cache and is available for offline browsing. For example, in the PointCast browser, we simply indicate the areas of interest we'd like to read about, and the server then "pushes" that information to us periodically and stores it on the local cache. We can then browse through the information at our own pace. Figure 1.2 shows how the PointCast browser lets users customize the topics in which they are interested. An application of XML known as the Channel Definition Format (CDF) is used to richly encode the information sent to and from the client. Similar and grander applications of push technology will be engendered by XML.

Advanced search engines.   This is one of our favorite applications. A typical search on the Web today results in several hundred thousand matches because search engines don't have a way of differentiating content due to the limited number of HTML tags (see Figure 1.3). Instead, they perform searches based on the entire document's text or, at best, on the information contained in the *meta tags*. Meta tags are reserved tags in HTML that are not used for display per se; they are a kind of placeholder for people to use as they see fit. Many search engines look for information contained in the meta tags when responding to a query.

When XML is widely adopted, search engines will be able to search based on the content of particular tags, for example `<subject>`.

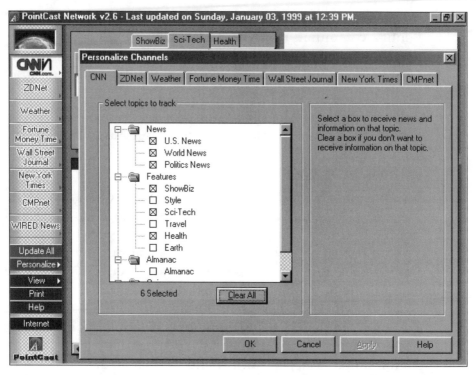

Figure 1.2   Selecting areas of interest you want pushed to you in the PointCast Network's browser.

Let's say you're interested in articles with the `<subject>` tag of Operations Research, a branch of industrial engineering. The search results will include only matches to pages that have a `<subject>` tag and whose contents of that tag include "Operations Research." In doing so, you eliminate all the hundreds of thousands of pages that may have the words *operations* and *research* mentioned somewhere in the document (for example, in an article on medicine or defense that's not relevant for your purpose).

Web-based control systems.   This is one of the most exciting areas for XML applications. Because your information is now meaningfully structured, you can encode it to mean anything. Why not use the Web to control your kitchen appliances, bathroom faucet, and home lighting while you are at the office? Thousands of people will be creating applications like these in the near future, and our bet is that the background technology will be XML.

Agents.   This is another of our favorite applications and probably one of the most fascinating applications of artificial intelligence. Agents

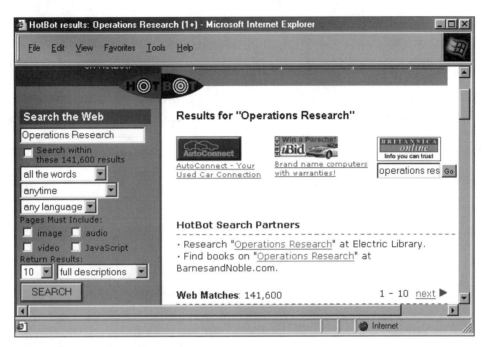

Figure 1.3 Results from a typical search engine.

are expressions of consciousness dissociated from your corporeal form. They are essentially software-based assistants that perform tasks for you based on your individual preferences, for example, performing specific research for you, controlling your schedule, and managing your stock portfolio. Agents are still relatively new, and people are doing a lot of great work in this area to use software to translate human preferences, at the same time conforming to existing information site structures. Translating human preferences is, generally speaking, very complicated, and you need a very rich way of describing information before you can communicate your desires to a piece of software. XML gives developers the flexibility they need to create more powerful agents.

Who Makes the XML Standard?

No single company makes the XML standard. It is an *open standard* like HTML, which means that a group of companies, individuals, and organizations get together and agree on what should or should not be included in the standard. The XML standard, like the HTML standard, is an official recommendation of the World Wide Web Consortium (the W3C). This consortium is comprised of many companies, including

Microsoft, Netscape, IBM, Sun, and Oracle; organizations such as the computer science department at MIT; and individuals. When the W3C approves a standard, it becomes the standard adopted by the professional world. Keep in mind, however, that these standards are not legally binding like traffic laws or building codes; some companies may choose to modify them, which is why the same page may look different in Netscape Navigator from Microsoft's Internet Explorer. By and large, though, companies stick to the recommendations of the W3C.

We've Heard of Super Technologies Before. Why Is XML Different? Why Will the World Accept It?

Good question. We believe that XML is here to stay for several reasons.

XML is an open standard ratified by the World Wide Web Consortium and, more important, almost all the major industry players have already announced their commitment to the XML standard. To date, companies that have announced support of the XML standard include Sun Microsystems, Netscape Communications, Microsoft Corporation, IBM, Oracle Corporation, Adobe Systems Inc., Hewlett Packard Co., and Corel Corporation.

This kind of mass commitment doesn't happen very often. These companies have agreed to a standard because each has a voice in it and each has the ability to track the development of the standard. By having their internal development teams follow the progression of the standards, these companies can have their products ready at the same time the standard is announced. None of the consortium members has a clear advantage over the others, ensuring a level playing field.

HTML, despite the incalculable benefits it bestowed to the Web, inadvertently created a huge hole in the arena of exchanging of structured information. The Web has very quickly become messy and difficult to navigate; if the same underlying technology were to persist, it would quickly become an unusable chaotic mess. Necessity is the mother of invention and, quite simply, XML is needed and needed now.

If XML Is a Universal Information Exchange Format, What Happens to Existing Databases?

XML is an information *exchange format*. XML information, like HTML, is the vehicle for exchanging information over the Web. The diagram in Figure 1.4 illustrates this concept more clearly.

Current information exchange model between client and server.
NOTE: Requires constant exchange of formatting information.

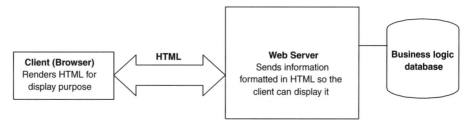

Information exchange model between client and server with XML.

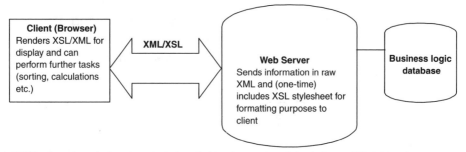

NOTE: Once the stylesheet is cached, the only thing that needs updating is the raw XML information.

Figure 1.4   Old and new models for information exchange.

Someday (and that day may never come) database companies may agree to a common primary data format. Presently, however, most information is stored in a variety of proprietary database formats. RDBMs (relational database management systems) are excellent for data storage and retrieval; however, sharing the information they contain remains a problem. Most organizations are quickly recognizing the tremendous need to make the information contained in their internal databases accessible via the Web. Various reasons exist for doing so, including better communication between employees, roving executives who need information for their meetings, and the movement toward e-commerce. The idea is that you don't want or need the entire database at your fingertips as you query the database from the Web. At the same time, you don't want the information "dumbed down"—that is, devoid of structure—so much that you can't perform further analysis at your end (say, generate graphs). The solution, therefore, is to use

XML as a transport mechanism for sending the data from your database to clients via their browsers, for example, where they can perform further manipulation. The client and the server will exchange information in XML, and the server and the database engine will have translators between them to convert the XML information such as a query into a format used by the database engine (say, SQL).

How Does XML Affect the Way We Think of Documents?

Traditionally, we've thought of a document as a holistic entity in which elements such as content, organization, and display are all merged into one unit. This model dates back to the codex and papyrus scrolls and has persisted in most of today's WYSIWYG (what you see is what you get) word processors (for example, WordPerfect and Microsoft Word). This model existed as a function of the technology we had available to us. With today's technology, it behooves us to start storing information in more natural and instinctive ways (see "Vanevar Bush").

A new model for storing information entails a distinction between content, organization, and display. Figure 1.5 illustrates these two models.

By separating base elements of a document, we can treat them independently and perform more efficient and advanced manipulations. For instance, we can sort content without worrying about how it looks. Once we've sorted the data the way we want it, we can then focus on displaying it. Breaking systems into simpler pieces is what engineering is all about. XML is continuing the same philosophy by extending it to the world of information exchange.

If XML Is Only Concerned with Content and Structure, How Do I Display It?

There are many ways to display XML. One of the major initiatives is the XML Stylesheet Language (XSL). Part Three of this book goes into more details about XSL, but for now, suffice it to say that XSL is another open standard under consideration by the W3C. It is specifically devoted to displaying XML and, therefore, is simpler and more powerful than other ways of displaying XML data. XSL gives you the ability to manipulate the data (for example, sorting or selective display), at the same time letting you format it using syntax similar to HTML.

Other ways of displaying XML data include using somewhat traditional techniques (anything that is more than two years old in the computer world is considered traditional) like Dynamic HTML (DHTML) with Cascading Stylesheets (CSS) and many new initiatives with even longer acronyms. XSL, however, is likely to emerge as the dominant way to display XML content.

The key advantage to displaying data with XSL—or any other initiative—is that you can display the same information in many ways without having to make a call to the server to generate a view for you. If the data is in XML, clients can choose whether they want to view it as a table, a bulleted list, a pie chart, or even in a different language! Figure 1.6 illustrates this feature.

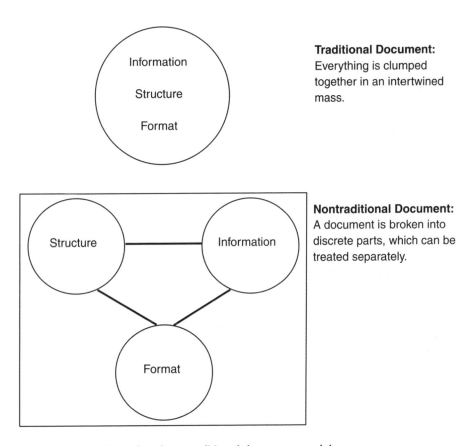

Figure 1.5 Traditional and nontraditional document models.

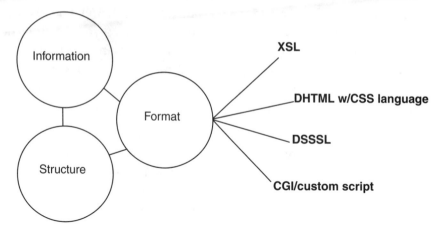

Figure 1.6 Ways of displaying XML.

Too Many Acronyms! How Do They All Relate to One Another?

In the business of computer-related technologies, there are never enough acronyms. However, we feel your pain. Figure 1.7 should help clarify things a bit.

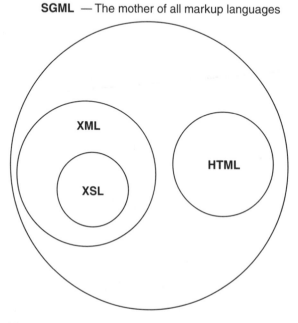

Figure 1.7 SGML, XML, XSL, and HTML genealogy.

Is There Any Way of Making Sure that Data Is Structured in a Particular Way? Can the Structure of an XML Document Be Checked?

Yes, there is. Since we're talking about applications like e-commerce where the data being exchanged must be according to a rigid form, it is necessary to ensure that the data we're sending or receiving conforms to a particular structure.

Currently the most common way to structure XML documents is to use an SGML template format called a *Document Type Definition* (DTD). A DTD is an ugly piece of code that defines the allowable structures in an XML document. We call it ugly because its format is nonintuitive and extremely rigid. The analogy is that DTDs are to XML interpreters (parsers) what the Rosetta stone was to archeologists looking to translate hieroglyphics.

Having a DTD is not enough—there has to be something that performs the actual check. A software engine called a *parser* performs the actual check on the data to make sure it conforms to the DTD. This process is called *validation*. An XML document that conforms to a DTD is called a *valid* XML document. We take a closer look at creating valid XML documents in Chapter 3.

As we mentioned above, we don't like DTDs because they're hard to work with. In the same way that we think the best way for displaying XML is to use an XML-based language (XSL), we believe that a schema syntax based on XML is the best way to describe the structure of a XML document. Currently there are two proposed specifications being looked at to remedy the shortcomings of DTDs: the XML Data and XML Data Content Description (DCD). Schemas based on XML are similar in purpose to DTDs, but the syntax is more friendly and intuitive.

What If I Don't Want the Data Validated?

If you don't want your XML data validated, don't link it to a DTD or schema. Provided the XML document is *well formed*, you won't have any problems. The diagram in Figure 1.8 shows the general scheme of how a parser interprets XML.

What Does "Well Formed" Mean? What Are the Details I Need To Know about Writing XML Syntax?

Well formed refers to properly structured markup syntax. Most HTML parsers (yes, browsers have HTML parsers for interpreting HTML) are

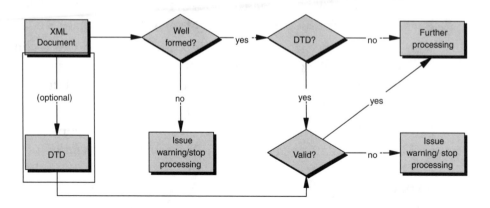

Figure 1.8 How a parser interprets XML.

kind to a fault in terms of tolerating poorly formatted markup syntax (for example, unclosed tags or tags nested out of sequence). The powers that be have decided that XML is not going to be that forgiving, which is very important because it forces authors to structure their information correctly. Recall the blueprint analogy we used earlier. Imagine your blueprint didn't contain a pillar where it was needed—the whole building could collapse. Well formed XML documents are documents that are structurally correct. Using the same analogy, a valid XML document is a blueprint of a building that is structurally correct and passes all government regulations.

When you create XML documents, you have to be very particular about closing all tags, nesting them properly, and using the right syntax. Also, the W3C recommends (recommendations by the W3C can be considered specifications) XML parsers to be case sensitive; thus, the following code clip would not be acceptable:

```
<ADDRESS>110 Main Street</address>
```

However, each of the following examples would be acceptable:

```
<address>110 Main Street</address>
<Address>110 Main Street</Address>
<ADDRESS>110 Main Street</ADDRESS>
```

Each of these three samples would be treated as separate entities altogether by an XML parser. Chapter 3 goes into more details about these issues.

Why Do We Need a Universal Data Format? Why Can't We Just Make Our Own Formats for Individual Projects?

You could make your own formats for individual projects. In fact, in some cases where secrecy is very important and you don't want to share information outside your organization under any circumstances, you may well want to create your own proprietary formats. In that case, XML may not be what you need. However, you should be aware that it is possible to encrypt your XML stream, thus preserving security and giving you flexibility in programming.

A basic philosophy needs to be accepted before you embark on using XML: We live in a world where communication is the key to success. The better the communication infrastructure your company deploys internally (that is, between employees) and externally (that is, with customers and suppliers), the better its prospects for success.

Once you accept this belief, you quickly realize that at present, there is no way to engender communication with everyone. Fluency in English and German won't help you a lick if you're in France trying to do business. In the computer world, HTML has been remarkably successful for creating a way for us to display information for one another to see. Though seeing may be believing, it is a form of one-way communication. For communication to be truly successful, it must be at least bilateral and preferably multilateral.

Although many languages purport to be cross platform in nature, they only handle the computer aspect of control and communication. What about the human form? Where does that go? What about the information that we want and need? XML is the missing link that completes the promise of languages like Java and Perl.

How Does XML Affect the Nature of Businesses Today? Are Browsers Going to Disappear? Are Relational Database Management System (RDBMS) Packages Going to Disappear? Is XML the Herald of Next-Generation Applications?

If we only had a crystal ball! The honest truth is that we don't know for sure. We can, however, make some intelligent guesses by looking at the big picture.

We think that XML is going to revolutionize the way information is exchanged by enabling the exchange of intelligent data. In doing so, the information processing will be more efficient and more intelligent.

Loosely translated, everything gets multiplied by X, where X is an acceleration factor of orders of magnitude.

The effect that XML is likely to have on browser technology in the long term may be to increase client dependency on the browser—the browser could start housing more and more applications. Eventually, full-blown applications may be run out of your browser. Imagine using your browser as a word processor or for spreadsheet analysis that can analyze data acquired from anywhere on the Web. XML could have a very positive reaction on the browser market. Some experts call this the birth of "OS agnostic machines."

Alternatively, because an XML stream is universally parseable, it is possible that you could just as easily bypass the browser altogether and create your own standalone application without the overhead of a browser. If you want to use XML as an instruction media for your remote home lighting system, does it really have to be tied to a browser?

For high-level programming languages like Java, XML is a boon. As some executives say, "XML gives Java something to do." Using XML as the standard format for exchanging information, programs written in these languages can easily exchange information with one another.

For the makers of database engines, it is a blessing because it removes much of the standards wars involved in exchanging information between different systems and making it available on the Web. Of course, it does mean that they will still have to agree on universal DTDs, but it is certainly a major step in the right direction.

Summary

What it all boils down to is this: XML is a universal format for exchanging information between software components that is legible to both computers and human beings. XML creates a lingua franca for the computer world that has been missing for the longest time. To illustrate how truly significant this is, imagine a world in which everyone could speak the same language and at the same time, maintain their societal customs, norms, and values. Imagine the tremendous potential for world peace and global prosperity that would be engendered by a universal language and a ubiquitous communication structure. Since everyone could communicate with one another, the sum total of human research would become immediately accessible. War would become redundant. Okay, call us idealists, but we believe that if everyone could communicate with one another perfectly, we'd have no conflicts and live in a world of global prosperity and happiness for all. That being true, XML is the closest thing we can see as being the tool for engendering utopia among computer users.

CHAPTER 2

Pioneering the Electronic Frontier

I n Chapter 1, we talked a little about XML and where it fit in the grand scheme of things. This chapter is geared toward Chief Information Officers (CIOs), managers, technical consultants, management consultants, and people are interested in the big picture of where XML can and will fit in your organization. In this chapter, we explore in some detail how XML is and will continue to affect the electronic frontier. XML has had a lot of hype surrounding it, and this chapter tries to separate myth from reality. We look at several applications of XML in an attempt to help you visualize how XML fits your particular information exchange needs. We also talk about some of the latest up-and-coming so-called killer apps that are based on XML. Finally, we provide you with enough information to decide whether now is the best time for your organization to deploy XML solutions.

The Philosophical Spiel

"Okay, so XML seems pretty cool, but why should I bother?" If you're asking yourself this question, you've come to the right chapter.

Humanity is continually trying to push the frontiers of what it considers its sphere of influence. Initially, this was manifested in the exploration of physical space—sailing the oceans, domesticating animals for transportation, learning to fly, building rockets to leap into outer space. And while we continue our exploration of physical space, we've started exploring more than just the physical world. Over the past few decades, we have started creating our own world, now affectionately called *cyber-space*. In exploring it, we have begun the most interesting journey yet: the exploration of our own inherent potential. The frontier, as a concept, has moved beyond physical exploration to the discovery of our minds.

As a civilization grows, it learns the benefits of cooperation. It learns the simple rule that many minds, working together, are better than one working in isolation. It also finds that the way to engender cooperation is to use communication as a tool. The Internet is perhaps the greatest example of the realization of this philosophy.

The potential of the Web has been harped upon by the best minds. To us, the best part of the Web is that we can order a pizza without having to dial the phone. However, we do concede that the Web is good for more than just ordering pizza. People far more qualified than us have been predicting for the longest time that the Web will be used for every-thing, including playing games, socializing, performing banking trans-actions, paying utility bills, buying anything from anywhere, or getting medical consultations. Virtually every facet of life is predicted to be associated with the Web in some form or fashion. You could make a very strong argument that technologically, we've reached the point where we can enable such ideas. For almost every example we've enu-merated, at least one or more Web sites currently provide such services. However, the reality is that while you can do a lot of this, you can't do all of it in an integrated fashion. There is no connectivity between these small islands of technology.

Figures 2.1 and 2.2 summarize the general problem for which XML is expected to provide a solution.

One reason we cannot do it is because of the nonubiquitous representa-tion of data. Let's face it, at just about every level, human communica-tion is flawed. We are rarely able to say things in a way that always appeals to everyone and certainly not in a way that everyone will accept. Some of it has to do with language differences, cultural differ-ences, our perceptions, or our current mind-set. The same rationale applies to the information technology world. Although we have a digi-tal format for digitizing and representing nearly every form of data, no

Figure 2.1 The general problem—islands of technology without ubiquitous intercommunication.

universal convention exists. While the Internet certainly is a universal information transmission media, it is not yet a ubiquitous *communication* media, that is, it does not provide a universal language that all users (clients) are able to process.

The net result is that we have created many isolated pockets of technology. Although it may be safe to say that all of these pockets conceivably hold keys to communication, none of them provides a complete solution that is ubiquitously usable. How many times have you had problems working with files in different formats, say opening Microsoft

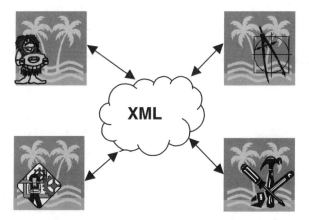

Figure 2.2 The general solution—use XML as a communication language for exchanging information between the islands.

Word documents on a Unix machine or processing information started in Oracle database in a complicated CAD package or simulation model? Similarly, why isn't it possible to convert all your accounting information from Excel, Quicken, or Microsoft Money into line items for calculating the taxes you owe the IRS (with automated reflection of updated rules) and then file that over the Internet? Sure, there are ways to get around these problems (usually involving a lot of manual "cut and paste" operations), but rarely is there a complete solution. Any solution almost always involves of large degree of customization and human interaction and is thus, inherently piecemeal at best. (We're not trying to knock humans here—we think humans are great—however, we believe they really ought to be doing more useful work than cutting and pasting.)

This is not a new problem; engineers and computer scientists have been aware of this for several decades. The extremely popular solution was—and persists as—"Live with it." When HTML came along, it was not as significant a technological leap as it was a leap in the standardization of technology. It provided a standard way for *displaying* information on virtually any computer—one where no private licensing was required nor any royalties due. XML, as a solution, is not so much a technological breakthrough, again, as it is a *standardization of technology* breakthrough.

XML: The Mother of All Web Languages

In the most basic sense, XML is not so much a computer language as a standard for defining all other markup languages. *Markup languages* is a generic term that is roughly applied to all information transmission languages that are text-based and use special text characters (markup) that contain additional information about the content from the raw content (data) itself.

To put things in perspective, let's use a concept with which we're pretty familiar: human languages. Just as the human speech apparatus can create an infinite number of sounds, only a finite set of those sounds when used in a finite set of arrangements can be understood in terms of human speech. You can make many noises with your mouth but in order to communicate, you need to speak words and sentences, all of which are members of the set called language. There are many languages. Languages are defined by society and each society is different. For each language, a finite (though expandable) list of words is created in the shape of dictionaries. In addition, the language dictates something called grammar, which classifies and controls the way these words can be arranged. One part of grammar is punctuation, which gives us additional information to help us differentiate sentences and words.

Coming back to the computer world, we've come to accept that alphanumeric text is the easiest format to transmit data so that computing devices can interpret it (using Unicode, we're not limited to English characters—more on that later in this chapter). In terms of our analogy, think of these alphanumeric characters as sounds that the human speech apparatus can create. Think of markup as punctuation.

XML comes in at a level above society (something that humans would never accept). XML dictates exactly how languages can be created; that is, it defines a grammar that all other languages must follow. The key point here is that the grammar the XML defines is flexible enough for each language to create its own dictionary and grammar.

This is incredibly important. Using our analogy again, XML has essentially achieved the equivalent of describing a way for creating virtually all human languages such that each can functionally remain as it is now and simultaneously provide a way for everyone to understand one another. Essentially, all languages become dialects of one base language. Figure 2.3 illustrates this idea.

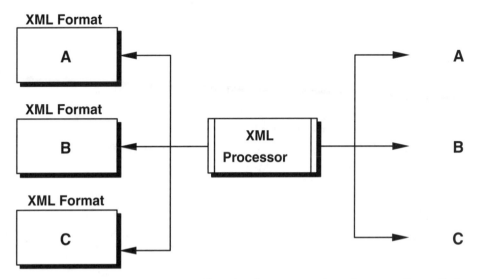

Figure 2.3 XML defines a way for all markup languages to be unique yet allows all of them to be interpreted the same way.

What this means is that if you have a tool that can understand XML, you have a tool that can understand all other markup languages. The implications and implementations of this are entirely what this book is about.

Why Not HTML?

In case you're wondering why, if we've already agreed that HTML is a universal method of exchanging information over the Web, we can't continue to use it for more complicated information exchange, the answer lies in the nature of HTML.

HTML was invented with the specific purpose of providing a universal set of tags for *displaying* information. If you take a look at any HTML source code, you notice that it consists of a finite set of tags (for example, <p>, <b>, <table>), each of which provides a special piece of formatting information about the contents (text) of the tag. Therein lies the answer. HTML tags only tell you what to make the information they contain *look* like. They don't give you enough information to know anything more than that about the contents. For example, is the content a name, an address, or a chemical formula?

You might think a solution would be to develop more tags that can comprehensively represent all the information you want represented. Unfortunately, that idea just doesn't cut it. It simply won't work because you cannot create a comprehensive and yet finite number of tags to represent all kinds of information. What is possible, however, is to create a finite number of ways of creating tags such that all tags you create are in a format that is universally understandable. That is what the XML 1.0 specifications seek to do. XML defines a standard way of creating markup that is simple and *extensible* so you can use it to richly describe any kind of data. Many applications can then process the same data in different ways to produce useful information (information, by definition, is processed data).

In some senses, you could say that XML is a political solution to today's data communication problems. However, to simply call it a political solution would be inadequate and inaccurate. Technologically, it is no mean feat to unite so many fronts, and though XML is not a ubiquitous solution—yet—it has every potential of becoming one.

Where Does XML Fit?

Moving away from the abstract model we outlined in the preceding section, let's talk technical: What exactly is XML for? The short answer is that XML is a universal, standardized language used to represent data such that it can be both processed independently and exchanged between programs and applications and between clients and servers. The keywords here are *information exchange*.

Let's limit our discussion for now to how XML fits in as an information exchange medium between applications and as an information exchange medium between clients and servers.

XML as an Information Exchange Format between Applications

Today, organizations possess vast amounts of information in documents. Even so far back as two decades ago most companies accepted that the best way to store data was to digitize it. Companies went about creating electronic documents with the hope that it would cut down on paper-based storage of information and thus avoid all the hassles associated with exchanging information in a paper world (for example, paper degradation and multiple copies). Around the same time, we figured out that certain documents contained standard types of information that could be stored in forms. Furthermore, much of this information could be broken down and stored in fields. From there, databases became a natural extension. Then came a couple of decades of database technology development to the point where now we tend to believe that relational databases are the de facto standard of data storage and retrieval. Figure 2.4 summarizes this process.

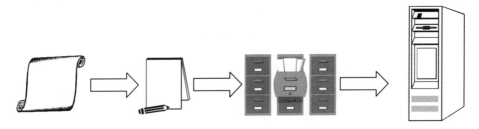

Figure 2.4   The move from paper documents to relational databases.

That takes care of one aspect (some would argue the most important aspect) of collecting, digitizing, and storing data but once you've got information, how do you exchange it? That's not as trivial as it seems. In one sense you'd think, okay, we have tons of *data*, and we know how to sift through it and extract *information* in an attempt to add to our *knowledge* (for those of you familiar with Information Systems theory, that's all of it in a nutshell). All that's left is to present the information to the user. However, the problem is that we don't have a way of universally trading or *exchanging* data between different users and applications *in a format that they can all perform further processing*. After all, what is *information* to one user could just as easily be *data* to another.

Managing your data is primarily the concern of your database management system, but creating and disseminating information is primarily the responsibility of an organization. How you choose to manipulate data to construct information depends primarily on what format your data is in. The reality is that there is an infinite number of ways of representing data, many of which are intuitive and many more that are counterintuitive yet efficient. If the format of data presented to you is proprietary, then you need corresponding proprietary information on how to decipher that data to manipulate it. You cannot open up a Microsoft Excel spreadsheet and extract information unless you've actually got the application programming interfaces (API) to Microsoft Excel.

If complex simulations are your game, then you often need to perform many independent operations on the same data. For the following scenario, let's assume that our data is stored in a common relational database management system, let's say a SQL Server. You may want to perform both complex statistical analysis and simulation analysis on your data. Programs specifically devoted to each part are available (for instance, Minitab and Arena), and each application is easy to use in its own right. The only problem is that you don't have a constant way of exchanging information between the two. Minitab processes data in its own native format and Arena does the same. For argument's sake, let's say that the results of one are dependent on the other (that is, they need to exchange information between each other). One alternative (and this is what usually happens) is for each program to do more than just one type of processing and to essentially perform the same tasks as the other does, but that's a really bad solution. It results in a lot of redundant resource allocation as well as maintaining inherent inefficiency; after all, each of these programs is specialized.

Another solution is for each vendor to create a translation program that allows it to directly access information stored in your database. However, this is more difficult than it sounds, and the vendor has no way of knowing up front that the information you have is stored in Microsoft Access, Oracle, Sybase, or any other DBMS vendor. Figure 2.5 summarizes this dilemma.

If each vendor decides to support third-party formats, say Microsoft Excel, then you've got a solution except that legally, you are bound to buy a copy of Microsoft Excel. From the perspective of an organization, things are really getting more expensive than they need. It's like saying to get from point A to point B, you have to go to point C first, but to get to point C, you have to go through points D, E, and F first. That's just not fair and beyond that, it's inefficient. Figure 2.6 summarizes this dilemma from your organization's perspective.

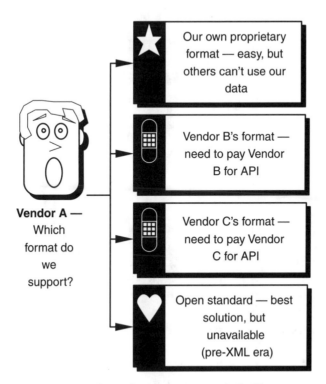

Figure 2.5 Independent software vendor's dilemma.

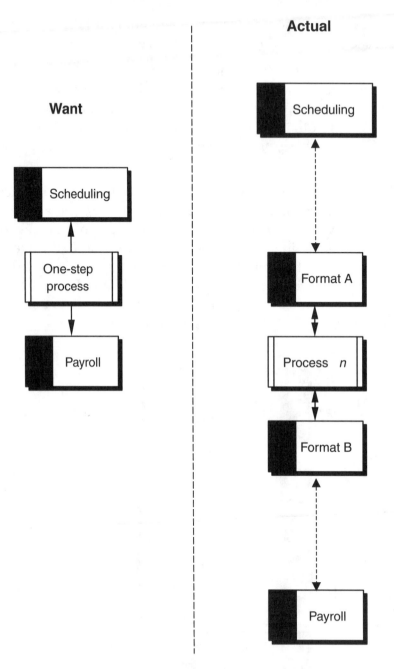

Figure 2.6 Organization's information exchange dilemma.

The ideal solution therefore is to present data to each application in such a way that it can be intelligently processed. Here's where XML comes in handy. Without going into the technical details for now (we go into more details in later chapters in this book) XML acts as an ideal exchange format between applications. Here's how XML is deployed to create a comprehensive solution (summarized in Figure 2.7):

1. You convert the information stored in your database (from any format) to an XML format. XML documents can handle textual information as well as pointers to binary files so if your database is a multimedia database with lots of graphics, sounds, or other binary formats, XML documents can still handle it.

2. Once it is in an XML format, vendors are able to universally parse (read) your XML document, which is made up of your initial data. They use freely available XML parsers to reduce their development time so that they can almost immediately begin to process the data stored in your XML documents.

XML as an Information Exchange Format between Clients and Servers

You've certainly seen information being exchanged between clients and servers. Every time you surf the Web, you download a page off the Web by making a request to a server and viewing the results of your request from your server (see Figure 2.8).

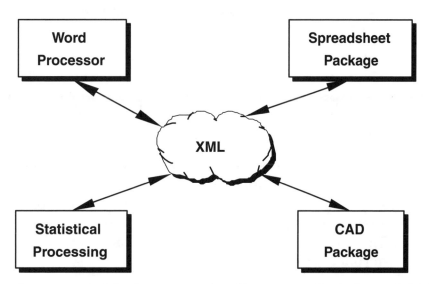

Figure 2.7 A minimalist representation of how XML can be used as a solution for exchanging information between applications.

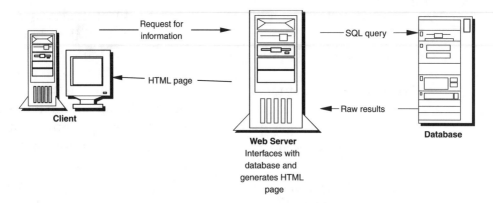

Figure 2.8 Standard client/server exchanges involving static HTML pages.

Now ask yourself this question: How often do you request information from the same site? For example, how often do you go visit a site like cnn.com? Every time you visit it, you hope that the contents of the same site have changed, say for news updates or stock quotes or for sports scores/updates/highlights. In this example, you are interested in *dynamic* information. You are primarily interested in getting the raw information (scores, stock quotes, news updates), but the server sends you a complete HTML page in which most of the page consists of formatting information (see Figure 2.7). The information you're interested in getting is probably only a few kilobytes at most, but the formatting information can be as large as several orders of magnitude times the necessary content (logos, styling information, advertisements).

Beyond that, how much can you really do with the information that a server sends you? Let's say you've requested the names and e-mail addresses of a series of vendors. If the list is really long, you have to manually sift through the information to find a particular piece of information. If you're lucky, the content provider gives you some sort of an advanced search or sort feature that forces the server to regenerate an HTML page organized the way you want it (sorted on a particular field name); but more often than not, that's wishful thinking. If the information were in a tabular form, you could copy and paste the data into an Excel spreadsheet and perform sorting, but then you need Microsoft Excel. That's not a complete solution. Why can't you just rearrange things in your browser?

How does XML figure in here? Most of the discussion surrounding this is contained in Parts Two and Three of this book; for now, we skim over much of the technical detail to put things in perspective. One of the more interesting working drafts under deliberation at the W3C is the XML Stylesheet Language (XSL). XSL Stylesheets are used for providing a simple, yet powerful set of tools for formatting XML cascading style sheets (CSS) except that the syntax is XML-based and fairly easy to use. The idea is for users to perform a one-time download of a stylesheet that will help them display information from the original content provider (for example, your news agency or broker). Once that stylesheet is downloaded and cached on the client's PC, then the content provider's server serves only raw XML data to the client. The client then has enough information to render (that is, generate a view of) the information in their browser. Figure 2.9 summarizes this process.

The benefits accrued to both the client and the content provider are enormous.

From the client's perspective the benefits include the following:

- Download time is minimized. Once the stylesheet is downloaded and cached, you only need to download a few kilobytes of information. This can improve your download time by orders of magnitude *while using your existing connection.*
- You can have several stylesheets, each of which displays the same information in a different way (for example, with tabular formatting versus paragraph or with charts and graphs).

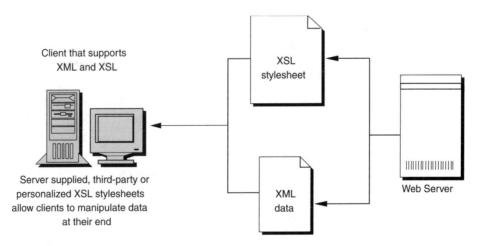

Client that supports
XML and XSL

XSL
stylesheet

Web Server

XML
data

Server supplied, third-party or
personalized XSL stylesheets
allow clients to manipulate data
at their end

Figure 2.9 Using XML with XSL to reduce client/server interaction.

- Once information is downloaded, you don't have to remain online to perform further manipulation of data. If you have the right stylesheets or applets downloaded/cached, you can make use of your PC's standalone strengths, that is, perform client-side processing.

- You can perform intelligent rearrangement of your data at the client's side (for example, sort by highest gains).

From a content provider's perspective the benefits include the following:

- The server is taxed less. Your server only has to deliver smaller portions of data to your clients, therefore your server is taxed less and can perform faster.

- The server doesn't need to develop HTML pages. All it does is forward raw XML information to the client, and the stylesheet takes care of all formatting issues.

- Because XML is Unicode compliant (that is, tags can be in virtually any language) you can create separate stylesheets in different languages (for example, French or German) and continue to serve only data to clients around the world. To put this in simpler words, you can make your services accessible to anyone in the world, no matter what language they speak, with very little overhead.

In Short

In slightly more abstract terms, by treating the user interface separately from structured data (as is otherwise done in Word Processors/WYSIWIG editors), XML allows you to easily integrate data from diverse sources. In doing so, you can compile information from purchase orders, invoices, research data, billing information, medical records, catalog data, or anywhere else by converting it to XML in the middle tier of a three-tier system. Because XML is exchanged the same way that HTML is, you can exchange all this information in a virtually ubiquitous manner over the Web to any Web client (desktop PC, workstation, PDA, WebTV unit). Your existing data can stay in its current database without your having to retrofit it.

Once the data is sent to clients, they can perform manipulation, editing, and rendering at their end without having to request the server to regenerate a new view for them. This frees up the server a great deal and immediately increases its availability and per-capita performance.

Similarly, because this exchange medium is multidirectional, information can travel backward the same way, that is, encoded in XML. Therefore, you can collect data from a huge variety of sources (for example, all the Web clients) and perform infinitely more interesting data processing.

We talk about all of these benefits and more in greater detail later in this chapter as we go through more examples of applications of XML.

XML—Changing the Nature of Documents

In Chapter 1, we briefly mentioned how XML changes our basic concept of what a document is. Now's the time to go into more detail about this.

Ever since human beings began recording information, we've been forced to create records that were independent, cohesive entities that were entirely self-describing—content, data, and structure are all thought of as being melded into a single document. Cave dwellers painted images in caves that recorded the story of the hunt. In this case, the cave wall itself was the document. The medium was the cave wall, the content consisted of the actual characters, and each author defined his or her format independently.

As we made the move to papyrus, paper, the codex, the printing press, and recently, electronic word processing, we've tried to keep all facets of information (content and format) together, in complete packages, that is, in complete documents.

When we made the move to electronic media, we continued this philosophy. Today's word processors are reflections of the paper printing industry and require you to concentrate on the content, format, and structure of the document all at the same time.

Some would argue that in the good old days when all we had was text editors, report writing hardly took any time. If you don't believe this, ask yourself how much time you spend writing an e-mail update versus the time you spend writing a proper memo that does the same. Transmission time aside, when you write the e-mail update, you don't spend a lot of time worrying about spelling or grammar mistakes. All you care about is getting your point through. Once written, a spell checker checks spellings in a batch process and—poof—your e-mail is sent to its destination.

When you write the memo, you invariably spend time worrying about formatting and spelling and grammar checking of your document *as you write it*. This cumulative, all-at-once approach, though seemingly powerful, inevitably slows you down. Sure, we humans are multiprocessing entities—there's no denying that—but when it comes to outputting your thoughts, sometimes it is better to get everything that's in your mind out before you start worrying about what it looks like. Certainly this is arguable, and a strong case can be made either way, but a common theme emerges: Breaking things into more manageable chunks is a smarter way of doing things. Cognitive science tends to suggest the same thing.

Breaking documents into more manageable chunks that can be processed separately and more efficiently is what XML is all about. In an XML document, a document can go through several stages of processing by different processors. For example, if we treated this book with an XML approach the following steps would occur:

- As authors, we would worry about writing meaningful and accurate content.
- Our editors would ensure that the content is grammatically correct.
- Layout experts would focus on making sure that the document is stylistically appealing.
- Publishing experts would focus on ensuring the document is printed correctly.
- Marketing experts would make sure that the book is marketed properly.
- Distribution experts would focus on making sure that the book is distributed to the right retailers.
- Retailers would focus on placing the book in the right spot so it sells.

But wait a minute! That's exactly how this book is being treated in any case! Now you've picked it up: an XML approach mimics the real world better. XML ensures that the data being exchanged between each pair of processors is in a common language so that everyone can focus on what they have best.

In XML, the document is broken into three generic parts:

- Content
- Structure
- Format

We talk about how you can create and work with these separate parts throughout this book.

Business Concerns

If you're a CIO or in an organizational post where you have to be cost conscious, you probably have some of the following concerns.

Who Owns XML? If I Use It, to Whom Do I Pay Royalties?

No single company or individual owns the XML standard. The World Wide Web Consortium develops the XML standard. This is the same organization that creates the HTML standard. Both standards are open standards, and you do not have to pay anyone to use the standard for your applications. These standards are created with the hope of engendering multilateral exchanges of information between computing applications. Thus, you don't really have to pay royalties to anyone for using the XML standard.

Why Should My Company Invest in Developing/Applying XML Solutions?

Good question. No business has more hyped technologies than the information technology business. However, we maintain that XML is the real deal. Every day, both established and new companies are announcing programs/applications that are based on XML.

Your firm should be prepared to invest in XML and its related technologies for several reasons:

The costs involved are minimal. The XML standard is open; therefore, you won't need to invest in expensive licensing agreements to use XML. The tools to support open standards are usually free or shareware, so your development costs are minimized.

The major vendor browsers have all pledged wide-scale support of XML. This being true, you can immediately market your products/services to the Internet browsing community (that is, to almost anyone who has a computer).

XML is uniquely suited to support localization into virtually every language. Because it is completely Unicode compliant, you are not limited to only supporting Web users who understand English.

The opportunity cost of *not* supporting XML is huge. If your firm only supports proprietary formats, it doesn't matter what services you provide, you are going to face tremendous communication problems in transferring information both internally and externally.

Specifically, What Benefits Do I/My Clients Stand to Gain?

Entire volumes could be written about this topic alone. Though woefully incomplete, here are a few points to ponder:

The ability to deliver your data over the Web. We mentioned this before, but it seemed an important benefit to reiterate again. XML information is transferred using the same protocol as HTML, that is the Hypertext Transfer Protocol (HTTP). Therefore, every benefit accrued from transferring HTML over the Web is directly, if not more, applicable to XML—and all without having to change your existing network.

The benefit of open standards. Because XML is an open standard, supporting it is very cost-effective. Tools and support of XML products are virtually free. The open standards-based HTML coupled with Web browsers enables thousands of businesses to communicate (at least in a unidirectional manner) with millions of clients with very little overhead. Similarly, an open standards-based XML enables the same low overheads to be incorporated by everyone again, only with bigger and better possibilities this time around.

The tools for developing XML applications will be available as easily and cheaply as they are for developing HTML pages today. Oodles and oodles of developers will be working with it and openly exchanging their experiences so the learning curve drops tremendously. In short, with open standards, you've opened up an endless array of support and compatibility that even the most expensive paid standards won't ever provide.

Client-side processing and manipulation of data. XML documents do not inherently contain user interface information in them and are structured such that the raw data contained in them can be easily parsed and edited using standards-based parsers at the client's side. The Document Object Model (DOM) provides a ubiquitous way for manipulating data using scripting or high-level programming languages, such as C++ or Java. Thus, clients can perform processing of XML data at their side completely independent of the server, which means users can now perform calculations, graphical interpretation of data, statistical processing, or virtually any other manipulation of the XML data at their end.

This means that clients have many extra degrees of freedom and power that enable them to take advantage of their own hardware instead of depending on the server to do the processing for them. That's good if you want to be able to realize some tangible benefits of having a spruced-up top-of-the-line PC while browsing the Web (normally, you're limited to the speed of the Web servers since they do all the processing for you).

Generate several views of your data. As we mentioned in Chapter 1, XML is more a blueprint of data than a picture of it (as HTML is). As with any blueprint, you can do a lot of things with it, and the ability to generate different views (graphical, tabular, 3-D, multiple layout) is thus inherent.

Better search results. We touched upon this in Chapter 1. If data providers employ a flexible and descriptive markup scheme in their documents using XML, then search engines are able to perform more accurate searches that allow you to find what you want with an accuracy that is unprecedented today. So when your clients search your Web site for an article on how to tackle a specific problem, they aren't simply fed back a list of pages with matching keywords (which is pretty darn annoying if you're looking for information in a hurry). Instead, they get a list of documents that contains documents that are specifically *about* the subject they've asked for (for example, all documents *about* Operations Research as opposed to all documents that *contain* the words *Operations* or *Research*).

The ability to develop real Web applications. Today, very few real "Web applications" exist. By that we mean full-blown, three-tier applications. It's not as if people aren't trying or lack the skills to get around obstacles. The fact is that the set of building blocks needed to create them was missing. With XML, the set of blocks is complete. XML provides a universal data exchange format complete with a common object model for interacting with it. Couple this with HTML for displaying information and scripting for providing decision/business logic (both of which exist and are ubiquitous already), we've now got the complete set of tools to go about creating full-blown Web applications.

The ability to collect and integrate data from multiple sources. Today, collecting information from disparate sources is very hard. Most places resort to rekeying data from one system to another just to get around the limitations of current data structures. Because XML is so flexible, richly structured data can be easily and faithfully represented, exchanged, and interpreted across virtually all electronic data systems at middle-tier servers from back-end servers and other applications or devices. The reverse flow can also occur; that is, clients can disseminate information in XML that can then be converted to the primary storage database after conversion through the middle tier.

Getting piecewise data updates. Today, when you want to update the information in your browser—for example, to look at new stock quotes or get a new article—you end up getting the entire HTML page rebuilt from the server and completely redelivered to you. This seems like a process that kills servers, and it does. With XML, you have the ability to get *only* the *updated* information sent to you instead of the entire data set (for example, the entire page with extra formatting information). Think of it as going grocery shopping: Instead of having to buy everything all at once, you only buy the things you need and go through the 10-items-or-less lane.

Virtually unlimited scalability. It's built into the name. XML documents are extensible and let you include as much markup information as you want, so you can code in any extra information you want the client/application to know. This prevents the server from having to be pinged repeatedly to get all the necessary information. Also, because of the granular update ability mentioned above, the server's scalability implicitly increases because it has less work to do.

Large documents are compressible. HTTP 1.1 includes the specifications for compression of information that translate really well with XML. Because typical XML documents consists of repetitive tags, they can be compressed fairly easily. (If you're not familiar with compression algorithms, repetitive entities are really easy to compress.) This is probably more interesting to you if you transfer large amounts of data over the Web so you can take advantage of the repetitive nature of XML elements. For smaller transfers, the results are less remarkable and are about the same fat (uncompressed) kilobyte for fat kilobyte as HTML transfers.

If you're still not convinced, let's look at where XML is, can, and will be applied.

Applying XML

By now your interest in XML may be piqued but you may not still be clear on where and how XML fits in. Allow us to present some scenarios—some general, some specific, some hypothetical, and some real—with their general XML-based solution outlines. By the way, the hypothetical ones are free potential seeds for business ideas.

General Uses of XML: Making Database Information Available on the Web

The following outlines a business scenario and then provides the XML solution.

Problem/Scenario

One of the first things you learn when you get into information systems is how wonderful database systems are and how many wonderful opportunities abound by using the Internet to interface with your database. One of the last things people mention is how hard it is to translate information back and forth between the two. There is currently no standard way of marrying the Internet to existing databases. Sure, there are plenty of custom solutions that involve many, many lines of code in the form of CGI (common gateway interface) scripts, but there isn't a really standardized way of making an SQL query and generating a report over the Internet. Furthermore, once you've generated the query, the results that come back to you are not necessarily the most useful. Sure they may be in a pretty HTML page, but then what? How do you export that data into Excel or some other package for further processing? Cutting and pasting is an option, but it is cumbersome and irritating and scales very poorly with larger data sets. Figure 2.10 illustrates this problem.

A lot of this has to do with the way that information is exchanged over the Internet and the vehicles that we use to traverse the Web (that is, usually the browser). Usually, information transfers are made using HTTP, the hypertext transfer protocol, which is a standardized way of transferring information (typically HTML pages) over the Internet (or an intranet for that matter). Typically, the information transferred is mostly marked-up text and the markup itself contains pointers to which binary files also need to be transferred (for example, pictures or sounds). The client (browser) receives the markup and, as it receives markup, starts making further requests based on the pointers and renders everything together in the shape of an HTML page.

When making database queries, a database server normally receives a query (usually in SQL syntax) and gives you back a table that you use to generate a report. If your client has direct access to the database server, then it's a fairly mundane process. Typically, however, you don't want the user to have direct access to the engine both for security reasons (and because you normally want to isolate the database logic from

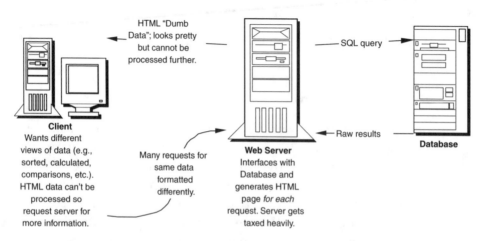

Figure 2.10 The problem of integrating databases with the Web.

the direct user). Instead, the user has to access a gateway to the database, which both generates the query and packages/transforms the results of the query into an HTML page, which is then sent to the client. If you're thinking in terms of processing overhead (which you should), then you are quickly realizing that a lot of steps are implicit and take up significant resources (processor overhead, excess network traffic, and throughput time). Figure 2.11 illustrates the typical database-to-Web solution.

This solution is extremely involved, and there are many ways of doing it. Unfortunately, very few of those ways are reproducible, and all tax the server intensively. The key is in the gateway. The gateway has to be able to do the following:

1. Convert the request from the client (usually posted in HTML or plain text) into a SQL query.
2. Send the query to the database and wait for the results.

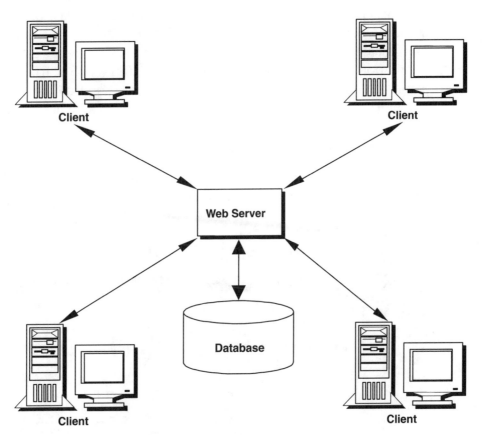

Figure 2.11   Current database-to-Web solutions.

3. Receive the results and transform them into an HTML page.

4. Send the HTML page to the client.

The client's browser gets a result from the server that is human viewable but cannot be used to generate further information without taxing the server further. To put it plainly, you receive dumbed-down data that you can see and that's it (the bad part of the WYSIWYG concept is that what you see is *all* you get). You can't take the information and do anything else with it, such as sorting, regrouping, calculating, rendering. Also, the power of your host machine (that is, your PC) is pretty much being wasted. Even though you have a Pentium III with an infinite amount of RAM, it doesn't help you a lick if the server is bogged down by traffic. Table 2.1 lists the limitations of getting HTML pages served up to you from a database.

All said and done, though, this solution, however clunky, works. Nevertheless it remains clunky, and, as your clientele increases, your Web server is going to get more and more bogged down over time. Your Web master will come to you very quickly with customer complaints about poor performance, and your competitors will start receiving some of your clients very quickly. Perish that thought. You've got to come up with a better solution! Let's see how XML can help out.

The XML-Based Three-Tier Solution

In our discussion above, the real bottlenecks are at the server's end. One of the primary reasons for this is that the size of each page sent to the

Table 2.1 Limitations of HTML Pages Served from a Database

NO.	LIMITATION
1.	Server is heavily taxed, resulting in poor performance for many users.
2.	Difficult to implement/program.
3.	Information client receives is WYSIWYG. The client cannot easily perform any processing with it except view it.
4.	For every request, the server has to spend a lot of resources formatting information.
5.	Every page sent to the client invariably contains more formatting information than raw content. This results in large files and slow data transfers.

client is inflated by formatting information. By using a system that employs XML coupled with XSL stylesheets, users perform a one-time download of the stylesheet. On every ping to the Web server thereafter, users receive only raw content information (articles, stock updates, sports scores), and the formatting is applied by the stylesheet(s) that is cached at their end.

Figure 2.12 shows XML in a classic three-tier solution model. You still need your Web server and several other classic modules. What XML does is add in an abstract layer that connects the Web server with the

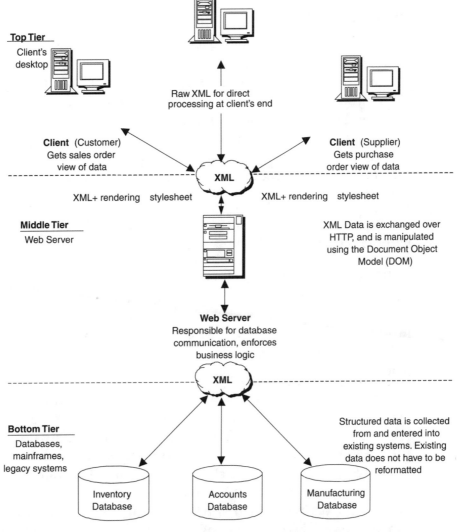

Figure 2.12   XML as applied in the classic three-tier application model.

client in a richer way than is currently possible. Using the middle tier, you are able to integrate information from many disparate information sources.

The following example is used to illustrate how XML can, will, and is being used and all uses are based on a similar model.

Specific Uses of XML: Creating Comparative Shopping Scenarios

The following outlines a business scenario and then provides the XML solution.

Problem/Scenario

It seems that you can never win when it comes to buying something. No matter how much you pay for an item, someone always tells you that they got the same thing for a better deal. The media is filled with stories of how you can use the Internet to find better deals for everything from books and cars to real estate and groceries. However, you will quickly realize that finding a better deal can take a long time, and time is a cost in and of itself. Thus the market was created for people to create Web sites that let you compare the prices of many separate vendors. The more vendors they support, the more choices you have to choose from.

The problem, however, is that collecting information from so many disparate sources is hard. Assuming that a particular vendor has an online site, one way of interfacing with the vendor's information is to ping its Web site, receive its HTML-generated page, carefully parse it, and extract the information you want (item name, price, and so on). You would then repeat this process for as many vendors as you want to include. This process is fairly tedious, and you have to become familiar with the vendor's system before you can parse the HTML data that is being output.

Assuming that you've somehow collected all this information, you then need to consolidate it and display it to your customer who wants to see the comparative prices before making a purchase. Again, assuming you've stored your results in a format that you can use (encoded with your own logic and set of tricks like separating data values with white spaces or special characters), you then need to generate an HTML page at your server and serve that back to your client. This entire process, though doable, is both irritating and messy. Figure 2.13 illustrates the non-XML approach.

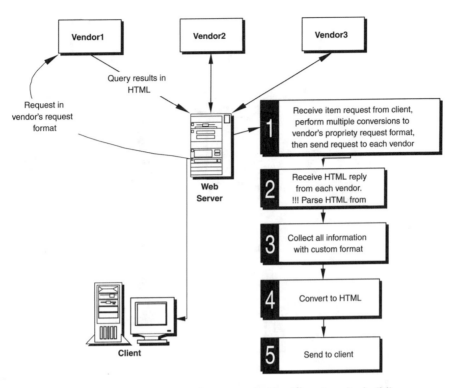

Figure 2.13   The non-XML approach to comparative shopping site building.

The XML-Based Solution Scenario

It would be much easier if everyone were using XML. With XML, you can immediately tell the structure of the data you are receiving from a client and can deal with it accordingly. Because standard parsers are easily and freely available, using the DOM, you could easily navigate and extract information from the results received from each vendor. Once you store the results as another XML document, then, by associating the document with a stylesheet (CSS or XSL), you can send back the results to clients. Those clients can then perform further analysis at their site (for example, sorting or filtering) and decide which product they want to purchase. Figure 2.14 summarizes this process. Another key point of this example is that by using XML throughout, you have the ability to include a much richer set of information. You can provide links to the vendor's product information pages with minimal program adjustment.

This example is purely minimalist in its approach, and we've intentionally left it a little vague. Parts Two and Three of this book provide

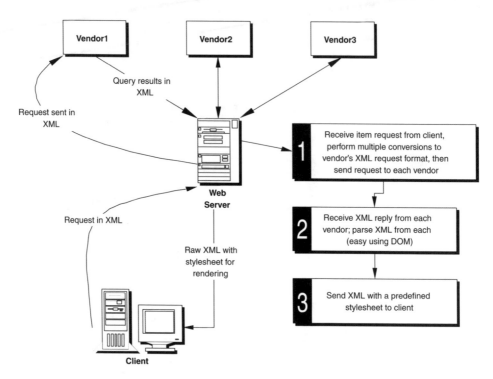

Figure 2.14   An XML solution approach.

you with the hands-on syntax you need to create such applications yourselves.

Industry Support: XML Vehicles

"The proof of the pudding is in the eating" or so the old saying goes. We've talked a lot about scenarios in which you use XML, but a key issue remains: What is the XML target platform? That is, how do your users interface with your XML solutions? Succinctly put: any way computers are used by computers; we do not mean only standard PCs.

For the most part, however, your users will use three classes of vehicles to access your XML solutions: the Internet, standalone, and "other" ways. The issue of your user's vehicle is important, so let's spend a little time talking about it.

Internet Vehicles

For the most part, your XML users will be using a standard Internet browser. However, it is important to mention that your clientele is not limited to accessing XML solutions through a browser. The major browsers that have announced XML support include Microsoft Internet Explorer 5 and Netscape Navigator 5. Here's more information on each of the browsers and also information on the "other" kind of Internet vehicles that you can use.

Microsoft Internet Explorer 5

Microsoft took the lead in the browser world in terms of its support of the standards-based XML. Remarkable as this may seem, at this point, it has the best implementation of XML in its browser as compared to any other vendor. Internet Explorer 5 includes complete support of the XML DOM and support of the transformation tools of XSL (see Part Three of this book). However, it does not fully support the Cascading Stylesheets standard (CSS), which is thought to be the best way of displaying XML data in a browser. Also, there are several extra XML support features available in Internet Explorer 5 that, though not standards-based, are interesting and worth taking a look at.

It should be noted that Internet Explorer 5's support is not perfect and is not 100 percent up to standards; however, it is pretty close. For now, we think it's okay to use it as a target vehicle, though we don't suggest enterprise-wide adoption of it until it is completely standards compliant.

Netscape Navigator 5

Netscape's support of XML comes in its browser engine called Gecko. Strictly standards speaking, Gecko has the tightest conformance, however, because of the current status of the standards, that doesn't mean you can do a lot. Certainly everyone (including us) believes that Netscape will provide developers with the most standards-compliant browser in the market. Unfortunately, seeing is believing to us, and we haven't yet seen much beyond hype.

At the time of writing this, Navigator 5's beta version had not been released while Internet Explorer 5's release version had. As a result, we spent more time playing with Internet Explorer 5 because it is much less likely to change than the pre-pre-prerelease versions of Navigator 5 to which we had access. We're not trying to knock Netscape here: They are a great company and produce the most standards-compliant browsers in the market. However, until the Navigator 5 preview comes out, there's not a lot we can write about, though we're pretty sure that once Navigator 5 comes out, it will be a great browser and have tons of XML support.

"Other" Internet XML Vehicles

Other Internet vehicles include scaled-down browsers, such as Opera, and "lite" browsers deployed in PDAs and palmtop computers. Currently, these vehicles don't offer much support for XML, but that will change in so-called Internet time. Once this support is available, however, expect a lot more interesting applications to occur—especially once small data collection devices have direct plugs to the Internet and use XML as their information exchange format. Concepts such as smart appliances will skyrocket into mainstream businesses.

Standalone Applications

XML does not have to be deployed over the Internet or over intranets, although that is primarily where XML's benefit lies (that is, as an over-the-wire format). You can use XML as a standalone data format as well whereby you use XML as a primary data storage format. This is often useful when you want to distribute large volumes of data and want to provide the users with a way of accessing that data without their having to install a database engine at their end. Using the DOM, you have an effective way of navigating your way through your data without having to install anything other than an XML-compliant browser or, if you don't want even that, a shell on top of an XML parser. Here are several example applications where you could create such systems:

- **Product catalogs.** Distributing large catalogs of merchandise, components, or hardware on CD-ROMs and DVDs becomes a snap using a standalone XML model. Your development and distribution costs are minimized immediately.

- **Reference books.** You could use XML as a primary storage format for storing reference information for distribution on CD-ROMs or DVDs. Because of the extensible nature of the documents, you could add in all kinds of keywords and references to other articles within the same disk and provide a very comprehensive reference set. Examples of target applications would include encyclopedias, dictionaries, medical references, and scientific research publications.

- **Directories.** Yellow pages, white pages, membership lists, associations lists—all could be easily indexed and searched for using standalone XML documents.

Moreover, you can use XML as a primary data format for your own applications to ensure interoperability with other applications. One of the promises of Microsoft for its Office suite of applications is that it will be using XML as the primary data format. Although its implementation of this promise is slow, other vendors will be joining this bandwagon very quickly.

Not too long ago, the entire Internet community was buzzing with the news of a new Microsoft Word macro-based virus called Melissa. One of the primary reasons this virus proliferated so much was because the data format (the Microsoft Word file) relied on executable content. Though a lot of argument has gone on in the recent past about this, the fundamental flaw lay in the fact that the document contained its own executable content and therefore took control of system resources in order to operate. You can make several arguments in favor of such a document model, but you cannot argue that XML presents users with meaningful data that does not seize system resources—all processing is left in the browser. That adds a lot of system security to XML documents. You are virtually assured that they will not grab hold of your system resources.

Industry Support: XML Applications

Like any big-picture-savvy businessperson, you probably want some assurance that XML is the right technology to invest in and to start supporting in your organization. You want examples of other companies that are currently investing in XML and want to know what they are doing with it right now. If you're the entrepreneurial sort of person, you already know that now is the time to be developing XML tools and applications and are looking for niche areas where you can develop products and solutions.

To help support our contention that XML is the real deal and to help convince you that the industry has already warmed up to it, we've taken the liberty of reviewing a few XML applications that some of the industry bigwigs have introduced recently. Unfortunately, due to the fact that anything written on paper in the IT industry is obsolete almost before the ink dries, many of you may find this as old news. Neverthe-less, these are excellent examples of XML applications; however, it is extremely important to realize that the most important and impressive XML applications have not yet even been dreamed of. These are just the first generation of a long line of applications to come!

Microsoft BizTalk

Microsoft announced its plans of releasing a new framework for e-com-merce whereby software would play a much larger role in business than it does today. This is perhaps one of the largest applications of XML with very far-reaching implications if it works.

The idea behind BizTalk is very simple: to provide a universal vocabu-lary for software among businesses that describes all their processes. You can see how XML as universal method for describing information fits in here very well.

What Microsoft realized was that the reason that businesses aren't doing a lot of e-commerce with each other right now is because they lack the standards that are both comprehensive and cost-efficient. EDI, the Electronic Data Interchange format, though very comprehensive, is expensive to implement and has thus been used mostly by large corpo-rate customers. EDI provides an excellent way of describing standard business transactions, such as purchase orders or invoices, but isn't very good at describing nonstandard procedures. Nevertheless EDI is the preferred method of choice for business transactions in the corpo-rate world. BizTalk does not seek to change that.

BizTalk focuses on a very large number of business processes going beyond where Enterprise Resource Planning (ERP) systems go. They not only encompass business procedures within an organization, but also preclude knowledge level systems. (Knowledge level systems include technical processing systems, such as engineering systems and manufacturing systems.) The idea is to make all aspects of the data used within an organization accessible to each branch of the organization. This stage is achieved by ensuring that all documents within the orga-nization either are in a native XML format or can be easily converted back and forth to XML. Microsoft hopes that all application vendors will start supporting XML as an information exchange medium. This makes sense—after all, XML is an open standards system.

Current e-commerce systems give you a really boring look at what you're buying. Half the fun of shopping is finding out all the details about the product before you buy it. You talk with a salesperson about the product and find out whether it works in certain conditions or what products are complementary to it. That richer information experience is currently not entertained in most e-commerce experiences. By melding information from all parts of an organization with XML, online shoppers get all the information they want about the product before they purchase it. This makes the online shopping experience that much more comprehensive. Figure 2.15 summarizes our understanding of BizTalk.

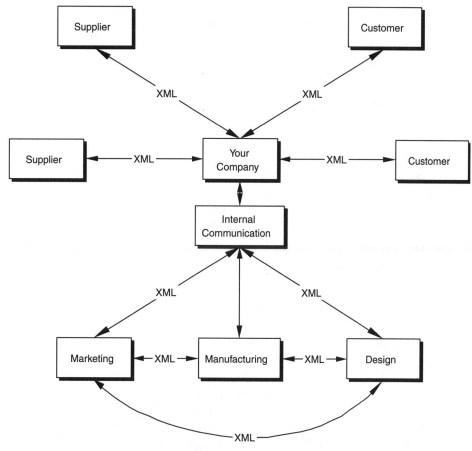

Idea: All communication, internal and external, occurs using XML documents. All external XML communication occurs using Microsoft BizTalk Schemas. In addition, Microsoft will leverage MS BizTalk Server and Transaction Server to facilitate implementation.

Figure 2.15   Microsoft BizTalk.

BizTalk works by defining a set of schemas or data-structures that are intended to comprehensively describe standard business procedures, such as purchasing, product catalogs, promotional campaigns, and invoices, as well as nonstandard standard business operations (for example, what we do when supplier X can't deliver because of manufacturing difficulties?). In doing so, a standard vocabulary for business is set. Our first reaction is that something like this would be very difficult for any business to accept. After all, no business wants to be told how to define its standard business operations by a software vendor. Microsoft's strategy includes working with many industry moguls to bolster support for this initiative. Each schema is supposed to be open to periodic industry design reviews, something that we believe should keep things real.

Here's an incomplete list of companies that Microsoft is working with to develop the BizTalk initiative:

- 1-800-FLOWERS
- barnesandnoble.com
- Best Buy Company Inc.
- Clarus Corp.
- Dell Computer Corp.
- DataChannel Inc.
- Eddie Bauer Inc.
- J.D. Edwards & Co.
- PeopleSoft Inc.
- Procter & Gamble
- SAP AG
- Sharp Electronics Corp.
- WebMethods

Though these are some pretty impressive names, Microsoft's goal is to get more than one million businesses online.

Will it work? Cautiously, we say yes, but we should qualify this by stating that we don't think it will meet the levels of success that Microsoft feels it will—at least not in the short run (two to four years). However, we think it's a great idea and are pretty sure that there will be a similar, clashing framework proposed by some other company or consortium in the near future.

Regardless, any new initiative will also base itself heavily on the support of XML. Bottom line, XML is going to be central to all e-commerce initiatives of the future.

IBM Speech Markup Language: SpeechML

IBM's alphaWorks (a Web site devoted to introducing IBM's research work to developers) introduced SpeechML in February 1999. SpeechML provides a framework in which Web-based applications can integrate interactive speech capabilities.

SpeechML provides tags for defining spoken output and input as well as tags for triggering actions to be taken on a given spoken input (such as "open window" or "copy to disk"). SpeechML elements are identified and linked by URLs in an attempt to keep everything familiar to HTML developers. It builds on Java Speech Markup Language (JSML) for spoken output (that is, text to speech) and uses a combination of markup and Java Speech Grammar Format (JSGF) to define the spoken input (that is, speech to text.)

IBM would like developers to be able to use tags to add interactive speech capability to Web sites without being experts in speech technology. Just as you'd mark up a paragraph with a <b> tag to make its contents bold, using a vocabulary of tags defined in SpeechML, you'd mark up sections of text with particular tags to make them audible.

The alphaWorks Web site includes a downloadable conversational browser that is written in Java and builds on Java's Speech API and IBM's XML parser.

This is exciting stuff. The realm of possibilities is virtually endless here. Imagine Web sites that give you their content without your having to look at the screen. You could perform multitasking like never before—listen to information from one page and type a report about it as you write.

In and of itself, text-to-speech capability built into a browser is pretty cool; however, other companies have tried the same. SpeechML adds the extra component of accepting voice input from users, which makes things really interesting. Imagine being able to talk to your browser, to tell it how to navigate for information, and to have it speak back to you as you surf the net. Things can get pretty wild.

The SpeechML implementation, as it currently exists, works only through an aural browser (called conversational browser), which provides the real text-to-speech functionality. For it to be a successful technology, SpeechML needs to be approved by the W3C. IBM intends to formally propose SpeechML to the W3C.

The spin-offs of voice markup languages are really cool. Once approved as a standard (we don't see any reason for it not to be—if not SpeechML, some similar standard will be approved), the implementations of its interpreters will extend far beyond the formal PC browser per se. Imagine doing things such as browsing the Web through your telephone, or having driving instructions read to you as you drive in your car, or having your refrigerator and other home appliances talk to you—granted, now we're bordering on being really being geeky, but it certainly is a possibility. The possibilities are extremely exciting.

To be fair, we should mention that at least two other similar voice applications of XML that we know about are in the pipeline: Motorola's VoXML and AT&T's VXML. All of these have similar intentions and all are XML-based. Our one fear is that a standards war may emerge. But even if there is one, after the dust settles, one standard will emerge and developers will be dreaming of hundreds of thousands of applications to use it with.

Figure 2.16 shows what voice markup languages look like from a systems-level perspective.

The bottom line is that we think this is way too cool a technology not to succeed, and the spin-offs of it are nothing less than incredible.

W3C Recommendation: MathML

This is for the academic reader wondering why a technology that started with academia (the Internet did after all take root in CERN, the international center for theoretical physics) doesn't pay as much attention to it anymore. MathML is currently an XML application that is also an official W3C recommendation. Its intention is to provide a low-level format for communicating mathematics between machines.

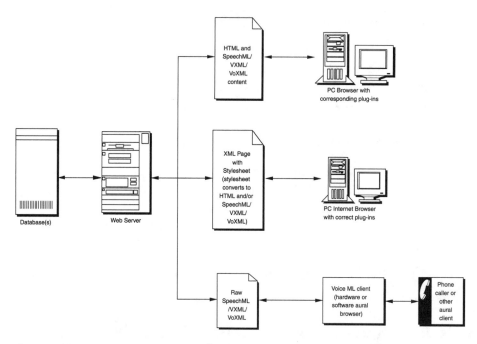

Figure 2.16 Voice markup languages from a systems-level perspective.

MathML, like every application of XML, consists of an XML vocabulary of tags. These tags can be used to mark up an equation in terms of its presentation and its semantics from a computational engine's perspective. In other words, MathML attempts to capture the meaning behind equations rather than concentrating on how they are going to look on the screen, which could otherwise be achieved through different fonts, images, or special characters.

The core philosophy is that a syntax is needed for describing mathematic functions over the Web. MathML syntax, though as human legible as any XML application, is not intended for direct human editing; rather it is to be used by specialized applications such as equation editors or math packages (for example, Maple).

As much as we may deny it, we need math. The more intricate details there are in the business world, the greater the desire and need for math becomes. Complex financial analysis using statistical processing, matrices, differential equations, and everything you never wanted to know that existed in Calculus III is necessary in today's business world. From an engineering perspective, converting a Fast Fourier Transform for a signal processing application from a simple gif to code is extremely tedious.

Though a computer vocabulary for performing complex math has been important in academia for years, it is the market that drives development. MathML will be used to facilitate the use of mathematical and scientific content on the Web. Its other uses include applications such as computer algebra systems, print typesetting, and voice synthesis.

Currently, there is no inherent browser support of MathML in popular browsers such as Internet Explorer or Netscape; however, plug-ins are available to both render MathML data and applications like it. A standalone browser for both HTML and MathML, called the Amaya browser, is available from the W3C.

Necessity being the mother of invention, this application has succeeded by virtue of existing.

W3C Recommendation: Synchronized Multimedia Integration Language

Synchronized Multimedia Integration Language (SMIL, pronounced "smile") was designed to enable the simple authoring of TV-like multimedia presentations such as training courses on the Web.

SMIL is another application of XML and, as such, has its own vocabulary of tags. SMIL presentations are extremely flexible and can consist of virtually any media, including streaming audio, streaming video, and static images, of virtually all formats. The idea is to enable Webcasts of media in a very informative and unique manner. This is the stuff that pundits dreamed about decades ago.

The syntax is very easy to use and places a lot of emphasis on the positioning of different media objects and then setting the order in which they are triggered or played. SMIL is intended for users of high-bandwidth systems and won't be completely usable to all Web users for some time.

Provided SMIL takes root in the industry, it could revolutionize the educational and entertainment processes across the Web. Students could listen to or watch a professor give a lecture and get a simultaneous list of annotations to follow to get more information. Imagine hearing a term you don't know the meaning of and seeing its meaning pop up in front of you as the speaker says the term. Or imagine if the speaker makes a reference to some process you are unfamiliar with and a list of links that you can follow comes up during that portion of the speech.

Figure 2.17 shows a hypothetical SMIL page with various components that can be constructed given today's level of technology.

Similarly, imagine a SMIL page from an entertainment perspective. Imagine watching a football game and being able to get statistics of a player by clicking on that player with a picture-in-picture type of view. Imagine further that while watching the game, you can video conference with your friend on the same screen and exchange expert comments on how the game's going.

These aren't bleary-eyed fantasies anymore: They're real live applications that can be enabled through a standards-based language, SMIL.

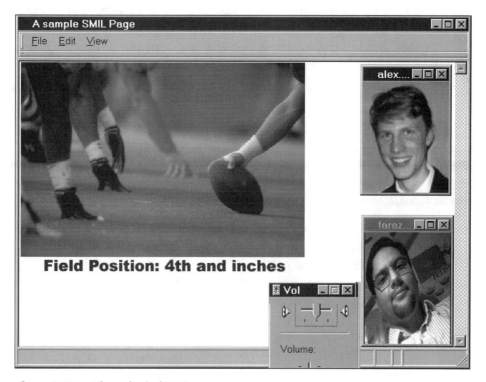

Figure 2.17   A hypothetical SMIL page.

SMIL's backing has teeth (pun intended). The members of the W3C working group who worked on the SMIL recommendation include members from RealNetworks (as in RealPlayer), Apple (as in QuickTime), Netscape, Philips, and other top-of-the-line multimedia players. The recommendation was passed in June 1998, and since then several SMIL players have been released, including RealNetwork's G2 player.

As cool as this technology is, it is slightly ahead of the market. Let's face it, only a select few of us have T1 or higher access to the Net (blessed be our universities for they are our providers of high bandwidth). We think it will go through several revisions before mainstream users are able to reap benefits from it.

XML Developer Support

Ah, yes, the all-important stuff. If you're a developer looking to create XML solutions, we have to tell you that the XML developer support is still pretty weak. However, if you've got strong programming resources and are looking to introduce early niche market applications of XML, it's great. You've got an edge because you can introduce solutions before anyone else can. If you've got your entrepreneurial hat on, you just realized that now is a great time to start introducing tools for developers.

The appendices provide an updated list of XML developer support resources. Right now we'd like to talk about some of the general developer support that is currently available in the market.

Parser Support

Currently, plenty of XML 1.0-compliant parsers are available. There is some variation in parsers—some are validating while others are not, and most are DOM compliant. Right now all companies would like you to be using their parser in the hopes that you will include it as a core component of whatever XML application you develop (then they can charge you royalties). Here's a list of a few parsers that we used and were somewhat comfortable with:

- Microsoft's XML parser (included in Internet Explorer 5)

- Microsoft/Data Channel's Java Parser
- IBM's XML for Java

Languages Supported

Virtually all programming languages have hooks into XML and the DOM. Here are a few for which we know software interfaces exist:

- Java
- C++
- C
- Perl
- Python
- Visual Basic

Major Vendor Support

You can't really invest in a new technology unless the so-called big boys are there already. (Well, you can, if you've got that entrepreneurial spirit and a lot of moxy.) Below we talk a bit about the support of XML that some of the largest vendors are providing. If you're a major vendor and we haven't listed you, please forgive us.

Sun's XML Support

Sun has been a champion of XML since its inception. Sun recently announced its intention to create Java Standard Extensions for XML (a Java-based API) through the Java Community Process. XML and Java seem to have a natural symbiotic relationship in that both are intended to be platform independent and portable. Industry pundits often cite the call "XML gives Java something to do." After working with both for some time, we concur! Using XML with Java, you can finally start to make real applications that actually do something meaningful as opposed to making things just look cool. Using XML+Java combinations, Web pages have the potential to become full-blown applications and not just applets.

Sun also has a strong presence on the W3C and is playing a major role in shaping the XML standards.

Microsoft's XML Support

Microsoft has taken the most visible lead in supporting XML. Here are some of Microsoft's XML friendly actions (or promises to be turned into actions):

- Implementing the most comprehensive browser support of XML, Internet Explorer 5
- Implementing the XML transformation part of XSL, Internet Explorer 5
- Using XML as a primary data storage format for all of Microsoft's Office suit applications
- Developing the BizTalk framework for using XML as a medium for exchanging information throughout all businesses in an effort to enable wide-scale e-commerce
- Having a seat on the W3C and playing a major role in shaping XML and its related standards

IBM's XML Support

IBM has created an entire array of XML applications in the works. We were pretty impressed with the huge array of things they have going (either that or they're the only folks who talk about what they're up to). Here are some of the things they've got going:

- **Bean Markup Language (BML).** BML is an XML-based component configuration language customized for controlling JavaBeans.
- **DataCraft.** This is an application that provides an XML view of existing databases in IBM DB2 and Microsoft Access and enables publishing XML forms to the Web. This is very interesting stuff.
- **Dynamic XML for Java (DXMLJ).** This is a processor to seamlessly embed Java within XML to provide dynamic data.
- **LotusXSL.** This is a partial XSL processor that implements the transformation functionality of XSL.

- **RDF for XML.** This is an RDF processor written in that builds, queries, and manipulates RDF structures by reading and writing them in XML.

- **Speech Markup Language.** We talked about SpeechML in an earlier section. This is a very exciting XML application.

- **TaskGuide Viewer.** This is an XML tool that helps you create Wizards.

- **Xeena.** The name was such that we had to comment on it. It's a GUI-based XML editor for editing valid XML documents.

- **XML BeanMaker.** This is pretty cool. It takes a DTD and generates the code for JavaBean classes.

- **XML Parser for Java.** This is probably the best Java parser available. Tightest conformance to standards and written in 100 percent pure Java.

Netscape's XML Support

Netscape's support of XML has huge promises, and while we think it will deliver the best implementation of the standards, at the time of writing this book, we could not get our hands on anything. What it intends to support includes the following:

- An Internet browser (Gecko) with the most comprehensive standards support

- A browser that is platform independent and soon device independent (i.e., for use with PDAs and similar devices)

Oracle's XML Support

Oracle has been quite vociferous in its support of XML. It views XML as a portal to the world of data. It intends to include in its support tight integration of XML in with Oracle 8i. Its core support in 8i includes:

- **The Oracle XML Parser.** Oracle intends to enable programmers to process XML documents and/or document fragments.

- **XML Support in iFS.** Oracle intends to support XML in its Oracle Internet File System to enable automated parsing and rendering of data between XML and the database.

These are only tips of the iceberg. Everyone has jumped onto the XML bandwagon. What are *you* waiting for?

Summary

We've given you a lot to think about in this chapter. We've tried to present a comprehensive overview of XML and where it fits in the grand scheme of things. We've also tried to help stimulate you to dream about where you can take it further.

The beauty of XML is in its sheer simplicity. It's not something that is abstract and difficult to envision—far from it. Simple things work, and the ubiquitous nature of HTML proves that incontrovertibly. As Dan Connolly wrote, "XML is like HTML with the training wheels off" (in the "Web matters" section of *Nature* magazine's online site). In other words, XML takes the concepts that millions of people implicitly learned while making Web sites and develops them a little further to empower all computer users to do more.

Moreover, it's not just us who believe in XML; virtually every industry leader has pledged support to XML. With the kind of support that XML has mustered in the last year alone, it is a sure bet that people who today invest millions as soon as they hear the words *e-commerce* or *dot-com* are going to be willing to pump money into ventures that use the buzzword *XML*.

Seven years ago, the Internet Revolution began, and its promise of a new future for every facet of human life was made by all industry pundits. The reality is that we are not there yet. We've certainly come a long way, but we are still at the beginning. HTML was a tremendous leap forward, but it was not enough. XML fills in where HTML could not. The support that XML has mustered from all facets of the industry is unprecedented by every measure. This is a technology that has success written all over it, so much so, that we will go so far as to say that the only way it could fail is if humanity were to unplug the Internet.

In a few years, XML is going to be as commonplace as HTML is, and *that's a good thing* because it means that *now* is the best time to get into it. Those who get there first win the prize, and the nice part is that everyone gets to share in the winnings. XML is the next cycle of the information revolution.

Details, Details

In this chapter, we delve into the more technical aspects of XML. Although this chapter introduces you to a lot of the XML jargon, it is not a replacement for reading the entire specifications of XML 1.0 from the W3C. Our intention here is to prepare you for creating XML documents. As we mentioned in Chapters 1 and 2, XML has the inherent goal of representing information in a universal format so that it can easily be interchanged and processed further. Parts Two and Three of this book address how to process the information stored in XML documents. This chapter covers a description of the XML syntax with a special emphasis on how to create an XML document. We had to deal with a lot of chicken-and-egg situations; this chapter has some forward referencing to concepts. As a result, you may want to skim through the whole chapter once before reading it in detail.

What Makes Up an XML System?

Every XML system is primarily concerned with processing information that is stored in a standardized format. It doesn't matter what the objective of the system is per se. We talked extensively about the applications of XML in Chapter 2 and throughout all of the applications, the underlying assumption for each has been that it is based on an XML system.

An XML system is composed of three generic parts and one unique part. In nontechnical terms, they can be expressed as content, structural definition, conformity checking, and customized application. The first three are the generic parts while the last, customized application is unique to the objective of the system.

Though we cannot anticipate the entire gamut of unique objectives that your XML system will achieve, we can help you generate the first three parts of your system, which makes the construction of the last part of your system less code intensive. Bringing things back into technical terms, an XML system typically consists of the following:

- XML Document (content)
- XML Document Type Definition—DTD (structural definition; this is an optional part)
- XML Parser (conformity checker)
- XML Application (uses the output of the Parser to achieve your unique objectives)

Figure 3.1 shows how these interrelate.

The actual data that an XML system processes comes from an XML document that makes use of a rich description of information using the XML syntax. To ensure that the information is actually expressed in the XML syntax, the document is run through an XML processor called an XML parser that rigorously checks whether that document is

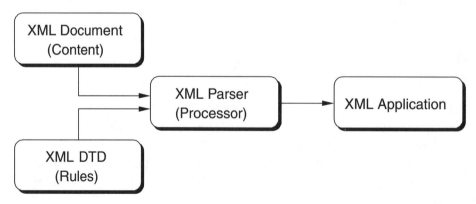

Figure 3.1   A typical XML system.

syntactically correct and then replicates the structure of the information in memory. This memory representation is then ready for customized processing through an XML application.

Often, we are interested in information being more than just syntactically correct. Sometimes we want it to possess a certain logical and physical structure. Certainly from a programmer's perspective, most problems arise from information that though syntactically correct is not necessarily logically or structurally correct (hence the many, many lines of error checking). The way to define the structure of an XML document is to create a Document Type Definition (DTD). When a DTD is either linked to or embedded in an XML document, the parser performs additional conformance checks of the XML document to determine its structural conformance. Once cleared for both syntactical correctness and structural integrity, the parser presents the XML application with an in-memory representation of the information.

Let's take a look at each one of these in more detail.

XML Document

As we mentioned earlier, an XML document is based on entities that can consist of content and markup. Content is the actual information, such as the price of melons, a paragraph of an essay, or the headline of a newspaper. Content is also referred to as *character data*.

Content is encased in markup. If you are familiar with HTML, then you already know that markup in the computer world consists of tags, such as start tags, end tags, and comments. We go into much more detail later on in this chapter.

XML Document Type Definition

Often, it is desirable to have information structured in a particular way. For example, you may want an address in an address book to include a ZIP code or a bibliography to include the name of the publisher. To insure that information is structured properly, you can create a set of rules for your XML documents through Document Type Definitions (DTDs.) DTDs are a series of expressions that define the logical structure of your XML document. The DTD is an optional part of your XML system. By and large, though, for any serious application, you would want to include a DTD, especially in instances where you are gathering information from a customer, for example, while gathering name information in a form submission. A name can consist of a first name and a last name. Identifying a person on the basis of the last name becomes more difficult when both the first and last names are put together, so often they are represented by two fields. By explicitly declaring that a name must consist of two parts, the parser is able to perform error checking for you so you don't have to write your own code to insure that the user has put in the right information.

In Chapter 1, we talked a little about DTDs and how we don't particularly care for them. Nevertheless, they are the only officially recommended way for creating rules in XML documents; thus we spend some time going over how to create an XML DTD in this chapter.

XML Parser

An XML parser is a software engine that checks your XML document to insure that it is syntactically correct. If you have chosen to include a DTD, the XML parser also checks your XML document against the DTD to insure that it is also structured correctly.

A parser reads the XML document's information and makes it accessible to the XML application. All parsers are supposed to behave the same but the reality is that they don't. Most of them have their own quirks and nuances (also known as features). For the most part, this book uses the parsers included with Microsoft's Internet Explorer 5 and Netscape Navigator 5 (alpha). A list of easily available parsers is included in Appendix B.

Choosing which parser to use is important and a lot depends on the language in which you are writing your application. Some parsers are written for C++, while others are written in Java. We talk a lot about interfacing with parsers through code in Part Three. For now though, you should be aware that using standard parsers makes programming much easier as the parser does a lot of the grunt work for you.

XML Application

The XML application is what you, the programmer, make. XML applications typically process information encased in XML documents, but there is virtually no limit to what you can do with an application. Companies like Microsoft and DataChannel are betting that you, as a programmer, will be creating XML applications using their XML parser (this makes sense; writing a comprehensive parser is tedious and expensive in terms of manpower). We're not going to talk much about how to make an application in this chapter. Fear not, Parts Two and Three of this book give you more than enough information about how to create your own hard-core superduper XML applications.

The XML Standard—Design Goals

The XML standard is an *open standard.* This means that no single company creates or owns it. The XML standard is a project of the World Wide Web Consortium (W3C) that is overseen by W3C's XML Working Group, which began work in 1996. You can get a copy of the latest official specifications from www.w3c.com/xml. Although the actual specifications document makes for some pretty heavy reading, the objectives of the standards are (as one would hope) very clear. They are reproduced here with permission:

1. XML shall be straightforwardly usable over the Internet.
2. XML shall support a wide variety of applications.
3. XML shall be compatible with SGML.
4. It shall be easy to write programs which process XML documents.
5. The number of optional features in XML is to be kept to the absolute minimum, ideally zero.
6. XML documents should be human-legible and reasonably clear.
7. The XML design should be prepared quickly.
8. The design of XML shall be formal and concise.
9. XML documents shall be easy to create.
10. Terseness in XML markup is of minimal importance.

By and large, the committee has been pretty true to its goals. We take our hats off to all the working group members. It is not easy to make something that is useful *and* relatively easy to work with.

XML Documents Overview: The Panoramic Perspective

At the most basic level, XML documents are made of at least one—though usually many—*entities*. An entity is a flexible information storage unit. Until parsed, XML files are really just text files, so essentially every XML document is an entity (XML documents can be made up of many other entities too). However, entities can also be non-XML related. Any binary file (for example picture, sound, video, or database) can be an entity too.

In levels of abstraction, a document is at the highest level (also called *root level*) and is referred to as the *document entity*. An XML parser reads a document entity and follows all references contained therein to piece together the complete document.

Entities that are made of XML syntax contain two parts, the content (raw information, also called character data) and the XML markup. We briefly touched on what markup was in Chapter 1. Markup is information about content that helps us use the content. In XML, the actual markup serves several purposes:

- It provides a fairly simple and standardized syntax that XML parsers can use for resolving the information it describes.
- The markup provides a rich method of describing the hierarchical structure of the content by breaking the content information (character data) into chunks called *elements* that in turn are further described by *attributes*. The hierarchical structure of the entire document is described through the usage of markup.

An XML document can be roughly broken down into three generic sections of markup collections:

- Prolog
- Document Type Definition (optional)
- Root Element

Each of these sections is further broken down into more detailed structures. Figure 3.2 shows all of these generic markup sections with their subsections. We go into some detail about all of these in this chapter.

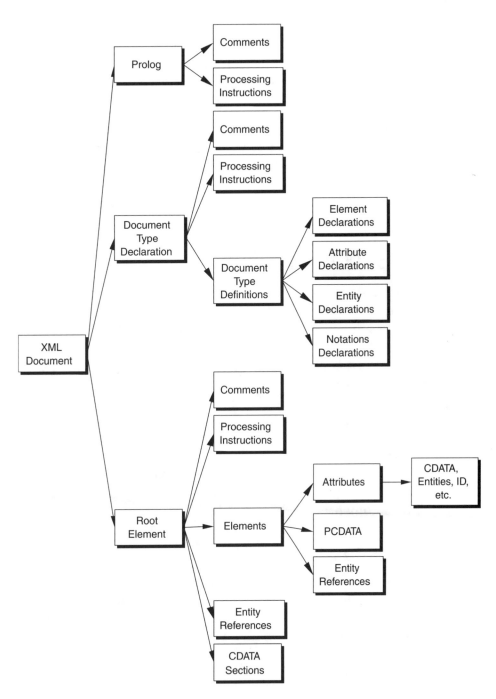

Figure 3.2 Putting XML documents in perspective: The Panoramic Perspective.

XML Documents in Depth

Now that we've had a brief introduction to the overall structure of an XML system, let's start breaking things down into greater detail.

XML documents are logical, hierarchically structured information chunks. Recall our analogy of XML documents as blueprints from Chapter 1. XML documents are not solutions in themselves. Remember, unlike HTML documents whose specific purpose is the display of information, XML documents have the agenda of presenting information so that it can be further processed. Therefore, an XML document includes a lot of markup to describe the content (raw information) it contains.

XML Concept: Well Formed

In Chapter 1, we briefly touched upon the concept of well formed XML documents. Well formed XML documents are those XML documents that are syntactically correct. XML, unlike HTML, is extremely picky about syntax. Fortunately, it's not that hard to write syntactically correct XML. The following are general guidelines for writing well formed XML documents.

Case Sensitivity

Unlike HTML, XML is case sensitive. You must be very careful when writing markup. Spelling mistakes can sometimes take a long time to detect, especially if you are using a plain text editor for creating your XML document.

Closing Tags

Another thing that the XML specification is rather picky about is that every open tag must be closed. So, though it's quite acceptable to begin an HTML document with an <HTML> tag and to not bother to close it, an XML parser will set off all kinds of red flags for not closing a tag.

No Overlapping Tags

It is easy to confuse overlapping tags with nesting tags. *Nesting tags* is a way of developing a logical hierarchy of information similar to the BODMAS (brackets of division, multiplication, addition, subtraction—

wouldn't our teachers be proud of us for remembering?) rules of eighth grade math. Nesting tags in XML documents is fine and is strongly encouraged from a design perspective. However, you cannot overlap tags. Here's an example of an XML clip that contains nested tags:

```
<first_tag>
     <second_tag>
          <third_tag>Contents of third tag</third_tag>
     </second_tag>
</first_tag>
```

There is a hierarchy that is implicitly defined by the above structure.

Here's an example of an unacceptable (that is, not well formed) XML snippet with overlapping tags.

```
<first_tag>
     <second_tag>
</first_tag>
          <third_tag>Contents of third tag</third_tag>
     </second_tag>
```

The term *overlapping* means that a tag that is not a child of the first starts before the other ends. Do you see how in the above case that an overlap occurs between `<first_tag>` and `<second_tag>`? In the XML world, this is a definite no-no. For those of you who are experienced in HTML, this may seem a little inconvenient; after all, most HTML parsers don't care when you overlap (they just act weird when you overlap tags). If you think about it for a minute from the parser's perspective, however, things could get very confusing with overlapping tags. If you intend to write your XML own documents, we strongly encourage you to watch out for overlapping tags.

Several tools out in the market take care of fussing around with the markup syntax. Tools like Vervet Logic's XML Pro and Microsoft's XML Notepad allow you to visually create your structures and fill in content. The advantage of these programs is obvious; you don't have to worry about well formed nonconformities. However, we must forewarn you that should you use any of these programs (or ones similar to these), you may end up losing several degrees of flexibility in your documents (for example, XML Notepad doesn't let you work with processing instructions very easily). For an updated list of tools for editing XML documents, check out this book's companion Web site.

XML Concept: Valid XML and Validation

Two categories of XML documents exist: those that are *well formed* and those that are well formed and *valid*. A valid XML document is one whose structure can be checked off against a Document Type Definition (DTD).

A parser performs two levels of checking on an XML document. After checking for syntactical correctness (that is, whether the document is well formed) the parser then checks to see if the document's contents are structured according to the rules set out in the DTD.

If the parser can verify that an XML document's content is in accordance with the rules specified in the DTD, the document is said to contain valid XML. The process of insuring that the structure is valid is called—you guessed it—*validation*.

XML Goodie: Unicode Compliance

If you develop a lot of Web pages in languages other than English, you'll be very happy to learn that XML is specified to be *Unicode compliant*. Unicode (also called double-byte characters) is a standard for text in all languages. Normal (ASCII) text uses 8 bits to represent each character. As a result, it can only represent 256 (2^8) unique characters. Unicode, on the other hand, uses 16 bits to represent each character, and is thus able to represent up to 65,536 (2^{16}) characters: virtually enough to represent all characters of all languages known to humanity (excluding Klingon and a few others).

In terms of writing XML documents, provided you have the right Unicode editor, you can create your documents in any language with which you are comfortable. XML parsers are specified to be language independent.

For more information on Unicode in general, check out the Unicode Consortium's Web site at www.unicode.org.

By default, parsers automatically recognize whether a document is in Unicode. If you want to include an explicit statement, your XML declaration should include the encoding = "UTF8" attribute.

```
<xml encoding = "UTF8" >
```

Creating XML Documents

Okay, you've waited patiently enough. Let's get our hands dirty and start exploring the nitty-gritty details. We begin by going over the XML document syntax.

XML Document Syntax

As we mentioned earlier, an XML document is made of content (character data) encapsulated in markup. There are seven types of markup that can be used in an XML document:

- Element start and end tags
- Attributes
- Comments
- Entity references
- Processing instructions
- Character data sections (CDATA)
- Document type declarations

In the next few sections, we go over each type of markup with examples of how to use them.

Element Start and End Tags

Elements are the most basic building blocks of XML documents. They can be used to both contain information and define structure. An element starts out with a starting tag and ends with a corresponding ending tag.

The start tag consists of a single word (no spaces allowed) surrounded by the < and > characters. If you're familiar with HTML, <h1> is an example of a start tag. Similarly, an end tag example is </h1>. Table 3.1 shows some examples of element tags and their usage.

Keep in mind that XML is case sensitive. Element names must therefore open and close with identical cases. For example:

Table 3.1 Element Start and End Tag Syntax

TAG	DESCRIPTION
`<first_tag>`	An allowable starting tag for the first_tag element
`</first_tag>`	The corresponding ending tag for the first_tag element
`<first tag>`	Incorrect usage—element names cannot include spaces
`<1st_tag>`	Incorrect usage—element names cannot begin with a number
`</ first_tag>`	Incorrect usage—spaces are not allowed between the forward slash and element name

```
<ADDRESS>110 Main Street</address>
```

is not acceptable whereas each of the following examples is acceptable:

```
<address>110 Main Street</address>
<Address>110 Main Street</Address>
<ADDRESS>110 Main Street</ADDRESS>
```

Also keep in mind that each of these is treated separately. From a parser's point of view, each of these examples is a different type of element.

Using Elements to Define Hierarchy

The hierarchy of information is encoded by the nesting of tags. Tags can be nested to an arbitrary length in XML documents. By using nested elements, you automatically introduce a hierarchical (and rich) description of your information.

If that sounds too abstract, allow us to solidify the concept with an example. Let's use the example of an address book. An address from this book consists of people, individually referred to as *contacts*. Each contact consists of a name, a telephone number, and an address. Each telephone number consists of an area code and a phone number. Each address consists of a street name, a city, a state, and a ZIP code. Figure 3.3 shows what the structure of our address book looks like conceptually.

XML can be represented in many ways, but since we are trying to illustrate how to use elements, we are going to limit ourselves to using only elements.

```
<ADDRESS_BOOK>
    <CONTACT>
```

```
      <NAME>Alley Gator</NAME>
      <PHONE>
         <AREA_CODE>515</AREA_CODE>
         <PHONE_NUMBER>5551235</PHONE_NUMBER>
      </PHONE>
      <ADDRESS>
         <STREET_ADDRESS>112, Main Street</STREET_ADDRESS>
         <CITY>Mudy Waters</CITY>
         <STATE>FL</STATE>
         <ZIP>55544</ZIP>
      </ADDRESS>
   </CONTACT>
</ADDRESS_BOOK>
```

As you can see, some elements (ADDRESS_BOOK, CONTACT, PHONE, ADDRESS) are used only to provide structure while other elements (NAME, AREA_CODE, PHONE_NUMBER, STREET_ADDRESS, CITY, STATE, ZIP) actually contain information. Intuitively, you can see that because the data is so richly structured, given a complete database of contacts, you could perform searches or sorting based on city information, area code, or name. Intuitively, you can also see that because the NAME element is not broken up into a FIRST_NAME and LAST_NAME, simple sorting involving the content of the NAME element would be done on the basis of the contact's first name.

Figure 3.4 shows how Internet Explorer displays the above raw XML file. Internet Explorer 5.0 has a built-in MIME Type viewer that allows you to dynamically view the contents and structure of raw XML files.

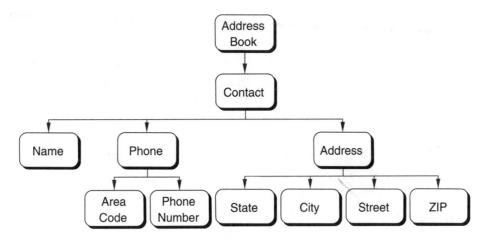

Figure 3.3　Conceptual structure of address book.

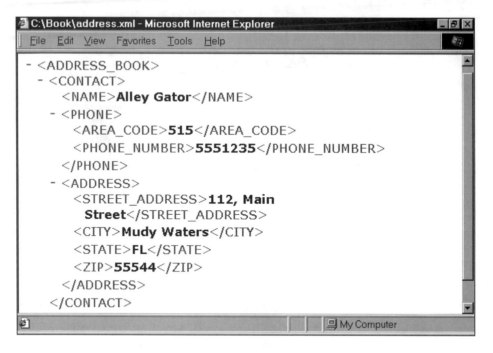

Figure 3.4 Raw XML display in Internet Explorer 5.

The red (gray in the picture) hyphens preceding the parent element names are handles that you can click on to collapse or expand portions of the XML document tree.

While this discussion may seem fairly complicated for something as small as a single contact entry, think of it in terms of scalability. This model scales very well for larger data sets, say for a contact database of several thousand contacts.

Finally, every so often, you have elements that are not being used for containing content but are being used as placeholders or to signify information by virtue of their existence (for example, the line break `<br/>` tag in HTML). For such empty elements, you can represent them in one of two ways. Let's say a particular contact has no address information. In that case, you could represent the contact as follows:

```
<ADDRESS></ADDRESS>
```

Or, if you prefer, as:

```
<ADDRESS/>
```

Both are acceptable and considered well formed.

Attributes

Attributes are usually small, descriptive bits of information used for describing elements. Again, if you are familiar with HTML, then the concept of attributes is also familiar. For example, an attribute of the `<table>` element would be `align = "center"`. If you're not familiar with HTML, then think of attributes in their literal sense: as adjectives used to describe nouns (elements).

You can use attributes in several ways to further describe your data. They are contained within the start tag of an element after the element name (remember the rule from Table 3.1, "no spaces allowed in element names"?—now you know why) and are followed by an = sign, which is followed by the value of the attribute in quotes (""). Table 3.2 describes some syntax and interpretations.

Comments

Comments are exactly the same as in HTML: They are a place to write a note to yourself; a reminder that is not displayed to the user. Think of comments as virtual Post-It Notes for software. Comments are great for reminding yourself about little details that you tend to forget while writing.

Table 3.2 Attributes and Their Syntactical Usage

ATTRIBUTE USAGE	DESCRIPTION
`<marble color = "red">`	A marble element that has a color attribute whose value is red. This is an example of a well formed attribute expression. The corresponding closing tag would be </marble>.
`<marble color = "red" size = "big">`	A marble element that has a color attribute whose value is red and a size attribute whose value is big. You can create as many attributes as you like.
`<marble color = "red" />`	A marble element with a color attribute whose value is red that has no other content.
`<marble color = red>`	Not well formed. The parser throws a fit because the attribute values must be contained in quotes.
`<marble color>`	Not well formed. XML parsers reject valueless attributes.

Here's what a comment looks like:

```
<!-- I wrote this so I could demonstrate what a comment looks
like -->
```

XML parsers ignore everything within comment tags, so you can pretty much use any characters in a comment; however, make sure you don't include the -- string inside the comment itself. For example:

```
<!-- I wrote this --so I could demonstrate what a comment looks
like -->
```

would be considered not well formed, and any XML parser worth its salt would reject it.

Comments can also be arbitrarily long; that is, there is no limit to their size. They can span several lines:

```
<!-- Here is my really long comment that has
     absolutely no meaning whatsoever other
     than to take up a lot of space -->
```

You can also use comments to *comment out* sections that you don't want the parser to read, for example:

```
<!-- here is a comment that is being used to comment out an element -->
<!-
<my_element> this element and its contents are being ignored by the
parser </my_element>
-->
```

If you're in the habit of commenting out code while writing C++ or Java applications, you will almost certainly appreciate how useful comments can be for debugging purposes—especially if you are using a parser that has terse error reporting (for example, "Error in document. Please correct and then retry."). A few words of advice: Please don't ever use a parser that reports errors as tersely as that.

Entity References

Entity references are pointers to entities. In XML, entities are units of text, where each unit could be anything from a single character to an entire document or even a reference to another document. Instead of forcing you to merge all your entities into a single chunk, entity references allow you to tell the parser where to go to find whatever entities you want included. The parser then goes to that location, fetches its contents, and stuffs it into the slot previously used by the entity reference. You could think of entity referencing as something that enables you to stay object oriented in your approach: Make your entities your objects and your entity references your pointers. Entity references can point to both external and internal entities. Internal entities are usually defined in the DTD (see the entity declarations portion later in this chapter). Figures 3.5 and 3.6 show how external entity references work.

One of the most common uses of entity references is to include content that contains characters that would otherwise confuse the parser. Once again, if you've worked a lot with HTML, you've probably already

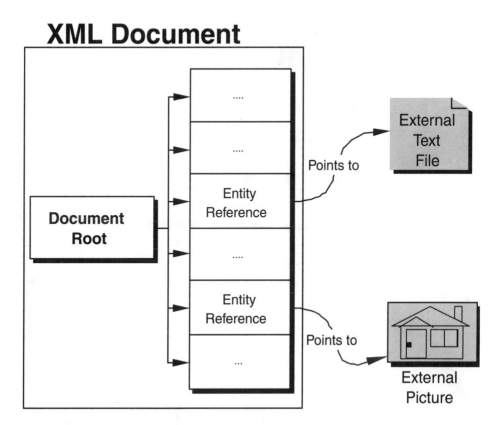

Figure 3.5   How entity references work—before parsing.

XML Document

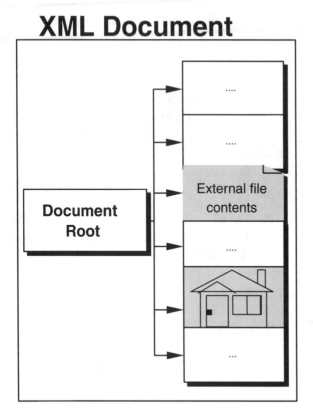

Figure 3.6 How entity references work—after parsing.

used entity references in the shape of the "&lt" to represent the less than sign (<).

For example, say you want to mathematically express that one of us authors is shorter than the other; Alex is 6' 2" and Faraz is 6' 0". Mathematically that would be:

Faraz < Alex

In XML, you might think to express it like this:

```
<height_comparison>
Faraz < Alex
</height_comparison>
```

But if you did that, the parser would get upset after reading Faraz because, as we mentioned before, this isn't well formed (there is a stray < character). In fact, you'd get an annoying error message, depending on which parser you are using to read the file, and wouldn't be able to do any further processing (take a look at Figure 3.7).

There are several ways of getting around this. One way is to use the entity references built in to XML (expressed in Table 3.3).

In the easiest case, the XML snippet would look like this:

```
<height_comparison>
Faraz &lt; Alex
</height_comparison>
```

Once run through an XML parser, the text output of the above would look like this:

```
Faraz < Alex
```

This is precisely what we want it to be.

In general though, entity references are used for representing bigger entities like files, documents, or text sections. The parser follows the references and pieces together the entire document. So, let's say you were

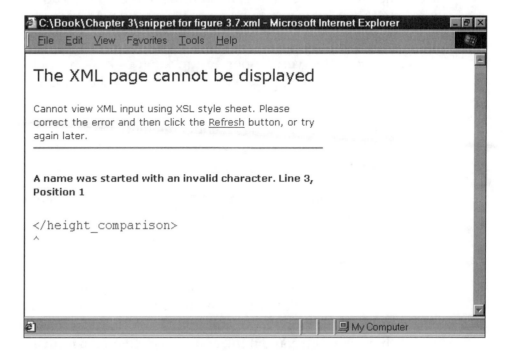

Figure 3.7 Errors occur when you use illegal characters.

Table 3.3 Built-in XML Entities and Their References

ENTITY	DESCRIPTION	ENTITY REFERENCE
<	Less than sign	<
>	Greater than sign	>
"	Quotation mark	"
'	Apostrophe	'
&	Ampersand	&

writing an essay consisting of an introduction, a body, and a conclusion. If you were to prepare each section separately, declaring each as an entity in your DTD, your XML document would refer to it as follows:

```
<my_essay>
&introduction;
&body;
&conclusion;
</my_essay>
```

The parser would then track down and read the actual introduction, body, and conclusion entities and stuff them into a single document in memory. This enables you to take an object-oriented approach to your XML documents.

If you're asking the very important question of how we defined the entities, wait a few more pages: We get into that in the "Making DTDs" section.

So, the generic syntax of using an entity reference is as follows:

```
&entity_name;
```

It is an ampersand, followed by the entity's name (declared in the DTD), followed by a semicolon. No white spaces are allowed.

Processing Instructions

Processing instructions (PI) are a hand-me-down syntax from SGML. The syntax is used to clearly mark up information sections that are specific to your application/application processor (for example, a parser) and nothing else. You could think of it as a coded memo format for your particular processor/application. You use the memo to write specific instructions to your application, instructions that you want to make sure are not thought of as conventional data.

PIs are particularly useful if your XML document is being processed by more than one parser (say a rich text format [RTF] engine or a CDF display engine). In that case, you may want to include some specific instructions to one engine that you don't want the other to pay attention to. The way this is done is to express processing instructions in a markup syntax that is different from elements, comments, or attributes. Processing instructions are of the following generic format:

```
<?processor specific_instruction = "value of instruction" ?>
```

It is a greater-than sign, followed by a question mark, followed by the name of the processor/application the PI is intended for, followed by the instruction and its value. The instruction need not have a value, though it could.

Let's take a look at an example. XML uses a PI for one of its most fundamental operations: the XML declaration. In order to tell an XML parser that the document you are passing though it is in XML, you use a PI expressed as follows:

```
<?xml version = "1.0"?>
```

Remember to keep it case sensitive; using XML in capitals causes the parser to go ballistic.

If you were using an RTF engine to insert a page break, here's the processing instruction you would include in your XML document.

```
<?rtf \page?>
```

Character Data Sections

When we talked about entity references, we mentioned that there was more than one way to fix the problem of the parser getting confused by content containing illegal characters or non-well formed syntax. One way to duck past the watchful eye of the parser is to make the parser simply assume that your content is nothing more than character data by dumping that information into a character data (CDATA) section (hence the name!). Think of the CDATA section as a cover under which contraband material (content containing characters that would otherwise cause non-well formed syntax errors) can be smuggled across customs (the XML parser).

Let's look at our original problem. We want to declare that Faraz is shorter than Alex using simple, standard math symbols. Unfortunately, the parser gets upset when we use the < character. Well, let's simply toss our errant statement into a CDATA section. Then, our XML snippet would look like this:

```
<height_comparison>
<![CDATA[Faraz < Alex]]>
</height_comparison>
```

The parser would then be tricked into ignoring the content of the CDATA section and simply reproducing it as:

```
Faraz < Alex
```

Again, this is precisely what we wanted it to look like.

Another example of using CDATA sections is to encode markup itself. Say your XML document contains information on how to create HTML pages. In that case, you're going to want to include a lot of markup sections in the document that you would want displayed as markup. Let's say you want to tell a reader how to create a div element within a span element in your HTML. Here's how you could include that information in your XML document such that it wouldn't throw the parser:

```
<example_code>
Here is how to put a &quot;Div&quot; into a &quot;Span&quot; :
<![CDATA[
        <Span id= "my_span">
            <div id= "my_div">contents of my_div</div>
        </Span>
]]>
</example_code>
```

Figure 3.8 displays what the parser spits out when it sees the above snippet.

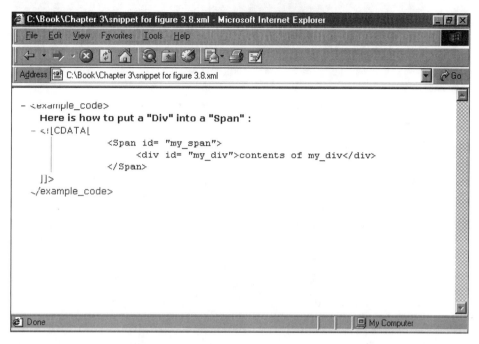

Figure 3.8 Parser output of CDATA snippet.

Generically, CDATA sections are expressed as follows:

```
<![CDATA[markup or special characters that are to be considered
as character data only]]>
```

Document Type Declaration

A *document type declaration* is a statement embedded in an XML document whose purpose is to herald the existence and location of a document type definition (DTD). Read that statement twice. A document type *declaration* is different from a document type *definition*. The first is a statement that points to the second. A DTD is a set of rules that defines the structure of an XML document. A document type declaration is a statement that tells the parser which DTD to use for checking and validation.

Let's say we have an XML document called myfile.xml that we want the parser to validate against a DTD called my_rules.dtd. The way to associate (that is, tell the parser to check) the content structure of myfile.xml against the rules specified in my_rules.dtd is to insert the following line after the XML declaration:

```
<!DOCTYPE myfile SYSTEM "my_rules.dtd">
```

The above simply states that for this particular document, whose root element's name is myfile (note: the root element name MUST match the root element declared in the declaration), a DTD is available, and its name and path is my_rules.dtd. Intuitive, isn't it? Seriously though, now you have a glimpse as to why we detest DTDs so much.

Document Type Declarations can have external and internal components; that is, they can refer to Document Type *Definitions* that are either declared within the XML document itself (so the structural rules are contained within the XML document itself) or described in an external file/location (that is, it points to an external document that contains structural information about the document, just as a model number refers to specifications contained in an external manual).

If the DTDs are internal, the syntax to use is this:

```
<!DOCTYPE root_element [
<!-- internal type definitions -->
]>
```

Even though we're getting ahead of ourselves (internal subsets are discussed later on in this chapter), here's an example of an internal subset declaration and its usage:

```
<!DOCTYPE good_guys [
<!ELEMENT good_guys (#PCDATA)>
]>
<good_guys>Alex, Faraz</good_guys>
```

Similarly, for external subsets, the syntax found in the XML document is:

```
<!DOCTYPE SYSTEM "external_file.dtd">
<root_element>
...
</root_element>
```

To exemplify this, we need to have two documents: the external DTD and the XML document. The XML document looks like this:

```
<!DOCTYPE SYSTEM "good_guys.dtd">
<good_guys>Alex, Faraz</good_guys>
```

while the DTD, good_guys.dtd looks like this:

```
<!ELEMENT good_guys (#PCDATA)>
```

A document can have *both* internal and external document type declarations so that you can further define your structure. In keeping with the same theme as above, our good_guys.dtd should look like this:

```
<!ELEMENT good_guys (#PCDATA)>
```

If we further wanted to define the structure of our good_guy element, our good_guys.xml XML file could look like this:

```
<!DOCTYPE SYSTEM "good_guys.dtd"[
<!ATTLIST good_guys who_are_they CDATA #REQUIRED>
]>
<good_guys who_are_they="the authors">Alex, Faraz</good_guys>
```

Hold on to your hats; it gets worse before it gets better. But rest assured—it does get better!

DTD Basics—The How Tos

We now enter the realm of creating XML DTDs. We've already mentioned what DTDs are, but we haven't stressed enough yet why they are important.

DTDs are important because they provide a way for explicitly declaring the structure of your XML documents. From a programming perspective, dealing with unstructured XML is pretty difficult because you can't really predict what information is going to be coming next. Even intuitive structures can take on different forms; for example, in an address data set, you may have name, address, and telephone as your fields, but who's to say that address can't be preceded by telephone? Thus you end up having to create programming instances to accommodate as many scenarios as you can to further process information. But that solution doesn't scale well; after all, the permutations of markup structures increases exponentially as data sets increase in size and complexity. Imagine what a nightmare that would be.

To make things easier, DTDs are a method for explicitly and completely defining the structure of a given XML document. DTDs are used by validating parsers that read a DTD, interpret the rules dictated within, and rigorously check to see if the XML data contained within the document is in conformance with the DTD.

Now we're ready to take a closer look at what XML DTDs are made of and how to make your own custom DTD.

A DTD can consist of the following parts:

- Element type declarations
- Attribute list declarations
- Entity declarations
- Notations declarations

Let's take a more detailed look at each of these declarations and their subsections, which we've illustrated with many examples for your convenience. If some sound silly, bear with us.

Element Type Declarations

XML documents are primarily concerned with elements. The structure of your XML documents is implicitly defined by the nesting of elements. However, at some point, an explicit description of the desired information structure has to be made. The DTD is the place to do it, and the *element type declaration* is the syntax that is used to make the structure official.

An element type declaration is a statement that heralds the existence and defines the structure of a class (type) of elements. In general, it provides the parser with three important pieces of information about each element type that occurs in your XML document:

- Its name
- The type of information (content) that it can contain (also called the element type's *content model*)
- The attributes associated with it

In a DTD, the order in which declarations are made makes a big difference. This is important to keep in mind when you are defining elements with nesting.

In general, the syntax of an element type declaration looks like this:

```
<!ELEMENT element_name (content_model)>
```

A content model is the type of data that the element can contain. Granted, that sounds a little vague. Allow us to make things more lucent.

There are several ways of declaring element structures. Generally an element can be made of other elements, character data, or a mixture of both. Let's take the simplest case: when you want to declare the existence of a single element that contains character data (that is, text). Let's say you'd like to have an element called First_Name that should contain the text of a person's name. Here's the simplest way of declaring it in your DTD:

```
<!ELEMENT First_Name (#PCDATA)>
```

Simple, right?

Table 3.4 walks through several examples of element type declarations and their equivalent interpretations and is included in case you want to use it as a quick reference guide. We go through all of these (and more) in our description of the content model.

Table 3.4 Element Type Declarations and Their Meanings

ELEMENT TYPE DECLARATION	MEANING
`<!ELEMENT Name (#PCDATA)>`	An element called *Name* must contain *character data* (that is, text). Under this declaration, an allowable element would look like this:
	`<Name>Faraz Hoodbhoy</ Name>`
	However, under this declaration, the following would be unacceptable even though it is well formed:

	`<Name>`
	`<First_Name>Faraz</First_Name>`
	`<Last_Name>Hoodbhoy</Last_Name>`
	`</Name>`

	Continues

Table 3.4 Element Type Declarations and Their Meanings *(Continued)*

ELEMENT TYPE DECLARATION	MEANING
`<!element Name (#PCDATA)>`	Beep! Parser error. The element type declaration must be in CAPITALS.
`<!ELEMENT Order ANY>`	The loosest declaration possible. An Order element can contain any mixture of character data and other elements that are *declared in the current DTD*.

`<!ELEMENT Order (appetizer, main_course, dessert)>`	An order *must* consist of one appetizer, one main_course, and one dessert item *in that order*. An acceptable example (though not necessarily a healthy one) would be:
	
	`<Order>`
	`<appetizer>Cream of Asparagus Soup</appetizer>`
	`<main_course>Fillet Mignon</main_course>`
	`<dessert>Apple Pie ala mode</dessert>`
	`</Order>`
	
	Under this order format, you would not be able to skip dessert; that is,
	
	`<Order>`
	`<appetizer>Bread rolls with butter</appetizer>`
	`<main_course>Fillet Mignon</main_course>`
	`</Order>`
	
	would be unacceptable. Nor would you be able to order food out of sequence; that is,
	
	`<Order>`
	`<dessert>Apple Pie ala mode</dessert>`
	`<appetizer>Bread rolls with butter</appetizer>`
	`<main_course>Fillet Mignon</main_course>`
	`</Order>`
	
	would also be disallowed by the parser.

`<!ELEMENT Order (appetizer?, main_course?, dessert?)>`	An order *may* consist *only* of one appetizer, one main_course, and/or one dessert item *in that order*. For example:
	`<Order>`
	`<appetizer>Bread rolls with butter</appetizer>`
	`<main_course>Fillet Mignon</main_course>`
	`</Order>`
	
	is acceptable to the parser, while
	
	`<Order>`
	`<dessert>Apple Pie ala mode</dessert>`
	`<appetizer>Bread rolls with butter</appetizer>`
	`</Order>`

Table 3.4 *(Continued)*

ELEMENT TYPE DECLARATION	MEANING
	is unacceptable because the order of *occurrence* of the elements is contrary to what was specified.

`<!ELEMENT Dessert (ice-cream|Coffee)>`	Dessert elements consists of either a *single* ice-cream element *or a single* coffee element. For example:
	
	`<Dessert>`
	`<ice-cream>vanilla<ice-cream>`
	`</Dessert>`
	
	is a valid Dessert element while
	
	`<Dessert>`
	`<pie>Apple</pie>`
	`</Dessert>`
	
	is not. It is well formed but not valid under this element type declaration.

`<!ELEMENT ice-cream (vanilla|chocolate |strawberry)+>`	An ice-cream element consists of *at least one or more* vanilla, chocolate, or strawberry elements.
	
	For example:
	
	`<ice-cream>`
	`<vanilla>...</vanilla>`
	`<vanilla>...</vanilla>`
	`<strawberry>...</strawberry>`
	`</ice-cream>`
	
	is valid while
	
	`<ice-cream>`
	`</ice-cream>`
	
	is not.

`<!ELEMENT ice-cream (vanilla|chocolate |strawberry)*>`	An ice-cream element consists of *at least zero or more* vanilla, chocolate, or strawberry elements.
	
	For example:
	
	`<ice-cream>`
	`<vanilla>...</vanilla>`
	`<vanilla>...</vanilla>`
	`<strawberry>...</strawberry>`
	`</ice-cream>`
	
	is valid and so is

Continues

Table 3.4 Element Type Declarations and Their Meanings (Continued)

ELEMENT TYPE DECLARATION	MEANING
`<!ELEMENT ice-cream (vanilla|chocolate |strawberry)*` *(continued)*	`<ice-cream>` `</ice-cream>`
`<!ELEMENT Order (#PCDATA|menu_item)*>`	This notation is used for elements with mixed content, that is, character data and further elements. In this case, an order element can consist of a mixture of at least zero or more character data and menu elements in any order. For example: `<Order>` `Madame will have:` `<menu_item>Cream of asparagus` `soup</menu_item>` `<menu_item>Sweet` `Potatoes</menu_item>` `<menu_item>Apple Pie</menu_item>` `</Order>`
`<!ELEMENT cupboard EMPTY>`	Used for elements that do not contain content. In this case, the cupboard element contains nothing.

Descriptions of Element Type Content Models

If you've skimmed over Table 3.4, you have an idea of what we're talking about. This section is more of a reference section in case there is something specific you didn't find in the table or want further clarification.

Describing the content model is key to defining the structure of your XML document. We wish there was an easier way to do it than to use the unintuitive DTD syntax, but for now we're all stuck with it. The content model essentially tells the parser what an element can contain. For example, you might want an element to be made of text only, such as:

```
<First_Name>...</First_Name>
```

Perhaps you want it to be made of other elements:

```
<Name>
    <First_Name>...</First_Name>
    <Last_Name>...</Last_Name>
</Name>
```

Perhaps still further, you want a mixture of both (technical name: *mixed content*):

```
<Name>
     Some text that adds further information
     <First_Name>...</First_Name>
     <Last_Name>...</Last_Name>
</Name>
```

There are so many ways of representing information that we make no pretensions about the best way of structuring your information. You're not going to get away from creating those pesky tree diagrams and story boards of your data—sorry. What you will find below are several common scenarios that should be able to help you create your own DTDs for enforcing whatever structure it is that you finally do decide upon.

Scenario: Specifying an Element with No Content

When an element has no content (that is, an empty element) the content model is described by the word EMPTY. The Element Type Declaration for an element called *vessel* whose contents are empty is:

```
<ELEMENT vessel EMPTY>
```

When creating the actual XML document itself, the `vessel` element would appear as this:

```
<vessel/>
```

or

```
<vessel></vessel>
```

If any content is found in the `vessel` element, the parser indicates an error.

Scenario: Specifying an Element That Can Contain "Any" Elements and Character Data

The ANY content model descriptor is the most loosely defined way of describing an element. ANY implies that the element can be an undefined mixture of elements that have been declared in the DTD as well as character data.

The Element Type Declaration for an element called catch_all is:

```
<!ELEMENT catch_all ANY>
```

A word of caution when using the ANY descriptor: Elements that inherit their complete characteristics can not be overridden by an undefined element. If you include a flavors element that has been previously defined to contain a choice of vanilla, chocolate, or strawberry, you can not override the flavors definition by putting in an unspecified flavor element, for example cookie_crumble.

Scenario: Specifying a Single Element That Contains Character Data

This is probably one of the most common declarations you will be using. This type of element simply has a name and can contain PCDATA (that is, text only). Here's the Element Type Declaration:

```
<!ELEMENT name (#PCDATA) >
```

Once declared in your DTD, any name element in your XML document would look like this:

```
<name>Faraz Hoodbhoy</name>
```

Under this type definition, name elements cannot contain subelements, for example:

```
<name>
    <first_name>Faraz</first_name>
    <last_name>Hoodbhoy</first_name>
</name>
```

is not allowed by the parser.

Scenario: Specifying an Element to Contain Subelements: Exactly One Occurrence Allowed

Suppose we wanted to make a name element such that it consists of first_name and last_name subelements (as in the above case that was disallowed). The Element Type Declaration would be:

```
<!ELEMENT name (first_name, last_name)>
```

Furthermore, because we want the `first_name` and `last_name` elements to contain PCDATA, we'd have to declare them as such. Their type declarations have been discussed above, but here is what the DTD portion defining the entire `name` element would look like:

```
<!ELEMENT name (first_name, last_name)>
<!ELEMENT first_name (#PCDATA)>
<!ELEMENT last_name (#PCDATA)>
```

The parser would interpret this declaration as follows: Elements of type `name` must consist of exactly two subelements called `first_name` and `last_name` *in that order and nothing else*. `first_name` elements can contain character data. `last_name` elements can contain character data.

As expected, a legal XML expression of the `name` type of elements would look like this:

```
<name>
    <first_name>Faraz</first_name>
    <last_name>Hoodbhoy</last_name>
</name>
```

Although the actual content of the names can differ (that is, Faraz and Hoodbhoy), nothing else could be changed with this declaration. For example,

```
<name>
    <last_name>Hoodbhoy</last_name>
    <first_name>Faraz</first_name>
</name>
```

would not work because the order is not as declared.

Also,

```
<name>
Faraz Hoodbhoy
</name>
```

would not work because the element type name was declared to explicitly have element content only.

A few notes about PCDATA usage:

- All PCDATA type content models are called *mixed content* models regardless of whether they have other elements specified.

- The (#PCDATA) content model inherently implies zero or more characters. For example, for our above example, both first_name and last_name elements could be left blank and the parser would not be upset. It would get upset if the either the first_name or the last_name or both element tags were omitted.

Scenario: Specifying a List of Subelements: Only One Occurrence Allowed

To specify a case where only a single selection is allowed (for example, answers to a multiple choice question) your element type declaration would look like this:

```
<!ELEMENT answer (choice1|choice2|choice3)>
```

The parser would interpret this declaration as: Elements of type answer can contain either one element of type choice1, or one element of type choice2, or one element of type choice3.

For this declaration, a legitimate XML representation would be:

```
<answer>
<choice1>…</choice1>
</answer>
```

Other legal answers would be only choice2 or choice3. Thus,

```
<answer>
<choice1>...</choice1>
<choice3>...</choice3>
</answer>
```

would be unacceptable as the declaration specifies *only* one occurrence of the elements specified can occur. Similarly,

```
<answer>
<choice4>…</choice4>
</answer>
```

is not allowed because choice4 has not been specified in the list of acceptable choices.

Scenario: Specifying a Subelement That Occurs Once or Not at All

Suppose you create an online form that requires information from a user, some of which is optional. For example, say you're asking for personal information and that title is not a required field, while the user's name and e-mail address is required. You only want one occurrence of each field and you want it in a particular order. Here's how to specify it:

```
<!ELEMENT user (name, e-mail_address, title?)>
```

According to this, the parser thinks an element of type user consists of one element of type name, one element of type e-mail, and optionally one element of type title.

Here's what a valid user element looks like:

```
<user>
    <name>Austin Sours</name>
    <e-mail_address>austins@being_silly.com</e-mail_address>
    <title>International Man of Tartness</title>
</user>
```

An equally valid user could look like this:

```
<user>
    <name>Austin Sours</name>
    <e-mail_address>austins@being_silly.com</e-mail_address>
</user>
```

A nonvalid user element would be:

```
<user>
    <name>Austin Sours</name>
    <title>international man of tartness</title>
</user>
```

This example is not valid because the necessary e-mail_address element is missing.

Scenarios: Specifying Subelements That Occur at Least Once and Possibly More

Let's say in our above scenario that typical users have more than one e-mail address and, for some inexplicable reason, want e-mail sent to both addresses. Though we require only one e-mail address element, why restrict them from giving us another one? Here's how you'd declare a subelement to occur at least once, possibly many times:

```
<!ELEMENT user (name, e-mail_address+, title?)>
```

The parser thinks that user elements consist of one name element, at least one e-mail_address element—possibly more—and one optional title element.

Valid user elements look like this:

```
<user>
    <name>Austin Sours</name>
    <e-mail_address>austins@being_silly.com</e-mail_address>
    <e-mail_address>austins@being_even_sillier.com</e-mail_address>
    <title>International Man of Tartness</title>
</user>
```

or this:

```
<user>
    <name>Austin Sours</name>
    <e-mail_address>austins@being_silly.com</e-mail_address>
    <title>International Man of Tartness</title>
</user>
```

or even this:

```
<user>
    <name>Austin Sours</name>
    <e-mail_address>austins@being_silly.com</e-mail_address>
</user>
```

but not like this:

```
<user>
    <name>Austin Sours</name>
</user>
```

Scenario: Specifying a Subelement That Occurs Zero or More Times

Suppose you decide that the person's name is sufficient information and that their e-mail address is no longer required. You still want them to be able to submit one or more e-mail addresses should they desire, but they are no longer necessary. In that case, your declaration would look like this:

```
<!ELEMENT user (name, e-mail_address*, title?)>
```

The parser now thinks that a user element is made of one name type element; none, one, or several e-mail_address type elements; and one optional title element.

Here's what a valid user looks like:

```
<user>
    <name>Austin Sours</name>
    <e-mail_address>austins@being_silly.com</e-mail_address>
    <e-mail_address>austins@being_even_sillier.com</e-mail_address>
    <title>International Man of Tartness</title>
</user>
```

It could also look like this:

```
<user>
    <name>Austin Sours</name>
    <title>International Man of Tartness</title>
</user>
```

or even this:

```
<user>
    <name>Austin Sours</name>
</user>
```

A nonvalid user element would look like this:

```
<user>
    <e-mail_address>austins@being_silly.com</e-mail_address>
    <title>International Man of Tartness</title>
</user>
```

We just described most of the simple element type descriptions, and nothing is stopping you from using more complicated combinations of the "zero or one" (?), "zero or more" (*), and "one or more" (+) content model operators.

Again, we recommend keeping things as simple as possible—we're big fans of the KISS (keep it short and simple) philosophy—but we realize some scenarios won't let you do that. Table 3.5 lists some examples of how you can make elements with more specialized content models.

It can get a little confusing, but if you design your structures properly, you can represent just about any content model using these notations.

Attribute List Declarations

Attributes, as we mentioned earlier, can be thought of as adjectives that further describe a noun—in this case, an element. An attribute list declaration allows us to constrain the range and types of adjectives we use to further define elements. If you've written a lot of HTML documents, then you've been using attributes for quite some time. For example, you know how to tweak the width of a table column or row by varying the value of the width attribute. You also can change the alignment of text in a cell by putting a right, left, or center value in the align attribute. But how do HTML parsers recognize these attribute names and values? One explanation is that the HTML DTD has all those values specified in it.

As in the previous section, we have summarized attribute list declarations in a table for a quick look and have detailed this information in the paragraphs that follow.

For the parser to ensure that the attributes contained in the XML document have real meaning (that is, are valid), the attributes need to be declared in your DTD. This is accomplished by using *attribute list declarations*, which generally describe four key aspects:

1. The element to which the attribute is associated
2. The name of the attribute
3. The type of the attribute
4. What the parser should do in case an attribute value is not supplied (that is, the default value)

Table 3.5 Examples of More Specialized Content Models

ELEMENT TYPE DECLARATION	MEANING AND EXAMPLES

`<!ELEMENT dessert ((ice_cream| Apple_Pie_ala_mode), scoops+)>`	Dessert type elements are made of either one *ice_cream element* or one *Apple_Pie_ala_mode* element, followed by one or more *scoop* elements. For example:
	
	`<dessert>`
	`<ice_cream></ice_cream>`
	`<scoop>vanilla</scoop>`
	`<scoop>chocolate</scoop>`
	`</dessert>`

`<!ELEMENT e-mail_header (to+,cc*,bcc*)>`	An *e-mail_header* element contains at least one or more *to* elements, followed by zero or more *cc* elements, followed by zero or more *bcc* elements. For example:
	
	`<e-mail_header>`
	`<to>faraz@some_school.edu</to>`
	`</e-mail_header>`

`<!ELEMENT comments ((good*|bad*) |(bad*|good*)*)>`	*Comments* can contain zero or more *good* elements and/or zero or more *bad* elements in any order. For example:
	
	`<comments>`
	`<good>a funny movie</good>`
	`<bad>but with very cheesy special effects.</bad>`
	`<good>But it has its moments</good>`
	`<good>You will never guess the ending</good>`
	`</comments>`

`<!ELEMENT year (junior|senior|> (#PCDATA))`	A *year* element can either have a *junior* element, a *senior* element, or contain character data. For example:
	
	`<year>`
	`it's summer -- so I am not quite a senior and no longer a junior`
	`</year>`

The general form of an attribute list looks like this (italics imply areas where specific syntax is used):

```
<!ATTLIST element_name
          attribute_name
              attribute_type
                  attribute_defaults
  >
```

The white space is tossed in to make things more legible; it has no syntactical value. The parser doesn't care about white space. If you have more than one attribute for a single element, you simply repeat the last three space holders in the same order, that is, the general form for declaring two attributes:

```
<!ATTLIST element_name
                attribute_name
                    attribute_type
                        attribute_defaults
            attribute2_name
                    attribute2_type
                        attribute2_defaults
    >
```

and so on.

Associating the attribute with the element is pretty easy. We've given you the general form; now here's an example (we leave the type and default characteristics in the general form for now):

```
<!ATTLIST student name
                name_type
                    name_default
    >
```

If we wanted to have students be described by their name and class attributes, we'd declare them like this:

```
<!ATTLIST student name
                name_type
                    name_default
            class
                class_type
                    class_default
    >
```

Table 3.6 summarizes attribute type declarations.

After we've associated the element and the attribute, we need to declare the attribute's type or class. The list of attribute types is fairly long—ten in total—but many are very similar. Here's the complete list of allowable attribute types:

1. Strings (text values)

2. Enumerated (one of specified values)

3. ENTITY

4. ENTITIES

5. ID

6. IDREF

7. IDREFS

8. NMTOLKEN

9. NMTOLKENS

10. NOTATION

Let's take a look at each type (or groups of types since several are similar) in greater detail.

String Attributes

Strings in attribute types are like strings in all programming languages—they are a series of character data. In XML, string lengths not defined and can be arbitrarily long. From a design perspective, however, we do not recommend using long strings in your attributes.

To assign a string type to an attribute called authors to an element of type book, here's what you'd do:

```
<!ATTLIST book author CDATA default>
```

The CDATA keyword implies a string. Strings can contain all text characters except for special characters like quotation marks and

Table 3.6 Attribute Type Declarations Part 1: Associating an Element with an Attribute

PARTIAL ATTRIBUTE TYPE DECLARATION	INTERPRETATION
`<!ATTLIST car manufacturer type default>`	An element of type *car* has an attribute called *manufacturer* associated with it.
`<!ATTLIST car manufacturer type default model type default >`	An element of type *car* has two attributes, one called *manufacturer* and one called *model,* associated with it.

ampersands. These exceptions are noted in Table 3.3. You can include these characters by using the entity references specified in Table 3.3.

Here's what a book element, as specified above, could look like (assume the element type declaration has already been made to allow PCDATA):

```
<book author= "J.R.R. Tolkein">The Hobbit</author>
```

Enumerated Attributes

Enumerated attributes are perhaps the most interesting and useful of attribute types. An enumerated attribute is one that can take on values from a specified list of set values. These values are specified in the declaration as well. The general form is as follows:

```
<!ATTLIST element_name attribute_name  (value1|value2|value3)
default>
```

This sort of an attribute type is useful in many instances in which you want to use attributes to slot elements, for example, based on priorities. Here's how to assign a priority attribute with three values (urgent, normal, low) to a mail_item element:

```
<!ATTLIST mail_item Priority (urgent|normal|low) default>
```

A valid mail_item element could look like this:

```
<mail_item  Priority  =  "urgent">more  mail_item  information<
/mail_item>
```

You can specify as many values as you like; however, please keep in mind that XML is case sensitive. In the above example, if Priority = "URGENT", the parser would declare it invalid because "URGENT" is in the incorrect case. One way of getting around this is to include both cases in your list of acceptable values. A better way is to take care of it in the XML application itself.

ENTITY and ENTITIES Attributes

We're treating both ENTITY and ENTITIES together because ENTITIES is the plural of ENTITY. The ENTITY and ENTITIES attribute types are a way of inserting entities into attribute values. To use these types, you must have previously declared an entity in your DTD (read the section on entities in this chapter for details on how to do this). The ENTITY/ENTITY keyword is used in the declaration to tell the parser to go find the unparsed entity and pop it into the value of the attribute.

For example, if you wanted to insert a picture entity in to the value of a priority attribute (say an up arrow), the following steps show you how to do it.

First, remember that the graphic needs to be declared as an entity somewhere in your DTD. Though we haven't yet talked about Entity declarations in detail, here's a possible declaration of it:

```
<!ENITY up_arrow SYSTEM "up_arrow.gif" NDATA gif>
```

Now that the up_arrow entity has been declared, the attribute declaration could look like this:

```
<!ATTLIST mail_item Priority ENTITY default>
```

By declaring this, we've now said that a priority attribute can contain any previously declared entity. Thus, a valid mail_item element under the above declaration could look like this:

```
<mail_item Priority = "up_arrow">more mail item information<
/mail_item>
```

The ENTITIES type essentially tells the parser that a particular attribute can have one or more entities. Continuing our mail_item theme, if you wanted to include two entities in the priority attribute (say an up arrow and a flag), you'd declare the attribute list as follows:

```
<!ATTLIST mail_item Priority ENTITIES default>
```

Assuming that up_arrow and flag are previously declared entities, a valid example of mail_item under this declaration is:

```
<mail_item Priority = "up_arrow flag">
```

ID, IDREF, and IDREFS Attributes

ID, IDREF, and IDREFS are similar. ID attributes are unique identifiers of an element. Once you declare an element to have an attribute of type ID, its ID value must be unique for every element of that type in your XML document. Think of them as primary keys from database theory. The good thing about IDs is they ensure that each such element can be uniquely identified (if you have elements with the same ID attribute value in your XML, the parser lets you know). The bad thing if you're writing the XML document yourself is that you've got to make sure you create a unique ID for each element (though that's not too tough to do as a programmer, so long as you have a well defined nomenclature/scheme).

It is important that the value of an ID attribute has a particular format. It must start with either a letter, an underscore (_), or a colon (:). An ID cannot be a pure numerical value. This is good at many levels, yet frustrating at others.

Here's how to declare assign an ID type attribute to a part element:

```
<!ATTLIST part code_number ID default>
```

A valid part could look like this:

```
<part code_number = "A106">more part information</part>
```

An IDREF is a pointer to the any of the unique IDs previously stated in the document. If the above part element has been included in the document (with its unique code_number), then it is possible to refer to it only on the basis of its ID value. Here's the attribute declaration:

```
<!ATTLIST part_to_order refers_to IDREF default>
```

A valid part_to_order element would be:

```
<part_to_order refers_to = "A106">more part_to_order information </part_to_order>
```

The IDREFS type is similar except that it allows multiple references to IDs. An attribute declaration of a parts_to_order element could look like this:

```
<!ATTLIST parts_to_order refers_to IDREFS default>
```

The corresponding valid element could look like this:

```
<parts_to_order refers_to = "A106 B308"> more parts_to_order information </parts_to_order>
```

NMTOKEN and NMTOKENS Attributes

Again, a similar relationship exists between NMTOKEN and NMTO-KENS attribute types. These types are essentially strings except that they do not allow the existence of white-space characters. This can be useful in instances when you want to ensure that a user inputs correct values, such as a license plate number, social security number, or credit card number. They ensure that you don't get erroneous values due to spaces between characters.

The NMTOKEN attribute type allows the existence of a single NMTOKEN value. Let's take the example of an element of type *car* that has an NMTOKEN attribute called *license*. Here's a plausible attribute declaration:

```
<!ATTLIST car license_plate_number NMTOKEN default>
```

A valid element under this declaration could be:

```
<car license_plate_number= "HGD3532">more car info</car>
```

By using the NMTOKEN attribute type, we've ensured that:

```
<car license_plate_number= "HGD 3532">more car info</car>
```

will not be allowed in our XML document.

As you've probably guessed, the NMTOKENS attribute type allows one or more NMTOKEN values. Each value in this case is separated by white space.

NOTATION Attributes

Notation attribute types essentially specify a list of predeclared notations, which are defined earlier in the Document Type Declaration. In doing so, the value of the attribute is constrained to one of these notation values. It is a little like the enumerated attribute type with two exceptions. First, you are declaring the values as notations instead of text. Second, the default value is implicitly defined; therefore, it is not followed by our mysterious *default* statement. Notations are discussed later in this chapter, but let's look at an example of how they are used in the context of declarations of notation attribute types.

For this notation declaration:

```
<!NOTATION  my_format  SYSTEM  "http://mysite.com/my_format
_processor.exe">
```

this NOTATION attribute declaration could be used:

```
<!ATTLIST my_code format NOTATION (my_format) >
```

and this element would be considered valid:

```
<my_code format = "my_format">
```

If you have several notations declared beforehand, you can specify a list of choices in your attribute declaration. For example, in

```
<!ATTLIST  my_code  format  NOTATION  (my_format|some_other
_format)>
```

my_code elements have the format attribute values of either my_format or some_other_format. That is, both

```
<my_code format ="my_format">
```

and

```
<my_code format ="some_other_format">
```

are considered valid under this declaration.

Table 3.7 summarizes these attribute type declarations.

Attribute Defaults

The last part of the attribute declaration list is the default value of the attribute. Defaults come in four variations:

Required.   You must supply a value for the attribute (that is, the document cannot leave it blank).

Implied.   The parser tells the XML application that no value was supplied, and it is up to the XML application to decide what value, if any, to fill in.

Table 3.7 Attribute List Declarations Part 2: Assigning an Attribute's Type

PARTIAL ATTRIBUTE TYPE DECLARATION	INTERPRETATION
`<!ATTLIST car manufacturer` **`CDATA`** *`default`*`>`	A string type attribute. An element of type *car* has a *manufacturer* attribute associated with it that contains string information.
	Acceptable XML document entries for *car*:
	`<car manufacturer = "Japanese">`
	or
	`<car manufacturer = "unknown at present">`
`<!ATTLIST car manufacturer` **`(American|European|Japanese)`** *`default`*`>`	An enumerated attribute type. An element of type *car* has a *manufacturer* attribute associated with it that can only contain one of the following values: American, European, or Japanese.
	Acceptable XML document entries:
	`<car manufacturer = "American">`
	or
	`<car manufacturer = "Japanese">`
	or
	`<car manufacturer = "European">`
	Unacceptable entry:
	`<car manufacturer = "Korean">`
`<!ATTLIST car logo` **`ENTITY`** *`default`*`>`	An ENTITY attribute type. An element of type *car* has a *logo* attribute associated with it that can hold one previously declared entity.
	Acceptable XML document entry (assume *pentagon* is a previously declared entity):
	`<car logo = "pentagon">`
	Unacceptable entry:
	`<car logo = "`*`undefined_entity`*`">`
`<!ATTLIST car logo` **`ENTITIES`** *`default`*`>`	ENTITIES attribute type, similar to ENTITY types. An element of type *car* has a *logo* attribute associated with it that can hold one or more previously declared entities.

Continues

Table 3.7 Attribute List Declarations Part 2: Assigning an Attribute's Type *(Continued)*

PARTIAL ATTRIBUTE TYPE DECLARATION	INTERPRETATION
`<!ATTLIST car logo` **`ENTITIES`** `default>` *(continued)*	Acceptable XML document entries (Assume *pentagon* and *arrow_head* are previously declared entities): `<car logo = "pentagon arrow_head">` or `<car logo = "pentagon">` Unacceptable entry: `<car logo = "pentagon undefined_entity">`
`<!ATTLIST car chassis_number` **`ID`** `default>`	ID attribute type. An element of type *car* has a *chassis_number* attribute associated with it that holds a value that is unique throughout the entire XML document. IDs start with either a letter(A–Z), an underscore (_), or a colon (:). Acceptable XML document entry (assume *C12345* hasn't been used before): `<car chassis_number = "C12345">` Unacceptable entry (assume above element is included in document): `<car chassis_number = "C12345">`
`<!ATTLIST car_to_recall Reference` **`IDREF`** `default>`	IDREF attribute type. An element of type *car_to_recall* uses a *Reference* attribute associated with it that points to another element in the document bearing a unique ID value. Acceptable XML document entry (assume *C12345* has been uniquely assigned to a element—possibly *car*, though not necessarily so): `<car_to_recall Reference = "C12345">` Unacceptable entry: `<car_to_recall Reference = "unused_ID">`
`<!ATTLIST cars_to_recall Reference` **`IDREFS`** `default>`	IDREFS attribute type, plural of IDREF. An element of type *cars_to_recall* uses a *Reference* attribute associated with it to point to one or more other elements in the document bearing unique ID values. Acceptable XML document entries (assume *C12345* and *B67890* have been uniquely assigned to some elements in the document): `<cars_to_recall Reference = "C12345 B67890">`

Table 3.7 *(Continued)*

PARTIAL ATTRIBUTE TYPE DECLARATION	INTERPRETATION

	or
	
	`<cars_to_recall Reference = "C12345">`
	
	Unacceptable entries:
	
	`<cars_to_recall Reference = "unused_ID">`
	
	or
	
	`<cars_to_recall Reference = "C12345 unused_ID">`

`<!ATTLIST car`
`hubcap_type`
NMTOKEN *default*`>`
	NMTOKEN attribute type. An element of type *car* has a *hubcap_type* attribute whose values contain no white space.
	
	Acceptable XML document entry:
	
	`<car hubcap_type= "S112R">`
	
	Unacceptable entry:
	
	`<car hubcap_type= "S 112R">`

`<!ATTLIST car`
`hubcap_types`
NMTOKENS *default*`>`
	NMTOKENS attribute type. Plural of NMTOKENS. An element of type *car* has a *hubcap_types* attribute that contains one or more values, each without white space.
	
	Acceptable XML document entries:
	
	`<car hubcap_types= "S1123 B2133">`
	
	or
	
	`<car hubcap_types= "S1123">`

`<!ATTLIST car`
`transmission_format`
NOTATION
`(automatic|manual)>`
	NOTATION attribute type. NOTATIONS specify allowable notations that have been previously declared (see NOTATION section for details). An element of type *car* has a *transmission_format* attribute that can contain a notation value of either *automatic* or *manual*. Note: This is a complete attribute list declaration—defaults are supplied in the declaration.
	
	Acceptable XML document entries:
	
	`<car transmission_format = "automatic">`
	
	or
	
	`<car transmission_format = "manual">`
	
	Unacceptable entry:
	
	`<car transmission_format = "undefined_notation">`

Fixed. The values of the attributes are included in the declaration itself. If no value is supplied, the parser plugs in and passes on the default value. If a value is supplied, it has to be the same as specified in the declaration or else the parser issues an error.

Supplied. In this case (the most common), the DTD supplies the default value of the attribute if it is not supplied in the XML document.

Let's take a more detailed look at each default type.

Required Attribute Values

Required attributes tell the parser that the XML document has to have a value specified for the attribute. If it doesn't, then it detects an error. This is a useful way for ensuring that you get a value from your document.

Here's how to declare the presence of a value for a string type attribute called license_number belonging to an element called *car*:

```
<!ATTLIST car license_number CDATA #REQUIRED>
```

Note that we no longer have any italics. This is a complete attribute list declaration.

Here's what a car's license number can look like:

```
<car license_number = "ADP453">
```

If your car element looks like this:

```
<car/>
```

the parser issues an error. However, you should be aware that if your element looked like this:

```
<car license_number = "">
```

the parser does not issue an error. Why? Because CDATA attribute types can contain zero or more characters.

Implied Attribute Values

An implied default is one that doesn't have to be explicitly defined: The parser is told to pass on a blank value to the XML application and let it decide what to do next. In doing so, you give yourself as an application developer more flexibility (and responsibility).

Here's how you assign an implied default to an attribute.

```
<!ATTLIST person gender CDATA #IMPLIED>
```

Essentially, we've told the parser that a person element has a gender attribute of type CDATA and that no value is supplied; therefore, let the XML application decide what to do next (for example, issue an error or toss in a default value). Thus, although the parser doesn't mark it as an error, the XML application can if the developer wants it to.

Fixed Attribute Values

Attributes with fixed defaults completely define an attribute and do not allow any changes to the attributes values in the XML document. If the attribute value in the XML document is left blank, the parser passes the specified default value to the parser. If the attribute has a value other than that specified, the parser reports an error. Finally, if the attribute value in the document matches the specified value, no error is detected, and the specified value is passed on to the application.

Here's how to fix an attribute:

```
<!ATTLIST person mood CDATA #FIXED "Happy">
```

This tells the parser that by default every person element's mood attribute *must* be Happy (wouldn't that be great!) Thus, there are two possible ways of representing the person element:

```
<person mood = "Happy"/>
```

or

```
<person/>
```

In both cases, the XML parser tells the XML application the same thing—that the person element's mood attribute value is happy.

Supplied Attribute Values

The term *supplied value* is not an official one. It's one we cooked up, but perhaps you will agree with our nomenclature after you've heard our reasoning.

With supplied value attribute defaults, the DTD supplies a default value if one is not provided in the XML document. Where it differs from any of the other values is that if the document contains a valid value, it gets passed on; if the attribute value (or even the attribute itself) is missing, supplied values get passed on to the application using the parser.

Here's what the supplied value attribute default looks like:

```
<!ATTLIST jelly_bean color (Red|Green|White) "Red">
```

Another example:

```
<!ATTLIST jelly_bean color #CDATA "Red">
```

Table 3.8 summarizes the usage of attribute defaults.

Table 3.8   Attribute List Declarations Part 3: Assigning an Attribute's Default Values

ATTRIBUTE TYPE DECLARATION	INTERPRETATION

`<ATTLIST car manufacturer CDATA #REQUIRED>`	#REQUIRED default. The XML Document must supply the value of the attribute *manufacturer;* otherwise the parser issues an error.
	
	Acceptable XML document entry:
	
	`<car manufacturer = "Korean">`
	
	Unacceptable entry:
	
	`<car/>`

`<ATTLIST car manufacturer CDATA #IMPLIED>`	#IMPLIED default. The XML document doesn't have to supply a value (the parser disregards value). The XML application decides what to do next.
	
	Acceptable XML document entries:
	
	`<car/>`
	
	or
	
	`<car manufacturer = "Korean">`

`<ATTLIST car manufacturer CDATA #FIXED "Korean">`	#FIXED default. The *car* attribute can have only one value: Korean. The XML Document must supply either no value or the exact same value. *Continues*

Table 3.8 (Continued)

ATTRIBUTE TYPE DECLARATION	INTERPRETATION

	Acceptable XML document entries:
	
	`<car manufacturer = "Korean">`
	
	or
	
	`<car/>`

`<ATTLIST car manufacturer CDATA "Korean">`	Supplied default. If a value is supplied, the parser passes it on. If no value is supplied, the parser passes on the default value *Korean*.
	
	Acceptable XML document entries:
	
	`<car manufacturer = "American">`
	
	or
	
	`<car manufacturer = "Korean">`
	
	or
	
	`<car/>`

Entity Declarations

Entities become more and more important as your applications grow more complex. As we mentioned before, entities are essentially objects that you can point to in your XML document using an entity reference. The actual declaration of the entity is made in the DTD.

Entities have their own types as well. While we talked briefly about internal and external entities in the entity reference section, we need to mention that both of these can furthermore be subsets of two types of entities:

Parameter Entities. Entities that are used only inside the DTD itself (sort of shorthand for programming ease). Their general form is:

```
<!ENTITY % entity_name "entity_type">
```

General Entities. Entities that are used in the XML document itself (that is, under the root element). Their general form is:

```
<!ENTITY entity_name "entity">
```

Realistically, you most likely will be dealing with external entities of the general form. However, in the interest of completion, we've described each type.

Internal General Entity Declaration

As we mentioned before, a general entity is one that is used in the XML document itself as opposed to being referenced internally in the DTD. `One common use of internal general entities is creating a shortcut to typing long words/acronyms. Here's an example (Note: this is a complete XML document with an internal DTD; keywords are in boldface):

```
<!DOCTYPE mail [
<!ELEMENT mail (letter)+>
<!ENTITY SDS "Same Day Service">
<!ENITITY NDS "Next Day Service">
<!ENTITY Alex "Alex Ceponkus, Canada">
<!ENTITY Faraz "Faraz Hoodbhoy, USA">
<!ELEMENT letter (to, from, content+)+>
<!ELEMENT to (#PCDATA)>
<!ELEMENT from (#PCDATA)>
<!ELEMENT content (#PCDATA)>
<!ATTLIST letter priority ENTITY #REQUIRED>

]>

<!-- Comment: XML document (that is, content) starts here-->

<mail>
    <letter priority = "SDS">
        <to>&Alex</to>
        <from>&Faraz</from>
        <content>Hi Alex. Good luck on the exam!</content>
    </letter>
    <letter priority = "NDS">
        <to>&Alex</to>
        <from>&Faraz</from>
        <content>How did the exam go?</content>
    </letter>
</mail>
```

During parsing, the parser follows all the entity references and pieces the document together in memory so that (in memory) it now looks like this:

```
<mail>
    <letter priority = "Same Day Service">
```

```
            <to>Alex Ceponkus, Canada</to>
            <from>Faraz Hoodbhoy, USA</from>
            <content>Hi Alex. Good luck on the exam!</content>
      </letter>
      <letter priority = "Next Day Service">
            <to>Alex Ceponkus, Canada</to>
            <from>Faraz Hoodbhoy, USA</from>
            <content>How did the exam go?</content>
      </letter>
  </mail>
```

The key point in this example is that we used entities that were declared and defined inside the DTD, in the main XML document.

Internal Parameter Entity Declaration

Parameter Internal Entity declarations are essentially useful for making your DTD more human readable and accessible. Why should this be an important consideration? It makes going back and changing your DTD easier (after all, who remembers what they've written months ago?). The argument could be made that you could just as easily accomplish this with extensive commenting. Nevertheless, it is a more comprehensive option than commenting. And like most structural things, it's harder to do the first time, but makes life much easier in the long run.

Let's say, for example, that you have a DTD of an XML document with a root element of cars. Each car element has a product_code attribute of string type that you later decide, should be of type NMTOKENS (to ensure that each product_code is devoid of white space—makes comparisons easier for the XML application.) Furthermore, let's say that you've got several attributes (say delivery_code and distributor_code), all of which are supposed to have the same format (say string or NMTOKEN). Instead of changing each attribute from CDATA to NMTOKEN, you could assign an internal parameter entity called code_format that is referenced each time for each attribute's type. Similarly, let's say you do the same for each attribute's default value. By changing the internal parameter entity statements, you instantly change the attribute type and default value for all concerned attributes.

For example:

```
<!DOCTYPE cars [
<!ENTITY % code_format "CDATA">
<!ENTITY % default_value "#REQUIRED">
```

```
<!ELEMENT cars (car)+>
<!ELEMENT car (#PCDATA)>
<!ATTLIST car product_code %code_format %default_value
            delivery_code %code_format %default_value
            distributor_code %code_format %default_value>
]>
<cars>
    <car product_code = "A432 0001" delivery_code = "B2121" distributor⌐
    code ="J3 4212">
     Model 2100ZX3
     </car>
</cars>
```

To force all the attribute values to have values without white space (that is, NMTOKEN), you'd simply change the

```
<!ENTITY % code_format "CDATA">
```

line to:

```
<!ENTITY % code_format "NMTOKEN">
```

You could do a similar change with the %default_value line to change the default value of the attributes.

External General Entity Declaration

General External entities declarations are made when you want to declare the existence of an external object (e.g., a picture or another XML document) as an entity in your document.

Let's say we've got a proposal document that consists of an executive summary, a discussion section, and a conclusion section. Each of these has been prepared and stored as external documents. In that case, our external entity declarations could look like this:

```
<!DOCTYPE proposal [
<!ENTITY executive_summary SYSTEM "executive_summary.xml">
<!ENTITY discussion SYSTEM "discussion.xml">
<!ENTITY conclusion SYSTEM "conclusion.xml">
<!ELEMENT proposal (#PCDATA)>
]>
<proposal>
&executive_summary;
&discussion;
&conclusion;
</proposal>
```

See the elegance of it all? Each of these sections (executive_summary, discussion, conclusion) can be treated separately and all joined together by the parser. They keyword SYSTEM tells the parser that the item in quotation marks is an URI (universal resource indicator), which is a pointer to the location of the file.

External Parameter Entity Declaration

External Parameter Entity Declarations are great for sharing DTD components among many XML DTDs. The idea is this: If you have common elements/entities/attributes, why bother declaring the same thing each time?

Following is an example of how to share DTD components. Let's say we're working with a bookstore environment. In our current document, we have a contact database that contains information on the person's name, address, and telephone number. Let's also say that we've previously used a particular structure for address and name information and that, in the interest of consistency, we'd like these fields to maintain the same structure. Here's an example of what our main XML document, including internal DTD, could look like:

```
<!DOCTYPE contacts [
<!ELEMENT contacts (contact)*>
<!ELEMENT contact (name, address, telephone)>
<!ENTITY % name SYSTEM "name.dtd">
<!ENTITY % address SYSTEM "address.dtd">
<!ELEMENT telephone (#PCDATA)>
]>
<contacts>
    <contact>
        <name>
            <first_name>Faraz</first_name>
            <last_name>Hoodbhoy</last_name>
        </name>
        <address>Karachi, Pakistan</address>
        <telephone>(555)123 4567</telephone>
    </contact>
</contacts>
```

You probably noticed that first_name and last_name elements are explicitly declared in the internal DTD. For this snippet to work, we need to have external DTD files name.dtd and address.dtd. Here's what name.dtd could look like:

```
<!ELEMENT address (first_name, last_name)>
```

```
<!ELEMENT first_name (#PCDATA)>
<!ELEMENT last_name (#PCDATA)>
```

address.dtd probably looks like this:

```
<!ELEMENT address (#PCDATA)>
```

Again, the parser follows the references/pointers to different locations, pieces together a comprehensive DTD in memory, and then checks whether the document is in compliance.

Table 3.9 summarizes the types of Entity declarations and their use.

Notations Declarations

Finally, the last items to mention about DTDs are Notations Declarations. We briefly touched upon them in the attribute list declaration section, but let us now talk about them in a little more detail.

Very often you may find the need to process a external information that is not in XML format (binary files, image files, sound files, or perhaps database files). In that case, more likely than not, your XML parser will not be able to process the information you are including. Theoretically, that could kill your application altogether.

Fortunately, there is a way around this using *notations*. Notation declarations allow to tell the parser what to do with information of a particular format or *notation*, usually by assigning an external application to process it for you. The parser tells the application what program is usually associated with that particular data so the application knows where to find it should it wish to execute it. Here's an example:

```
<!NOTATION    my_format    SYSTEM    "http://my_website.com
/my_application.exe">
```

If the XML document wants to use a file (or data) in my_format, it can refer to it in one of two ways. First, it can reference it with an external entity. Second, it can include it directly in the content of an element by assigning an attribute of type NOTATION (as described it the Attribute Declaration List section) and setting the value of that attribute to my_format.

You can also explicitly tell the parser that the contents of an entity are of a non-XML format by using the keyword NDATA followed by the

Table 3.9 Entity Declaration Types and Their Use

TERM	MEANING/DESCRIPTION
Parameter	Entities that are used solely within the DTD (that is, not in the XML document).
General	Entities that are used within the XML document itself.
Internal	Declared internally and used in the same document.
External	Declared in an external file and used in the internal XML document (DTD section or markup section).
Internal Parameter Entity Declaration	Entities that are internally referenced in the DTD section of your XML document. Useful for making your DTD more human readable and accessible. Very helpful in creating classes of attributes or elements, which make future changes very easy.
Internal General Entity Declaration	Declaring entities that are internally referenced in the markup portion of your XML document. Useful for creating entities that contain either text or markup (or both), for example, acronyms, short forms, or markup sections, which can later be referenced into the markup section of your XML document.
External Parameter Entity Declaration	Declaring entities that have been further described in an external DTD. Useful for sharing XML DTD components across many XML documents.
External General Entity Declaration	Declaring external objects as entities. Useful for maintaining an object-oriented approach in your XML documents and pulling in non-XML information (for example, images and sound clips).

declared notation. The advantage of doing so is that you explicitly tell the parser not to bother parsing the entity itself, rather than letting it read through it and issue an error. Again, an example:

```
<!DOCTYPE applicant [
<!NOTATION resume_format SYSTEM "resume-whiz notation">
<!ENITITY resume_file SYSTEM "faraz.rsm" NDATA resume_format>
<!ELEMENT applicant (name)>
<!ATTLIST applicant resume ENTITY #REQUIRED>
<!ELEMENT name (#PCDATA)>
]>

<applicant resume = "resume_file">
<name>Faraz Hoodbhoy</name>
</applicant>
```

The important thing to note here is that because the NDATA section explicitly states that the resume_file entity contains non-XML data, resume_file entities cannot be referenced from within an element's content as opposed to the usual way by using an entity reference. NDATA sections are hence only referenced as the value of the ENTITY or ENTITIES type attributes.

Concluding Thoughts on DTDs

We've gone through a lot of details about the guts of an XML document and stressed a lot on how to create DTDs to ensure structural integrity of your XML documents. Using DTDs you can define even fairly complex structures with the syntax we've described.

However, DTDs leave a lot to be desired. They are not terribly intuitive, nor are they particularly easy to use. Even more important than the niceties of convenience, DTDs have a serious deficiency in that they do not address datatyping, which is constraining data to a particular format such as an integer, floating point, or date. Furthermore, it does not allow you to limit the number of entries (sure, you can specify "zero," "zero or more," and "one or more" instances, but you cannot specify "let only 2 occurrences happen" or "let there be less than 10 occurrences").

More often than not, as a programmer, you are going to want more control of your datatyping. String information (#PCDATA and CDATA), while useful, usually requires further processing before you can do anything interesting such as calculations with it. The result is that you end up having to do a lot of grunt programming to make things happen, which is pretty ridiculous when you think about it—just about every programming language gives you the ability to datatype your variables. If XML is going to succeed in being the universal way of representing and exchanging information over the Web, datatyping is critical.

The W3C is aware of this very basic need and has a working group called the XML Schema Working Group. According to its Web site, it is currently working on creating a formal recommendation; however several proposals have been submitted to the group. The current proposals listed include the XML-Data proposal submitted by representatives from Microsoft, Inso Corporation, DataChannel, ArborText, and the University of Edinburgh.

The reason we mention this proposal is that Microsoft has included complete support of this proposal, which was later included as a subset to the Document Content Description proposal in August of 1998, in Internet Explorer 5. However, because this is NOT currently a W3C approved recommendation, we do not spend a lot of time writing about how to use it. Nevertheless, we do encourage you to take a look at it and perhaps write some sample code around it. It's neat and it gives you an idea of what alternative content description syntaxes to DTDs might look like. You can get details on the current proposals under consideration at the W3C's XML Schema Working Group at www.w3.org/XML/Activity.html.

Namespaces

We've stressed over and over how great XML is because you can create your own tags and how you can use an object-oriented approach toward documents and import data from various sources. However, in our glee, we would be remiss if we didn't mention the possibility of importing data from various sources that use the same element and attribute names. This is not as uncommon as you'd think. In fact, once you do think about it, you may end up being upset with us for not having mentioned it earlier.

Let us create a scenario for describing how and when namespaces are important. Let's say that you are creating a comparative shopping application displaying information about books from different vendors. The vendors we are interested in are, for lack of better names, Narnes&Bobel and Mamazon.com. The vendors you are dealing with are able to supply information to you in the form of XML markup, but it is your job to put information from both vendors into a single XML document.

It is extremely likely that you will come across information from both vendors that utilize the same tag names, for example, book, author, title, price, and isdn. It is also likely that information from each is going to be defined by DTDs, and there is no guarantee that both bookstores are going to be using the exact same DTD as the other one is (after all, they're competitors).

For instance, let's say that the Narnes&Bobel site uses the following structure to represent information about a particular book:

```
<book  author = "J.R.R. Tolkein"
       title = "The Hobbit"
       price = "$3.50"
</book>
```

while Mamazon may choose to use this format:

```
<book>
    <title>The Hobbit</title>
    <author>J.R.R. Tolkein</author>
    <price currency = "US$">3.25</price>
</book>
```

Both are legitimate ways of representing information. Both structures can be defined in a DTD. But how does one differentiate between these book types? This example is intentionally scaled down, but you can easily imagine what much more complicated real-life situations could be. For example, when the same attribute name is used in a single document with many elements:

```
<book name = "The Rabbit">
<author name = "Dr. Jameson"/>
<reviewer name = "Martial Law"/>
</book>
```

Furthermore, when you decide to do special formatting on the book's name, how do you distinguish it from the reviewer name attribute? Things can get pretty nasty very quickly, but lest you think we're evil people for making you read this entire chapter only to tell you that an insurmountable obstacle prevents you from making a real-world XML application, rest assured! There is a solution.

Fortunately, the good people at the W3C have been giving a lot of thought to this situation. The solution they recommend was finalized in January 1999 and is expressed in the concept of *namespaces*. Namespaces are a way of uniquely qualifying element and attribute names on the Web, thus avoiding conflicts between elements (and attributes) that have the same name.

The idea is to declare a namespace and a corresponding prefix for each DTD or schema (see the section "Concluding Thoughts on DTDs") and to preface every element or attribute that is from a particular DTD with its corresponding namespace prefix.

We see the look of consternation on your face, which means its time for another example. In this one, we've combined the information from both our vendors:

```
<Results xmlns:mama="http://mamazon.com/schema"
        xmlns:nab="http://NarnesAndBobel.com/book.dtd"
        xmlns:e_com_org="http://e_com_org.com/schema">
  <mama:book>
      <mama:title>The Hobbit</mama:title>
      <mama:author>J.R.R. Tolkein</mama:author>
      <mama:price e_com_org:currency = "US$">2.75</mama:price>
  </mama:book>

  <nab:book
          nab:author = "J.R.R. Tolkein"
          nab:title = "The Hobbit"
          nab:price = "$3.50"
  >
  </nab:book>
  <our_recommendation>
  You should buy the book from Mamazon.com
  </our_recommendation>
</Results>

@
```

Other than looking much messier, what does this example actually indicate? Let's take a look under the hood and see what's going on.

Breaking Down Our "Results" Example

Let's take a closer look at what's going on:

```
<Results xmlns:mama="http://mamazon.com/schema"
        xmlns:nab="http://NarnesAndBobel.com/book.dtd"
        xmlns:e_com_org="http://e_com_org.com/schema">
```

Our root element is *Results*.

The xmlns keyword is part of the reserved vocabulary in XML used for declaring the *namespace prefix* (in this case mama, nab, and e_com_org) and the location (a UUID, URN, URI, or URL) of the respective DTD or schema.

UUID, URN, and URI

All of these are ways of representing the complete address and route for locating a file across electronic networks.

A UUID is a Universally Unique IDentifier. It is similar to a GUID (Globally Unique IDentifier), which is used for identifying COM (Component Object Model) objects.

A URN is a Uniform Resource Name. It defined by the IETF (Internet Engineering Task Force) as "resource identifiers with the specific requirements for enabling location independent identification of a resource, as well as longevity of reference." Simply put, they provide permanent, unique addresses for files over a network.

A URI is a Uniform Resource Identifier. The IETF defines a URI as a scheme that allows resources to be uniquely named over time and space using Universally Unique Identifiers (UUIDs). It consists of a series of characters.

The namespace prefix mama is used to distinguish every attribute and element whose description (document type definition) comes from the http://mamazon.com/schema file. The namespace prefix nab is used to distinguish every attribute and element whose description comes from the DTD file located at http://NarnesAndBobel.com/book.dtd. Similarly, the prefix e_com_org is used to describe standard elements and attributes that are defined by the mythical E-commerce Organization.

The xmlns: attribute's value is the location of the DTD or schema. The parser goes to those locations, reads through their definitions, and commits them to memory so that whenever an element or attribute bearing the namespace prefix appears in the Results element, it is validated against the respective DTD or schema.

The region or *scope* where you can use elements and attributes of the types defined in the given schemas and DTD is limited to the child elements and attributes of the Results element. This is called scoping the namespace. You could locally scope the namespaces by assigning the xmlns: keyword in each element, but the following is a much more efficient way of doing this:

```
<mama:book>
```

Here we're using a book element whose definitions are described in the http://mamazon.com/schema file. When parsed to check for validity, the parser checks this element against the type definitions expressed in the schema. Thus, the rest of the book element's structure has to look exactly like it would if it were working in isolation. We've prefixed all the mama:book elements with the mama prefix to tell the parser that each component used is to be validated against the Mamazon.com schema.

```
<mama:price e_com_org:currency = "US$">2.75</mama:price>
```

We're trying to illustrate that it is possible to use components described across many different schemas and DTDs. Here, we've made up a mythical electronic commerce organization that globally defines standards for currency units. While the mama:price element is subject to validation against Mamazon's schema, its currency attribute is subject to validation against the E-commerce Organization's schema.

Also, we should clarify that we're assuming that the mama schema has a provision for allowing a currency attribute in it whose definition comes from the E-commerce Organization.

```
<nab:book>
```

Here we're using a book element whose definitions are described in the http://NarnesAndBobel.com/book.dtd file. When this element is parsed to check for validity, the parser checks it against the type definitions expressed in that DTD. Thus, the rest of the nab:book element's structure—in this case its attributes—have to look exactly as it would if it were working in isolation. We've prefixed all of the nab:book attributes with the nab prefix to tell the parser that each component used is to be validated against the NarnesAndBobel DTD.

```
<our_recommendation>
   You should buy the book from Mamazon.com
</our_recommendation>
```

Wait a minute; these elements don't have any prefixes! That's fine. Remember that you don't *have* to validate everything. In this case, because this element is our own and we have control over it, we decided not to validate it against anything. Our Result element is not limited to only containing elements and attributes defined in the xmlns: attribute values.

General Points

Here are some general points of discussion about this example and namespaces:

- When you use a namespace prefix, you are telling the parser to validate the markup against the DTD or schema to which the prefix points. Thus you can create complex structures that use components described from several sources. Just as we made up the E-commerce Organization, real organizations (for example the ISO and W3C) could publish similar standard definitions for XML markup terms like date, time, and measurement units (miles versus kilometers and pounds versus kilograms).

- Namespace prefixes are inherited from parent elements to child elements by default. Once you declare a namespace for a parent, you don't need to turn it on again (that is, restate the xmlns: statement). To turn off the default namespace that a child inherits from its parents, simply add an xmlns: attribute to the child and set the attribute value to null. For example,

```
<child_element xmlns: "">...</child_element>
```

turns off the default namespace it inherited from its parent.

- Using namespaces, you can include information from many different sources—even sources that use the same element and attribute names to describe different data. For example, Title may refer to a book's name or describe how to address a person (Mr., Mrs., or Ms.).

- Namespaces are easy to use; however, they are not necessarily less verbose. Recall the W3C's intentions behind XML: "Terseness in XML markup is of minimal importance."

- Namespaces give you a unique way for naming each attribute and element. This feature gives you a great amount of control over manipulating the values of attributes and elements for unique formatting purposes or for taking the values and performing further processing.

Summary

In this chapter, we went through a lot of effort trying to describe the basics and underlying semantics of the XML syntax as well as how to go about making DTDs for describing the structure of your data. These basics are useful as they help you create XML applications. Nothing is worse than making an application for something whose specs are not well understood. We hope that after reading this chapter, you've eliminated that problem.

We also made many references to what the parser's reaction to syntax is like. These are important to you as a programmer because the parser can do a lot of the grunt work associated with making applications. The parser can take care of basic error-checking functions—checking that the markup is well formed and that it is valid against the DTD or schema—which often make up more than half the code of an application. You can bypass a lot of this by using a standard parser, which is why we spent so much time describing the parser's reactions to different scenarios.

Finally, all the information in this chapter is a building block to help you on your way to creating the next generation of applications across the Web. Now that you've got the basics nailed down, you can move on to the more challenging aspects of creating applications with XML.

XML Document Object Model (DOM)

Introduction to Document Object Model (DOM)

XML was introduced to alleviate interoperability problems across platforms and networks. A standard language, combined with a DTD (or another schema construct), provides a standard data way of exchanging data. Not only does data need to be in a standard format, but the way data is accessed should also be standardized. XML provides the constructs for putting data into a standard format, and as we shall soon see, the Document Object Model provides a standard way of accessing data. A Web developer, who provides some script inside a Web page that makes use of an XML document, shouldn't have to recode the script to work in every browser.

Some overhead is involved when using XML documents, because extracting data from the tags in an XML document can be arduous. A parser is used to take care of checking a document's validity and extracting the data from the XML syntax. A layer of abstraction between the application and the XML document is made possible by the XML Document Object Model (DOM) specification, which has been standardized by the W3C. This layer of abstraction comes in the form of interfaces that have methods and properties to manipulate an XML document. In other words, when using the DOM, you don't need to worry about the XML syntax directly. For example, the methods, getAttribute(...) and setAttribute(...), allow you to manipulate the attributes on an element in an elegant fashion. Legacy systems can use these interfaces to provide access to legacy data as if the data was natively stored in XML. In other words, your legacy data can be made to look like an XML document by implementing the DOM interfaces on top of the legacy database.

What Is an Object Model?

An object model represents a document by providing a set of interfaces (methods and properties) to the programmer. This set of interfaces completely shields a programmer from the actual syntax of the data behind this interface. The data behind the interface can be an XML document, legacy database, or an application that provides an XML stream. In the case of an XML document, a parser is used to check a document's validity, to build an in-memory representation of the document, and to expose the object model to the programmer. For a legacy database, an object that can read the database in its native form sits on top of the database, allowing programmers to use the DOM to access the original data. This method allows an existing database to provide on-the-fly conversion to XML.

An analogy of the object model in the car industry is how every car is used in a similar fashion. Each car has a steering wheel, gas pedal, and brake pedal. The number of cylinders, the number valves, and the horsepower rating of the engine don't matter to the interface; the way a driver uses a car remains the same. All compliant XML DOM implementations expose the same set of classes to the programmer, regardless of the internals. Of course, some cars have air bags, CD players, and other features. In the XML world, as we see later on, some parsers have included additional functionality that you can't guarantee in every parser.

A standard object model is necessary to alleviate the many problems that occurred when Netscape and Microsoft provided different implementations of the HTML object model known as Dynamic HTML (DHTML). Web sites that make heavy usage of DHTML through scripting engines often need to have multiple versions of the Web site—one for Navigator and one for Internet Explorer. Also, a standard object model allows developers to write programs that use XML without committing themselves to one company's parser.

Types of DOM

The DOM also addresses the need for an Object Model in HTML as well as in XML. A well formed HTML document is also an XML document. This relationship is shown in the DOM, where the XML DOM is referred to as the Core DOM, and the HTML DOM is an extension to the Core specification.

DOM Level 2 (working draft).   At the time of writing, this specification was a working draft. Its main purpose is to give a glimpse into what the future holds for the DOM. There is no implementation of this specification; the disclaimer at the top of the spec states that the contents are guaranteed to change. Rather than risk having you get mad at us for covering a nonstandard specification, we won't be covering this document. Rest assured, when the new DOM is standardized, we will have a revised version.

DOM Level 1 Core.   This specification defines the methods and properties that can be used to manipulate XML. This specification outlines the XML DOM that is covered in later chapters.

DOM Level 1 HTML.   This specification extends the Level 1 Core specification to provide additional functionality for HTML, known as Dynamic HTML. Script authors can use these interfaces to manipulate an HTML page.

DOM Level 0.   This specification doesn't exist, but the title refers to the combination of the HTML DOMs exposed in Microsoft Internet Explorer 3 and Netscape Navigator 3.

The Tree Model

XML is a hierarchical language: The tags contained within an XML document have parent-child relationships (see Figure 4.1). The hierarchical nature of an XML document naturally leads to a tree for the representation of an XML document. The DOM specification does not state that the internal structure of the XML document should be a tree; rather the set of interfaces that are presented leads directly to a conceptual model of a tree. In other words, the parser uses whatever internal structure programmers see fit. On the other hand, users of this parser see a tree representation of the XML document as provided by the DOM inter-

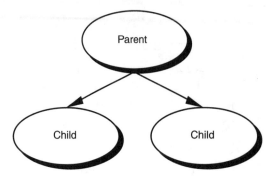

Figure 4.1 Tree model.

faces. Each construct in an XML document, such as an element or an attribute, is represented as a node in the tree. This tree representation is designed with object-oriented principles. The nodes that represent the XML document constructs each have their own set of properties and methods, and share functionality from a base class. Some of the functionality present in all nodes includes the mechanism to navigate through the tree and the ability to manipulate the contents of nodes.

DOMifier

While reading Chapters 4 and 5, you are encouraged to try to see for yourself what the DOM exposes for different XML documents. We have put together a learning utility called the DOMifier to show what the DOM exposes. This utility can be found on the CD, and the source code to the DOMifier is in Chapter 10 to show how the DOM can be used from Visual Basic. The diagrams presented in the next section can be easily verified by copying the XML snippets into a file and then loading them in with the DOMifier. Changing a few lines around and reloading can help you get a feel for what the DOM exposes much faster than just reading alone. Figure 4.5 shows an example of the DOMifier output.

Different Node Types

A brief description of each node type is given below, and an in-depth look at each node is provided in later chapters.

Each of the following node types is derived from a base class called Node. A developer never creates a generic node, but rather creates one of the following nodes to model the appropriate behavior of a fragment of an XML document. Each of these nodes can identify themselves through

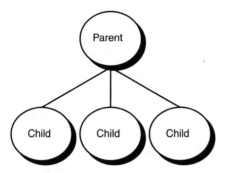

Figure 4.2   Conceptual model of a tree.

the nodeType property. A numerical value is assigned to every node, and the nodeType returns the numerical value associated to a particular node. Details about the nodeType property are described in Chapter 5.

Document.   The Document node is the master node; only one of these nodes can exist for an XML document. This node is the topmost parent node and represents the XML document as a whole. In other words, the document node doesn't represent any specific piece of the XML document. This node has the special functionality to create other nodes, which can then be inserted into the tree.

NodeList.   A NodeList node is used to hold a collection of child nodes. This node can also tell the parent how many children are present, a feature that is useful in loops. Not all nodes can have children; that is, not all nodes can have a NodeList collection. Conceptually, the

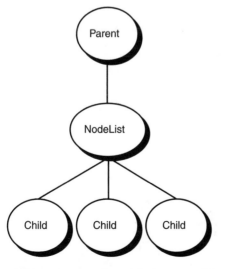

Figure 4.3   Actual model of a tree using a NodeList.

NodeList is just a facility to gain access to the children of a given node. Figure 4.2 shows a simple tree: a parent and three children. Figure 4.3 shows how a NodeList node is like any other node in a model, but is used only to group the children. This NodeList facility provides a uniform mechanism for accessing child nodes.

NamedNodeMap. This node is similar to NodeList, but possesses additional functionality for accessing child nodes using their name. This functionality is necessary for accessing attributes; as a result, NamedNodeMap nodes are used to hold attribute nodes.

Element. The Element node type (see Figure 4.4) contains an element from an XML document. It has special facilities, which are described in Chapter 5, for accessing and managing the attributes declared within the element. Element nodes are children of other element

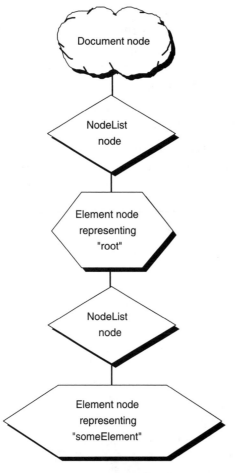

Figure 4.4 Tree model of Element example.

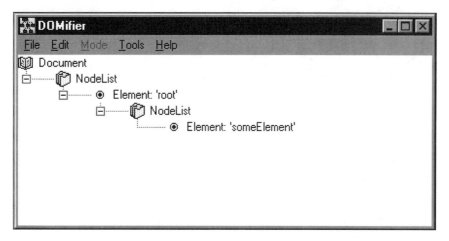

Figure 4.5 DOMifier display of Figure 4.4.

nodes, except for the topmost element node, which is a child of the document node. This topmost element node is referred to as the documentElement. The following XML document would have two Element nodes: root and someElement. The root Element node would be a child of the Document node, and the someElement Element node would be a child of the root Element node.

```
<root>
        <someElement/>
</root>
```

Text. Text nodes are used to represent the text that is contained within element tags (see Figure 4.6). The following XML document produces a Text node that is a child of the name Element node. This text node contains the value "Alex."

```
<name>Alex</name>
```

Attr (Attribute). The Attr node type represents the attributes that are declared within the scope of an element (see Figure 4.7). Attribute nodes can also be children of nodes other than Element nodes, such as Entity and Notation nodes. The following XML document produces an Element node for root and an Attribute node for myAttribute. The myAttribute Attribute node is a child of the root Element node. A NamedNodeMap collection is used instead of the NodeList collection to hold attributes. Also, a Text node representing someValue is exposed.

```
<root myAttribute="someValue" />
```

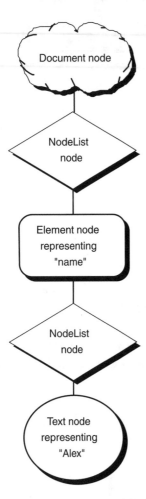

Figure 4.6 Tree model of Text example.

CDATASection. A CDATASection node is similar to a Text node, but can contain markup. In other words, special characters such as < and > can be used within the XML document without being interpreted as tags. This example yields a similar result as the Text node example, except the node type of the bottommost node is CDATASection instead of Text (see Figure 4.8). <B> and </B> are left as text and not interpreted as element tags.

```
<name> <![CDATA[<B>Alex</B>]]> </name>
```

DocumentType. The DocumentType node (see Figure 4.9) represents a small subset of a Document Type Definition (DTD). Unfortunately, only the <!ENTITY> and <!NOTATION> tags from the DTD are exposed through the DOM. The representation of only these two nodes

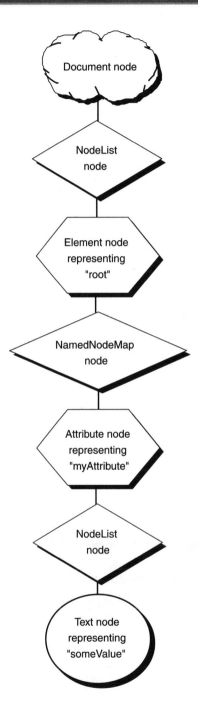

Figure 4.7 Tree model of Attribute example.

is a known limitation of the DOM specification. The DocumentType node is always a child of the Document node and is, in turn, a parent

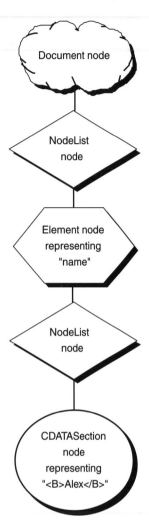

Figure 4.8 Tree model of CDATASection example.

to a collection of both Entity nodes and Notation nodes. The following XML document ends up creating a DocumentType node.

```
<!DOCTYPE root [
    <!ELEMENT root (#PCDATA)>
]>
<root>some text</root>
```

Entity. The Entity node (see Figure 4.10) provides a representation of the <!ENTITY …> tag used in a DTD. This Entity node can be accessed from the parent DocumentType node. The various proper-

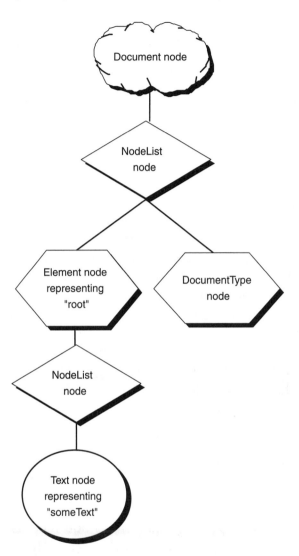

Figure 4.9 Tree model of DocumentType example.

ties of the entity, such as the system id, public id, and notation name, are modeled as Attr nodes and located as children of the Entity node.

Notation. The Notation node (see Figure 4.10) provides a representation of the <!NOTATION ...> tag used in a DTD. This node is placed at the same level in the tree as the Entity node, as a child of the DocumentType node. The public id and system id of the notation are turned into Attr nodes and placed under the Notation node. Figure 4.10 shows how <!ENTITY ...> and <!NOTATION ...> tags are modeled using nodes. In Chapter 5, we show that there is another method to access Entities and Notations. Although the model shown here is correct, it should be noted that often other ways of accessing elements could make Figure 4.10 change slightly.

```
<!DOCTYPE root [
  <!ELEMENT root (#PCDATA)>
  <!ENTITY section1 SYSTEM "http://www.xmlsite.com/section1.xml">
  <!NOTATION gif SYSTEM "http://www.xmlsite.com/gifviewer.exe">
]>
<root></root>
```

EntityReference.   An EntityReference node (see Figure 4.11) represents a reference to an entity that is declared in a DTD. For the following XML document, an EntityReference node is created to represent "&xml;." This node is inserted as a child of the root Element node. Figure 4.11 shows how the DOM would expose the following XML document. It could be argued that the two Text nodes that represent Extensible Markup Language are the same node. It doesn't matter in this diagram, because when you reach a NodeList, it is the Text node that you see in the child list. Also, the Text nodes under EntityReferences are read-only, rendering the argument meaningless, because you can't change the node.

```
<!DOCTYPE root [
  <!ENTITY xml "Extensible Markup Language">
  <!ENTITY dom "Document Object Model">
  <!ELEMENT root (#PCDATA)>
]>
<root>&xml;</root>
```

ProcessingInstruction.   A ProcessingInstruction node models a processing instruction, such as <?xml version="1.0" ?>. This node is located as a child of the Document node.

Comment.   A Comment node represents the comment construct <!-- comment here -->. Comment nodes are inserted in the tree with respect to the XML construct located in within an XML document.

DocumentFragment.   The DocumentFragment node is a stripped-down version of the Document node. It's used as a placeholder when moving nodes around. This node does not have the full facility of the Document node, because it's just temporary storage for nodes that will be reinserted into the tree.

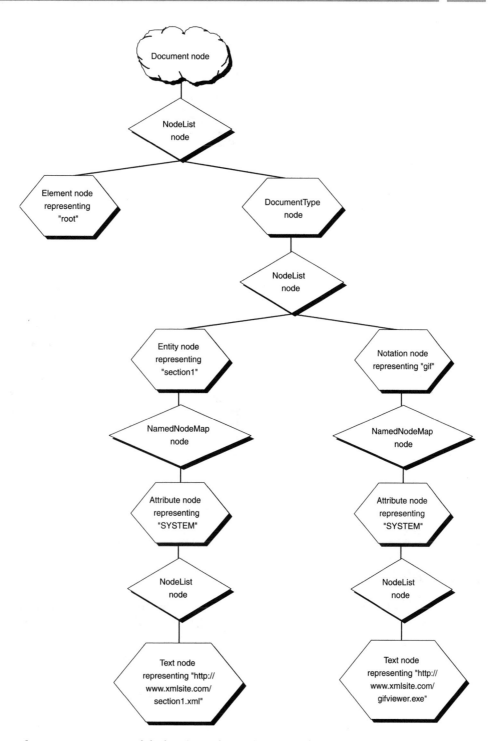

Figure 4.10 Tree model of Entity and Notation example.

Figure 4.11 Tree model of EntityReference example.

Tree Model Example

The following is a simple example to show the tree representation that would be exposed through the DOM on an actual piece of XML. (See Figure 4.12.)

```
<?xml version="1.0"?>

<itemlist>
  <!-- Result from a query -->
  <item id="1012945">
```

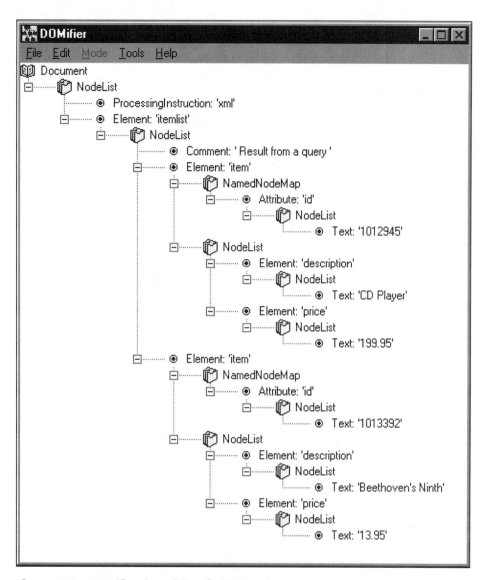

Figure 4.12   DOMifier view of "itemlist" XML snippet.

```
    <description>CD Player</description>
    <price>199.95</price>
</item>
<item id="1013392">
    <description>Beethoven's Ninth</description>
    <price>13.95</price>
</item>
</itemlist>
```

The Big Picture

These nodes somehow need to fit together in the DOM tree. All the different nodes have restrictions as to which nodes can be their children. The parent-child relationships can be easily shown using a tree diagram, which has been split up among Figures 4.13 through 4.19. Figure 4.13 starts with the Document node, and the remaining figures flow from there. The property, such as childNodes, that is used to get access to a node is written in the line between nodes. These properties are described in greater detail in Chapter 5. Nodes that reside under

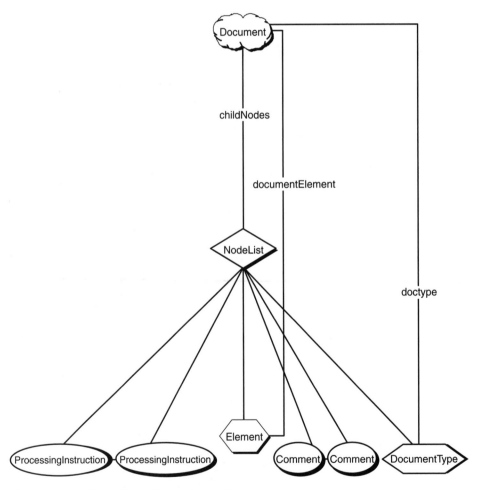

Figure 4.13 Allowable nodes under the Document node.

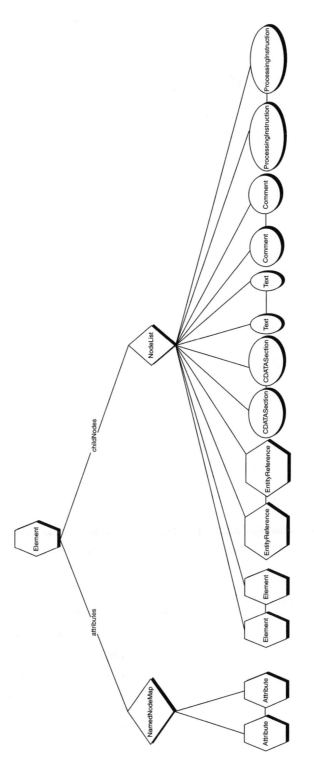

Figure 4.14 Allowable nodes under the Element node.

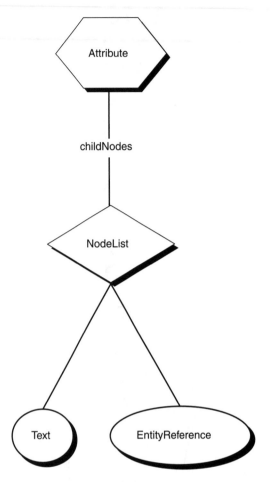

Figure 4.15   Allowable nodes under the Attribute node.

NodeList or NamedNodeMap collections don't have a property name because they are accessed with the item(x) method.

DOM Applications

You might be wondering why the DOM is needed to display an XML document in a browser. In fact, the DOM doesn't always need to be used when accessing XML data. A Web page that simply wants to display the contents of an XML document can just point the URL to that page. An XSL stylesheet can be associated with that XML document to provide a certain view of the data. Also, CSS can be used to render the

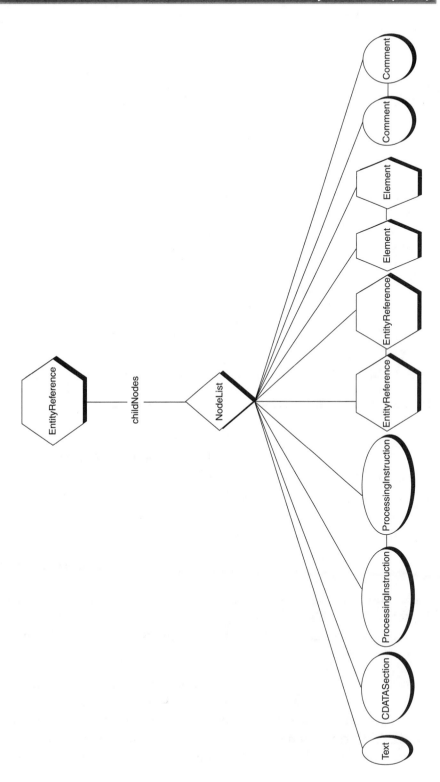

Figure 4.16 Allowable nodes under the EntityReference node.

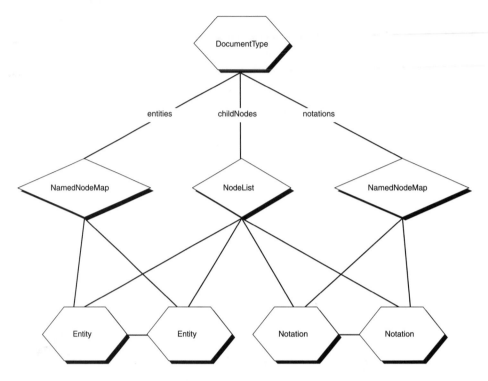

Figure 4.17 Allowable nodes under the DocumentType node.

display of the XML document. The DOM comes into play from a script when the XML document needs to be modified or when the script needs access to some of this data. For example, a script might need to calculate the tax on a given item at an online shopping site. Any application that requires the manipulation of the data contained within an XML document needs to use the DOM interfaces.

On the server side, the DOM is used heavily to process XML documents. For example, the online shopping application included with this book sends an XML document that represents a client's order down to the server. The object on the server uses the DOM to view the contents of this document and then applies the necessary business logic to complete the transaction.

Another server-side application would be to provide a translation mechanism from legacy databases to XML (see Figure 4.20). The DOM interfaces can be implemented on top of this database to make it seem like an XML document to users of this data. In effect, the users of this database don't need to know that the data is not natively stored in XML.

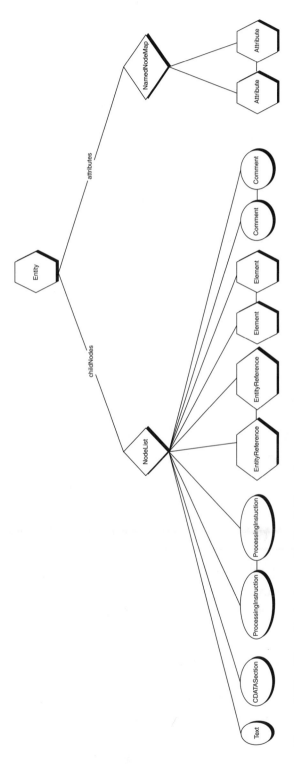

Figure 4.18 Allowable nodes under the Entity node.

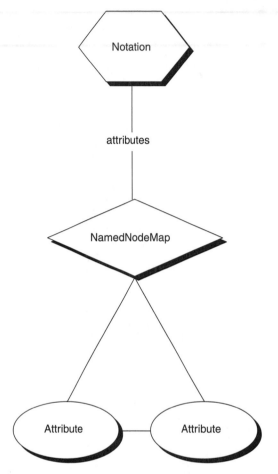

Figure 4.19 Allowable nodes under the Notation node.

The Future of the DOM and Its Current Limitations

The current DOM Level 1 specification defines only the necessary constructs to expose and manipulate an XML document. Future versions are in the works to address some of the following limitations:

- DTD or Schema validation support
- A multiple user mechanism to allow an XML document to be edited by multiple users in a structured manner
- XSL stylesheet support
- An event model

The DOM is currently in its infancy, which has given rise to some extensions to DOM implementations. Using nonstandard extensions in DOM implementations may provide much needed functionality, but also limits an application's target platform to only one implementation of the

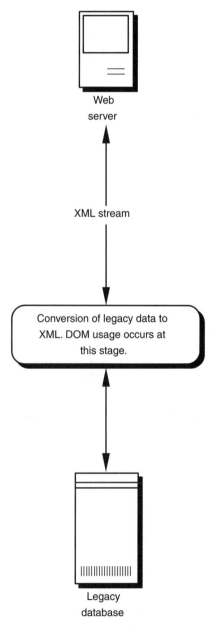

Web
server

XML stream

Conversion of legacy data to
XML. DOM usage occurs at
this stage.

Legacy
database

Figure 4.20   Conversion of legacy data to XML.

DOM. In other words, extensions should only be used when there's no standard way of doing the same thing.

Microsoft Extensions

In the Microsoft XML parser bundled with Internet Explorer 5, the parser adheres to the DOM Level 1 Core specification. In addition to DOM Level 1 Core compliance, some extensions have been added that might be useful or destructive to an application. Some of these extensions are useful because they compensate for some of the limitations in the DOM specification.

DOM limitations that the parser addresses include:

- A definite way of loading an XML document. Unfortunately, the specification does not specify the syntax for loading an XML document.
- A mechanism for persisting the XML tree model to an XML document.
- Support for datatypes in elements and attributes.
- Stylesheet transformations from script.
- Identification of parse errors.
- Asynchronous XML document downloading capability.

As interesting as some of these features sound, be forewarned that these extensions can prove to be destructive to your application, because the application only works with the MSXML parser. A Web page that uses the DOM interfaces could suffer from using extensions, since those extensions won't be available in other browsers.

Summary

In this chapter, we went over what the DOM is and why you may want to use it as your application programming interface. It is important to understand what a node is and how it interacts with other nodes to form a tree. In this chapter, we presented a conceptual model; details on how to use the model are discussed at length in the next chapter.

DOM Reference

In the preceding chapter, we discussed why the DOM is used and from which environments it can be used. We also talked briefly about of the various nodes present. In this chapter, we drill down into the details of these various nodes. A description of node properties and methods is presented, including sample code in JavaScript. A scripting language is used in the examples because scripting languages are easier to follow. Also, while most developers who write in C++ or Java are able to follow JavaScript, the reverse isn't necessarily true. The script examples are all HTML that run under Internet Explorer 5, because, at the time of writing, Internet Explorer 5 was the only browser that provided support for the DOM. This chapter should be read somewhat like a reference, where a quick glance at the method descriptions and sample code reveals most of the usage of the different DOM nodes.

The nodes that are most commonly used when working with the DOM are Document, Element, and Attribute because they directly represent a construct found in an XML document. Nodes that are essential, but that do not represent XML syntax constructs, are Text, CDATASection, NodeList and NamedNodeMap. These seven nodes are presented first, followed by the remaining nodes.

Appendix A contains a concise reference of the methods and properties of each node.

At first, the plethora of methods and properties for each node type might seem a little daunting. We've added sample code to the descriptions to illustrate the most commonly used methods and properties. Some methods might seem redundant, and others might seem plain old useless. On top of that, some methods that people would have liked to see may have be omitted from the specification altogether. By and large, these inconsistencies occurred because the W3C DOM committee is made up of industry players who occasionally have conflicting perspectives for the use of the DOM. That being said, we've included *all* the DOM methods and properties for the sake of thoroughness. As you read through this chapter, keep in mind that the usage of some of these methods is open to your own interpretation.

Understanding the Examples

Most of the examples in this section are HTML documents that have JavaScript and XML documents embedded within them. These HTML examples can be pasted into a file and loaded with Internet Explorer 5 to view the intended result. In Chapter 6, we talk about using the XML DOM usage within different environments including Microsoft's Internet Explorer 5. This section provides an introduction to help you follow the examples in this chapter.

XML documents embedded within HTML pages/documents are called *data islands*. Let's say that we'd like to create a data island using the following XML document.

```
<root>
  This is my XML document.
</root>
```

The above simple XML document is embedded into a data island by using a new, reserved HTML tag called (you guessed it) "<xml>". Here's how to use it:

```
<xml id="xmlID">
  <root>
    This is my XML document.
  </root>
</xml>
```

An *id* is provided so the script can reference the XML document. The *id* becomes especially useful when the HTML document contains more than one XML data island.

```
<script language="javascript">
  var documentNode = xmlID;
  var rootNode = documentNode.documentElement;
</script>
```

The above script is embedded with an HTML document and shows how to make use of the data island. xmlID is the Document node and, in this case, is assigned to a variable called documentNode. For those unfamiliar with JavaScript, JavaScript is not a strongly typed language. var allows you to create a variable, and you can then assign any kind of variable or object to it. In this case, we assigned a Document object to documentNode. The same syntax would be used if we were to assign a integer value to a variable.

```
<script language="javascript">
  var myInt = 5;
  var someString = 'hello';
</script>
```

The above code shows how easy variable declarations are in JavaScript. myInt contains an integer value, whereas someString contains the string "hello." In the examples to follow, the alert(...) function is used to display a string to a dialog box. This function allows us to show the reader the behavior of many DOM methods and properties by displaying their results to the screen with an alert(...) box.

```
<script language="javascript">
  var someString = 'hello';
  alert(someString);
</script>
```

This piece of code produces an alert box that contains the string "hello" (see Figure 5.1).

Figure 5.1 Alert box.

For those completely new to programming, especially with JavaScript, a primer might be necessary. Briefly, a property is a variable that is attached to the object and is usually a string, an integer, or another node object like a NodeList. For example, the nodeName property on nodes is a string that represents the name of a node. On the other hand, a method performs some sort of action and usually has parameters and a return value. For example, the method called insertBefore(...) is used to place nodes into the tree. Methods and properties can be accessed from the main object by using a period. someNode.nodeName produces the nodeName property of the someNode node. Objects can also be cascaded in this fashion. For example, someNode.childNodes.length produces the length property found on the childNodes property, where childNodes is a property of someNode. someNode.childNodes.length is a shortcut for assigning childNodes to a variable and then using it.

```
<script language="javascript">
  var childCollection = someNode.childNodes;
  alert(childCollection.length);
</script>
```

Enough about JavaScript. The examples in this section are quite straightforward, because only one property or method is displayed at a time. The more involved scenarios in later chapters bring the various concepts together in one place.

Some basic knowledge of the DOM is also needed to understand the examples. The chapter is organized in a reference style for easy access while programming. For the first-time reader, a few methods and properties need to be briefly explained to understand the examples. The documentElement property found on the Document node points to the top most XML element. Looking at the following the XML data island, root is the top most element; therefore documentElement is the root Element node.

```
<xml id="xml">
  <root>
    <element1/>
    <element2/>
    <element3/>
  </root>
</xml>
```

Moreover, understanding the childNodes property is also necessary. The childNodes property is a NodeList node that allows the programmer access to a node's children. The following script shows how a programmer would use the childNodes collection to gain access to the root element and the children of the root element. Figure 5.2 shows what the DOM exposes and can help follow the script below.

```
<script language="javascript">
  var rootNode = xml.documentElement;
  var alsoRootNode = xml.childNodes.item(0);

  var element1 = xml.documentElement.childNodes.item(0);
  var element2 = rootNode.childNodes.item(1);
  var element3 = xml.childNodes.item(0).childNodes.item(2);
</script>
```

There also exists an attributes property that points to a NamedNodeMap node, which is used to hold a collection of Attribute nodes.

Everything Is a Node (Well, Almost Everything)

The chart in Figure 5.3 is not to be confused with Figures 4.13 through 4.19 (The Big Picture). Figure 5.3 depicts the class inheritance. In other words, all classes that have a parent (for example, node is the parent of Element) get all the properties and methods that the parent class has. Figures 4.13 through 4.19, on the other hand, show how the DOM exposes these various nodes. Note that in these figures, node is not found anywhere. Node is used only to derive other classes and is not directly exposed.

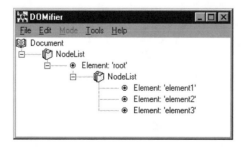

Figure 5.2 DOM representation of above XML document.

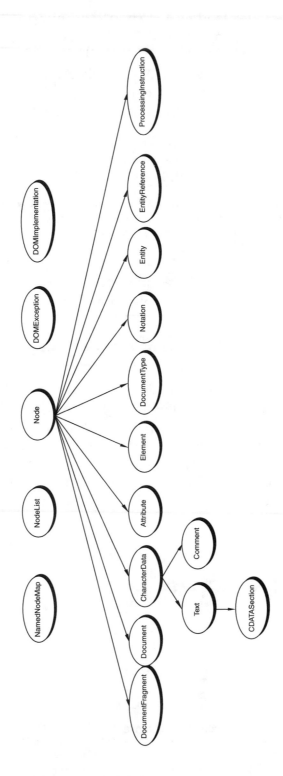

Figure 5.3 DOM Class hierarchy.

Node

Parent: None

Almost all the nodes described in the preceding chapter are derived, either directly or indirectly, from a base class called Node. The exceptions are the NodeList and NamedNodeMap nodes, which don't have a base class. A class that is derived from another class (referred to as the base class) inherits all the methods and properties of the base class. For example, the Node class defines the method childNodes, which every class derived from Node can use without redefining childNodes. Even though most of the nodes are derived from Node, a Node cannot exist on its own; only the specialized nodes can be created.

A description of the properties and methods that are available to all classes (except NodeList and NamedNodeMap) is presented in the following section.

Node Properties

nodeName

Type: String

Description: This string property represents the name of the node. Depending on the type of node that this property is used on, the results will vary.

Comments: Table 5.1 shows that the only node types that have nontrivial usage of nodeName are Element and Attribute. It is not recommended to use nodeName to find out what kind of node you have a hold of. The property nodeType provides that functionality and is described later in this section. If nodeName is called on an element with a namespace, such as <foo:root xmlns...>, then nodeName will be foo:root, whereas the baseName (described later) will be root.

Example:

```
<html>
<script language="javascript" for="window" event="onload">
  alert(xml.documentElement.nodeName);
  alert(xml.documentElement.attributes.item(0).nodeName);
```

Table 5.1   nodeName Behavior for Different Node Types

NODE TYPE	NODENAME PROPERTY
Document	#document
Element	tag name
Attribute	attribute name
Text	#text
CDATASection	#cdata-section
Comment	#comment
Entity	entity name
Notation	notation name
EntityReference	name of entity referenced
ProcessingInstruction	target (the first word following the <?)
DocumentType	document type name (also the name of the top-most element)
DocumentFragment	#document-fragment

```
</script>
<xml id="xml">
  <someElement someAttribute="hello" />
</xml>
</html>
```

The first alert produces *someElement*, and the second alert produces someAttribute. The documentElement property is described in the Document section later in this chapter. Briefly, this property points to the top-most element, in this case the someElement element. The nodeName property is then called on this topmost element, returning the string someElement to the alert method, which in turn displays the tag name in a dialog box.

nodeValue

Type: String

Description: This string property represents the data that is contained within a node. Depending on the type of node that this property is used on, the results will vary. Table 5.2 describes behavior for nodeValue.

Comments: Notice that Element is not included in the list in Table 5.2. Element has been omitted because an Element node contains a Text node to hold the data. It might seem annoying to have to dig one level deeper in the tree to get at the elements contents, but this behavior occurs because

Table 5.2 nodeValue Behavior for Different Node Types

NODE TYPE	NODENAME PROPERTY
Attribute	attribute value
ProcessingInstruction	text (typical processing instruction: <?target text?>)
Comment	comment text
Text	text
CDATASection	text
Other node types	null

multiple Text nodes can exist under an Element. To make matters more complicated, an EntityReference node might exist between two Text nodes, and all three nodes will be children of an Element node. This behavior exists for all nodes that can have Text nodes as children, please refer to Figures 4.13 through 4.19 (The Big Picture) to see which nodes have Text nodes as children. Also, if the nodeValue property is written to, then all the previous nodes under the Attribute node are deleted and one text node is created with the new contents.

Example:

```
<html>
<script language="javascript" for="window" event="onload">
  alert(xml.documentElement.attributes.item(0).nodeValue);
  alert(xml.documentElement.childNodes.item(0).nodeValue);
</script>
<xml id='xml'>
  <someElement someAttribute="hello">
    element contents
  </someElement>
</xml>
</html>
```

For the above example, the first alert produces hello as the result, and the second alert produces element contents. Figure 5.4 shows Named-NodeMap attributes collection and the NodeList childNodes collection. Notice that the attribute someAttribute and the Text node containing element contents are both the first child of their collections. It should also be noted here that to access the contents of an element, you need to drill down to the Text node and check the Text node's nodeValue property. For attributes, the nodeValue property on the Attribute node can give the contents of the attribute. Of course, you could also drill down to the

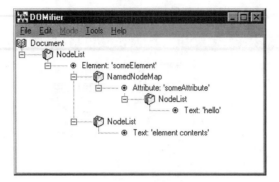

Figure 5.4 DOMifier output of nodeValue XML example.

Attribute's Text node and get the nodeValue off that node for the same result. In other words, the following two lines produce the same result.

```
xml.documentElement.attributes.item(0).nodeValue
xml.documentElement.attributes.item(0).childNodes.item(0).nodeValue
```

nodeType

Type: Unsigned short integer

Description: This property is an integer value that represents the type of the node. Table 5.3 shows the correlation between nodeType and the different nodes.

The following six properties—parentNode, childNodes, firstChild, lastChild, previousSibling, nextSibling—refer to other nodes in the same tree. Figure 5.5 shows their relationship to a node picked out at random called CURRENT NODE. Also, nodes that have their description in parentheses are not directly accessible from CURRENT NODE, but are still accessible indirectly through another node.

childNodes

Type: NodeList node

Description: This property is a NodeList collection that holds all the children of this node. A NodeList is still returned, even if the node doesn't have any children; the length property on childNodes will just be set to 0. The reader is encouraged to take a quick peek at the NodeList description found in this chapter.

Table 5.3 nodeType Definition

NODE TYPE	NODETYPE
Element	1
Attribute	2
Text	3
CDATASection	4
EntityReference	5
Entity	6
ProcessingInstruction	7
Comment	8
Document	9
DocumentType	10
DocumentFragment	11
Notation	12

attributes

Type: NamedNodeMap node

Description: This property is a NamedNodeMap collection that holds all the attributes of a node. The attributes property is set to null for all nodes that aren't Elements, Entities, or Notation, because only these nodes can have attributes. A NamedNodeMap is still returned, even if the node doesn't have any attributes. The NamedNodeMap is described in detail further in this chapter.

parentNode

Type: Node

Description: This property is a pointer to the parent of the node. Figures 4.13 through 4.19 show the relationships between the parents and children of nodes. Note that, in the figure, a NodeList collection is often directly above a node, but parentNode points to the node above the collection. The following example illustrates this behavior.

Example:

```
<html>
<script language="javascript" for="window" event="onload">
  alert(xml.documentElement.nodeName);
```

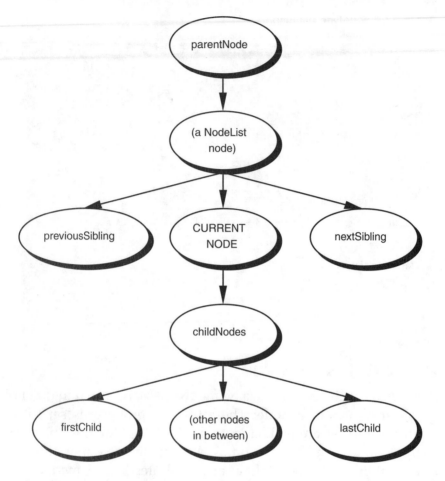

Figure 5.5 Node property hierarchy.

```
    alert(xml.documentElement.childNodes.item(0).parentNode.nodeName);
</script>
<xml id="xml">
  <element1>
    <element2/>
  </element1>
</xml>
</html>
```

Both alerts in this example return element1, because the parentNode property allows a programmer to walk up a tree in addition to moving down. Figure 5.6 gives further insight by showing what the DOM exposes for the above example.

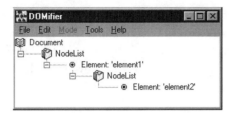

Figure 5.6 DOM tree of parentNode example.

firstChild

Type: Node

Description: This property represents the first child of the node. If the node does not contain any children, then this property is set to null.

Comments: This property is just a short cut for accessing the first item in a NodeList collection. In other words, myNode.firstChild and myNode.childNodes.item(0) represent the same node.

lastChild

Type: Node

Description: This property represents the last child of the node. If the node does not contain any children, then this property is set to null.

Comments: This property is a short cut for accessing the last item in a NodeList collection. In other words, myNode.lastChild and myNode.childNodes.item(myNode.childNodes.length - 1) represent the same node.

Example:

```
<html>
<script language="javascript" for="window" event="onload">
  var myNode = xml.documentElement;
  alert(myNode.lastChild.nodeName);
  alert(myNode.childNodes.item(myNode.childNodes.length-1).nodeName);
</script>
<xml id="xml">
<root>
  <element1/>
  <element2/>
  <element3/>
</root>
</xml>
</html>
```

Both alerts from the above example produce element3. The first alert comes from using the lastChild property. The second alert finds the number of elements in the collection; subtracts 1 because the collection is indexed from 0, then goes to that item. Both methods go to the last child in the collection.

previousSibling

Type: Node

Description: This property represents a node that has a common parent and is the child of this parent that precedes the current node. If this child does not exist, then this property is set to null.

nextSibling

Type: Node

Description: This property represents a node that has a common parent and is the child of this parent that follows the current node. If this child does not exist, then this property is set to null.

ownerDocument

Type: Document node

Description: This property represents the Document node of the DOM tree in which the current node resides.

Comments: The Document node is the highest level parent for any node, and it always exists. The ownerDocument property is useful because it is a shortcut to the node that has special capabilities to create other nodes. A detailed description of the Document node is included in this chapter.

Node Methods

Most of the methods described in this section are used to manage and manipulate children of nodes. Not all nodes—for example, text nodes—are allowed to have child nodes. Since all the different node types are nodes, they inherit the following methods, even if the use of those methods doesn't make sense. Using a method that would affect the children of a node that can't have children results in an error. Please consult

Figures 4.13 through 4.19 for details concerning which nodes can have children and what kind of children are allowable.

insertBefore(newChild, refChild)

Parameters: newChild and refChild are both Nodes.

Return value: Node

Exceptions thrown: DOMException

Description: This method inserts the node newChild before an existing child node refChild, and newChild is then returned. If refChild is set to null, then newChild is inserted at the end of the list of children. An error occurs if refChild does not exits or if newChild is not an allowable node to a given parent.

Comments: Consult Figures 4.13 through 4.19 to see which nodes are allowed to be inserted. For example, if you try to insert a Document node into an Element's list of children, an error is thrown. Please note that Attr nodes cannot be inserted into an Element's child list using this method. Consult the methods found on the Element node for managing attributes.

replaceChild(newChild, oldChild)

Parameters: newChild and oldChild are both Nodes.

Return value: Node

Exceptions thrown: DOMException

Description: oldChild is removed from the list of children, and newChild is inserted into its place. oldChild is then returned.

Comments: Consult Figures 4.13 through 4.19 to see which nodes are allowed to be inserted.

removeChild(oldChild)

Parameters: oldChild is a Node.

Return value: None

Exceptions thrown: DOMException

Description: oldChild is removed from the list of children. If oldChild does not exist, then an error is raised.

Comments: In Internet Explorer 5, oldChild is returned.

appendChild(newChild)

Parameters: newChild is a Node.

Return value: None

Exceptions thrown: DOMException

Description: newChild is added to the end of the list of children. If newChild was located somewhere else in the tree, then it is first removed from that location before being added to the current list of children.

Comments: In Internet Explorer 5, newChild is returned.

Example:

```
<html>
<script language="javascript" for="window" event="onload">
  var elem1 = xml.documentElement.childNodes.item(0);
  var elem2 = xml.documentElement.childNodes.item(1);
  elem1.appendChild( elem2.childNodes.item(0) );
</script>
<xml id="xml">
  <rootElement>
    <elem1>
      <childElement1/>
    </elem1>
    <elem2>
      <childElement2/>
    </elem2>
  </rootElement>
</xml>
</html>
```

After the script is run, the resulting XML document is:

```
<rootElement>
  <elem1>
    <childElement1/>
    <childElement2/>
  </elem1>
  <elem2>
  </elem2>
</rootElement>
```

The appendChild method automatically removed childElement2 from the child list of elem2, before inserting it into the child list of elem1. Figures 5.7 and 5.8 shows the before and after DOM representation of this XML document.

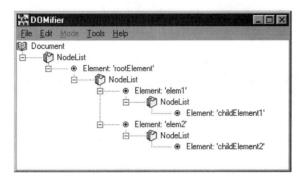

Figure 5.7 DOM representation of original XML document in appendChild example.

hasChildNodes()

Parameters: None

Return value: Boolean

Exceptions thrown: None

Description: This method returns *true* if this node has children and *false* otherwise.

cloneNode(deep)

Parameters: *deep* is a Boolean value.

Return value: Node

Exceptions thrown: None

Description: cloneNode is used to produce a copy of the node that it is called on. For those familiar with object-oriented programming terminology, this function fulfills the role of a copy-constructor. If deep is false, then the node is copied, but its children are ignored. If deep is true,

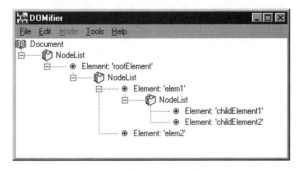

Figure 5.8 DOM representation of XML document after childElement2 is moved.

then a complete replica of the subtree starting at the current node is returned.

Comments: Calling cloneNode(true) can result in a very processing-intensive operation, especially if called on the Document node of a large document.

Document

Parent: Node

The Document node is not an element; rather it represents the document as a whole. In data islands, the id attribute on the <xml> tag is a reference to the Document node.

The Document node is the root node that contains the facilities to manage the various nodes beneath it. More specifically, the Document node is used to create nodes that can later be inserted into the tree. Also included is a basic searching mechanism. In addition to these facilities, the Document node contains pointers to other important nodes in the tree, such as the root Element node and the DocumentType node.

Document Properties

documentElement

Type: Element node

Description: This property represents the highest level Element in the document.

Example:

```
<html>
<script language="javascript" for="window" event="onload">
  alert(xml.documentElement.nodeName);
</script>
<xml id='xml'>
  <rootElement>
    <someElement/>
  </rootElement>
</xml>
</html>
```

This very simple example produces rootElement in the alert box. Notice that the keyword xml is the Document node and xml.documentElement is the Element node that represents rootElement.

doctype

Type: DocumentType node

Description: This property represents the DocumentType node in the document. The DocumentType node contains a small subset of the contents of a DTD. The DocumentType node is discussed in greater deal in a later section in this chapter.

implementation

Type: DOMImplementation node

Description: This property represents the DOMImplementation node in the document. The DOMImplementation node provides a mechanism for version checking and is described in greater detail in the DOMImplementation section in this chapter.

Document Methods

createElement(tagName)

Parameters: tagName is a string value.

Return value: Element

Exceptions thrown: None

Description: Creates and returns an Element node with the nodeName property set to tagName.

createDocumentFragment()

Parameters: None

Return value: DocumentFragment

Exceptions thrown: None

Description: Creates and returns a new DocumentFragment node.

createTextNode(data)

Parameters: *data* is a string value.

Return value: Text node

Exceptions thrown: None

Description: Creates and returns a new Text node that contains the string *data*.

createComment(data)

Parameters: *data* is a string value.

Return value: Comment

Exceptions thrown: None

Description: Creates and returns a new Comment node that contains the string *data*.

createCDATASection(data)

Parameters: *data* is a string value.

Return value: CDATASection

Exceptions thrown: None

Description: Creates and returns a new CDATASection node that contains the string *data*.

createProcessingInstruction(target, data)

Parameters: *target* and *data* are string values.

Return value: ProcessingInstruction

Exceptions thrown: None

Description: Creates and returns a new ProcessingInstruction node and sets the ProcessingInstruction properties target and data to the given parameters *target* and *data*. See the ProcessingInstruction section later in this chapter for an explanation of target and data.

createAttribute(name)

Parameters: *name* is a string value.

Return value: Attribute

Exceptions thrown: None

Description: Creates and returns a new Attribute node and sets the nodeName property to *name*. The nodeValue property is left blank.

createEntityReference(name)

Parameters: *name* is a string value.

Return value: EntityReference

Exceptions thrown: None

Description: Creates and returns a new EntityReference node and sets the nodeName property to *name*.

getElementsByTagName(tagname)

Parameters: *name* is a string value.

Return value: NodeList

Exceptions thrown: None

Description: Returns a list of Element nodes that have a property tagName (or nodeName) that matches the parameter name *name*. This method searches the whole tree that belongs to the Document node. If name equals "*", then all the Element nodes are returned.

Comments: This method performs the same operation as the getElements-ByTagName(name) method that is found on the Document node. The Document node's getElementsByTagName(name) searches the whole tree, whereas the Element's method searches only the subtree of the Element on which it was called.

Tree Management Examples

A few examples of using the Node and Document methods are presented here to bring together some actual scenarios of DOM usage.

Creating Nodes

This example shows how to create a new Element node and insert it into the tree. createElement(...) is used to create the new Element node, and insertBefore(...) is used to insert it into the tree. The second parameter is set to null because we want to insert new Element node to the end of the list. The xml property on the Document node, also called xml, is used to show the resulting XML document. The xml property is a Microsoft extension, which means it only works in MSXML (it is described in more detail in Chapter 7).

```
<html>
<script language="javascript" for="window" event="onload">
  // Create a new Element node.
  var newNode = xml.createElement("element2");

  // Insert the new Element node under the root element.
  xml.documentElement.insertBefore(newNode, null);

  // Display the resulting XML document
  alert(xml.xml);
</script>
<xml id="xml">
  <rootElement>
    <element1/>
  </rootElement>
</xml>
</html>
```

The resulting XML document appears as follows:

```
<rootElement>
  <element1/>
  <element2/>
</rootElement>
```

Deleting Nodes

This example takes the node we added from the previous example to get back to the original XML document. The removeChild(...) method from the Node class is used to delete the node.

```
<html>
<script language="javascript" for="window" event="onload">
  // Find node to delete
  var nodeToDelete = xml.documentElement.childNodes.item(1);

  // Delete the node
  xml.documentElement.removeChild(nodeToDelete);

  // Display the resulting XML document
  alert(xml.xml);
</script>
```

```
<xml id="xml">
  <rootElement>
    <element1/>
    <element2/>
  </rootElement>
</xml>
</html>
```

The resulting XML document appears as follows:

```
<rootElement>
  <element1/>
</rootElement>
```

Moving Nodes

This example shows how to move nodes around in the tree. The append-Child(...) method from the Node class is used to move element2 around. Of course, a combination of removeChild(...) and insertBefore(...) could have been used to achieve the same result.

```
<html>
<script language="javascript" for="window" event="onload">
  // Find node to move
  var nodeToMove = xml.documentElement.childNodes.item(1);

  // Move the node
  xml.documentElement.childNodes.item(0).appendChild(nodeToMove);

  // Display the resulting XML document
  alert(xml.xml);
</script>
<xml id="xml">
  <rootElement>
    <element1/>
    <element2/>
  </rootElement>
</xml>
</html>
```

The resulting XML document appears as follows:

```
<rootElement>
  <element1>
      </element2>
    </element1>
</rootElement>
```

Element

Parent: Node

Just as the name implies, the Element node represents the element construct from an XML document. Most of the methods that exist solely for Elements are for managing attributes.

Element Properties

tagName

Type: String

Description: This string property represents the tag name of the Element.

Comments: This property is the same as nodeName on Elements. When dealing with Elements, the two can be used interchangeably.

Element Methods

getAttribute(name)

Parameters: *name* is a string value.

Return value: String

Exceptions thrown: None

Description: This method returns a string that contains the contents of the attribute named *name*.

setAttribute(name, value)

Parameters: *name* and *value* are strings.

Return value: None

Exceptions thrown: None

Description: If the attribute named *name* doesn't exist, then it is created and given the value *value*. If this attribute already exists, then the previous value is overwritten with *value*.

removeAttribute(name)

Parameters: *name* is a string value.

Return value: None

Exceptions thrown: None

Description: The Attribute node named *name* is removed from the tree.

getAttributeNode(name)

Parameters: *name* is a string value.

Return value: Attribute node

Exceptions thrown: None

Description: This method returns the Attribute node that is named *name*. If no such attribute exists, then *null* is returned.

Comments: This method differs from getAttribute(name) by returning the actual Attribute node and not just a string. Also, getAttribute(name) is a shortcut for getAttributeNode(name).nodeValue.

removeAttributeNode(oldAttr)

Parameters: oldAttr is an Attribute node.

Return value: None

Exceptions thrown: None

Description: Removes the attribute oldAttr from the element's attribute list.

Comments: In Internet Explorer 5, this method returns oldAttr.

setAttributeNode(newAttr)

Parameters: newAttr is an Attribute node.

Return value: None

Exceptions thrown: None

Description: The node newAttr is added to the attribute list of the Element node.

Comments: An Attribute node can be created from scratch using the Document node. An Attribute node that has been removed from another Element node can be used in this method. In Internet Explorer 5, this method returns newAttr.

Example:

```
<html>
<script language="javascript" for="window" event="onload">
  var attrNode = xml.documentElement.getAttributeNode("myAttr");
  xml.documentElement.removeAttributeNode(attrNode);
      xml.documentElement.childNodes.item(0).setAttributeNode(attrNode);
</script>
<xml id="xml">
  <rootElement myAttr="hello">
    <myElem/>
  </rootElement>
</xml>
</html>
```

This example takes the attribute myAttr=""hello" off rootElement and puts it on myElem. If the tree was to be persisted (saved to disk), then the XML document would appear as follows:

```
<rootElement>
  <myElem myAttr="hello">
</rootElement>
```

In Internet Explorer 5, if the line xml.documentElement.remove-AttributeNode(attrNode) was removed from the script, an error would be issued saying that the node must first be removed from before inserting into another element.

getElementsByTagName(name)

Parameters: *name* is a string value.

Return value: NodeList

Exceptions thrown: None

Description: Returns a list of Element nodes that have a property tagName (or nodeValue) that matches the parameter name *name*. This method searches the whole subtree of the Element that it was called on. If *name* equals "*", then all the Element nodes are returned.

Comments: This method is performs the same operation as the getElementsByTagName(name) method that is found on the Document node. The Document node's getElementsByTagName(name) searches the whole tree, whereas the Element's method searches only the subtree of the Element that it was called on.

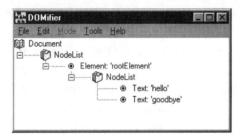

Figure 5.9 DOM tree before normalize().

normalize()

Parameters: None

Return value: None

Exceptions thrown: None

Description: Collapses adjacent Text nodes into one node. This view is reference as the normal form where only another type of node can separate a Text node.

Example: If a programmer ended with a DOM tree as depicted in Figure 5.9, which can be done easily when moving nodes around, a call to normalize() on rootElement would produce the DOM tree shown in Figure 5.10.

Element Usage Examples

The following are several examples of element usage.

Iterating through Children

Often it is necessary to perform some sort of action to every child of a node. Using the childNodes collection and a for loop, visiting each child

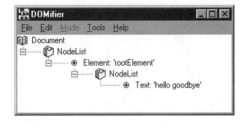

Figure 5.10 DOM tree after normalize().

is quite easy. The start() method is automatically called when the document is loaded because of the onload event on the <body> tag. The function then visits each child node to check if it's an Element node. If so, the tag name is displayed. A true iterating facility would indeed be a nice addition to the DOM specification. For those who are unfamiliar with iterators, an iterator facility would allow a programmer to ask for the next child through a method instead of with indexes.

```html
<html>
<body onload="start()">
<script language="javascript">

// Define a constant to represent the Element nodeType.
var ELEMENT_NODE = 1;

// Start the process with the next line.
// This function is called when the document is loaded.
// Note that this function responds to the onload event on the <body>
// tag.
function start() {
  // Putting the number of children of the node is a
  // seperate variable greatly increases the performance.
  var length = xml.documentElement.childNodes.length;

  // This for loop visits each node in the childNodes collection.
  for (index = 0; index < length; index++) {

    var childNode = xml.documentElement.childNodes.item(index);

    // Check if the child is an Element node.
    // If so, display the tag name.
    if (childNode.nodeType == ELEMENT_NODE) {
      alert(childNode.nodeName);
    }
  }
}

</script>
</body>
<xml id="xml">
    <rootElement>
    <elem1/>
    <elem2/>
    <elem3/>
  </rootElement>
</xml>
</html>
```

This script produces three alert boxes in the contents in following order: elem1, elem2, and elem3.

Displaying Element Contents

Elements can contain multiple Text and CDATASection nodes. To display the contents of such Element nodes, all the children must be checked if they are either Text nodes or CDATASection nodes. This example uses the idea of visiting each child node that was introduced in the previous example. At that point, their contents can be added to a buffer. Once all contents of all the Text and CDATASection nodes have been collected in a buffer, then the contents can be displayed. In the script that follows, the displayContents(...) function performs those actions.

```
<html>
<body onload="start()">
<script language="javascript">

// nodeType constants.
var TEXT_NODE = 3;
var CDATASECTION_NODE = 4;

// Start the process with the next line.
// This function is called when the document is loaded.
// Note that this function responds to the onload event on the <body>
tag.
function start() {
  displayContents(xml.documentElement);
}

// This function displays all the Text and CDATASection nodes of a
// given node.
function displayContents(node) {

  var length = node.childNodes.length;
  var index;
  var outputBuffer = "";

  // Visit every child of node.
  for (index = 0; index < length; index++) {
    var childNode = node.childNodes.item(index);

    // If the child node is of type Text, then
    // add its contents to the output buffer.
    if (childNode.nodeType == TEXT_NODE) {
      outputBuffer += childNode.nodeValue;
    }
```

```
      // If the child node is of type CDATASection, then
      // add its contents to the output buffer.
      if (childNode.nodeType == CDATASECTION_NODE) {
         outputBuffer += childNode.nodeValue;
      }
   }

   // Now that we have built up the output buffer, it can be
   // displayed through an alert box.
   alert(outputBuffer);
}

</script>
</body>
<xml id="xml">
  <rootElement>
  Some text
  <![CDATA[<B>Bold text</B>]]>
  More text
  </rootElement>
</xml>
</html>
```

The result of this script is an alert box with the following contents: "Some text<B>Bold text</B>More text." Figure 5.11 shows the three nodes that make up this string, making the display of an element's contents slightly nontrivial.

Navigating through Trees

Depending on the XML document, it is often useful to visit every element in a document or in a subset of the document. For example, the DOMifier utility visits every node, checks what type the node is, and displays the result. The following code illustrates, using recursion, how this action is performed. For those unfamiliar with recursion, a function

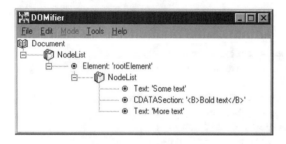

Figure 5.11 DOM representation of XML document in the Displaying element contents example.

is recursive if it calls itself. To stop this process, a stop case is needed. In this case, the process stops if there aren't any children under the node the function visit(...) is working on. The process starts with the start() function that is automatically called when the document is loaded, because of the onload event on the <body> tag. start() then passes visit(...) the first element, the documentElement, and then visit(...) takes over. visit(...) checks if the node that is passed to it is an Element node; if so, the tag name for the element is displayed to the user through an alert box. The function then performs the same action on the children with a depth-first traversal of the tree. Depth-first means that the function goes as deep as possible before visiting siblings. The other type of traversal is referred to as a breadth-first traversal, where all the siblings are first visited and then the children.

```
<html>
<body onload="start()">
<script language="javascript">

// Define a constant to represent the Element nodeType.
var ELEMENT_NODE = 1;

// Start the process with the next line.
// This function is called when the document is loaded.
// Note that this function responds to the onload event on the <body>
// tag.
function start() {
  visit(xml.documentElement);
}

// This function recursively visits all nodes.
// If the node is an Element node, then its tag name is displayed.
function visit(node) {

  // Check if the node is an Element node.
  if (node.nodeType == ELEMENT_NODE) {
    // This next line could be substituted to perform the needed
    // action.  For example, "string += node.nodeName" could have
    // been used to build a string of all the tag names.
    alert(node.nodeName);
  }

  var length = node.childNodes.length;

  // Check if this node has any children.
  if (length > 0) {
    var index;

    for (index = 0; index < length; index++) {
```

```
        visit( node.childNodes.item(index) );
    }
  }
}

</script>
</body>
<xml id="xml">
  <rootElement>
    <elem1>
      <deepelem1/>
    </elem1>
    <elem2/>
    <elem3>
      <anotherDeepElement/>
    </elem3>
  </rootElement>
</xml>
</html>
```

This script results in six alert boxes in the following order: rootElement, elem1, deepelem1, elem2, elem3, and anotherDeepElement.

Managing Attributes

Most of the functionality that is included with the Element node is the management of attributes. This example kills two birds with one stone by showing how to put new attributes on an Element node and how to view attribute contents. Creating Attributes can be accomplished with the Document method createAttribute(...). It can then be inserted into the tree with setAttributeNode(...). An even simpler method exists by using the setAttribute(...) method on the Element node. This method allows the programmer to work with attribute names that are strings instead of Attribute nodes.

```
<html>
<body onload="start()">
<script language="javascript">

function start() {
  var rootElement = xml.documentElement;

  // Put the attribute myAtt='hello' on rootElement.
  rootElement.setAttribute('myAtt', 'hello');

  // Check to see if the attribute was added with an alert box.
  alert(rootElement.getAttribute('myAtt'));
}
```

```
</script>
</body>
<xml id="xml">
  <rootElement/>
</xml>
</html>
```

This script produces an alert box with contents of *hello*.

Attr (Attribute)

Parent: Node

Attribute nodes shadow the attributes that are placed on elements in XML documents. Also, the attributes placed on Entities and Notations from DTDs are modeled by the Attribute node. The Attribute node itself does not contain many methods or properties; instead the Element node contains the facilities for manipulating Attribute nodes. Of course, the Node properties such as nodeName and nodeValue apply to Attribute nodes.

Attribute nodes are really defined as Attr. For script programmers, this naming does not matter. However, for those who are working in a strongly typed language such as C++, this naming does make a difference. The IDL in Appendix A reflects the actual naming.

Attr Properties

name

Type: String

Description: This string property represents the name of the Attribute node.

Comments: This property is the same as the nodeName property that is inherited from Node.

specified

Type: Boolean

Description: This property is set to *true* if this attribute was specified in the XML document before being loaded by a parser; otherwise, the value is *false*.

value

Type: String

Description: This string property represents the value of the Attribute note.

Comments: This property is the same as the nodeValue property that is inherited from Node.

NodeList

Parent: None

The NodeList class is a crucial component for navigating through the DOM tree. The examples in this section use the childNodes property from Node class to show the usage of the NodeList class.

NodeList Properties

length

Type: Unsigned long integer

Description: This property returns the number of children contained in the NodeList.

NodeList Methods

item(index)

Parameters: *index* is an unsigned long integer value.

Return value: Node

Exceptions thrown: None

Description: Returns the Node that is at the position index in the list of children. The first child is index = 0 and last child is index = length -1.

Comments: A shortcut in Internet Explorer 5 exists: someNode.childNodes-(index) can be used instead of someNode.childNodes.item(index).

NamedNodeMap

Parent: None

A NamedNodeMap is used to hold collections of attributes together and is the type for the attributes property that is defined in the Node class.

NamedNodeMap Properties

length

Type: Unsigned long integer

Description: This property returns the number of children contained in the NamedNodeMap.

NamedNodeMap Methods

getNamedItem(name)

Parameters: *name* is a string value.

Return value: Node

Exceptions thrown: None

Description: getNamedItem returns the Node that has the nodeName property equal to the parameter *name*. *null* is returned if the requested node cannot be found.

setNamedItem(node)

Parameters: node is a Node.

Return value: Node

Exceptions thrown: DOMException

Description: This adds the node specified with the parameter *node* to the list and then returns *node*. If a node with the same nodeName as *node* exists, then *node* replaces the old node and the old node is returned. An exception can be thrown for any of the following three reasons: *node* was created in another document, the NamedNodeMap is read-only, or *node* is currently an attribute on another Element.

Comments: In Internet Explorer 5, an Attribute can be created with createAttribute with one Document node, then the Attribute node can be inserted into another Document node's tree without an exception being raised.

removeNamedItem(name)

Parameters: *name* is a string.

Return value: Node

Exceptions thrown: DOMException

Description: Removes the node with the nodeName that equals *name* from the list and returns the node. *null* is returned if this node does not exist. An exception is raised if the specified node cannot be found.

Comments: In Internet Explorer 5, an exception is not raised if the node cannot be found.

item(index)

Parameters: *index* is an unsigned long integer value.

Return value: Node

Exceptions thrown: None

Description: item(index) returns the Node that is at the position index in the list of children. The first child is index = 0 and last child is index = length -1.

Comments: A shortcut in Internet Explorer 5 exists: someNode.attributes(index) can be used instead of someNode.attributes.item(index).

CharacterData

Parent: Node

The CharacterData node is never used directly, similarly to the Node node. As shown in Figure 5.3, the methods and properties defined by the CharacterData node are used by Text, Comment, and CDATASection nodes. This node defines methods and properties that are used to manage text strings.

CharacterData Properties

data

Type: String

Description: This property returns text stored in a node that inherits from CharacterData.

Comments: Text nodes inherit from CharacterData and for Text nodes. The data property returns the same value as the nodeValue property.

length

Type: Integer

Description: This property represents the number of characters of the text string stored in this node.

CharacterData Methods

substringData(offset, count)

Parameters: offset and count are both unsigned long integer values.

Return value: String

Exceptions thrown: DOMException

Description: Returns the count characters from the text string starting from offset. An exception is thrown if offset and count are invalid. They must both be positive and offset cannot exceed length.

Comments: Setting offset to 0 and count to length would return the entire string.

appendData(appendString)

Parameters: appendString is a string value.

Return value: None

Exceptions thrown: DOMException

Description: This method appends the string appendString to the existing text string in the node. An exception is thrown if the node is read-only.

insertData(offset, newString)

Parameters: offset is a unsigned long integer and newString is a string value.

Return value: None

Exceptions thrown: DOMException

Description: This method inserts newString into the existing text string at the offset *offset*. An exception is thrown if offset is invalid or if the node is read-only.

deleteData(offset, count)

Parameters: offset and count are both unsigned long integer values.

Return value: None

Exceptions thrown: DOMException

Description: This method deletes count characters from the existing text string starting from the offset *offset*. An exception is thrown if offset or count are invalid or if the node is read-only.

replaceData(offset, count, data)

Parameters: offset and count are both unsigned long integer values and *data* is a string value.

Return value: None

Exceptions thrown: DOMException

Description: This method replaces count characters with data from the existing text string starting after offset number of characters. An exception is thrown if offset or count are invalid or if the node is read-only.

Text

Parent: CharacterData

A Text node contains the nonstructural related text in an XML document. A simple XML document, such as <root>some Text</root>, would create a Text node that contains some Text. This Text node would be a child of the Element node root. Multiple Text nodes could exist as children of the same element. For example, the below XML document would create two Text nodes with an Element node in between (see Figure 5.12).

```
<root>text1
<elem/>text2
</root>
```

Text Methods

splitText(offset)

Parameters: offset is a long value.

Return value: None

Exceptions thrown: None

Description: This method produces two text nodes from the text node on which it was called. The first text node contains all the text up to the offset point, and the second text node contains the text at the offset point and after.

Comments: Internet Explorer 5 returns the created Text node, which contains that text at and after the offset point. This method is useful if another type of node, for example, a CDATASection, needs to be inserted in between a text string.

CDATASection

Parent: Text

The CDATASection node is derived from the Text node, meaning that this node behaves very similarly to the Text node. The only difference is

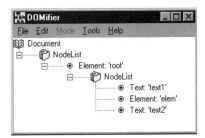

Figure 5.12 DOM tree of two Text nodes example.

that CDATA sections can be stored in it; otherwise, the node behaves exactly like a Text node. An example of a CDATA section is as follows:

```
<![CDATA[<B>Alex</B>]]>
```

These CDATA sections are used to so that markup characters (< and >) can be used within text.

DocumentType

Parent: Node

The DocumentType node is used to represent a schema (a DTD) for an XML document. Currently, the DOM only exposes the entities and notations that are declared in a DTD. The future might bring DOM representations of DTDs so that a programmer could use the DOM to check a documents structure. Only one DocumentType node exists for any given DOM tree, and it is accessed using the doctype property found on the Document node.

DocumentType Properties

name

Type: String

Description: This read-only property represents the name that follows directly after the DOCTYPE in an XML document, which is also the name of the root element.

entities

Type: NamedNodeMap

Description: This read-only property represents the collection of Entities for this document. Each Entity node models an entity declaration that is present in the DTD.

notations

Type: NamedNodeMap

Description: This read-only property represents the collection of Notations for this document. Each Notation node models a notation declaration that is present in the DTD.

Entity

Parent: Node

Entity nodes model an entity declaration provided in a DTD. In the DOM tree, Entity nodes are found only under DocumentType nodes that represent the DTD. Please consult Chapter 3 for specifics about creating and using entities.

Entity Properties

systemId

Type: String

Description: This property represents the system identifier that is associated with the entity. If the system identifier was omitted from the declaration, then systemId is null.

Example:

```
<!DOCTYPE root [
  <!ELEMENT root (#PCDATA)>
  <!ENTITY section1 SYSTEM "http://www.xmlsite.com/section1.xml">
]>
<root/>
```

The above XML document would cause the parser to create an Entity node. The systemId property would be set to http://www.xmlsite.com/section1.xml.

publicId

Type: String

Description: This property represents the public identifier that is associated with the entity. If the public identifier was omitted from the declaration, then publicId is null.

notationName

Type: String

Description: This property represents the name of the notation for unparsed entities. In the case of an parsed entity, this property is set to null.

Notation

Parent: Node

Notation nodes model notation declarations provided in a DTD. In the DOM tree, Notation nodes are found only under DocumentType nodes that represent the DTD. Please consult Chapter 3 for specifics about creating and using notations.

Notation Properties

publicId

Type: String

Description: This property represents the public identifier that is associated with the notation. If the public identifier was omitted from the declaration, then publicId is null.

Example:

```
<!DOCTYPE root [
  <!ELEMENT root (#PCDATA)>
  <!NOTATION abc PUBLIC "http://www.somewebsite.com/abcviewer.exe">
]>
<root/>
```

The above XML document would cause the parser to create an Entity node. The publicId property would be set to http://www.somewebsite.com/abcviewer.exe.

systemId

Type: String

Description: This property represents the system identifier that is associated with the notation. If the system identifier was omitted from the declaration, then systemId is null.

EntityReference

Parent: Node

An EntityReference node is used to point to a corresponding Entity node. This node type does not extend any of its own methods or properties; therefore, only the properties and methods that are declared in Node can be used with EntityReference nodes. The nodes found under an EntityReference node are read-only.

Figure 5.13 shows how the DOM exposes an Entity and its associated EntityReference for the following XML document. An EntityReference node for title is created as a child of root. The contents of the EntityReference node are identical to the contents of its associate Entity node.

```
<!DOCTYPE root [
  <!ELEMENT root (#PCDATA)>
  <!ENTITY title "Applied XML">
]>
<root>&title;</root>
```

EntityReference nodes can be used to contain a multitude of nodes, including entire subtrees. Figure 4.16 shows the allowable child nodes for EntityReferences nodes.

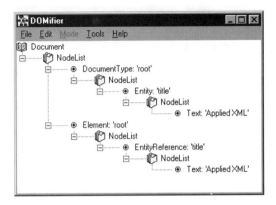

Figure 5.13 DOM tree of EntityReference example.

ProcessingInstruction

Parent: Node

ProcessingInstuction nodes are used to shadow processing instructions from XML documents. Processing instructions found in XML documents take the following form: <?target text?>. For example, a common processing instruction found at the beginning of most XML documents is: <?xml version="1.0" ?>.

ProcessingInstruction Properties

target

Type: String

Description: This property represents the target of the processing instruction that is in the form <?target text?>.

Comments: This property behaves exactly like the nodeName property for ProcessingInstuction nodes.

Example: The target property for the following processing instruction is xml.

```
<?xml version="1.0" ?>
```

data

Type: String

Description: This property represents the text of the processing instruction that is in the form <?target text?>.

Comments: This property behaves exactly like the nodeValue property for ProcessingInstuction nodes. In Internet Explorer 5, this property does not return anything, nodeValue should be used instead.

Example: The data property for the following processing instruction is version="1.0".

```
<?xml version="1.0" ?>
```

Comment

Parent: CharacterData

As the name implies, the Comment node is used to represent comments that have been inserted in an XML document. This node behaves similarly to a Text node, since it only contains strings that represent comments. The Comment node contains all the text found between <!— and —>.

DocumentFragment

Parent: Node

The DocumentFragment node does not represent any XML document construct. Instead, it is used as a place holder when moving nodes around. A Document node could be used for this purpose, but depending on any given DOM implementation, creating Document nodes might be expensive. The DocumentFragment is considered a scaled-down version of the Document node that can only be used as a place holder. Those who create DOM implementations understand that creating DocumentFragment nodes should not be a behind-the-scenes, extensive task. The DocumentFragment does not have any extra methods or properties, but it does have a special capability. When inserting a DocumentFragment node into some node's (either a Document or Element node) child list, only the children of the DocumentFragment and the DocumentFragment itself are inserted. A DocumentFragment would be most likely used to gather Elements that already exist in a tree. Once the collection of Elements has been created in the DocumentFragment, the children would be transferred to a subtree.

Example: This is a slightly contrived example, because it doesn't serve any purpose other than showing how to use a DocumentFragment. As mentioned above, the DocumentFragment would be used to collect Element nodes from different parts of an already existing tree. In this case, we just create the nodes to keep the script simple.

```
<html>
<body onload="start()">
<script language="javascript">
```

```
// This function is called when the document is loaded.
// Note that this function responds to the onload event on the <body>
// tag.
function start() {
  // First create a DocumentFragment node.
  var myDocFrag = xml.createDocumentFragment();

  // Let's also create two elements.
  var elem1 = xml.createElement("elem1");
  var elem2 = xml.createElement("elem2");

  // Now let's insert these two Element nodes into
  // the DocumentFragment.
  myDocFrag.insertBefore(elem1, null);
  myDocFrag.insertBefore(elem2, null);

  // Now that we have finished collecting nodes
  // let's insert them under the rootElement Element.
  xml.documentElement.insertBefore(myDocFrag, null);

  // Now let's view the resulting XML document.
  alert(xml.xml);
}

</script>
</body>
<xml id="xml">
  <rootElement/>
</xml>
</html>
```

The result is shown in Figure 5.14. Notice that there isn't any evidence that a DocumentFragment was ever used. If the DOMifier was used to show the DOM tree at this point, the DocumentFragment node would not be present.

Figure 5.14 Result of DocumentFragment example.

DOMImplementation

Parent: None

DOMImplementation class is used to hold on to implementation details that are independent of any particular instance of the DOM. Currently, only one method exists, and it is used to provide version checking.

DOMImplementation Methods

hasFeature(feature, version)

Description: This method takes a *feature* and a *version* and returns either *true* or *false*, depending on whether the specified version exists for the specified feature. Legal values for feature are "HTML" and "XML." Currently, this method returns true only for the version value of "1.0." At this time, this method serves little purpose since only one version of the DOM exists. In the future, it will be important to check versions as future versions of the DOM will contain added functionality.

Nitty-Gritty Details

This section lists two more classes: DOMString and DOMException. Knowledge of these classes is not necessary to work with the DOM; however, they are included for thoroughness.

DOMString

Parent: None

Throughout this chapter, *string* has been used whenever a method or property uses string values. In fact, a DOMString is used and not just a string. Actual implementations will most likely not use a DOMString, but rather, the string facilities that are available. For example, COM environments (Microsoft XML DOM implementation) uses BSTRs. In Java, the String class would be used. The only requirement for DOMString is that the string be a 16-bit quantity, which uses the UTF-16 encoding. For most programmers (especially when working with script), this information is probably useless. As a result, this chapter uses string in place of DOMString.

DOMException

Parent: None

Exceptions are thrown by methods when something irregular has occurred, such as a parameter that was passed was invalid. Exceptions can be caught using try...catch blocks. The usage of exceptions is not be covered in detail, since it is a language-dependent topic. The IDL in Appendix A lists the various exceptions that can be thrown.

Summary

This chapter has covered the W3C DOM Level 1 Core specification. All the defined methods and properties have been listed in a fashion to facilitate lookup while programming. Implementation-specific methods and properties, also known as extensions, are covered in later chapters. Also, specifics associated with using these methods and properties in languages other than JavaScript are covered in the next chapter.

Using the DOM in Different Environments

J ust as XML is here to alleviate interoperability problems, the DOM is here to facilitate XML access on any platform. The DOM has been designed to work with more than one programming language and it is encouraged to port the DOM compliant parser to various languages and platforms. Because we do not live in a perfect world, DOM usage varies across different parsers. In this chapter, we provide a taste of the various parsers available and show how they are used in their respective languages. Because the number of available parsers seems to be growing constantly, we could not cover them all. Instead, we selected a small subset that show how the DOM can be used from your favorite language.

Script within Internet Explorer 5

Internet Explorer 5 can instantiate an XML parser from an HTML page to access XML documents. The parser can be created in two ways, either using data islands or creating an XML parser object from script. Chapter 7 explains in great detail what a data island is and how to use it. In this section, we focus on creating the XML parser object directly from JavaScript and from VBScript.

JavaScript

We have already seen plenty of JavaScript examples in Chapter 5, but we briefly review the basics. The XML parser that is shipped with Internet Explorer 5 is an ActiveX object; therefore, the standard ActiveX object instantiation routine can be used to create the parser object directly from script. An ActiveXObject object can be created using the *new* operator. The constructor for ActiveXObject requires an identifier to the actual ActiveX object you are trying to create. In this case, microsoft.xmldom is the identifier for the parser. The following line can be inserted into a script to create the parser:

```
var myXML = new ActiveXObject("microsoft.xmldom");
```

The myXML variable becomes the Document node and can used to reference the DOM methods and properties.

The following code sample shows how to create an XML parser object, load an XML document from the server, and display the name of the root element. In addition, this script turns off asynchronous downloading and checks to see whether the XML document was parsed successfully. Asynchronous downloading and parser error checking are features that have been included with Internet Explorer 5 and are not part of the standard DOM. More details about using these features are included in Chapter 7, where we cover the Internet Explorer 5 extensions. Parser error checking is included in this example to show how to produce well-behaved script. Asynchronous downloading, on the other hand, needs to be turned off, because the XML document might not have finished loading and parsing when the script tries to access the documentElement.

```
<HTML>
<BODY>
<SCRIPT LANGUAGE="Javascript" FOR="window" EVENT="onload">

  // Instantiate the XML parser
  var xml = new ActiveXObject("microsoft.xmldom");

  // Turn off asynchronous downloading
  xml.async = false;

  // Load an XML document from the server
  xml.load("http://spartus/xml/clients.xml");

  // Check if the XML document was parsed successfully
```

```
    if (xml.parseError.reason != "") {
      alert("ERROR: " + xml.parseError.reason);
    } else {
      // Display the name of the root element
      alert("The root element is: " + xml.documentElement.nodeName)
    }
</SCRIPT>
</BODY>
</HTML>
```

VBScript

Instantiating the parser in VBScript is very similar to the JavaScript method; the main difference is syntax. The parser ActiveX object, also known as an *Automation object*, is created by using the CreateObject(...) function. The following two lines are used to create the parser object:

```
Dim xml
Set xml = CreateObject("microsoft.xmldom")
```

As in the JavaScript method, we pass the string microsoft.xmldom to specify which ActiveX object to instantiate.

The following code sample produces a VBScript version of the example used in the JavaScript section. The XML parser is instantiated, then an XML document is loaded from the server, and finally the root element is displayed in a message box. Asynchronous downloading is turned off to insure that the document has been properly loaded and parsed before the script continues. *parseError.reason* is consulted to make sure that the XML document has been parsed successfully.

```
<HTML>
<BODY>
<SCRIPT LANGUAGE="VBscript" FOR="window" EVENT="onload">

  Dim xml

  ' Instantiate the XML parser
  Set xml = CreateObject("microsoft.xmldom")

  ' Turn off asynchronous downloading
  xml.async = false

  ' Load an XML document from the server
  xml.load("http://spartus/xml/clients.xml")
```

```
' Check if the XML document was parsed successfully
if (xml.parseError.reason <> "") then
  msgbox("ERROR: " + xml.parseError.reason)
else

  ' Display the name of the root element
  msgbox("The root element is: " + xml.documentElement.nodeName)
end if

</SCRIPT>
</BODY>
</HTML>
```

Java

The Java and XML team has been getting a lot of hype and rightfully so. XML provides the universal data mechanism, and Java provides the mechanism that allows code to run under any browser or platform. In a sense, the combination is universal data flow with universal data access. Since Java is hyped as the language of choice for XML programming, we are going to show how to use three different XML parsers. We are not reviewing the parsers, we are simply showing you how to get started using them and letting you choose which one best fits your application. The three Java-based XML parsers covered are the DataChannel XJParser, the Sun Technology Release 1 XML parser, and the IBM XML parser for Java.

DataChannel Parser

DataChannel has partnered with Microsoft to provide a Java port of Microsoft's XML parser. Both the standard DOM and Microsoft's extensions are implemented. The standard DOM classes are located in the package org.w3c.dom and are standard across all Java parsers. Appendix B outlines the semantics of Java-based DOM usage. The Microsoft extensions, which are covered in Chapter 7, are located in the package com.datachannel.xml.om. The classes found in org.w3c.dom and the classes that start with IXMLDOM in com.datachannel.xml.om are interfaces and cannot be used directly. Just a quick refresher, interfaces are abstract classes. They aren't used directly, but are implemented by classes. Classes implement the functions provided by an interface. The implemented classes are found in com.datachannel.xml.om and have the following names: Document, Comment, Element, Attribute, CDATASection, Entity, EntityReference, Notation, ProcessingInstruction, and Text. These are the same names found in org.w3c.dom, but they are not the same classes. If you are creating classes with the new operator, then you must use the classes found in com.datachannel. xml.om.

Loading a Document

To get you started with this parser, let's first load a document and check if it is valid. The following code sample creates a Document object called *doc*, then loads and parses an XML document using the load(....) function. The URL for the file to load is passed as a command line parameter, as in java DCValid http://server/document.xml.

```java
import com.datachannel.xml.om.*;
import com.datachannel.xml.tokenizer.parser.XMLParseException;

public class DCValid {

  public static void main(String argv[]) {

    // Create a Document node that is defined in the
    // com.datachannel.xml.om package.
    Document doc = new Document();
    boolean ok = true;

    // If you want the Document node in it's purest form
    // without any extensions, use the following line instead.
    // org.w3c.dom.Document doc = new Document();
    // In the above line, a com.datachannel.xml.om.Document node is
    // created and then casted (converted) into a W3C standard
    // Document node.

    // Load the document using a try..catch block.
    // We catch the XMLDOMException, which signifies that a
    // parsing error had occured.
    try {
      doc.load( argv[0] );
    } catch(XMLDOMException e) {
      // An error has occured during parsing.
      // Display the error to the output.
      System.out.println("\n\n" + e.getReason());
      ok = false;
    }

    if (ok == true) {
```

```
        System.out.println("Document is valid and here it is...");
        System.out.println( doc.getXML() );
    }
  }
}
```

First, you need to create an instance of the Document class. Now you can load your XML or use the DOM methods to build your own. Next, load the XML document specified by the URL in the first command line parameter. The parser takes care of creating the URLConnection object and downloading the document. An XMLDOMException is thrown if something goes wrong, either with the downloading or with the parsing of the XML. When running this example, if an error occurs, then the parser displays a stack trace from the TokenizerException exception. This exception does not halt the program, but takes away from the elegance of the program by dumping the error to the output. Instead, the program should process the error and display a message to the user only if necessary.

Using the DOM Methods

In this section, we produce a program that reads in an XML document and, using the DOM, display the structure of the document to the screen. First, we show you the code and then explain how it works. In the code that follows, some lines are bolded to show the DataChannel DOM functions and declarations.

```java
import com.datachannel.xml.om.*;
import org.w3c.dom.*;

// A naming clash occurs since there exists a Document node in
// both com.datachannel.xml.om and org.w3c.dom.
// We want to use the datachannel Document node, since we need
// the load(...) method. Let's tell the compiler which one
// to use.
import com.datachannel.xml.om.Document;

public class DCDisplay {

    private Document doc;

    public static void main(String argv[]) {
        DCDisplay myDCDisplay = new DCDisplay(argv[0]);
        myDCDisplay.display();
    }
```

```
public DCDisplay(String url) {
  doc = new Document();
  doc.load(url);
}

public void display() {
  displayRecursive(doc.getDocumentElement(), 0);
}

// This function will recursively visit every node in the tree.
// Element nodes are displayed with the proper indentation
// to indicate their location in the tree.
private void displayRecursive(Node node, int depth) {

  int i, childCount;
  NodeList children;

  // Check if the current node is an Element node
  if (node.getNodeType() == Node.ELEMENT_NODE) {
    spacer(depth);
    System.out.println(node.getNodeName());

    children = (NodeList) node.getChildNodes();
    childCount = children.getLength();
    for(i = 0; i < childCount; i++) {
      displayRecursive(children.item(i), depth+1);
    }
  }
}

// This function displays the specified number of spaces.
private void spacer(int spaces) {
  int i;

  for (i = 0; i < spaces; i++)
    System.out.print(" ");
}
}
```

The constructor DCDisplay(String url) creates a new DOM tree and loads the specified XML document. The display() function is then used to start the display process by passing the root most element to displayRecursive(...).

Next, we make use of the following XML document to see what the program produces.

```
<clients>
  <client>
```

```
      <name>John Server</name>
      <phone>425-5363-9989</phone>
   </client>

   <client>
      <name>Xavier M. Lee</name>
      <phone>416-978-7669</phone>
   </client>
</clients>
```

The following is the result that is displayed to the screen.

```
clients
  client
   name
   phone
  client
   name
   phone
```

Up to this point, we have shown you two programs written using the DataChannel XML parser, which should give you a good idea of where to start for your own applications. It is useful to check the API documentation for the names of methods, because they might not be exactly as described in Chapter 5. The naming of the methods might be slightly different because Java is not a script language, so many of the properties become functions. For example, the property *length* becomes getLength(). Appending *get* is usually the only change, but take a quick peek at the API documentation to verify this. Also, Appendix B contains the standard DOM definitions for Java. You need to understand how to use the DOM before looking at the API docs, because they often don't have descriptions for the properties and the methods.

IBM XML Parser for Java

The IBM XML parser for Java is currently in its second release. It comes with plenty of features, but we only show how to use the DOM from this parser. We don't show much here because this parser adheres very closely to the DOM specification. The Document node is called Document and not IDOMDocument. In fact, there are two DOM parsers: *validating* and *nonvalidating*. The validating parser checks whether the XML document adheres to a specified DTD; the nonvalidating does not.

We again revisit the same program we used with the Java parsers. If you would like to use a nonvalidating parser, you need only substitute

DOMParser for NonValidatingDOMParser. All the DOM interfaces are defined in the package org.w3c.dom. First, you need to create a DOMParser object and use the parse(url) method to load your document. When calling parse(url), the parser takes care of creating a URL and downloading the document. Two exceptions, SAXException and IOException, must be caught when using parse(url). Finally, use getDocument() to get the Document node. At this point, the DOM interfaces described in Chapter 5 can be used. Also, get must be appended to the properties to make them methods. For example, nodeValue becomes getNodeValue(). Some lines are bolded to distinguish the changes that are needed from the DataChannel parser to use the IBM parser.

```java
import com.ibm.xml.parsers.DOMParser;
import org.w3c.dom.*;
import org.xml.sax.SAXException;
import java.io.IOException;

public class IBMDisplay {

  private Document doc;
  private DOMParser parser;

  public static void main(String argv[]) {
    IBMDisplay myIBMDisplay = new IBMDisplay(argv[0]);
    myIBMDisplay.display();
  }

  public IBMDisplay(String url) {
    parser = new DOMParser();

    // Use the parse(...) method to load and parse an
    // XML document.  SAXException and IOException must
    // be caught.
    try {
      parser.parse(url);
    } catch (SAXException se) {
      se.printStackTrace();
    } catch (IOException ioe) {
      ioe.printStackTrace();
    }

    // The getDocument() method on the DOMParser object
    // is used to get the Document node.
    doc = parser.getDocument();
  }

  public void display() {
    displayRecursive(doc.getDocumentElement(), 0);
  }
```

```
    private void displayRecursive(Node node, int depth) {

      int i, childCount;
      NodeList children;

      if (node.getNodeType() == Node.ELEMENT_NODE) {
        spacer(depth);
        System.out.println(node.getNodeName());

        children = node.getChildNodes();
        childCount = children.getLength();
        for(i = 0; i < childCount; i++) {
          displayRecursive(children.item(i), depth+1);
        }
      }
    }

    private void spacer(int spaces) {
      int i;
      for (i = 0; i < spaces; i++)
        System.out.print(" ");
    }
  }
```

Sun XML Parser

Sun's XML Parser, also known as Java Project X, is currently in its Technology Release 1 version. Like the IBM parsers, the DOM specifics are contained in the package org.w3c.dom. The com.sun.xml.tree package contains the classes that are needed to load and parse an XML document. The XMLDocument class has a method, createXmlDocument(url, doValidation), that returns an XmlDocument object. A document object is created by casting the call to createXmlDocument(...). The doValidation parameter specifies whether the parser should check the XML document for validity. As with the other two Java parsers, the Sun parser takes care of creating the necessary URL object to download the XML document.

We are going to beat this example to death by showing it to you one last time. As you can see, very few changes from the IBM parser example were needed here. The two parsers have properly implemented the W3C DOM specification, and we benefit by having to rewrite less code. The display functions were left untouched, and only the few lines that deal with loading the document were changed. The bolded lines indicate Sun parser specifics.

```java
import com.sun.xml.tree.XmlDocument;
import org.w3c.dom.*;
import org.xml.sax.SAXException;
import java.io.IOException;

public class SunDisplay {

  private Document doc;

  public static void main(String argv[]) {
    SunDisplay mySunDisplay = new SunDisplay(argv[0]);
    mySunDisplay.display();
  }

  public SunDisplay(String url) {

    // The createXmlDocument(...) method loads and parses an XML
    // document, then returns the Document node.
    try {
      doc = (Document) XmlDocument.createXmlDocument(url, false);
    } catch (SAXException se) {
      se.printStackTrace();
    } catch (IOException ioe) {
      ioe.printStackTrace();
    }
  }

  public void display() {
    displayRecursive(doc.getDocumentElement(), 0);
  }

  private void displayRecursive(Node node, int depth) {

    int i, childCount;
    NodeList children;

    if (node.getNodeType() == Node.ELEMENT_NODE) {
      spacer(depth);
      System.out.println(node.getNodeName());

      children = node.getChildNodes();
      childCount = children.getLength();
      for(i = 0; i < childCount; i++) {
        displayRecursive(children.item(i), depth+1);
      }
    }
  }

  private void spacer(int spaces) {
    int i;
```

```
    for (i = 0; i < spaces; i++)
      System.out.print(" ");
  }
}
```

Java Summary

We have seen three companies' Java XML parser offerings. Let's not forget the other Java XML parsers out there. At the time of writing, these parsers were still in beta. We hope, in the future, that the DOM committee will address a standard way of loading XML documents; otherwise, as we have seen from the IBM and Sun parsers, very little code needs to change between parsers.

Visual Basic

Visual Basic provides a programmer-friendly environment when working with ActiveX objects. Of course, the final Visual Basic application runs much slower, but often the ease of application development outweighs the performance penalties. Because the Microsoft XML parser is a COM object, Visual Basic can be used to create applications that make use of XML documents. As long as Internet Explorer 5 is installed on your machine, Visual Basic can reference the XML DOM object. The first step to creating Visual Basic applications that use XML is to reference the XML DOM object by going to the Projects menu and selecting the *References...* item. The Microsoft XML object can then be selected, as shown in Figure 6.1. Version 2.0 of the object is necessary to use the DOM Level 1 methods and properties. Note: If Version 1.0 is the only available option, select it, and it will magically become Version 2.0 as long as you have Internet Explorer 5 Beta 2 or a more recent version installed on your machine.

Instantiating the XML DOM Object

Now that you have referenced the XML DOM object in your application, you can instantiate the parser and use the DOM methods and properties. The DOMDocument object is the Document node that was shown in Chapter 5. Once a DOMDocument object has been created, the familiar load(...) method can be called to load and parse an XML document. The following code from a Visual Basic form creates an XML parser object, parse some XML, and display the root element name in a message box. Asynchronous downloading is turned off to guarantee that the XML document is loaded and parsed before the program continues.

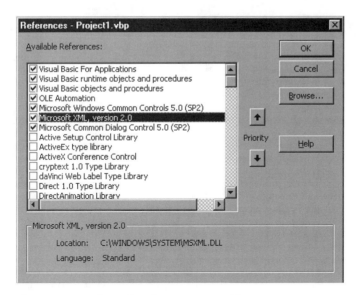

Figure 6.1 Referencing the XML DOM object.

```
' Global variable
Private xml As DOMDocument

Private Sub Form_Load()

    ' Create a new XML DOM object (aka: Instantiate the parser)
    Set xml = New DOMDocument

    ' Turn asynchronous downloading off to ensure that the XML
    ' document is loaded and parsed before the program continues.
    xml.async = False

    ' Load an XML document from a URL
    xml.Load ("http://spartus/xml/clients.xml")

    ' Display the root element name
    MsgBox (xml.documentElement.nodeName)

End Sub
```

A note for future debugging: If asynchronous downloading is left on, which is the default, you might receive the error shown in Figure 6.2. This error occurs because the parsing of the XML document has not completed yet; therefore, the documentElement property does not exist yet, causing an error.

When working the Internet Explorer 5 XML DOM object, it is convenient to use the Visual Basic Object Browser (shown in Figure 6.3) to

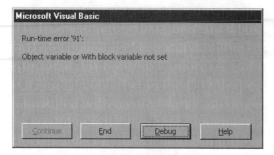

Figure 6.2 Object variable error.

check the names of classes and the return values of methods. If you look at the methods and properties included under DOMDocument, you will notice that the list is much longer than what described in Chapter 5. Both the standard DOM and the Microsoft DOM extensions are included in these classes. Chapter 7 covers the Microsoft extensions in detail.

Server-Side Usage

Interaction between a browser and a server has caused static Web pages to become dynamic Web sites, which is the foundation of e-commerce sites. Updating stock quotes, searching databases, and playing online games, just to name a few, require server-side assistance in delivering the content

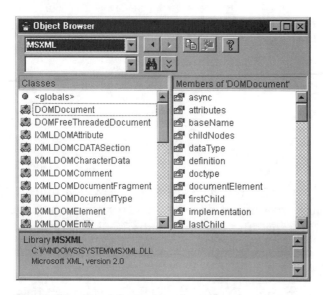

Figure 6.3 Visual Basic object browser.

that the user requires. Many technologies currently exist that allow the server to complete various tasks and return the results to the client. The DOM can be used on the server to create an in-memory XML tree and then persist the tree up to the client. For example, the DOM can create elements based on a query to an existing non-XML data source. A text version of the XML DOM tree can be created and sent to the client. At this point, the client reads in the XML data through a parser and performs the necessary processing. In this section, we will show how to use the DOM on the server with Active Server Pages (ASP) and from Java Servlets.

Active Server Pages

Active Server Pages (ASP) is a server-side scripting technology that can be used from Microsoft's Internet Information Server (IIS). ASP scripts have gained some popularity because it is simple to design these pages. When a browser requests an ASP page from the server, the script is executed on the server, and a dynamically generated page is returned. The returned page does not contain any script and appears to be a static page to the user. ASP technology allows ActiveX objects to be used within the script, allowing the Microsoft XML parser to be used. For the examples in this section, we use VBScript, because it has (unfortunately) become the standard language when working with ASP.

In ASP, instantiating the parser is similar to the VBScript example earlier in this chapter, except that the server object is used to provide the CreateObject(...) function. The following example shows how to instantiate the parser, build an XML document using the DOM methods, and then persist the XML tree into a XML text document.

```
<%@ LANGUAGE="VBSCRIPT" %>

<%
  ' Set the content type to XML
  Response.ContentType = "text/xml"

  ' Instantiate the XML parser
  Set xml = Server.CreateObject("microsoft.xmldom")

  ' Create an XML document with only one element
  xml.loadXML("<root/>")

  ' Create an element node
  Set elem = xml.createElement("myElement")
```

```
' Create a text node and place it under elem.
Set text = xml.createTextNode("data")
elem.appendChild(text)

' Insert the new element into the tree
xml.documentElement.appendChild(elem)

' The =xml.xml line is used to persist the xml
%>

<%=xml.xml%>
```

The result of this script is the following XML document:

```
<root><myElement>data</myElement></root>
```

This script sets the content type to text/xml, which tells the browser that an XML document is coming down the pipe. In Internet Explorer 5, an XSL stylesheet is applied to the XML document, as shown in Figure 6.4. The crucial step in this script is the <%=xml.xml%> line. The *xml* property on the Document node is a Microsoft extension that creates the XML text version of the DOM tree.

Our ASP example doesn't do very much. In fact, because it creates the same XML document, it would make more sense to make a static XML page. In this example, we are trying to show that you can access another data source and build an XML tree on the fly. This method can be used to convert existing data into an XML stream or to build an XML document from multiple data sources. On the other hand, the server might perform some calculations and then return the results in XML. This technology can be used in a multitude of ways, depending on the needs of the application. Next, we show how to do similar processing using Java Servlets.

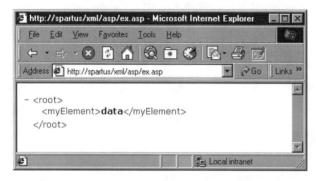

Figure 6.4 XML document display in Internet Explorer 5.

Java Servlets

Java Servlets are slowly moving into the mainstream for server-side processing. Unlike ASP, Servlets are not scripts, but rather are written in Java and need to be compiled before they are used. Servlets achieve greater efficiency over the usual CGI programs, which are usually written in Perl, because of the way the server handles the requests and manages the Servlets. Servlets need to run on special servers. If they run on existing servers, such as Apache or IIS, the server needs to have widely available extensions installed. To implement a Servlet, the HttpServlet abstract class needs to be implemented. The example in this section assumes that the reader is familiar with the basics of writing Servlets.

We figured it would be fitting to use the Sun XML parser for the Servlets example, but in fact any of the currently available Java-based XML parsers would work. The following Servlet example performs the same job as the ASP example. Some knowledge of Java Servlets might be necessary to follow this example. The *service* method is called to process an request from the client. The Sun parser is instantiated and the DOM is used to create the following XML document:

```
<root><myElement>data</myElement></root>.
```

An output stream is created and Sun's write(...) method on the Element-Node class is used to persist the XML document.

```
import javax.servlet.*;
import javax.servlet.http.*;
import java.io.*;
import com.sun.xml.tree.*;
import org.w3c.dom.*;

public synchronized class XMLServlet extends HttpServlet {

  // Here is the constructor for the XMLServlet.
  public XMLServlet() {
  }

  // service processes the HTTP request
  public void service(HttpServletRequest req, ⏎
  HttpServletResponse res) throws ServletException, IOException {

    // tempelem and temptext will be used for temporary
    // storage when creating nodes.
    ElementNode tempelem;
```

```
Text temptext;
Writer out;

// Create a new Document node
XmlDocument xml = new XmlDocument();

// Create the root element and add it to the tree
tempelem = (ElementNode) xml.createElement("root");
xml.appendChild(tempelem);

// Create another element
tempelem = (ElementNode) xml.createElement("myElement");

// Add myElement to the tree
xml.getDocumentElement().appendChild(tempelem);

// Create a text node and place it under myElement
temptext = (Text) xml.createTextNode("data");
xml.getDocumentElement().getChildNodes().item(0).appendChild ⏎
(temptext );

// Set the response content type to "text/xml"
res.setContentType("text/xml");

// Grab a hold of an output stream
out = new OutputStreamWriter(res.getOutputStream());

// Use Sun's proprietary method for persisting
// the DOM tree to an XML text document
tempelem = (ElementNode) xml.getDocumentElement();
tempelem.write(out);

out.flush();
out.close();
}

public String getServletInfo() {
  return "Creates and returns an XML document.";
}
}
```

Summary

We have seen how to access the DOM methods and properties from various languages on various settings. It becomes obvious why the DOM needs to be standard across all parsers. Many of the beta versions have quirks that you will discover when working with individual parsers. An overview of the various DOM settings is useful when building applications to understand the possibilities that XML and the DOM can provide.

In Chapters 8 through 10, we show scenarios that use DOM in a more detailed capacity. The three scenarios drill down further into using the DOM with JavaScript in Internet Explorer 5, Visual Basic, and Java.

XML Support in Internet Explorer 5

Microsoft Internet Explorer 5 comes with XML support through a bundled COM object. The XML support provided conforms to the W3C DOM Level 1 specification outlined in Chapter 5. Some of the limitations of the DOM have been addressed through various extensions. Unfortunately, these extensions are bundled only with the Microsoft XML parser and not with any other parser. For those who have committed themselves to Internet Explorer 5 with the use of some of the proprietary aspects of DHTML, these extensions are quite useful.

This chapter begins with an explanation of the various features of the Microsoft's XML support, which includes a tutorial on data island usage, a description of datatype support, namespace support, querying support, XSL stylesheet support, and thread safety support. The remainder of the chapter is organized in a similar reference style similar to the one in Chapter 5. Examples are included to show the various aspects of the extended properties and methods. The initial feature summary and tutorial provides a higher-level view of how the various methods and properties can work together, and the reference section shows the details. We encourage you to consult the reference section in addition to reading the introductory material, because in it, we describe examples of using the loading and saving mechanism, parser error trapping support, iterator support, and various other useful features.

Data Islands

In Internet Explorer 5, XML documents can be embedded directly into HTML documents by using data islands, which are denoted by the <XML> tag. A data island is the <XML> tag, and within this tag, an XML document can be inserted. A data island is a useful construct that provides access to an XML document that has been embedded within an HTML document. Also, the data island can be used as a pointer to an XML document that is located on the server. Currently, the <XML> tag is proprietary to Internet Explorer 5, but the W3C is considering adding it or a similar construct to the HTML specification. An XML document that is included with a data island can be accessed from script. The script can do anything with the XML document by using the DOM interfaces. In other words, the data island is a mechanism to get an XML document to the parser, which can then be accessed through the DOM. Any changes from script cannot modify the original HTML page that contains the data island. Let's see how the following simple XML document would look in a data island.

```
<root>
    <element/>
</root>
```

This XML document can then be inserted into an HTML document as follows:

```
<HTML>
<BODY>
    ...
</BODY>
<XML ID="myXML">
    <root>
        <element/>
    </root>
</XML>
</HTML>
```

Accessing the Data Island from Script

Embedding XML within HTML is useful, because an XML document can then easily travel with script that knows how to make use of this XML. From script, the XML in a data island can be accessed using the ID attribute on the <XML> tag. For those familiar with the HTML object model, the *id* becomes part of the *all* collection. When using the ID, it represents the Document node, the top of the XML DOM tree. Let's look at an example.

```
<HTML>
<BODY>
<SCRIPT LANGUAGE="Javascript" FOR="window" EVENT="onload">

// Method #1
var documentNode = myXML;
var root = myXML.documentElement;

// Method #2
var alsoDocumentNode = document.all("myXML");
var alsoRoot = document.all("myXML").documentElement;

// Method #3
var yetAnotherDocumentNode = document.all("myXML").XMLDocument;
var yetAnotherRoot = document.all("myXML").XMLDocument.documentElement;

</SCRIPT>
</BODY>
<XML ID="myXML">
<root>
     <item>speakers</item>
     <price>159.99</price>
</root>
</XML>
</HTML>
```

This example shows how to access the Document node and the root element in three different ways by using the ID attribute on the data island. Once the HTML page is loaded, the parser parses the XML document contained in the data island and exposes the DOM interfaces. At this point, the script can access the DOM interfaces, and the original data island is disregarded. Any manipulations through the DOM interfaces affect only the current tree in memory and not the original HTML document. If the changes need to be sent to the server, then a persistence mechanism needs to be used. The xml property provides this functionality and is described in more detail later in this chapter.

Loading an XML Document

A data island can also be used to reference an actual XML file that might be located on the server by using the SRC attribute. The SRC attribute is specified on the <XML> tag and refers to a URL. In this case, the data island does not contain an XML document and is only used to gain access to the XML parser. The following example shows how to use the SRC attribute to access an XML document located on the server.

```
<HTML>
<BODY>
    ...
</BODY>
<XML ID="myXML" SRC="http://www.livingcode.com/clients.xml" />
</HTML>
```

Support for Older Browsers

An older browser might have a hard time understanding what the XML tag is. <SCRIPT> tags are considered a safe haven for putting in new functionality, because the scripting engines only work with what they understand. On the other hand, if an older browser reaches a tag that it doesn't understand, an error can occur. Internet Explorer 5 supports a method of inserting a data island inside of a <SCRIPT> tag. The structure appears as follows:

```
<HTML>
<BODY>
<SCRIPT ID="myXML" LANGUAGE="XML">
  <root>
    <item>speakers</item>
    <price>159.99</price>
  </root>
</SCRIPT>

<SCRIPT LANGUAGE="Javascript" FOR="window" EVENT="onload">

  // Method #1
  var documentNode = myXML.XMLDocument;
  var root = myXML.XMLDocument.documentElement;

  // Method #2
  var alsoDocumentNode = document.all("myXML").XMLDocument;
  var alsoRoot = document.all("myXML").XMLDocument.documentElement;

</SCRIPT>
</BODY>
</HTML>
```

The LANGUAGE attribute is used to associate the <SCRIPT> tag with an XML data island. The ID can then be used to reference the data island, but the XMLDocument property must be used to get to the Document node.

Multiple Data Islands

Data islands are indeed very social, and more then one <XML> tag can exist in an HTML page. Data islands can coexist as long as each one has a unique ID to identify it. Having multiple data islands is particularly useful when using XSL with XML, because the XSL can be contained in a separate data island. Two data islands can be created—one for the XSL stylesheet, which is valid XML, and one for the XML document to which the stylesheet is applied. Details on how to apply an XSL stylesheet to an XML document with the transformNode(...) function are found later in this section and a full description of XSL can be found in Part Three. Following is a brief example to show how to get to the Document nodes of three XML documents.

```
<HTML>
<BODY>
<SCRIPT LANGUAGE="Javascript" FOR="window" EVENT="onload">
  var clientsDoc = clients;
  var clientsXSLDoc = clientsXSL;
  var productsDoc = products;
</SCRIPT>
</BODY>
<XML ID="clients" SRC="http://www.myXMLsite.com/clients.xml">
</XML>
<XML ID="clientsXSL" SRC="http://www.myXMLsite.com/clients.xsl">
</XML>
<XML ID="products">
  <products>
    . . .
  </products>
</XML>
</HTML>
```

Using the DOM Without Data Islands

The parser can still be instantiated in Internet Explorer 5 without using data islands. The XML support in Internet Explorer 5 comes in the form of an ActiveX object, and data islands provide a mechanism to access this object. The parser can also be loaded just like any other ActiveX object creating an ActiveXObject object. This example shows how to load an XML document that is located on the server. The string microsoft.xmldom identifies the object that provides the XML support. The load(...) method is a Microsoft XML parser extension and is described in the IXMLDOM-Document reference in this chapter.

```
<HTML>
<BODY>
<SCRIPT LANGUAGE="Javascript" FOR="window" EVENT="onload">

  // Create the object.
  var myXML = new ActiveXObject("microsoft.xmldom");

  // Turn off asynchronous downloading (explained later).
  myXML.async = false;

  // Load an XML document off the server.
  myXML.load("http://www.livingcode.com/clients.xml");

  // myXML is the Document node and we can use the
  // DOM methods and properties as before.

</SCRIPT>
</BODY>
</HTML>
```

Datatypes Support

One of the key aspects of XML is the very defined structure it gives to the data—with either a DTD or some other type of schema language. Knowing what type of data is contained in an element is also important for building applications with XML. A shortcoming of using DTDs is not having a clear mechanism for specifying what type of data is contained within an element. For example, if you have an element called *date*, the DTD does not specify that only a valid date can be contained within this element; the XML document is still be valid if you put any kind of text inside. Even worse, this tag can contain dates that are formatted differently. The following XML document is used to illustrate this point.

```
<!DOCTYPE root [
  <!ELEMENT root (date*)>
  <!ELEMENT date (#PCDATA)>
]>
<root>
  <date>1/5/99</date>
  <date>January 5, 1999</date>
```

```
<date>World DOMination</date>
</root>
```

This XML document shows that even though you'd expect a date in the date element, you could end up with sporadic results. Different date types show up in this element. Programming using this XML document is much more complicated than it needs to be. The same can occur for other datatypes, such as integers, floating point numbers, and currency types.

To alleviate this problem, two things are needed. First, we need a schema language, such as XML-Data or Document Content Description (DCD), that supports data types. Second, we need the DOM interfaces to check and set the data types that are contained in an XML document. Unfortunately, we are stuck with DTDs in the meantime. The following example shows how an attribute can be added to the date element in order to specify the type of date we would like the element to contain.

```
<root xmlns:dt="urn:uuid:C2F41010-65B3-11d1-A29F-00AA00C14882/">
  <date dt:dt="date">1999-01-05</date>
</root>
```

The xmlns:dt attribute on the root element defines the dt namespace, which specifies the data types. The UUID C2F41010-65B3-11d1-A29F-00AA00C14882 has been reserved for specification of the datatype namespace. On the date element, the dt attribute in the dt namespace specifies the datatype for this element. In this case, we use the date datatype, which is a subset of the ISO 8601 format. The Microsoft XML parser (MSXML) checks the date element to make sure that it contains the date in the specified format. For example, if 1/5/99 was specified instead of 1999-01-05, then a parser error would occur and the XML document would not be valid. This error is the same type as the XML document being malformed. See Chapter 3 for an explanation of namespaces and how they are specified on elements.

The IMSXML DOM exposes two additional properties on the node to provide data type functionality: datatype and nodeTypedValue. The datatype property specifies to which data type the node is set. From the above example, the date Element node would have its datatype property set to *date*. On the other hand, nodeTypedValue provides the functionality to access the contents of the node through the data types mechanism.

nodeTypedValue is easily explained with an example. For the following XML document:

```
<root xmlns:dt="urn:uuid:C2F41010-65B3-11d1-A29F-00AA00C14882/">
  <name>Alex</name>
  <age dt:dt="int">21</age>
</root>
```

accessing the nodeValue property on the age element would yield "21" as a text string whereas accessing the nodeTypedValue on this node would produce 21 as an integer and not a string. Knowing that age is an integer, a script author can use the nodeTypedValue directly in calculations without any casting. A full explanation of datatype and nodeTypedValue, including the behavior for different node types, can be found later in this chapter in the IXMLDOMNode interface section.

Using a schema language, such as the Internet Explorer 5 schema preview, data types can also be specified for attributes. Table 7.1 lists the allowable data types in MSXML.

Table 7.1 Allowable Data Types in Internet Explorer 5

DATA TYPE	DESCRIPTION
bin.base64	MIME style Base64 encoded binary data.
bin.hex	Hexadecimal digits representing octets.
boolean	0 or 1, where 0 is false and 1 is true.
char	A character.
date	Date in a subset ISO 8601 format, without the time data (for example, "1994-11-05").
dateTime	Date in a subset of ISO 8601 format, with optional time and no optional zone. Fractional seconds can be as precise as nanoseconds (for example, "1988-04-07T18:39:09").
dateTime.tz	Date in a subset ISO 8601 format, with optional time and optional zone. Fractional seconds can be as precise as nanoseconds (for example, "1988-04-07T18:39:09-08:00").
fixed.14.4	Same as *number* but no more than 14 digits to the left of the decimal point and no more than 4 to the right.
float	Real number, with no limit on digits; can potentially have a leading sign, fractional digits, and optionally an exponent. Punctuation as in U.S. English. Values range from 1.7976931348623157E+308 to 2.2250738585072014E-308.
int	Number, with optional sign, no fractions, and no exponent.

Table 7.1 *(Continued)*

DATA TYPE	DESCRIPTION
number	Number, with no limit on digits; can potentially have a leading sign, fractional digits, and optionally an exponent. Punctuation as in U.S. English. (Values have same range as most significant number, R8, 1.7976931348623157E+308 to 2.2250738585072014E-308.)
time	Time in a subset ISO 8601 format, with no date and no time zone (for example, "08:15:27").
time.tz	Time in a subset ISO 8601 format, with no date but optional time zone (for example, "08:1527-05:00").
i1	Integer represented in one byte. A number, with optional sign, no fractions, no exponent (for example, "1, 127, -128").
i2	Integer represented in one word. A number, with optional sign, no fractions, no exponent (for example, "1, 703, -32768").
i4	Integer represented in four bytes. A number, with optional sign, no fractions, no exponent (for example, "1, 703, -32768, 148343, -1000000000").
i8	Integer represented in eight bytes. A number, with optional sign, no fractions, no exponent (for example, "1, 703, -32768, 1483433434334, -1000000000000000").
r4	Real number, with no limit on digits; can potentially have a leading sign, fractional digits, and optionally an exponent. Punctuation as in U.S. English. Values range from 3.40282347E+38F to 1.17549435E-38F.
r8	Same as *float*. Real number, with no limit on digits; can potentially have a leading sign, fractional digits, and optionally an exponent. Punctuation as in U.S. English. Values range from 1.7976931348623157E+308 to 2.2250738585072014E-308.
ui1	Unsigned integer. A number, unsigned, no fractions, no exponent (for example, "1, 255").
ui2	Unsigned integer, two bytes. A number, unsigned, no fractions, no exponent (for example, "1, 255, 65535").
ui4	Unsigned integer, four bytes. A number, unsigned, no fractions, no exponent.
ui8	Unsigned integer, eight bytes. A number, unsigned, no fractions, no exponent.
uri	Universal Resource Identifier (URI). For example, urn:mywebsite-com:authors.
uuid	Hexadecimal digits representing octets, optional embedded hyphens that are ignored (for example, "333C7BC4-460F-11D0-BC04-0080C7055A83").

Continues

Table 7.1 Allowable Data Types in Internet Explorer 5 *(Continued)*

DATA TYPE	DESCRIPTION
entity	Represents the XML ENTITY type.
entities	Represents the XML ENTITIES type.
enumeration	Represents an enumerated type.
id	Represents the XML ID type.
idref	Represents the XML IDREF type.
idrefs	Represents the XML IDREFS type.
nmtoken	Represents the XML NMTOKEN type.
nmtokens	Represents the XML NMTOKENS type.
notation	Represents a NOTATION type.
string	Represents a string type.

Namespace Support

The namespace mechanism has been introduced briefly in Chapter 3 to alleviate the possibilities of element or attribute name clashes. In the same document, the element *name* could have different meanings, depending on the namespace that it comes from. For example, the name element from a book namespace would mean the book title, whereas the name element from the author namespace would mean the name of the author. A namespace is represented by a Universal Resource Identifier (URI) and has an XML specific prefix associated with it. Namespaces are specified as attributes using the xmlns attribute and are valid for all the elements and attributes of the subtree in which the namespace was declared. The XML document is used to illustrate the namespace syntax.

```
<booklist xmlns:book="urn:some.xml.repository:book"
  xmlns:author="urn:some.xml.repository:author">

  <book>
    <book:name>Applied XML</book:name>
    <author:name>Ceponkus</author:name>
    <author:name>Hoodbhoy</author:name>
  </book>
</booklist>
```

Notice that the name element is used twice, but the two name elements are considered completely different. The namespace notation mentioned up to this point is recommended by the W3C and will eventually be standard across all the parsers. In MSXML, functionality has been added to the DOM to take namespaces into account. The namespace, prefix and baseName properties have been added to the Node interface to specify which namespace a node belongs to. Also, two methods, getQualifiedItem(...) and removeQualifiedItem(...), extend the NamedNodeMap interface to access attributes that are associated to a namespace. These extensions are mentioned here, but are described in detail in the IXMLDOMNode and IXMLDOMNamedNodeMap sections later in this chapter.

Querying Support

One of the benefits of XML is the decoupling of data and the presentation for this data. Since XML is being used to hold data, a method of finding the data in a document is also needed. XML documents can be queried using the XSL pattern matching syntax that is described in the XSL part of this book. This query language can be used to locate an element or a collection of elements in a tree based on the given parameters.

The MSXML DOM comes with a mechanism that uses this query language to find elements in the DOM tree. Two functions, selectNodes(...) and selectSingleNode(...), are used to provide this querying support. They both take only one parameter, an XSL pattern matching string, and they return the requests node(s). Examples of the usage of these functions are found later in the reference section of this chapter.

XSL Support

As mentioned in the first chapter, XML is used to carry data, and another mechanism is used to describe the presentation of this data. One of the available presentation technologies for XML is the XML Stylesheet Language (XSL). XSL is described in great detail in Part Three, the XSL portion of the book. Instead of describing XSL in this section, we talk about how to use XSL from the MSXML DOM. The function transformNode(...) is used to apply an XSL stylesheet to an existing XML document. The result is a text string that can then be displayed to the screen. An example of the usage of transformNode can be found in the reference section of this chapter.

Asynchronous Downloading Support

As we all know, Web traffic often moves at a turtle's pace. This limitation is an annoying burden that Web site developers need to tackle in order to keep users from getting frustrated with their sites. MSXML comes with a mechanism that allows XML to be downloaded asynchronously, which means that while your XML document is being downloaded, you can do something else. Even better, you can start using the part of the document that has been retrieved while waiting for the rest of the document to download. This mechanism is particularly useful when dealing with large XML documents. For those who are familiar with concurrent programming, the parser assigns a separate thread to do the downloading, allowing the parser to start its work on the part that has come down from the server. In fact, asynchronous downloading has become the norm with HTML. Imagine if your browser just sat there until a Web page, including images, finished downloading and then displayed it. Most users would get fed up, turn off their computers, and go sell their Netscape and Microsoft stocks.

The following properties and method are extended to provide this functionality: async, readyState, abort(), and parsed. The first three can be found in the IXMLDOMDocument interface, and the parsed property is implemented in the IXMLDOMNode interface. async specifies whether asynchronous downloading should be enabled. parsed and readyState describe the state of the document. The details of these properties and method are left to the reference section in this chapter. A detailed example of asynchronous downloading is presented with the parsed property in the IXMLDOMNode section.

Thread Safety Support

A typical scenario is to have an XML parser on the server that exposes DOM interfaces to multiple users who are all working with the same XML document. It is important to allow only one person or program to manipulate the tree at a time. Threads are used by programs to execute tasks in parallel, and each task is assigned a thread. MSXML has the capability to only allow one thread to access the DOM tree at a time. This feature is necessary to prevent the XML tree from becoming corrupted and to allow each thread to see the modifications made by a previous thread.

In a nonthread safe parser the following could occur: Let's say that we have built an online shopping site that uses XML. Two users place an order simultaneously for a book. Two instances (A and B) of some ordering program on the server are started up to process the orders. Both instances of the program check to see whether any copies of the book are available and they both see that there are. Then they will both try to update the tree to reflect the orders. Let's say A starts updating the tree, then B also starts before A is finished. A thinks it has successfully placed the order and returns a confirmation to one of the users. In the meantime, B has also been updating the tree and has inadvertently overwritten what A did to the tree. Now B returns a confirmation to the user. As we can see, both users think they have placed an order, but only one of the two actually receives the book in the mail!

The solution: Let only one instance (or thread) of the program update the tree at a time. That way B would only go place the order until A is finished. Of course there is a penalty: performance. The parser needs to perform much more management to ensure that only thread updates the tree at a time, but on the server, thread management is necessary to ensure reliability. MSXML comes in two flavors: the rental model and the free-threaded model. The rental model does not provide any special thread management and is used throughout this book. The free-threaded model allows only one thread to access the DOM tree at a time. The progID for the rental model is Microsoft.XMLDOM, whereas for the free-threaded model it is Microsoft.FreeThreadedXMLDOM.

The free-threaded version of MSXML can be instantiated from Javascript using the following:

```
var xmldoc = new ActiveXObject("Microsoft.FreeThreadedXMLDOM");
```

It can also be instantiated from an ASP page using VBScript:

```
Set xmldoc = Server.CreateObject("Microsoft.FreeThreadedXMLDOM")
```

DOM Interface Extensions Reference

Extensions have been implemented by adding to the node classes that contain all the base functionality that is described in Chapter 5. In MSXML, all the class names begin with *IXMLDOM* and contain both the base DOM and the extended functionality. Figure 7.1 shows this

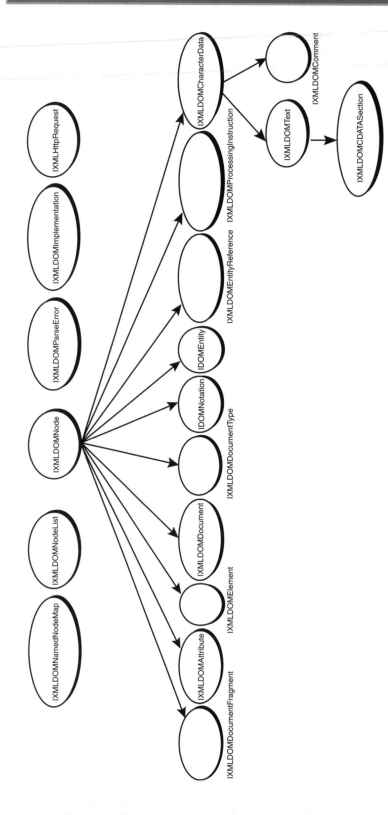

Figure 7.1   Microsoft XML DOM class hierarchy.

relationship. Notice the similarities between Figure 7.1 and Figure 5.1. If you find yourself working with interfaces that start with IXML or with IDOM, then you are probably working with a beta version of Internet Explorer 5. Now that we have an interface that has been handed down by the W3C, the old interfaces are obsolete and their use is discouraged. Because of this, they won't be covered in this book.

These extensions add facilities that many of you will find useful as well as other facilities that are crucial to working with XML documents. For example, the DOM specification leaves out the details for loading an XML document into the parser. Microsoft has added two methods, *load* and *loadXML*, to address this shortcoming. On the other hand, some extensions are just useful shortcuts. For example, the *text* property is added to give the programmer the ability to view the Text nodes under an Element node. With standard DOM interfaces, a programmer would need to go to the childNodes collection, iterate through all the Text nodes and combine them. Details about these methods are given in the interface descriptions later in this chapter.

IXMLDOMNode

Parent: IDOMNode (node)

The IXMLDOMNode class extends the base DOM functionality found in the Node interface. When using the MSXML extensions, this class would be used instead of the Node class. This class provides support for data types, namespaces, querying, XSL stylesheet transformations, persistence, asynchronous loading, and schema definitions.

IXMLDOMNode Properties

nodeTypeString

Type: String

Description: This string property represents the nodeType in a text string format. This property is different from nodeType, because nodeType returns a numerical value that represents the node type. Table 7.2 describes what nodeTypeString returns for the various node types.

Table 7.2 nodeTypeString Values for Various Node Types

NODE TYPE	nodeTypeString
Element	"element"
Attribute	"attribute"
Text	"text"
CDATASection	"cdatasection"
EntityReference	"entityreference"
Entity	"entity"
ProcessingInstruction	"processinginstruction"
Comment	"comment"
Document	"document"
DocumentType	"documenttype"
DocumentFragment	"documentfragment"
Notation	"notation"

definition

Type: Node

Description: A read-only property that represents a node in the schema (or DTD) that holds the definition for the current node.

Comments: Currently, only a small subset of a DTD is exposed through the DOM. This means that this property can only be called on EntityReference nodes. The definition property on any other node type returns *null*. This property becomes much more useful in the future when more of a schema or DTD is exposed through the DOM.

specified

Type: Boolean

Description: This read-only property is used only on Attr (Attribute) nodes, and it indicates whether an attribute was specified in the XML document. true is returned if this is the case; otherwise, false is returned, which signifies that the attribute was put there because it was specified in the DTD (or schema) as a #FIXED attribute.

Example: The following HTML page produces two alert boxes. The first contains true, while the second contains false. These results represent the call to specified for notFixedAtt and FixedAtt, respectively.

```
<HTML>
<SCRIPT LANGUAGE="javascript" FOR="window" EVENT="onload">
  // Check if notFixedAtt was specified. (true)
  alert(xml.documentElement.attributes.item(0).specified);

  // Check if FixedAtt was specified. (false)
  alert(xml.documentElement.attributes.item(1).specified);
</SCRIPT>
<XML ID="xml">
  <!DOCTYPE root [
    <!ELEMENT root (#PCDATA)>
    <!ATTLIST root
       notFixedAtt CDATA #IMPLIED
       FixedAtt CDATA #FIXED "some fixed value">
  ]>
  <root notFixedAtt="some value" />
</XML>
</HTML>
```

namespaceURI

Type: String

Description: This read-only property returns the URI associated with the namespace to which the current node belongs. A typical namespace declaration appears as follows, xmlns:prefix="uri". The uri portion of this declaration is returned by the namespaceURI property.

Example: Using the following snippet of XML, the namespaceURI property on the foo:root element is set to uri:foo.

```
<foo:root xmlns:foo="uri:foo" >
</foo:root>
```

prefix

Type: String

Description: This read-only property returns the prefix of a namespace declaration. In other words, *prefix* is returned from the following namespace declaration: xmlns:prefix="uri".

Example: Using the following snippet of XML, the prefix property on the foo:root element is set to foo.

```
<foo:root xmlns:foo="uri:foo" >
</foo:root>
```

baseName

Type: String

Description: This read-only property returns the node name without the namespace prefix.

Example: Calling nodeName on this XML snippet returns foo:root. Calling baseName returns root.

```
<foo:root xmlns:foo="uri:foo" >
</foo:root>
```

nodeTypedValue

Type: Type specified with dt:dt attribute.

Description: The nodeTypedValue property returns the contents of the node, but in the type that is specified on the dt:dt attribute. On the other hand, the nodeValue property returns the same contents but as a text string. nodeTypedValue applies only to Element, Attribute, and Text nodes. If this property is used on any of the other node types, nodeValue is returned. This property is not read-only.

Comments: nodeTypedValue is useful because the value that is returned can be used in calculations without any casting. There is an inconsistency between nodeTypedValue and nodeValue for Element nodes. nodeValue does not return anything for Element nodes—a programmer needs to go to child nodes of Element nodes to retrieve the contents of the element. nodeTypedValue, on the other hand, automatically finds the necessary child node and returns its contents.

Example: The following example shows how nodeTypedValue can be used from script. This script checks to see which of the two times, time1 or time2, is greater, and an alert box is used to tell the user the result. In this case, time1 is greater than time2, and this script reports that result accordingly. This example becomes interesting if you were to change nodeTypedValue to nodeValue in both cases. Now the variables time1 and time2 hold string text and not a time. As a result, the alert box says that time2 is greater because the string 03:45:03 is greater than the string 11:04:33. Naturally, the same is not true for the time they represent.

```
<HTML>
<SCRIPT LANGUAGE="javascript" FOR="window" EVENT="onload">
```

```
var time1 = xml.documentElement.childNodes.item(0).nodeTypedValue;
var time2 = xml.documentElement.childNodes.item(1).nodeTypedValue;

if (time1 > time2)
  alert("time1 is greater than time2");
else
  alert("time2 is greater than time1");

</SCRIPT>
<XML ID="xml">
<root xmlns:dt="urn:uuid:C2F41010-65B3-11d1-A29F-00AA00C14882/">
  <time1 dt:dt="time">11:04:33</time1>
  <time2 dt:dt="time">03:45:03</time2>
</root>
</XML>
</HTML>
```

dataType

Type: String

Description: This read/write property specifies the data type (see Table 7.1) of the current node. Only Element, Attr, and EntityReference nodes can have data types; all other node types return string. For Element, Attr, and EntityReference nodes, dataType can be used to set the data type. Also, if a data type has not been specified for one of these three nodes, *null* is returned.

xml

Type: String

Description: This property is used to convert the current node and its subtree into an XML document. This process is called persisting or saving out the tree and is particularly useful when the browser wants to send XML to the server.

Example: This example shows how to use the xml property by producing the XML for the whole tree and for the subtree of elem1. Figures 7.2 and 7.3 show the results of this script.

```
<HTML>
<SCRIPT LANGUAGE="javascript" FOR="window" EVENT="onload">

// Persist the whole tree
alert(xml.xml);
```

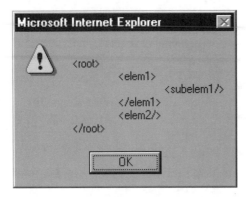

Figure 7.2   Alert box containing the whole tree.

```
// Persist only the subtree of elem1
alert(xml.documentElement.childNodes.item(0).xml);

</SCRIPT>
<XML ID="xml">
<root>
  <elem1>
    <subelem1/>
  </elem1>
  <elem2/>
</root>
</XML>
</HTML>
```

text

Type: String

Description: This property displays the contents of the node concatenated with all the contents in the nodes found in the childNodes collection. Nodes (for example, Comment) that don't have children behave exactly like the nodeValue property.

Figure 7.3   Alert box containing the subtree of elem1.

Comments: For Element nodes, this property behaves like the Displaying Element Contents example in Element Usage Examples section of Chapter 5. When an Element only has one Text node, the text property is a shortcut to the nodeValue of this node. Please note that the contents of child Element nodes is also displayed.

Example: The XML for this example is taken from the Displaying Element Contents example in Chapter 5. The same result occurs, which is: Some text<B>Bold text</B> More text.

```
<HTML>
<SCRIPT LANGUAGE="javascript" FOR="window" EVENT="onload">

alert(xml.documentElement.text);

</SCRIPT>
<XML ID="xml">
  <rootElement>
    Some text
    <![CDATA[<B>Bold text</B>]]>
    More text
  </rootElement>
</XML>
</HTML>
```

parsed

Type: Boolean

Description: A read-only property that represents whether a node and its children have been parsed. This property is used with the asynchronous loading mechanism.

IXMLDOMNode Methods

selectNodes(query)

Parameters: query is a string.

Return value: NodeList

Description: selectNodes returns a NodeList of Nodes that match the XSL pattern string query. Even if no nodes match the search criteria, a NodeList is still returned, even though it is empty. In other words, the length property of this NodeList is set to 0.

Example: In this example, we use selectNodes(...) to search through the tree and pick out all the elements with the nodeName set to *name*.

The XSL pattern ".//name" is the query string that satisfies this condition. (XSL patterns are described in Part Three, the XSL portion of this book.) We then display each name of each client using the nodeValue property on the text node of the current element in the NodeList.

```
<HTML>
<BODY>
<SCRIPT LANGUAGE="javascript" FOR="window" EVENT="onload">

  // Perform the query.
  var result = clientsXML.selectNodes(".//name");

  for(i=0;i<result.length;i++) {

    // Display the name of each client.
    alert(result.item(i).childNodes.item(0).nodeValue);
  }

</SCRIPT>
</BODY>
<XML ID="clientsXML">
<clients>
  <client>
    <name>John Server</name>
    <phone>425-536-9989</phone>
  </client>

  <client>
    <name>Xavier M. Lee</name>
    <phone>416-978-7669</phone>
  </client>

  <client>
    <name>Danny Otis Manning</name>
    <phone>905-778-4345</phone>
  </client>
</clients>
</XML>
</HTML>
```

selectSingleNode(query)

Parameters: query is a string.

Return value: NodeList

Description: The behavior of selectSingleNode(...) is identical to selectNodes(...), except that only the first node is returned.

transformNode(stylesheet)

Parameters: stylesheet is a node.

Return value: String

Description: The transformNode(...) method is used to apply a stylesheet transformation on the Node on which it is called. This function then returns a string that contains the formatted XML. In other words, the string that is returned contains a view of the XML that is defined in the XSL stylesheet.

Example: An example of using the transformNode(...) function follows, but an understanding of XSL basics is necessary to understand the example. XSL is covered in detail in Part Three of this book.

First we show the XML document that contains a list of clients:

```
<clients>
  <client>
    <name>John Server</name>
    <phone>332-536-9989</phone>
  </client>

  <client>
    <name>Xavier M. Lee</name>
    <phone>416-978-7669</phone>
  </client>

  <client>
    <name>Danny Otis Manning</name>
    <phone>905-778-4345</phone>
  </client>
</clients>
```

The following XSL stylesheet formats the above XML document into an HTML table.

```
<xsl:stylesheet xmlns:xsl="http://www.w3.org/TR/WD-xsl">
  <xsl:template match="/">
    <TABLE BORDER="1">
      <TH>Client</TH>
      <TH>Phone Number</TH>

      <xsl:for-each select = ".//client">
        <TR>
          <TD> <xsl:value-of select = "name"/> </TD>
          <TD> <xsl:value-of select = "phone"/> </TD>
```

```
            </TR>
          </xsl:for-each>
        </TABLE>
    </xsl:template>
  </xsl:stylesheet>
```

Notice that the XSL specific elements are in the xsl namespace. The value-of element is used to get the text associated with an element. The for-each element is used to build a row for each client element in the XML document. Finally, the stylesheet element is a container for an XSL stylesheet. Also, notice that the XSL stylesheet is a valid XML document. That means if you are to use HTML elements such as <P> (paragraph) and
 (hard return), then you must close these tags for the XSL to be valid.

Finally, the script that applies the XSL stylesheet to an XML document is as follows:

```
<HTML>
<BODY>
<DIV ID="tableDiv"></DIV>
<SCRIPT LANGUAGE="javascript" FOR="window" EVENT="onload">

   // Apply the XSL stylesheet to the XML
   var result = clientsXML.transformNode(clientsXSL.documentElement);

   // Put the result of the XSL into an HTML <DIV>
   tableDiv.innerHTML = result;
</SCRIPT>
</BODY>
<XML ID="clientsXSL" SRC="table.xsl">
</XML>
<XML ID="clientsXML" SRC="clients.xml">
</XML>
</HTML>
```

You might wonder why we would use the DOM to apply a stylesheet to XML. In this case, the example is contrived to show the usage of the transformNode(...) function. However, if you had more than one stylesheet, the Web page could present radio buttons for each view of the data. The DOM can then be used to process the selection by applying the appropriate stylesheet. Figure 7.4 shows the result of this script. For those unfamiliar with HTML <DIV> elements, a <DIV> can be used as a placeholder. In this case, this element does nothing until we place the HTML table into it using the innerHTML property.

Figure 7.4 XSL example.

IXMLDOMDocument

Parent: IXMLDOMNode

The IXMLDOMDocument extends the document interface that was presented in Chapter 5. Various methods and properties have been added with most of them falling into one of two categories: asynchronous downloading support and XML document loading support. Asynchronous downloading refers to downloading a document while doing something else in script. XML document loading support refers to the loading and the parsing the XML document, regardless of whether it is done synchronously or asynchronously. XML loading was unfortunately left out of the W3C DOM Level 1 specification, so Microsoft has introduced load(...) and loadXML(...) to take care of this task.

IXMLDOMDocument Properties

url

Type: String

Description: If the load(...) method was used to load the document, then the read-only property url represents the location of the XML document. If the document was loaded in any other fashion, then url is set to *null*.

parseError

Type: IDOMParseError

Description: Represents the error object for this document, which represents the last parsing error that occurred. Please see the IDOMParseError reference section for examples of using this object.

readyState

Type: Long integer

Description: This read-only property returns the state of the document (see Table 7.3), in terms of downloading and parsing progress. This property is used in conjunction with asynchronous downloading.

Comments: Writing a program that waits until the readyState of a document is COMPLETED is equivalent to turning asynchronous downloading off (async=false). In other words, you might as well just wait for load(...) to return synchronously instead of doing the checking yourself.

async

Type: Boolean

Description: async is set to true if asynchronous is turned on and false if asynchronous is off. This is a writeable property, and the default value is true.

Comments: If you want your script to flow logically and not have functions return before they are complete, you should set async to false. In other words, when async is set to false, the load(...)only returns when the document has been completely downloaded and parsed.

Example: This example shows how to use the asynchronous downloading mechanism. We make use of the onreadystatechange event that gets fired through the various stages of parsing (see Table 7.3). We wait until the readyState changes to COMPLETED (4) before we do anything with the tree. Notice that we are instantiating the XMLDOM object from script instead of using a data island. Data islands fire off

Table 7.3 readyState States

READYSTATE	STATE	DESCRIPTION
0	UNINITIALIZED	The XML Object has been created, but the download has not started yet.
1	LOADING	The loading of the XML document is in progress, but parsing has not been started yet.
2	LOADED	Finished loading the document, but the DOM tree has not been exposed yet.
3	INTERACTIVE	The DOM tree has been exposed, but only some of the document has been loaded and parsed. The parsed property should be checked on a node to see if that nodes' subtree is ready to be used.
4	COMPLETED	The XML document has been loaded and parsed, but an error might have occurred.

values for onreadystatechange events that are different than those defined for the readyState property on the IXMLDOMDocument node.

```
<HTML>
<BODY onload="init()">
<SCRIPT LANGUAGE="javascript">

// Global variable declarations
var xmldoc;
var COMPLETED = 4;

function init() {
  // Instantiate the XMLDOM object.
  xmldoc = new ActiveXObject("Microsoft.XMLDOM");

  // Turn on Asynchronous downloading.
  xmldoc.async = true;

  // Associate the done() event handler to the
  // onreadystatechange event.
  xmldoc.onreadystatechange = done;

  // Load the XML document from the server.
  xmldoc.load("http://spartus/xml/clients.xml");

  // At this point we can do tasks until our XML document
  // is downloaded and parsed.
  alert("Going to do other stuff");
}
```

```
// done() is called by xmldoc 4 times as it moves through the
// various stages in parsing.
function done() {

  // Check if the XML is ready to be used; otherwise, return.
  if (xmldoc.readyState != COMPLETED)
    return;

  // Document is ready to be used. Display the file to the
  // screen as proof.
  alert(xmldoc.xml);
}

</SCRIPT>
</BODY>
</HTML>
```

validateOnParse

Type: Boolean

Description: This writeable property tells the parser whether it should check if the XML document conforms to the specified DTD. However, validateOnParse doesn't turn off checking if an XML document is well formed. This property is set to true by default.

Comments: validateOnParse cannot be used in conjunction with data islands, because the XML in the data island has to be loaded before the validateOnParse property can be set to false. Instead, use the load(...) methods after validateOnParse has been set to false.

preserveWhiteSpace

Type: Boolean

Description: When this property is set to true, the parser ensures that all the white space (for example, spaces, tabs, and carriage returns) are saved and exposed in the DOM. Initially, preserveWhiteSpace is set to false.

resolveExternals

Type: Boolean

Description: This property informs the parser where externals (for example, external DTDs, external entities, and resolvable namespaces) are to be resolved during the parsing. If resolveExternals is set to false, then validation cannot occur if the DTD is external.

IXMLDOMDocument Methods

load(url)

Parameters: url is a string.

Return value: Boolean

Description: Loads the XML document that is pointed to by url and returns true if the loading was successful. load(...)uses the security restrictions that are set by the user through the Internet Explorer 5 security restrictions. There are various levels of security for Internet, intranet, trusted, and restricted sites, and they can be set from Tools...Internet Options...Security.

loadXML(xml)

Parameters: xml is a string.

Return value: Boolean

Description: loadXML(...)takes the string xml, parses it, and exposes the DOM tree. The parameter xml refers to an actual piece of XML and a url that points to an XML document.

Example: This example shows how to use loadXML(...) from script. Notice that single quotes (') and not double quotes (") were used to specify attributes. A double quote is used to mark the beginning and the end of the string. Using a double quote for attributes would render the script invalid.

```
<HTML>
<BODY>
<SCRIPT LANGUAGE="javascript" FOR="window" EVENT="onload">

  // Parse the XML document that is passed as a string.
  xmldoc.loadXML("<root><elem1 att='hello'/></root>");

  ...

</SCRIPT>
</BODY>
```

```
<XML id="xmldoc">
</XML>
</HTML>
```

save(destination)

Parameters: destination can be a string (filename) or an object (IXMLDOMDocument or ASP Response object).

Return value: integer error code

Description: save(...) is used to dump the DOM tree to a specified location, either to a file, another DOM tree, or to a Response object from ASP. Please note that security restrictions in Internet Explorer 5 prevent you from writing to a file from the browser. This method is intended to be used on the server.

createNode(type, name, namespaceURI)

Parameters: type is an integer; name and namespaceURI are strings.

Return value: Node

Description: This method creates a node with a node type of *type* and node name of *name*. The valid numerical node types are specified in Table 5.3. A node can also be created in the context of a namespace that is specified with namespaceURI. In this case, the name can be specified with a prefix, such as "prefix:name." If the prefix is omitted, the default namespace is assumed.

nodeFromID(id)

Parameters: id is a string.

Return value: Node

Description: This method returns the node that has an ID attribute that is equal to the parameter id. In a DTD, each element can only have one ID attribute.

Example: In this example, we must first define a DTD for the XML document. This step is required to tell the parser which attribute is the ID attribute, since it can have any name. In our example, elem has an ID attribute called elemID. The elem element is given an id equal to *b*, which nodeFromID(...) uses to find the necessary node. The example then just displays "elem" to prove that we did indeed get the node that we requested.

```
<HTML>
<BODY>
<SCRIPT LANGUAGE="javascript" FOR="window" EVENT="onload">

  // Grab a hold of the elem node using nodeFromID..
  var elemNode = xmldoc.nodeFromID("b");

  alert(elemNode.nodeName);

</SCRIPT>
</BODY>
<XML id="xmldoc">
  <!DOCTYPE root [
    <!ELEMENT root (elem)*>
    <!ATTLIST root
      id ID #REQUIRED>
    <!ELEMENT elem (#PCDATA)>
    <!ATTLIST elem
      elemID ID #REQUIRED>
  ]>

  <root id="a">
    <elem elemID="b" />
  </root>
</XML>
</HTML>
```

abort()

Parameters: None

Return value: None

Description: abort()stops an asynchronous download and discards any XML that has been downloaded. parseError.reason of the XML document specifies that the loading of the XML document was aborted.

IXMLDOMNodeList

The IXMLDOMNodeList interface extends the W3C DOM NodeList interface by adding support for iterators. In the Element Usage Examples section of Chapter 5, we showed how to iterate through a list of children by using the standard facilities. The iterator support that has been added to the IXMLDOMNodeList interface is a much cleaner way of doing roughly the same thing. In the example in Chapter 5, we first get the number of children in the NodeList using the length property. Based on that number of children, we visit each child of the collection. Things get complicated if nodes are added to or removed from the collection: If the length property changes and then we end up missing nodes or trying to access a node that doesn't exist anymore. Two methods, nextNode() and reset(), have been introduced to alleviate this shortcoming.

A for...each construct from Visual Basic and from VBScript can also be used. The following example shows how to use this construct. It is the only VBScript example in this chapter. The sample code results in three alert boxes, each with a client name. Notice how much cleaner this mechanism is compared with using a for loop that counts up to xmldoc.documentElement.childNodes.length.

```
<HTML>
<SCRIPT LANGUAGE="vbscript" FOR="window" EVENT="onload">
Dim node

For Each node In xmldoc.documentElement.childNodes
  MsgBox (node.childNodes.item(0).childNodes.item(0).nodeValue)
Next
</SCRIPT>
<XML ID="xmldoc">
<clients>
  <client>
    <name>John Server</name>
    <phone>425-536-9989</phone>
  </client>
  <client>
    <name>Xavier M. Lee</name>
    <phone>416-978-7669</phone>
  </client>
  <client>
    <name>Danny Otis Manning</name>
    <phone>905-778-4345</phone>
  </client>
</clients>
</XML>
</HTML>
```

IXMLDOMNodeList Methods

nextNode()

Parameters: None

Return value: Node

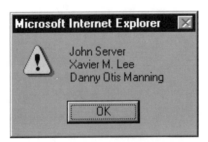

Figure 7.5 nextNode() example.

Description: nextNode() is used to iterate through a collection of nodes. The first time nextNode() is called, the first node in the list is returned. Every subsequent call returns the node adjacent to the one previously returned, until the end is reached. At that point, *null* is returned.

Example: This example uses nextNode() to visit each client in a list of clients and display the name of each client in an alert box. The result of this script is shown in Figure 7.5.

```
<HTML>
<BODY>
<SCRIPT LANGUAGE="javascript" FOR="window" EVENT="onload">

  // Make a shortcut to the NodeList that belongs to clients.
  var clientList = clientsXML.documentElement.childNodes;

  // stringBuffer is used to hold the list of names that will
  // later be displayed to the screen.
  var stringBuffer = "";

  // current is the node we are working with.
  // nextNode() keeps advancing current until we reach null.
  while ( (current = clientList.nextNode()) != null ) {

    // Make a shortcut for the client name.
    var clientName = current.childNodes(0).childNodes(0).nodeValue;

    // Append each client name to the StringBuffer.
    stringBuffer += clientName;

    // Also append a newline character.
    stringBuffer += "\n";
  }

  // Display the result to the user.
  alert(stringBuffer);
```

```
</SCRIPT>
</BODY>
<XML ID="clientsXML">
<clients>
  <client>
    <name>John Server</name>
    <phone>425-536-9989</phone>
  </client>

  <client>
    <name>Xavier M. Lee</name>
    <phone>416-978-7669</phone>
  </client>

  <client>
    <name>Danny Otis Manning</name>
    <phone>905-778-4345</phone>
  </client>
</clients>
</XML>
</HTML>
```

reset()

Parameters: None

Return value: None

Description: Sets the iterator back to the first node. In other words, if nextNode() is called after reset() was called, then nextNode()returns the first node in the collection.

IXMLDOMNamedNodeMap

The IXMLDOMNamedNodeMap interface extends the same iterator functionality as described in IXMLDOMNodeList. In addition, this interface also adds support for accessing attributes that are associated with a namespace.

IXMLDOMNamedNodeMap Methods

getQualifiedItem(name, namespace)

Parameters: name and namespace are both strings.

Return value: Node

Description: This method returns the node in the NamedNodeMap called *name* that has a namespace URI called *namespace*. If such a node doesn't exist, then *null* is returned.

Example: The example that follows shows how to access attributes using getQualifiedItem(...). Two alert boxes are displayed, the first with the contents "with namespace" and the second with the contents "without namespace." Notice that to access an attribute with this method that doesn't have a namespace, an empty string must be passed as the namespace URI.

```
<HTML>
<BODY>
<SCRIPT LANGUAGE="javascript" FOR="window" EVENT="onload">

// Create a shortcut to elem's list of attributes.
var elemAtts = xmldoc.documentElement.childNodes.item(0).attributes;

// Display the contents of the ax:myAtt attribute.
alert( elemAtts.getQualifiedItem( "myAtt", ↵
"uri:AppliedXML" ).nodeValue );

// Display the contents of the myAtt attribute that
// is without a namespace.
alert(elemAtts.getQualifiedItem("myAtt", "").nodeValue);

</SCRIPT>
</BODY>
<XML ID="xmldoc">
  <root xmlns:ax="uri:AppliedXML">
    <elem ax:myAtt="with namespace" myAtt="without namespace" />
  </root>
</XML>
</HTML>
```

removeQualifiedItem(name, namespace)

Parameters: name and namespace are both strings.

Return value: Node

Description: This method removes and returns the node in the NamedNodeMap called *name*, which has a namespace URI called *namespace*. If such a node doesn't exist, then *null* is returned.

nextNode()

Parameters: None

Return value: Node

Description: nextNode() is used to iterate through a collection of nodes. The first time nextNode() is called, the first node in the list is returned. Every subsequent call returns the node adjacent to the one previously returned, until the end is reached. At that point, *null* is returned.

Example: The behavior of this method is the same as the nextNode() method defined in the IXMLDOMNodeList interface. The example of the IXMLDOMNodeList nextNode() method shows how to use this nextNode() method. The only difference is that the childNodes collection is in a NodeList; to use this method, you need to access the attributes collection to obtain a NamedNodeMap.

reset()

Parameters: None

Return value: None

Description: Sets the iterator back to the first node. In other words, if nextNode() is called after reset() was called, then nextNode()returns the first node in the collection.

IDOMParseError

Parent: none

The IDOMParserError object is used to report errors that have occurred in the parser while an XML document was being parsed. You can gain access to this object by using the parseError property on the IXML-DOMDocument class. This object can then be used to pinpoint the exact cause of the error by finding the exact location of the error and the reason for the error.

IDOMParseError Properties

errorCode

Type: Long integer

Description: This read-only property returns the error code for the last parsing error.

url

Type: String

Description: This read-only property returns the URL of the XML document that had the parsing error.

Comments: This property is set only if an error occurs during the parsing of an XML document, whereas the url property on IXMLDOMDocument is always be set.

reason

Type: String

Description: This read-only property gives the reason for the last error.

Comments: We have noticed that the string that is returned already has a new line character ("\n") appended to it. In other words, if you want to append this string to another string without skipping a line, you need to strip out the new line character.

Example: This property returns one-line reasons like the following when you forget to properly close your tags: "The character '>' was expected."

srcText

Type: String

Description: This read-only property returns the line of text on which the parser found an error.

line

Type: Long integer

Description: This read-only property returns the line number on which the parser found an error.

linepos

Type: Long integer

Description: This read-only property returns the column number in the line on which the parser found an error.

filepos

Type: Long integer

Description: This read-only property returns the character position with respect to the beginning of the document.

IDOMParseError Example

Now that you have seen all the painful details of the IDOMParseError object, we show you a practical example. These properties on the IDOM-ParseError object can be used to produce useful output when a parsing error occurs. The XML in the data island should read "<root><elem att="myAtt" /></root>" and not "<root><elem att myAtt /></root>." Figure 7.6 shows the result of this sample.

```
<HTML>
<BODY>
<DIV ID="errorDIV"></DIV>
<DIV ID="errorDIVtext"></DIV>
<SCRIPT LANGUAGE="javascript" FOR="window" EVENT="onload">

  // Check if a parsing error occurred.
  if (xml.parseError.errorCode != 0) {

    var pe = xml.parseError;
    var stringBuffer = "";

    stringBuffer += "<B>A parsing error has occurred.</B><BR><BR>";

    // Display the reason
    stringBuffer += "<B>Reason:</B> " + pe.reason + "<BR>";

    // Check if the url property is null.
    if (pe.url != "") {
      stringBuffer += "<B>URL:</B> " + pe.url + "<BR>";
    }

    stringBuffer += "<B>Line:</B> " + pe.line + "<BR>";
    stringBuffer += "<B>Character:</B> " + pe.linepos + "<BR><BR>";

    // Dump what we have so far into a <DIV>
    errorDIV.outerHTML = stringBuffer;

    // Reset the buffer.
    stringBuffer = "";
```

```
        // Display the line of from the XML that the error occurred on.
        stringBuffer += "\"" + pe.srcText + "\"" + "\n";

        // Insert place holders.
        for ( i = 1; i < pe.linepos; i++ )
          stringBuffer += "-";

          // Show where the error occurred.
          stringBuffer += "/^\\";

          // Dump the result in a <DIV>.
          // Make sure that the font is fixed width.
          errorDIVtext.style.fontFamily = "monospace";
          errorDIVtext.innerText = stringBuffer;
        }

</SCRIPT>
</BODY>
<XML ID="xml">
  <root><elem att myAtt /></root>
</XML>
</HTML>
```

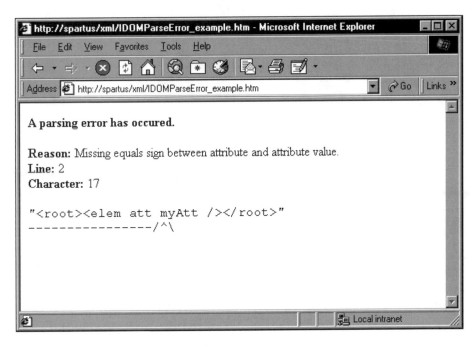

Figure 7.6 IDOMParseError example.

Summary

We have covered the inner details of the Microsoft XML extended DOM. To summarize, support has been added for the following items: data islands, datatypes, namespaces, querying, XSL, loading and persisting XML, parser error trapping, iterators, and thread-safety. In time, the standard DOM will evolve to support some of the items that have been listed. Currently, the drawback to using these extensions is that your programs only work with the Microsoft XML parser. If you are developing in a non-browser language that supports COM, such as C++ or Visual Basic, then using the additional support may save you some headaches.

Internet Explorer 5 and Server-Side Scenario: Online Shopping Demo

F or this chapter, we put together an online shopping site to show how XML can be used to create e-commerce sites. The user can browse through catalogs, accumulate items in a shopping cart, and then send the order to the server. This site is a demo, because the actual transaction doesn't take place. Don't worry if you just spent all your money on a new machine and high-speed Net access, because ordering doesn't cost anything.

Design Overview

The shopping demo is composed of three tiers: client tier, middle (Web server) tier, and the database tier. The three tiers and the data flow between them are depicted in Figure 8.1.

Microsoft's Internet Explorer 5 is used as the front end. Netscape Navigator could also be used, but at the time of writing, instantiating a parser from script was not yet possible in Netscape Navigator. The Microsoft XML parser is also used on the server, but only with the standard DOM methods and properties (see Chapter 5) and not the MSXML extensions (see Chapter 7).

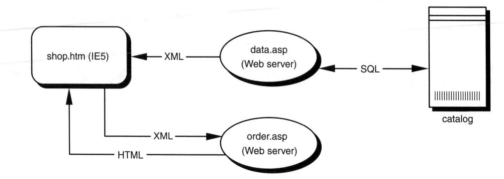

Figure 8.1 Shopping demo data flow.

Javascript and the Microsoft XML parser are used to obtain catalog information from the server. This catalog comes in XML format and is processed using the DOM to create a table as shown in Figure 8.2. Other technologies, such as XSL, CSS, or Databinding, could have been used to generate the table. In fact, using a stylesheet language (XSL) is considered better design, because higher level authoring tools could have been used to generate the view. These other technologies have not been covered yet; therefore, we stick to a DOM-only XML solution. Also, if any kind of calculating needs to be done, then the functionality that the DOM provides would be necessary.

Using DHTML, mouse events are captured to highlight the entry in the table that the mouse is over. The user can then click on an item, which adds the item to the shopping cart. For this scenario, we use a DOM tree to represent the shopping cart. When an item is added to the shopping cart, a node from the catalog DOM tree is copied to the shopping cart tree. The text version of the shopping cart tree is shown in the bottom text area of Figure 8.2. Figure 8.3 shows the structure of the data stream coming from the server that contains the catalog information. Figure 8.4 shows the XML structure of the shopping cart in the browser. The *name* element is the common node that is copied between the two trees and is the index for an item. A numerical id would be a better choice for an index, but for the purpose of this demo, the name of the item is easier to follow.

Finally, the transaction is complete when the order is sent to the server in the form of XML. The server then builds an HTML page confirming the order.

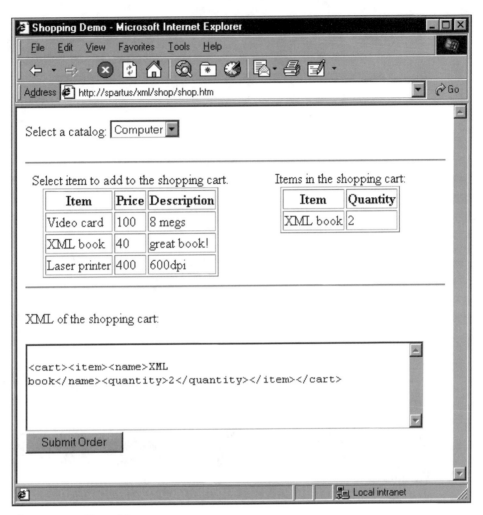

Figure 8.2   Client side.

On the server, Active Server Pages (ASP) send the catalog to the client and process the client's order. The ASP scripts use Structured Query Language (SQL) to access the database. Because of the way ODBC works, the database could be either an Access table or a SQL server. We have chosen to use an Access table because of its simplicity. The ASP script processes the result from the database and converts the data on the fly to XML. Server-side solutions most likely entail on-the-fly conversion of native data to XML. Storing data natively in XML is inefficient, and the whole scale conversion of existing data is expensive, leaving on-the-fly conversion the optimal solution.

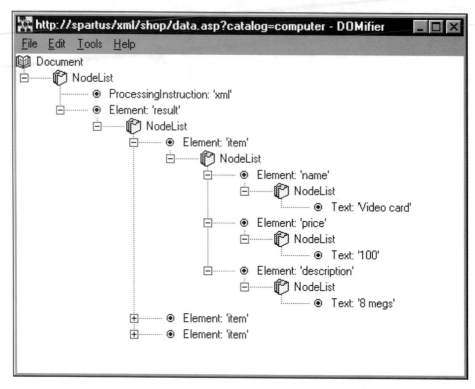

Figure 8.3 XML structure of catalog from server.

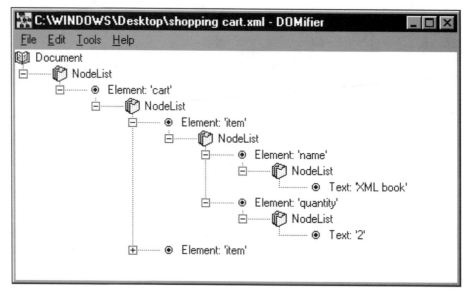

Figure 8.4 XML structure of shopping cart on the client.

Setting Up the Demo

Getting the demo to work on your local machine is a simple process. Since ASP is used, this demo only runs on Windows NT/95/98/2000 boxes. Internet Information Server (IIS) or Personal Web Server (PWS) is needed to host these pages. Also, Microsoft Data Access Components (DAC), including the Access ODBC driver, are needed to access the database. The demo files shop.htm, data.asp, order.asp, and catalog.mdb are located on the companion CD-ROM and need to be copied over into a directory that your Web server can host. Then, the ODBC Administrator (found in the Control Panel) is used to set up a System DSN for the Access table. For the demo to work, the Data Source Name must be *catalog*, as shown in Figure 8.5.

As long as shop.htm and the two ASP scripts are in the same directory, the demo is ready to run.

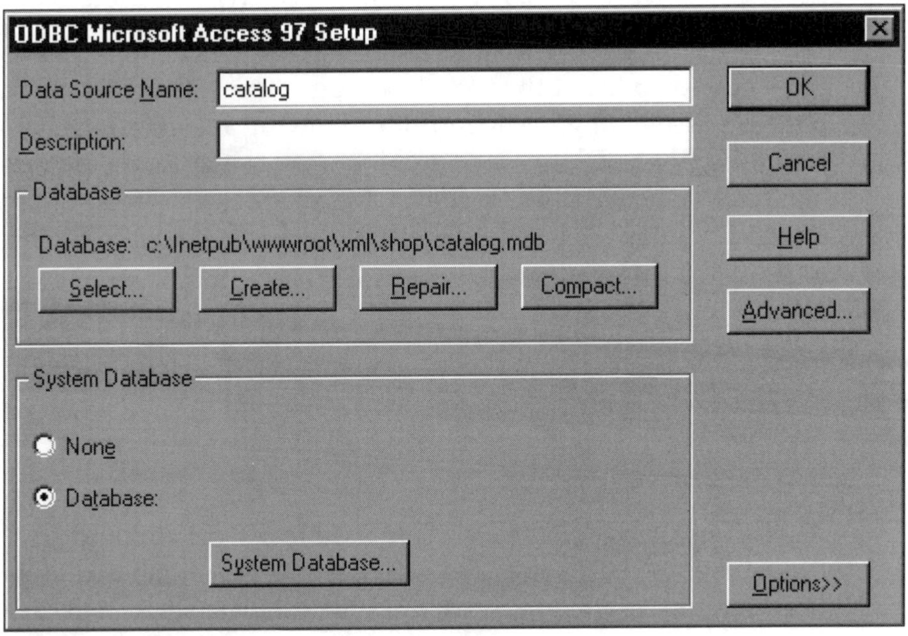

Figure 8.5   Demo settings in ODBC Administrator.

Designing the Client

This client is going to use XML, so we need some way to load up the parser. Two data islands are created to take care of this task.

```
<XML ID="itemsXML">
</XML>
<XML ID="cartXML">
<cart/>
</XML>
```

itemsXML holds the catalog of items that comes from the server. cartXML, on the other hand, holds the contents of the shopping cart that contains the user's order. Notice that the root element <cart/> is specified in the second data island and that the first one is empty. itemsXML loads XML from the server, which overwrites anything we put in there, whereas in cartXML, the DOM methods and properties are used to build an XML document on the fly, so no loading occurs.

The script contains seven functions: init(), displayCart(), catSelect(), inCart(itemName), mouseClick(), mouseOver(), and mouseOut().

catSelect() executes when the user changes the catalog selection from the drop-down list at the top of the page. The HTTP GET command is used by assembling a URL in the following format: data.asp?catalog =userselection. GET refers to passing data to the server by appending that data to the URL. Using the DOM, catSelect() creates a table view of the XML catalog. This table is then displayed to the screen by inserting it into an HTML DIV element.

DIV elements are commonly used as placeholders in HTML documents. Two DIV elements are used in this HTML page—displayDiv and cartDiv—to display the catalog and the shopping cart, respectively. We use the innerHTML property on the DIV element to insert the tables into the page.

displayCart() and mouseClick() are used to select items and add them to the shopping cart. As in catSelect(), the XML shopping cart is converted to a table and inserted into cartDiv. A view of the text version of the DOM tree is inserted into the bottom text area. Normally, that text area would not be shown, but it is useful to see what is going on behind the scenes.

mouseOver() and mouseOut() are common DHTML techniques that are used to highlight the item, on top of which the user has the mouse pointer. These functions aren't essential, but make the user interface a little easier to use.

It should be noted that the XML structure we chose, shown in Figures 8.3 and 8.4, might not be the best for any given application. Attributes are a viable alternative to using elements, and a combination of the two might be your best bet. One advantage of using attributes is that the DOM methods for accessing attributes are slightly easier to use. An attribute can be accessed with one command, getAttribute(...) or setAttribute(...). However, with elements, you need to dig down to the text node and then access the nodeValue property on that node, making the code hard to follow. Figure 8.6 shows the DOM tree of the following alternative to the catalog XML structure by using only attributes.

```xml
<?xml version="1.0"?>
<result>
 <item name="Video card" price="100" description="8 megs"></item>
 <item name="XML book" price="40" description="great book!"></item>
 <item name="Laser printer" price="400" description="600dpi"></item>
</result>
```

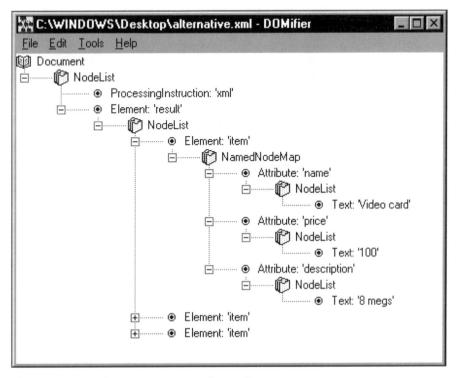

Figure 8.6 Catalog XML structure using attributes.

Client Code

As with all programs, the best way to learn what is going on is to look under the hood. The code for the browser is presented here with plenty of comments to facilitate reading the script. The comments, as well as some important tags, have been highlighted to assist you. This HTML document is structured in the following way: All HTML elements that have to do with the presentation are located at the beginning, followed by the script, and finally, the data islands.

```html
<HTML>
<HEAD>
<TITLE>Shopping Demo</TITLE>
</HEAD>

<BODY onload="init()">

<P>Select a catalog:
  <SELECT NAME="catalogSelect" SIZE="1" onchange="catSelect()">
    <OPTION VALUE="Computer">Computer</OPTION>
    <OPTION VALUE="Clothing">Clothing</OPTION>
 </SELECT>
</P>

<HR>

<TABLE BORDER="0" WIDTH="100%" HEIGHT="0">
 <TR>
  <TD WIDTH="50%" VALIGN="top" ALIGN="center">

    Select item to add to the shopping cart.
    <DIV ID="displayDiv"></DIV></TD>

  <TD WIDTH="50%" VALIGN="top" ALIGN="center">

    Items in the shopping cart:
    <DIV ID="cartDiv"></DIV>

  </TD>
 </TR>
</TABLE>

<HR>

<P>XML of the shopping cart:</P>

<FORM ID="orderForm" METHOD="POST" ACTION="order.asp">
 <p>
```

```
    <TEXTAREA NAME="order" ROWS="6" COLS="57" READONLY="true">
    </TEXTAREA>
    <INPUT TYPE="submit" VALUE="Submit Order" NAME="B1" ↵
      STYLE="float: left">
  </P>
</FORM>


<SCRIPT LANGUAGE="javascript">

/*********************************************************
* init()
*********************************************************/

/* Init performs some tasks at load time. */
function init() {
  /* Asynchronous downloading and parsing is turned off,
     because we don't want the script to continue until
     we have the XML downloaded and parsed.
  */
  itemsXML.async = false;
  cartXML.async = false;

  /* Refresh the display. */
  displayCart();
  catSelect();
}


/*********************************************************
* displayCart()
*********************************************************/

/* displayCart builds and displays the Shopping Cart table and
   updates the XML view of the Shopping Cart
*/
function displayCart() {

  /* stringBuffer is used to hold the Shopping Cart table
     before it is displayed */
  var stringBuffer = "";

  /* length represents the number of items in the cart */
  var length = cartXML.documentElement.childNodes.length;

  if (length == 0) {
  /* The cart is empty. */

    stringBuffer += "<p>Cart is currently empty.</p>";

  } else {
```

```
/* The cart is not empty. */

  /* Table headers */
  stringBuffer += "<table id=displayTable ⌐
  border=1><th>Item</th><th>Quantity</th>";

  /* Create a row in the table for each item in the DOM tree. */
  for (i=0; i<length; i++) {
    var itemElement = cartXML.documentElement.childNodes.item(i);

    stringBuffer += "<tr>";

    /* The name of the item. */
    stringBuffer += "<td>" + ⌐
    itemElement.childNodes.item(0).childNodes.item(0).nodeValue ⌐
    + "</td>";

    /* The quantity ordered of the item. */
    stringBuffer += "<td>" + ⌐
    itemElement.childNodes.item(1).childNodes.item(0).nodeValue ⌐
    + "</td>";

    stringBuffer += "</tr>";
  }

  stringBuffer += "</table>";
}

  /* Dump the table into an HTML DIV element to
     display the table to the screen. */
  cartDiv.innerHTML = stringBuffer;

  /* update the XML text area. */
  orderForm.order.innerText = cartXML.xml;
}


/******************************************************
 * catSelect()
 ******************************************************/

/* catSelect downloads the specified catalog and displays
   the data in table format. */
function catSelect() {

  /* index refers to selected catalog from the drop
     down list at the top of the page. */
  var index = catalogSelect.selectedIndex;

  /* selection refers to the name of the selected
     catalog pointed to by index. */
```

```javascript
    var selection = catalogSelect.options(index).text;

    /* Load the XML catalog using HTTP GET by specifying
       the catalog in the URL. */
    itemsXML.load("data.asp?catalog=" + selection);

    /* stringBuffer is used to hold the catalog table
       before it is displayed */
    var stringBuffer = "";

    stringBuffer += "<table id=displayTable border=1 ↵
BGCOLOR=white><th>Item</th><th>Price</th><th>Description</th>";

    /* length specifies the number of items in the catalog. */
    var length = itemsXML.documentElement.childNodes.length;

    /* Generate a row in the table for each item in the catalog. */
    for(i=0; i<length; i++) {

      /* itemElement refers to the current node */
      itemElement = itemsXML.documentElement.childNodes.item(i);

      stringBuffer += "<tr onMouseOver=mouseOver() ↵
onMouseOut=mouseOut() onClick=mouseClick()>";

      /* Name of the item */
      stringBuffer += "<td>" + ↵
itemElement.childNodes.item(0).childNodes.item(0).nodeValue ↵
+ "</td>";

      /* Price of the item */
      stringBuffer += "<td>" + ↵
itemElement.childNodes.item(1).childNodes.item(0).nodeValue ↵
+ "</td>";

      /* Description of the item */
      stringBuffer += "<td>" + ↵
itemElement.childNodes.item(2).childNodes.item(0).nodeValue ↵
+ "</td>";

      stringBuffer += "</tr>";
    }

    stringBuffer += "</table>";

    /* Display the table by putting the contents of
       stringBuffer into an HTML DIV element. */
    displayDiv.innerHTML = stringBuffer;
}
```

```
/*******************************************************
 * inCart()
 *******************************************************/

/* inCart(itemName) checks to see if the ordered
   item is already in the cart.
      - If the item is found return its index into the tree.
      - If not, then return -1.

   A query language such as the XSL pattern matching syntax used by
   selectNodes could have been used in this function. This
   functionality is not part of the standard DOM; therefore,
   the old-fashioned way is used.
*/
function inCart(itemName) {

  /* length is the number of items currently in the shopping cart.*/
  var length = cartXML.documentElement.childNodes.length;

  /* Go to each items in the DOM tree and compare the names. */
  for(i=0; i<length; i++) {
    var item = cartXML.documentElement.childNodes.item(i);
    var name = item.childNodes.item(0);
    var nameText = name.childNodes.item(0);

    if ( nameText.nodeValue == itemName )
      return i;
  }

  /* Item not found. */
  return -1;
}


/*******************************************************
 * mouseClick()
 *******************************************************/

/* mouseClick is executed when a user clicks on an item in
   the catalog table. The contents of the shopping cart are updated.
*/
function mouseClick() {

  /* Make sure we get the row and not just a column element of the
     row.
  */
  var row = window.event.srcElement;
  while (row.tagName != "TR")
    row = row.parentElement;

  /* rowIndex indexed on 1 instead of 0. */
```

```
var index = row.rowIndex - 1;

/* itemName is the name of the items that was clicked. */
var itemName = ↵
itemsXML.documentElement.childNodes.item(index).childNodes. ↵
item(0).childNodes.item(0).nodeValue;

var cartIndex = inCart(itemName);

/* Check if the item is already in the shopping cart. */
if (cartIndex == -1) {
  /* Item is not in the shopping cart. */

  /* Create a new item in the shopping cart. */
  var newItem = cartXML.createElement("item");

  /* cloneNode true to get text node. Copying the name
     of item only, not the price or the description.
  */
  var newItemName = ↵
  itemsXML.documentElement.childNodes.item(index).childNodes. ↵
  item(0).cloneNode(true);

  /* Insert the name to the tree of the item */
  newItem.appendChild(newItemName);

  /* Create the quantity element for the item */
  var newQuantity = cartXML.createElement("quantity");
  var newQuantityText = cartXML.createTextNode("1");
  newQuantity.appendChild(newQuantityText);

  /* Insert the quantity node to the item */
  newItem.appendChild(newQuantity);

  /* Insert the new item node into the shopping cart tree. */
  cartXML.documentElement.appendChild(newItem);

} else {
  /* The item is already in the cart, so just increment the
     quantity
  */

  /* Get the item element node */
  var item = cartXML.documentElement.childNodes.item(cartIndex);

  /* Get the item's quantity element node */
  var quantity = item.childNodes.item(1);

  /* Get the quantity value */
  var quantityText = quantity.childNodes.item(0);
```

```
/* Convert the quantity value from a string to an integer. */
var quantityInt = parseInt(quantityText.nodeValue);

/* Increment the quantity */
quantityInt++;

/* Put the new quantity back into the tree. Integer to string
   casting occurs automagically, not the other way around.
*/
quantityText.nodeValue = quantityInt;
}

/* Update the shopping cart display. */
displayCart();
}


/**********************************************************
* mouseOver()
**********************************************************/

/* mouseOver is called when the mouse moves over the catalog
   table. The row that the mouse is over gets highlighted.
*/

function mouseOver() {

  var element = window.event.srcElement;

  while (element.tagName != "TR")
    element = element.parentElement;

  element.style.backgroundColor = "yellow";
}


/**********************************************************
* mouseOut()
**********************************************************/

/* mouseOut is called when the mouse moves off a row in the
   catalog table. The highlighted row returns to normal.
*/

function mouseOut() {

  var element = window.event.srcElement;

  while (element.tagName != "TR")
    element = element.parentElement;
```

```
        element.style.backgroundColor = "white";
    }

    </SCRIPT>
    </BODY>

    <XML ID="itemsXML">
    </XML>
    <XML ID="cartXML">
    <cart/>
    </XML>
    </HTML>
```

Building the Server Components

Two server-side components are needed for this demo: data.asp and order.asp. data.asp takes care of querying the existing data source (the Access table), converting the data to XML, and sending it to the browser. order.asp receives an XML order from the browser and returns a success message. The order does not actually take place, but this script would normally take care of the transaction processing.

ASP scripts were chosen for this scenario because the script is easier to follow then C or Java code, allowing more people to follow the details. Also, the Internet Explorer 5 parser has been covered in great detail in the book, and ASP scripts allow ActiveX objects to be used, such as the Internet Explorer 5 parser.

Downloading the Catalog

To download the catalog, we use data.asp, which is used with the HTTP GET command. We can call either data.asp?catalog=computer or data.asp?catalog=clothing, depending on which of the two catalogs we would like to view. In the ASP script, Request.QueryString("catalog") is used to find out which catalog was specified on the URL.

The ActiveX Data Objects (ADO) are used to access the native data source with the specified SQL query. The data is returned in the form of record sets, which are in a relational table format. Methods on the Recordset object are used to move down the table while building the XML tree. Figure 8.7 shows the original table view of the computer catalog, and the following is the catalog in XML format.

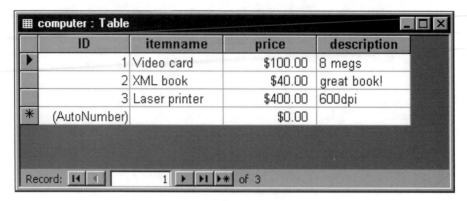

Figure 8.7   Access table of computer catalog.

```xml
<?xml version="1.0"?>
<result>
 <item>
  <name>Video card</name>
  <price>100</price>
  <description>8 megs</description>
 </item>
 <item>
  <name>XML book</name>
  <price>40</price>
  <description>great book!</description>
 </item>
 <item>
  <name>Laser Printer</name>
  <price>400</price>
  <description>600dpi</description>
 </item>
</result>
```

Here's the Code

We know you're dying for the details, so we follow the same format as before and highlight the comments throughout the script.

```asp
<%@ LANGUAGE="VBSCRIPT" %>

<%
  ' Set the content type to XML
  Response.ContentType = "text/xml"

  ' Instantiate the XML parser
  Set xml = Server.CreateObject("microsoft.xmldom")
```

```
' Create an XML document with only one element
xml.async = false
xml.loadXML("<?xml version='1.0' ?><result/>")

' Create a connection to the database
Set conn = Server.CreateObject("ADODB.Connection")
Set recordSet = Server.CreateObject("ADODB.Recordset")
conn.Open "catalog","sa",""

' Query the database for the requested catalog
catalog = Request.QueryString("catalog")
sqlstring = "SELECT * FROM " & catalog
recordSet.Open sqlstring, conn

' Convert the query result to XML
Do While Not recordSet.EOF

' Create element nodes
Set item = xml.createElement("item")
Set name = xml.createElement("name")
Set price = xml.createElement("price")
Set desc = xml.createElement("description")

' Create the text nodes
Set nametext = xml.createTextNode( recordSet("itemname") )
Set pricetext = xml.createTextNode( recordSet("price") )
Set desctext = xml.createTextNode( recordSet("description") )

' Insert the text nodes under their respective element nodes.
name.appendChild(nametext)
price.appendChild(pricetext)
desc.appendChild(desctext)

' Build the item's subtree
item.appendChild(name)
item.appendChild(price)
item.appendChild(desc)

' Insert the new element into the tree
xml.documentElement.appendChild(item)

' Move to the next row of the query result
recordSet.MoveNext

Loop

' The =xml.xml line is used to send the XML to the client.
%>

<%=xml.xml%>
```

Parserless Alternative

A design decision was made to use an XML parser on the server, but we could have created the script without the parser. The tags could have been designed manually, using the following script to produce exactly the same output.

```
<%@ LANGUAGE="VBSCRIPT" %>

<%
  ' Set the content type to XML
  Response.ContentType = "text/xml"

  ' Create a connection to the database
  Set conn = Server.CreateObject("ADODB.Connection")
  Set recordSet = Server.CreateObject("ADODB.Recordset")
  conn.Open "catalog","sa",""

  ' Query the database for the requested catalog
  catalog = Request.QueryString("catalog")
  sqlstring = "SELECT * FROM " & catalog
  recordSet.Open sqlstring, conn

%><result><%
    ' Go to each row of the table that matches the query
    Do While Not recordSet.EOF

%><item><name><%=recordSet("itemname")
%></name><price><%=recordSet("price")
%></price><description><%=recordSet("description")
%></description></item><%

    ' Move to the next row of the query result
    recordSet.MoveNext
    Loop
%></result>
```

Using this method would increase the speed of your script, but a typo in the script could produce malformed XML. For example, additional white space (spaces, tabs or carriage returns) could produce unexpected results. We built our scenario by using the DOM to produce the XML, but because efficiency is crucial on the server, it is probably best to manually generate the tags. On the other hand, the server should always use the parser when reading in XML, because the DOM provides a simple way of manipulating the document. Also, the parser ensures that the XML is valid. Now you might be wondering when you would want to use the parser to produce XML. Well, consider a situation where the server reads in some XML from the client and then manipulates the original XML sent by the client before sending it back. In this case, using a parser is the better alternative. When only converting an existing data source to XML, manually inserting the tags will significantly increase performance. Depending on the application, both alternatives can provide feasible solutions.

Submitting an Order

Submitting an order requires the client to send data to the server, so the HTTP POST command is used. For POST, the parameters are not specified on the URL the way they were in GET. Instead they are sent separately from the URL. In the script, Request.Form("order") is used to obtain the XML order that was sent by the client.

order.asp takes the XML order and produces a table to tell the user that the order was processed. In reality, this script would also complete the transaction by validating the credit card number, updating the inventory, and so on.

Code for the Last Time

Once again, we are going to subject you to the code for submitting the order. This last script is much simpler as a reward for nearing the end of the chapter.

```vbscript
<%@ LANGUAGE="VBSCRIPT" %>

<%
    ' Don't let the browser cache the result of this script.
    Response.Expires = 0

    ' Set the content type to XML
    Response.ContentType = "text/html"

    ' Instantiate the XML parser
    Set xml = Server.CreateObject("microsoft.xmldom")

    ' Load the XML order
    xml.async = false
    xml.loadXML( Request.Form("order") )
%>
```

```
<HTML>
<HEAD><TITLE>Order confirmation</TITLE></HEAD>

<BODY>

<H3>The order for the following items has been confirmed.</H3>

<TABLE BORDER="1">
  <TH>Item</TH><TH>Quantity</TH>

<%
  Dim i
  Dim length

  ' length is the number of items ordered
  ' minus 1 because the index starts on 0 and not 1
  length = xml.documentElement.childNodes.length - 1

  ' Generate a row for each ordered item
  For i = 0 To length
%>

<TR>

<TD>
<% ' Insert the name of the current item into the table. %>
<%=xml.documentElement.childNodes.item(i).childNodes.item(0). ↵
childNodes.item(0).nodeValue%>
</TD>

<TD>
<% ' Insert the quantity of the current item into the table. %>
<%=xml.documentElement.childNodes.item(i).childNodes.item(1). ↵
childNodes.item(0).nodeValue%>
</TD>

</TR>

<% Next %>

</TABLE>
</BODY>
</HTML>
```

Summary

We would like to note here that all the examples in this chapter use the standard DOM syntax as described in Chapter 5. Two additions to the DOM that would make this scenario even more feasible are a query language for XML and datatypes. A query language would be necessary if the catalogs were much larger, because the user would specify search criteria that would be sent to the server in the form of a standard XML search string. There are currently a few proposals on the table that are being considered by the W3C. Currently, XSL can be used to query XML, and this technique is described in Chapter 13.

Datatypes would allow the price element to be denoted as a currency type and the quantity as an integer type. As in the client-side script, a casting operation was required to convert the quantity string into an integer. A datatype mechanism would allow the process to be much cleaner.

From this scenario, we have seen that the DOM and DHTML combination can be quite effective. The scenario was kept simple to show the concepts, but can be easily augmented. For example, the following enhancements can be readily implemented: Allow the user to remove items from the shopping cart by selecting them, sort the items in the cart, and add up the prices of everything in the cart on-the-fly.

In this chapter, we have seen how to use XML to build a functional e-commerce site. Using XML between the client and server can allow other applications to use this data source. In the next chapter, we extend this scenario by providing a Java applet version of the client that uses the server scripts that were developed in this chapter.

CHAPTER 9

Java Scenario: Online Shopping Demo Continued

Now it's time to show you where XML really shines by extending the scenario from Chapter 8. We build on the server platform that we designed and make a new front end, but this time in Java. Designing your server to receive and send XML greatly increases your options for the front end. In fact, you don't even need a browser. Standalone applications written in Java, Visual Basic, or C++, just to name a few, can hook into the XML stream from the server. To take this one step further, you don't even need a front-end application from which a person orders. A state-of-the-art grocery store may have a computer system that automatically places an order when the check-out register records that an item has been sold. This example just shows that a good XML design on the server side can greatly improve the possibilities for your site. Figure 9.1 shows what the demo looks like in Netscape Navigator.

Design Overview

Although a good XML design on the server is crucial, the Chapter 8 scenario has a flaw. It was customized for use in a browser. When an order

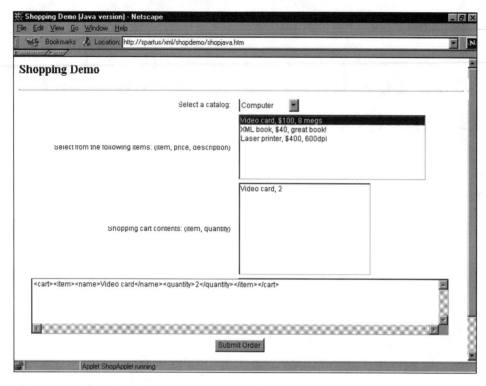

Figure 9.1   Shopping demo running in Netscape.

is placed, the result from the server is HTML and not XML. The Chapter 8 scenario can be easily augmented to take in the XML from the server and generate some sort of success/fail message. Figure 9.2 shows the data flow for a system that makes exclusive use of XML, and we encourage you to compare with Figure 8.1, the data flow diagram for the Internet Explorer 5 shopping demo.

The server-side ASP orderXML.asp is introduced to alleviate this shortcoming. This script will be shown toward the end of the chapter and

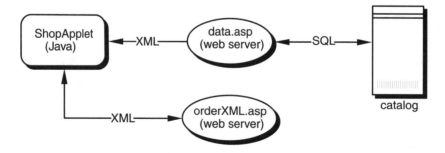

Figure 9.2   Shopping demo data flow.

merely returns the following XML to signify that the order was processed:

```
<orderresult status="ok" />
```

If you got the Chapter 8 demo running, then running this demo will be a snap. Copy shopjava.htm, ShopDemo.jar, and orderXML.asp to the same directory as the files from the Chapter 8 demo. Now point your browser to shopjava.htm, which downloads and decompresses ShopDemo.jar, a Java Archive file. ShopApplet.class, which is contained in ShopDemo.jar, is then executed by the browser. Make sure that you open shopjava.htm through a server and not as a local file; otherwise, the ASP scripts won't execute.

Now we look at the three parts of this demo: the HTML page, the Java Applet, and the new ASP script.

HTML Page

The HTML page (shopjava.htm) is used to tell the browser how to get the demo up and running. This functionality is achieved through the <APPLET> tag, which is bolded in the code that follows. The ARCHIVE parameter specifies which Java Archive to download, in this case ShopDemo.jar. A JAR file is a compressed file (using ZIP technology) that contains the *.class files that are needed to run the applet. The CODE parameter specifies which class to start after the downloading and uncompressing is complete; in this case, it's the ShopApplet.class. That's all the shopjava.htm does. Here are its contents:

```
<HTML>

<HEAD>
<TITLE>Shopping Demo (Java version)</TITLE>
</HEAD>

<BODY>
<H2>Shopping Demo</H2>
<HR>

<APPLET CODE="ShopApplet.class" ARCHIVE="ShopDemo.jar" WIDTH="760" ⌐
HEIGHT="500">
</APPLET>

</BODY>
</HTML>
```

Java Applet

The applet, ShopApplet.java, is the meat of this demo. It contains all the functionality for managing the user interface (UI) and the logic for communicating with the server. The code shown here was designed for the 1.1 version of the Java Virtual Machine (JVM). For those who are curious, we used Java Development Kit (JDK) version 1.1.7B to write this applet.

For the UI, the Abstract Window Toolkit (AWT) is used. The Swing components are usually used for UI, but our goal was to show XML usage from Java and not create a pretty interface. One of the limitations of the AWT is the lack of a table component. Instead, we use the List component.

This applet makes use of the Sun XML parser to generate the DOM trees. In fact, we use three DOM trees: itemsXML, cartXML, and resultXML. itemsXML keeps track of which items the user can order. cartXML keeps track of which items the user has selected for ordering. Finally, resultXML is used to hold the result from the server after an order is placed. Just a reminder: a DOM tree is represented by the Document node, so we define the three mentioned objects as Document objects.

Before jumping into the code, we first describe the basic operation of this applet. init() is the first function to be called and is used to set up the UI, which includes registering event handlers. An event handler is executed when a user selects a catalog, double-clicks an item to order, or clicks on the Submit button. These event handlers (located near the bottom of the code) are used to execute the necessary functions to respond to the user interaction.

The following list provides a brief synopsis of some of the important functions in the applet:

- **init()** Sets up the user interface. Also calls functions to clear the list boxes and the DOM trees.
- **catSelect()** Downloads the requested catalog from the server.
- **updateCart()** Adds the item that the user selected into the shopping cart.
- **displayCart()** Takes the contents of cartXML and inserts them in the shopping cart display list box. Also, the XML version of the shop-

ping cart is put in the order TextArea, which is located near the bottom of the screen.

- **postOrder()** Sends the order to the server. The result from the server is inserted into the order TextArea.

Here are the helper functions:

- **resetCart()** Empties the shopping cart by creating a new Document node, and then creates the root element for this new DOM tree. We don't need to worry about deleting the old tree, because the Java garbage collector takes care of discarded memory that is unassigned.
- **resetLists()** Resets the List displays in the UI.
- **inCart(String itemName)** Checks if an item called itemName exists, if so than the index of this item to the tree is returned; otherwise, -1 is returned.
- **catalogSelectListener** Calls catSelect() when a user selects a different catalog from the drop-down box.
- **displayListListener** Calls updateCart() when a user selects an item by double-clicking on it.
- **submitOrderListener** Sends the order to the server in the form of XML. The user is reminded to order something if the shopping cart is empty.

Code

Now that we have seen what this applet does from a design perspective, it's time to leap into the code and get a feel for the details. Almost every line in the code is commented, so even if your Java is a little rusty, you should be able to follow what is going on. To help ease the pain of reading code, the comments have been bolded.

```
/* Standard Java classes. */
import java.awt.*;
import java.applet.Applet;
import java.awt.event.*;
import java.net.*;
import java.io.*;
```

```
/* Classes that are specific to the Sun Java parser.
   We must be sure to include these into the JAR archive. */
import com.sun.xml.tree.XmlDocument;
import org.w3c.dom.*;
import org.xml.sax.SAXException;


public class ShopApplet extends Applet {

    /* User interface components */
    private Choice catalogSelect;
    private List displayList;
    private List cartList;
    private TextArea order;
    private Button submitOrder;

    /* We are going to need three DOM trees */
    private Document itemsXML;
    private Document cartXML;
    private Document resultXML;

    /* baseURL represents the server's URL */
    private String baseURL;

/********************************************************************/

    /* init() takes care of setting up the user interface. */
    public void init() {

        baseURL = getCodeBase().toString();

        /* Make the horizontal gap large, so that the
           panels will line up vertically. */
        FlowLayout myLayout = (FlowLayout) getLayout();
        myLayout.setHgap(800);

        setBackground(Color.white);

        /* Setup the catalog select UI */
        Panel catalogPanel = new Panel();
        catalogPanel.setLayout( new GridLayout(1,0) );
        catalogPanel.add( new Label("Select a catalog:") );
        catalogSelect = new Choice();
        catalogSelect.addItem("Computer");
        catalogSelect.addItem("Clothing");
        catalogSelect.addItemListener( new catalogSelectListener() );
        catalogPanel.add(catalogSelect);
        add(catalogPanel);

        /* Setup the catalog display UI */
        Panel itemsPanel = new Panel();
        itemsPanel.setLayout( new GridLayout(0,2) );
```

```java
    itemsPanel.add( new Label("Select from the following items:(item, ↵
    price, description)") );
    displayList = new List(7);
    displayList.setMultipleMode(false);
    displayList.addActionListener( new displayListListener() );
    itemsPanel.add(displayList);
    add(itemsPanel);

    /* Setup the shopping cart UI */
    Panel cartPanel = new Panel();
    cartPanel.setLayout( new GridLayout(0,2) );
    cartPanel.add( new Label("Shopping cart contents: ↵
    (item, quantity)") );
    cartList = new List(10);
    cartList.setMultipleMode(false);
    cartPanel.add(cartList);
    add(cartPanel);

    /* Setup the order UI */
    order = new TextArea(5, 100);
    order.setEditable(false);
    add(order);
    submitOrder = new Button("Submit Order");
    submitOrder.addActionListener( new submitOrderListener() );
    add(submitOrder);

    /* Do some initialization */
    resetLists();
    resetCart();

    validate();

    catSelect();
  }


/******************************************************************/

  /* catSelect() downloads the requested catalog from the server. */
  private void catSelect() {

    int length, i;

    /* Check what the user asked for. */
    String selection = new String( catalogSelect.getItem( ↵
    catalogSelect.getSelectedIndex() ) );
    selection.toLowerCase();

    try {

      /* Download the XML catalog */
      itemsXML = XmlDocument.createXmlDocument(baseURL + ↵
      "data.asp?catalog=" + selection, false);
```

```
        /* Check how many items are in the catalog. */
        length = itemsXML.getDocumentElement(). ↵
        getChildNodes().getLength();

        /* Reset the UI */
        displayList.removeAll();

        /* build the items list from the downloaded XML */
        for (i=0; i<length; i++) {
          Node node = itemsXML.getDocumentElement(). ↵
          getChildNodes().item(i);

          String name = node.getChildNodes().item(0). ↵
          getChildNodes().item(0).getNodeValue();
          String price = node.getChildNodes().item(1). ↵
          getChildNodes().item(0).getNodeValue();
          String description = node.getChildNodes().item(2). ↵
          getChildNodes().item(0).getNodeValue();

          /* Add the entry to the catalog list UI */
          displayList.add(name + ", $" + price + ", " + description);
        }

      } catch (SAXException se) {
      } catch (IOException ioe) {
      }
    }


/***************************************************************/

  /* updateCart() adds the item that the user selected
     into the shopping cart. */
  private void updateCart() {

    /* Check which item the user selected. */
    int index = displayList.getSelectedIndex();

    /* itemName is the name of the item that was clicked. */
    String itemName = itemsXML.getDocumentElement().getChildNodes(). ↵
    item(index).getChildNodes()..item(0).getChildNodes(). ↵
    item(0).getNodeValue();

    /* Check if the item is already in the shopping cart. */
    int cartIndex = inCart(itemName);
    if (cartIndex == -1) {
      /* Item is not in the shopping cart. */

      /* Create a new item in the shopping cart. */
      Element newItem = cartXML.createElement("item");
```

```
    Element newItemName = cartXML.createElement("name");
    Text newNameText = cartXML.createTextNode( itemName );
    newItemName.appendChild(newNameText);

    /* Add the new item to the shopping cart tree. */
    newItem.appendChild(newItemName);

    /* Create the quantity element for the item */
    Element newQuantity = cartXML.createElement("quantity");
    Text newQuantityText = cartXML.createTextNode("1");
    newQuantity.appendChild(newQuantityText);

    /* Insert the quantity node to the item */
    newItem.appendChild(newQuantity);

    /* Insert the new item node into the shopping cart tree. */
    cartXML.getDocumentElement().appendChild(newItem);

} else {
    /* The item is already in the cart, increment the quantity */

    /* Get the item element node */
    Element item = (Element) cartXML.getDocumentElement(). ↵
    getChildNodes().item(cartIndex);

    /* Get the item's quantity element node */
    Element quantity = (Element) item.getChildNodes().item(1);

    /* Get the quantity value */
    Text quantityText = (Text) quantity.getChildNodes().item(0);

    /* Convert the quantity value from a string to an integer. */
    Integer quantityInteger = new Integer( quantityText. ↵
    getNodeValue() );
    int quantityInt = quantityInteger.intValue();

    /* Increment the quantity */
    quantityInt++;

    /* Put the new quantity back into the tree. Integer to
       string casting occurs automatically, but not the
       other way around. */
    quantityText.setNodeValue( Integer.toString(quantityInt) );
}

    /* Update the shopping cart display. */
    displayCart();
}

/******************************************************************/
```

```
/* displayCart() takes the contents of cartXML and inserts them
   into the shopping cart list box. Also, the XML version of
   the shopping cart is put into the order TextArea. */
private void displayCart() {

  int length, i;

  /* Put XML version of the shopping cart into the order
     textarea. */
  order.setText( cartXML.getDocumentElement().toString() );

  /* Reset the cart UI */
  cartList.removeAll();

  /* Check how many items are in the shopping cart. */
  length = cartXML.getDocumentElement().getChildNodes().getLength();

  if (length == 0)
    cartList.add("Shopping cart is empty.");
  else {
    /* build the shopping cart list. */
    for (i=0; i<length; i++) {
      Element node = (Element) cartXML.getDocumentElement(). ⏎
      getChildNodes().item(i);
      String name = node.getChildNodes().item(0).getChildNodes(). ⏎
      item(0).getNodeValue();
      String quantity = node.getChildNodes().item(1).getChildNodes(). ⏎
      item(0).getNodeValue();

      /* Add the row to the display. */
      cartList.add(name + ", " + quantity);
    }
  }
}

/*****************************************************************/

/* postOrder() sends the order to the server.
   The result of the transaction is displayed in the order
   textarea. */
private void postOrder() {

  try {
    /* Create the connection to the server */
    URL url = new URL(baseURL + "orderXML.asp");
    URLConnection connection = url.openConnection();
    connection.setDoOutput(true);

    /* Setup an output stream and send the XML order. */
    PrintWriter out = new PrintWriter( connection.getOutputStream() );
```

```java
      out.print("order=" + cartXML.getDocumentElement().toString());
      out.flush();
      out.close();

      /* Get the result from the server */
      try {
        resultXML = XmlDocument.createXmlDocument( ↵
        connection.getInputStream(), false );
      } catch (SAXException se) {
        order.setText("An error occured during your order.");
      } catch (IOException ioe) {
        order.setText("An error occured during your order.");
      }

      /* Check the result that the server sent. */
      String str = resultXML.getDocumentElement(). ↵
      getAttribute("status");
      if ( str.compareTo("ok") == 0 ) {
        /* Order went through */

        /* clear the shopping cart, since the items
           have now been ordered. */
        resetCart();
        displayCart();

        /* Display the result into the order textarea. */
        order.setText("Your order has been processed.");

      } else {
        order.setText("An error occured during your order.");
      }

    } catch (MalformedURLException e) {
      order.setText("An error occured during your order.");
    } catch (IOException e) {
      order.setText("An error occured during your order.");
    }
  }

/******************************************************************/

  /* resetCart() empties the shopping cart by creating a new
     Document node, and creates the root element. */
  private void resetCart() {

    /* Create the shopping cart. */
    cartXML = new XmlDocument();
    Element root = (Element) cartXML.createElement("cart");
    cartXML.appendChild(root);
  }
```

```
/******************************************************************/

  /* resetLists() clears the list UI */
  private void resetLists() {
    displayList.removeAll();
    displayList.add("Catalog not downloaded yet.");

    cartList.removeAll();
    cartList.add("Shopping cart is empty.");
  }

/******************************************************************/

  /* inCart(...) returns the index of the item in the cart.
     If the item does not exist, -1 is returned. */
  private int inCart(String itemName) {

    /* length is the number of items currently in the shopping cart. */
    int length = cartXML.getDocumentElement(). ⏎
    getChildNodes().getLength();
    int i;

    /* Go to each item in the DOM tree and compare the names. */
    for(i=0; i<length; i++) {
      Element item = (Element) cartXML.getDocumentElement(). ⏎
      getChildNodes().item(i);
      Element name = (Element) item.getChildNodes().item(0);
      String nameText = name.getChildNodes().item(0).getNodeValue();

      if ( nameText.compareTo(itemName) == 0 )
        return i;
    }

    /* Item not found. */
    return -1;
  }

/******************************************************************/
  /* User interface handlers. */
  /* These handler catch the UI events and call the appropriate
     function to handle the event. */

/******************************************************************/

  /* Catalog selection handler */
  private class catalogSelectListener implements ItemListener {
    public void itemStateChanged(ItemEvent e) {
      catSelect();
    }
  }
```

```
/*****************************************************************/


  /* Items selection handler */
    private class displayListListener implements ActionListener {
      public void actionPerformed(ActionEvent e) {
        updateCart();
      }
    }


/*****************************************************************/


  /* Order button handler */
  private class submitOrderListener implements ActionListener {
    public void actionPerformed(ActionEvent e) {

      /* Check if there are any items in the shoppping cart. */
      if (cartXML.getDocumentElement().getChildNodes().getLength() < 1)
        order.setText("Nothing to order!");
      else

        /* Post the shopping cart to the server. */
        postOrder();
      }
    }
  }
```

Deploying the Applet

One last detail needs to be covered to get this applet running in your browser. ShopApplet.class depends on a bunch of classes that need to be packaged with the applet. These classes include the three event handler classes that are automatically generated with ShopApplet.class and should be located in the same directory as ShopApplet.class. More important, the XML parser needs to be sent with the applet. Unfortunately, the parser that we chose for this demo is quite large, so it adds to the initial download time for a user. The good news is that after the initial download, all subsequent XML transfers are very short. We hope that someday a Java accessible XML parser will become a standard component that is included with all the browsers, so you won't need to send it.

An archive file is used to package the necessary classes, which are then compressed to reduce the download time. The jar utility that comes with the JDK is used to create and manage these archives. Assuming that the Sun XML parser classes are located in the directory with the applet classes, the following line is used to create the archive:

jar cf ShopDemo.jar *.class org com. The size of the archive can proba-bly be reduced by taking out some of the classes, located in the org and com directories. Unfortunately, there is no easy way to generate a class dependence tree, so you have to take out one file at a time to see if your program still works. Don't forget to check the license of the parser that you are using to make sure that you are allowed to split up the binaries.

Server-Side ASP Scripts

The servers for most Web sites are designed to return HTML to the client. Generating HTML seems to cause problems when other sites try to access your data or try to interact with your servers. It's not an easy job to write programs that sift through HTML to locate some informa-tion that you requested. Also, if you ever want to give out a standalone application that interacts with your servers, then once again, you are in a bind. The solution is to send XML from your servers and let the client generate the display. In the XSL section, we show how this job can also be done with stylesheets.

In our example, we present a new ASP script, called orderXML.asp. It reads in the XML order from the client the same way that order.asp did, but sends back XML instead of HTML. Also, to keep this script simple, we return only a status message, instead of a complete list of ordered items. In fact, this server does very little because we don't actually do the transaction. In reality, credit card numbers need to be validated, taxes need to be calculated, inventory needs to be adjusted, and so on. Any one of those operations could fail, which would return a status message indicating the failure.

Here is the code behind orderXML.asp:

```
<%@ LANGUAGE="VBSCRIPT" %>

<%
    Response.Expires = 0

    ' Set the content type to XML
    Response.ContentType = "text/xml"

    ' Instantiate the XML parser
    Set xml = Server.CreateObject("microsoft.xmldom")
```

```
    xml.async = false
    xml.loadXML( Request.Form("order") )

    ' Do error checking and transaction here.
%>

<orderresult status="ok" />
```

Summary

We hope we have convinced you of the possibilities associated with providing XML streams from your servers. The benefits will be realized not only by your site, but also by others who try to hook into your site. In addition to augmenting your service, the information that your site provides is easily accessible. For example, search engines can be used to provide much more meaningful results when the content is properly described using XML.

Java and XML have been forecasted by many to be the dynamic duo of the net. Using some of the great features found in Java, some really impressive sites and applications can be put together that make use of XML. Let's not forget that Java is not limited to just applets, but that it can also be used for standalone applications. In the next chapter, we design a standalone application with Visual Basic that uses XML.

CHAPTER 10

Visual Basic Scenario: DOMifier

The DOMifier, shown in Figure 10.1, is a utility that reads in an XML document and displays the DOM tree structure to the user. This tool was written in Visual Basic and uses the Microsoft Internet Explorer 5 XML parser to access the XML documents. This scenario is different from those presented in Chapters 8 and 9 because it doesn't run in a browser. Limiting XML's usage to the browser is a common pitfall. In fact, its applications are much more far reaching. This standalone application can make use of the Internet, because a URL can be specified for an XML document.

In this chapter, we show you how to use XML from Visual Basic by using the Microsoft XML parser. Also, we briefly review how the TreeView Component works to display hierarchical data. Finally, we present working code that traverses a DOM tree and builds the desired output.

XML in Visual Basic

Let's quickly recap how to use XML from Visual Basic, which is presented in Chapter 6.

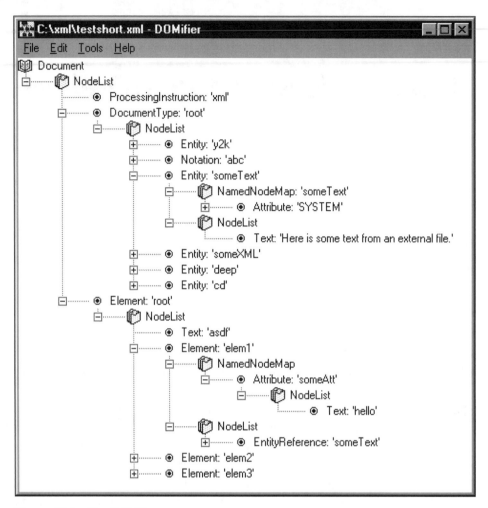

Figure 10.1 The DOMifier.

The Document node implementation for the Microsoft parser is called DOMDocument. In the DOMifier, we declare an object of type DOMDocument as a global so the parser can be used from anywhere in the program. The Load(url) method on the DOMDocument object is a proprietary extension of the Microsoft parser, which we use to download and parse an XML document. Another extension that we use is the xml property on the IXMLDOMNode class, which extends the standard Node functionality. The xml property gives us a text version of the DOM tree, which is referred to as *persisting the tree*. The following Microsoft extensions are used: loading a document, checking for parse errors, and persisting the tree.

TreeView Control

XML documents are arranged in a hierarchical tree format, which makes the TreeView control an ideal tool for representing XML documents. This control produces a collapsible tree that is commonly found when representing drives, directories, and files. In our case, we use folders to model the collection nodes: NodeList and NamedNodeMap. The remaining nodes are placed under these folders to make up the DOM tree. To use the TreeView control in Visual Basic, you need to select Microsoft Windows Common Controls 5.0 in the References dialog box, which is found in the Project menu option.

TreeView Basics

We're going to show you just enough of the TreeView control so you can follow the DOMifier code. If you need more information, check the Visual Basic Books Online that comes with Visual Basic. A tree that's been constructed using the TreeView control is made up of nodes, and these nodes have parent-child relationships with each other. Unfortunately, the object to represent these nodes is called Node, so be careful not to confuse it with the DOM Node object. The add method on the TreeView control is used to insert these nodes into the tree. The general form of the add method follows. Please note that all the parameters are optional and that this method returns a Node object.

```
TreeView.add(relative, relationship, key, text, image,
selectedimage)
```

First, you need to decide where to put a node, so relationship lets the function know where to put the new node with respect to an already existing relative node. Relative is an index that represents the already existing node; it can be a number or a string. Relationship takes on one of the following values: tvwFirst, tvwLast, tvwNext, tvwPrevious, or tvwChild. For example, if relationship is set to tvwChild, then the new node is a child of the existing node relative. For the DOMifier, we only use the tvwChild option.

That was the hard part; now we need to describe what our new node looks like. Key represents a unique index that can be used by another node as their relative. Text is the string that we want placed next to our node. Image refers to the index of the image in a ImageList control. The ImageList that we use for the DOMifier has only three images: a book to represent the Document, a folder to represent node collections, and a circle to represent all other nodes Their associated indexes are Document, List, and Node. Figure 10.2 shows the Property Page of our ImageList control, with the three images that are inside. Finally, we don't use the selectedimage parameter, but it can also used to reference an image.

Here is an example of how we use the TreeView control to add an element node to the display:

```
Set nodX = TreeView1.Nodes.Add("n" & parent, tvwChild, "n" & counter, _
"Element: '" & nodeList.Item(Index).nodeName & "'", "Node")
```

TreeView1 is the name of our TreeView control, and nodX is the name of a TreeView Node object. Add returns a Node, so we place it in nodX, but it is discarded because it is not needed for our application. For both relative and key, we generate indexes by prefixing the letter *n* to a unique number. A global Integer called counter is used to generate these unique numbers. Parent refers to the unique index of the node's parent. Since we are inserting an Element node, the parent is a NodeList. For

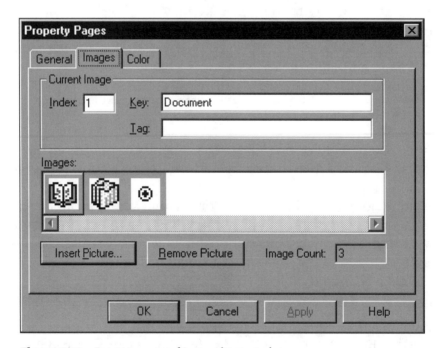

Figure 10.2 Property page of ImageList control.

the text, we put *Element*: and the name of the Element node. Finally, we use the image indexed by Node to represent this entry. In Figure 10.2, Node is the third image. To see what an element looks like after it has been inserted, take a look at the bottom of Figure 10.1.

One last feature of the TreeView control that we use is the ability to collapse and expand the trees. The user can do this by clicking on the minus or plus side next to the NodeList and NamedNodeMap entries. From the Edit menu we provide the functionality to expand or collapse the entire tree. To perform this task we set the Expanded property on each Node object to either true or false.

Building the DOMifier

The DOMifier project is split up into three files: main.frm, frmLoad.frm, and frmAbout.frm. The bulk of the code is found in main.frm, which represents the main window as shown in Figure 10.1. frmLoad.frm displays the *Load URL* dialog box shown in Figure 10.3 and calls the necessary function in main.frm to perform the loading. frmAbout.frm displays only the About box—it is not a crucial piece of the DOMifier.

Here are the DOMifier functions that are found in main.frm:

- **loadURL(url As String)** Downloads and parses the specified XML document. If an error occurs with either the downloading or the parsing, the user is notified. This function also does some minor UI: It shows the "please wait" message, hides the tree until it is ready to be displayed, and sets the window caption to let the user know which document we are currently looking at.

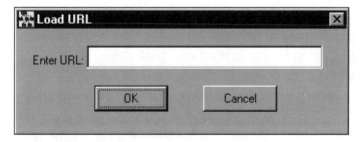

Figure 10.3   Load URL dialog box.

- **XMLloaded(state As Boolean)** Performs grunt work that needs to be done before and after a document is loaded. The menu options are grayed when an XML tree is not ready to be displayed. Also, the tree from the previous XML document is erased.

- **buildTree()** Kick starts the tree building process by displaying the Document node and calling NodeListRecursive(...) with the necessary parameters.

- **NodeListRecursive(nodeList As IXMLDOMNodeList, parent As Integer)** Takes care of displaying all the nodes that are located within a NodeList. This function uses recursion (calls itself) to traverse the tree.

- **NamedNodeMapRecursive(nodeList As IXMLDOMNamedNodeMap, parent As Integer)** Takes care of displaying all the nodes that are located within a NamedNodeMap. This function uses recursion to traverse the tree and is very similar to NodeListRecursive(...).

- **removeTree()** Tells the TreeView control to erase the current tree.

The following functions are associated with an event on the main DOMifier window:

- **Form_Load()** Performs some initialization when DOMifier first starts up, including the creation of a new DOM tree, and turns off asynchronous downloading.

- **Form_Resize()** This event is called when a user resizes the DOMifier window. The TreeView control is resized to its maximum size within the window.

- **Form_Unload(Cancel As Integer)** Kills the hidden About box and the "Load URL" window when the program dies.

The following functions are called when a user selects a menu option:

- **openURL_Click()** Displays the Load URL dialog located in frm-Load.frm when File..Open URL is selected.

- **openLocal_Click()** Shows the typical Open dialog box that is found in nearly every Windows program when File..Open local file is selected. The Open dialog box is a part of the Microsoft Common Dialog Control.

- **exit_Click()** Quits the DOMifier when the user selects File..Exit.

- **expandAll_Click()** Shows the entire tree display when the user selects Edit..Expand All.

- **collapseAll_Click()** Collapses the tree display down to the Document node when the user selects Edit..Collapse All.

- **showXML_Click()** Displays the text version of the DOM tree in a message box when Tools..Show XML is selected.

- **about_Click()** Shows the About box when the user selects Help..AboutDOMifier.

The User Interface

Before jumping into the XML details, we give a quick rundown of the UI. The main screen has one main component, the TreeView control, which is used to display the tree. There is also a "Building Tree...Please Wait" label that comes up when the tree is being built. A glance at Figure 10.4 shows two more components: the CommonDialog component and the ImageList component. The ImageList is used to hold the three images that can be associated with nodes: one for the Document node, one for NodeList and NamedNodeMap nodes, and the last for all other types of nodes. The CommonDialog is also located in the design area but is used only for the Open dialog box to select an XML document.

The DOMifier displays objects in the DOM tree in the way that they are stored. The shortcuts (that is, documentElement, doctype) are not shown. To get to the root element, you are used to using myDocumentNode .documentElement, whereas through the DOMifier, we access the root using myDocumentNode.childNodes.item(....). Both methods are valid, but using the shortcut is easier.

Traversing the DOM Tree

To construct the tree diagram in a TreeView control, we need a systematic way of visiting each node in a DOM tree. We use a concept called *recursion*, where a function can call itself until it reaches a stop case. In our example, the stop case occurs when the current node doesn't have any children. Two functions are used to traverse the tree: NodeListRecursive(...)and NamedNodeMapRecursive(...). Other designs can collapse all the functionality into one function, but we are going for simplicity here so we leave the two separate.

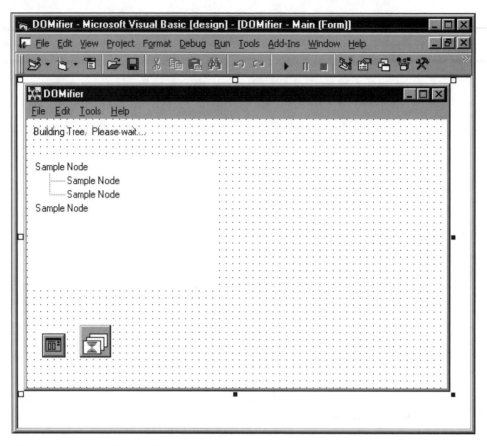

Figure 10.4 Main form object design.

Code

We know you're dying for the details, so we show you what's going on behind the scenes. This section contains the code for main.frm with all the comments highlighted. If you're interested in building or modifying the project, the complete source code can be found on the CD-ROM.

```
' Global variables
' xml is the DOM tree that represents the loaded XML document.
Private xml As DOMDocument
' isXMLloaded keeps track if there is currently an XML
' document on the screen.
Private isXMLloaded As Boolean
' counter is used to generate unique indexes for TreeView.
Private counter As Integer


' **************************************************************
```

```vb
' loadURL downloads and parses the specified XML document.
' If an error occurs with either the downloading or the parsing,
' the user is notified.
' This function also does some minor UI: Show the 'please wait'
' message, hides the tree until it is ready to be displayed,
' and sets the window caption to let the user know which document
' we are currently looking at.
Public Sub loadURL(url As String)

    ' Do some cleaning up of the previous document.
    XMLloaded (False)

    ' Show the 'Please wait' label, hide the TreeView control
    ' and reset the title.
    waitLabel.Visible = True
    TreeView1.Visible = False
    Main.Caption = "DOMifier"
    Main.Refresh

    ' Load the XML document
    If (xml.Load(url) = False) Then
        ' If an error occured during the loading,
        ' let the user know what happened.
        waitLabel.Visible = False
        TreeView1.Visible = True
        Main.Refresh
        MsgBox ("Parsing error: " & xml.parseError.reason)
    Else
        ' The load occured successfully.
        XMLloaded (True)

        ' Display the url in the title.
        Main.Caption = url & " - DOMifier"

        buildTree
    End If

    ' Show the tree.
    waitLabel.Visible = False
    TreeView1.Visible = True
End Sub

' ************************************************************

' XMLloaded() does some grunt work that needs to be done before and
' after a document is loaded. The menu options are grayed when an
' XML tree is not ready to be displayed. Also, the tree from the
' previous XML document is erased.
Private Sub XMLloaded(state As Boolean)
```

```
   isXMLloaded = state
   collapseAll.Enabled = state
   expandAll.Enabled = state
   showXML.Enabled = state

   ' Erase the tree
   If (state = False) Then
     removeTree

     'Refresh so user doesn't see old tree when loading new one.
     Main.Refresh
   End If
End Sub


' ************************************************************


' buildTree() kick starts the tree building process by displaying
' the Document node and calling NodeListRecursive(...)
Private Sub buildTree()

   ' Only build the tree if there is a loaded document.
   If (isXMLloaded = True) Then
     ' nodX is a TreeView node and NOT a DOM node.
     Dim nodX As Node

     TreeView1.ImageList = ImageList1

     ' Add the Document node and its NodeList.
     Set nodX = TreeView1.Nodes.Add(, , "n" & 0, "Document", "Document")
     nodX.Expanded = True
     Set nodX = TreeView1.Nodes.Add("n" & 0, tvwChild, "n" & 1, ⏎
     "NodeList", "List")

     counter = 2
     Call NodeListRecursive(xml.childNodes, 1)
   End If
End Sub


' ************************************************************


' NodeListRecursive(...) takes care of displaying all the nodes that
' are located within a NodeList.
' This function uses recursion (calls itself) to traverse the tree.
' Note: this function contains cases that should never occur, but we
' leave them in nevertheless.
Private Sub NodeListRecursive(nodeList As IXMLDOMNodeList, ⏎
parent As Integer)
   Dim nodX As Node
   Dim tempCount As Integer
   Dim nodeType As DOMNodeType
```

```vbnet
Dim forLength As Integer


' Using a separate variable for the length instead of putting
' it directly into the For loop statement, increases the
' performance dramatically.
forLength = nodeList.length - 1

' Do this loop for every node in the NodeList.
For Index = 0 To forLength
  nodeType = nodeList.Item(Index).nodeType
  tempCount = counter

  ' Check what type of node we are currently at
  ' and display it accordingly.
  Select Case nodeType

    Case NODE_ELEMENT:
      ' Add the element to the TreeView.
      Set nodX = TreeView1.Nodes.Add("n" & parent, tvwChild, ↵
      "n" & counter, "Element: '" & nodeList.Item(Index).nodeName ↵
      & "'", "Node")

      counter = counter + 1

      ' Check if this element has any attributes.
      ' If so, add the NamedNodeMap to the TreeView and
      ' call NamedNodeMapRecursive.
      If (nodeList.Item(Index).Attributes.length > 0) Then
        Set nodX = TreeView1.Nodes.Add("n" & tempCount, tvwChild, ↵
        "n" & counter, "NamedNodeMap", "List")
        counter = counter + 1
        Call NamedNodeMapRecursive(nodeList.Item(Index).Attributes, ↵
       counter - 1)
      End If

    Case NODE_ATTRIBUTE:
      ' Add the attribute to the TreeView.
      Set nodX = TreeView1.Nodes.Add("n" & parent, tvwChild, ↵
      "n" & counter, "Attribute: '" & nodeList.Item(Index).nodeName ↵
      & "'", "Node")
      counter = counter + 1

    Case NODE_TEXT:
      ' Add the text node to the TreeView.
      Set nodX = TreeView1.Nodes.Add("n" & parent, tvwChild, ↵
      "n" & counter, "Text: '" & nodeList.Item(Index).nodeValue ↵
      & "'", "Node")
      counter = counter + 1

    Case NODE_CDATA_SECTION:
```

```
                ' Add the CDATA section to the TreeView.
                Set nodX = TreeView1.Nodes.Add("n" & parent, tvwChild, ↵
                "n" & counter, "CDATASection: '" & ↵
                nodeList.Item(Index).nodeValue & "'", "Node")
                counter = counter + 1

        Case NODE_ENTITY_REFERENCE:
                ' Add the entity reference to the TreeView.
                Set nodX = TreeView1.Nodes.Add("n" & parent, tvwChild, ↵
                "n" & counter, "EntityReference: '" & ↵
                nodeList.Item(Index).nodeName & "'", "Node")
                counter = counter + 1

        Case NODE_ENTITY:
                ' Add the entity to the TreeView.
                Set nodX = TreeView1.Nodes.Add("n" & parent, tvwChild, ↵
                "n" & counter, "Entity: '" & nodeList.Item(Index).nodeName ↵
                & "'", "Node")
                counter = counter + 1

                ' Check if this entity has any attributes.
                If (nodeList.Item(Index).Attributes.length > 0) Then
                  Set nodX = TreeView1.Nodes.Add("n" & tempCount, tvwChild, ↵
                  "n" & counter, "NamedNodeMap: '" & ↵
                  nodeList.Item(Index).nodeName & "'", "List")
                  counter = counter + 1
                  Call NamedNodeMapRecursive(nodeList.Item(Index).Attributes, ↵
                 counter - 1)
                End If

        Case NODE_PROCESSING_INSTRUCTION:
                ' Add the processing instruction to the TreeView.
                Set nodX = TreeView1.Nodes.Add("n" & parent, tvwChild, ↵
                "n" & counter, "ProcessingInstruction: '" & ↵
                nodeList.Item(Index).nodeName & "'", "Node")
                counter = counter + 1

        Case NODE_COMMENT:
                ' Add the comment to the TreeView.
                Set nodX = TreeView1.Nodes.Add("n" & parent, tvwChild, ↵
                "n" & counter, "Comment: '" & nodeList.Item(Index).nodeValue ↵
                & "'", "Node")
                counter = counter + 1

                ' It's silly to check for the Document node here, but we'll
                ' leave it in for fun. (maybe we'll find Microsoft bugs :) )
        Case NODE_DOCUMENT:
                Set nodX = TreeView1.Nodes.Add("n" & parent, tvwChild, ↵
                "n" & counter, "Document: '" & nodeList.Item(Index).nodeName ↵
                & "'", "Node")
```

```
                    counter = counter + 1

         Case NODE_DOCUMENT_TYPE:
            ' Add the doctype to the TreeView.
            Set nodX = TreeView1.Nodes.Add("n" & parent, tvwChild, "n" & ↵
            counter, "DocumentType: '" & nodeList.Item(Index).nodeName ↵
            & "'", "Node")
            counter = counter + 1

         Case NODE_DOCUMENT_FRAGMENT:
            ' Add the Document Fragment to the TreeView.
            Set nodX = TreeView1.Nodes.Add("n" & parent, tvwChild, ↵
            "n" & counter, "DocumentFragment: '" & ↵
            nodeList.Item(Index).nodeName & "'", "Node")
            counter = counter + 1

         Case NODE_NOTATION:
            ' Add the notation to the TreeView.
            Set nodX = TreeView1.Nodes.Add("n" & parent, tvwChild, ↵
            "n" & counter, "Notation: '" & nodeList.Item(Index).nodeName ↵
            & "'", "Node")
            counter = counter + 1

            ' Check if this notation has any attributes.
            If (nodeList.Item(Index).Attributes.length > 0) Then
               Set nodX = TreeView1.Nodes.Add("n" & tempCount, tvwChild, ↵
               "n" & counter, "NamedNodeMap", "List")
               counter = counter + 1
               Call NamedNodeMapRecursive(nodeList.Item(Index).Attributes, ↵
               counter - 1)
            End If

      End Select

      ' Finally check if the current node has any children.
      ' If so, then add the NodeList to the TreeView and
      ' call NodeListRecursive again.
      If (nodeList.Item(Index).childNodes.length > 0) Then
         Set nodX = TreeView1.Nodes.Add("n" & tempCount, tvwChild, ↵
         "n" & counter, "NodeList", "List")
         counter = counter + 1
         Call NodeListRecursive(nodeList.Item(Index).childNodes, ↵
         counter - 1)
      End If

   Next Index

End Sub


' ****************************************************************
```

```
' NamedNodeMapRecursive(...) takes care of displaying all the nodes
' that are located within a NamedNodeMap.
' This function uses recursion (calls itself) to traverse the
' tree and is very similar to NodeListRecursive(...).
' Note: This function contains cases that should never occur, but we
' leave them in nevertheless.
Private Sub NamedNodeMapRecursive(nodeList As IXMLDOMNamedNodeMap, ↵
parent As Integer)

  Dim nodX As Node
  Dim tempCount As Integer
  Dim nodeType As DOMNodeType
  Dim forLength As Integer

  forLength = nodeList.length - 1
  ' Do this loop for every node in the NamedNodeMap.
  For Index = 0 To forLength
    tempCount = counter
    nodeType = nodeList.Item(Index).nodeType

    Select Case nodeType
      Case NODE_ELEMENT:
        ' Add the element to the TreeView.
        Set nodX = TreeView1.Nodes.Add("n" & parent, tvwChild, ↵
        "n" & counter, "Element: '" & nodeList.Item(Index).nodeName ↵
        & "'", "Node")
        counter = counter + 1

        ' Check if this element has any attributes.
        If (nodeList.Item(Index).Attributes.length > 0) Then
          Set nodX = TreeView1.Nodes.Add("n" & tempCount, tvwChild, ↵
          "n" & counter, "NamedNodeMap: '" & ↵
          nodeList.Item(Index).nodeName & "'", "List")
          nodX.Expanded = False
          counter = counter + 1
          Call NamedNodeMapRecursive(nodeList.Item(Index).Attributes, ↵
          counter - 1)
        End If

      Case NODE_ATTRIBUTE:
        ' Add the attribute to the TreeView.
        Set nodX = TreeView1.Nodes.Add("n" & parent, tvwChild, ↵
        "n" & counter, "Attribute: '" & nodeList.Item(Index).nodeName ↵
        & "'", "Node")
        counter = counter + 1

      Case NODE_TEXT:
        ' Add the text node to the TreeView.
        Set nodX = TreeView1.Nodes.Add("n" & parent, tvwChild, ↵
```

```
"n" & counter, "Text: '" & nodeList.Item(Index).nodeValue ↵
& "'", "Node")
counter = counter + 1


Case NODE_CDATA_SECTION:
   ' Add the CData Section to the TreeView.
   Set nodX = TreeView1.Nodes.Add("n" & parent, tvwChild, ↵
   "n" & counter, "CDATASection: '" & ↵
   nodeList.Item(Index).nodeValue & "'", "Node")
   counter = counter + 1


Case NODE_ENTITY_REFERENCE:
   ' Add the entity reference to the TreeView.
   Set nodX = TreeView1.Nodes.Add("n" & parent, tvwChild, ↵
   "n" & counter, "EntityReference: '" & ↵
   nodeList.Item(Index).nodeName & "'", "Node")
   counter = counter + 1


Case NODE_ENTITY:
   ' Add the entity to the TreeView.
   Set nodX = TreeView1.Nodes.Add("n" & parent, tvwChild, ↵
   "n" & counter, "Entity: '" & nodeList.Item(Index).nodeName ↵
   & "'", "Node")
   counter = counter + 1


   ' Check if this entity has any attributes.
   ' If so, then add a NamedNodeMap to the TreeView
   ' and call NamedNodeMapRecursive.
   If (nodeList.Item(Index).Attributes.length > 0) Then
      Set nodX = TreeView1.Nodes.Add("n" & tempCount, tvwChild, ↵
      "n" & counter, "NamedNodeMap", "List")
      nodX.Expanded = False
      counter = counter + 1
      Call NamedNodeMapRecursive(nodeList.Item(Index).Attributes, ↵
    counter - 1)
   End If


Case NODE_PROCESSING_INSTRUCTION:
   ' Add the processing instruction to the TreeView.
   Set nodX = TreeView1.Nodes.Add("n" & parent, tvwChild, ↵
   "n" & counter, "ProcessingInstruction: '" & ↵
   nodeList.Item(Index).nodeName & "'", "Node")
   counter = counter + 1


Case NODE_COMMENT:
   ' Add the comment to the TreeView.
   Set nodX = TreeView1.Nodes.Add("n" & parent, tvwChild, ↵
   "n" & counter, "Comment: '" & nodeList.Item(Index).nodeValue ↵
   & "'", "Node")
   counter = counter + 1
```

```
Case NODE_DOCUMENT:
    ' Add the document to the TreeView. This case should
    ' never occur.
    Set nodX = TreeView1.Nodes.Add("n" & parent, tvwChild, ↵
    "n" & counter, "Document: '" & nodeList.Item(Index).nodeName ↵
    & "'", "Node")
    counter = counter + 1

Case NODE_DOCUMENT_TYPE:
    ' Add the doctype to the TreeView.
    Set nodX = TreeView1.Nodes.Add("n" & parent, tvwChild, ↵
    "n" & counter, "DocumentType: '" & ↵
    nodeList.Item(Index).nodeName & "'", "Node")
    counter = counter + 1

Case NODE_DOCUMENT_FRAGMENT:
    ' Add the document fragment to the TreeView.
    Set nodX = TreeView1.Nodes.Add("n" & parent, tvwChild, ↵
    "n" & counter, "DocumentFragment: '" & ↵
    nodeList.Item(Index).nodeName & "'", "Node")
    counter = counter + 1

Case NODE_NOTATION:
    ' Add the notation to the TreeView.
    Set nodX = TreeView1.Nodes.Add("n" & parent, tvwChild, ↵
    "n" & counter, "Notation: '" & nodeList.Item(Index).nodeName ↵
    & "'", "Node")
    counter = counter + 1

    ' Check if this notation has any attributes.
    If (nodeList.Item(Index).Attributes.length > 0) Then
        Set nodX = TreeView1.Nodes.Add("n" & tempCount, tvwChild, ↵
        "n" & counter, "NamedNodeMap", "List")
        nodX.Expanded = False
        counter = counter + 1
        Call NamedNodeMapRecursive(nodeList.Item(Index).Attributes, ↵
        counter - 1)
    End If

End Select

' Check if the current node has any children by checking
' its childNodes collection.
' If it does, then add a NodeList to the TreeView and
' call NodeListRecursive.
If (nodeList.Item(Index).childNodes.length > 0) Then
    Set nodX = TreeView1.Nodes.Add("n" & tempCount, tvwChild, ↵
    "n" & counter, "NodeList", "List")
    counter = counter + 1
```

```vb
          Call NodeListRecursive(nodeList.Item(Index).childNodes, ↵
          counter - 1)
      End If

  Next Index

End Sub


' ***********************************************************


' removeTree() tells the TreeView object to erase the tree.
Private Sub removeTree()
        TreeView1.Nodes.Clear
End Sub


' ***********************************************************


' Performs some initialization when DOMifier first starts up, including
' creating a new DOM tree, and turning off asynchronous downloading.
Private Sub Form_Load()

  Set xml = New DOMDocument
  xml.async = False

  waitLabel.Visible = False

  ' No XML document is loaded yet.
  XMLloaded (False)

  ' Set up the TreeView top-left coordinates.
  TreeView1.Left = 0
  TreeView1.Top = 0
End Sub


' ***********************************************************


' This event is called when a user resizes the DOMifier window.
' The TreeView control resized to the size of the viewable main window.
Private Sub Form_Resize()

  If ((Main.Height > 750) And (Main.Width > 140)) Then
    TreeView1.Height = Main.Height - 750
    TreeView1.Width = Main.Width - 140
  End If
End Sub


' ***********************************************************


' Kills the hidden about box and 'Load URL' window
' when the program dies.
```

```vb
Private Sub Form_Unload(Cancel As Integer)
  Unload frmAbout
  Unload frmLoad
End Sub


' *************************************************************


' Displays the 'Load URL' dialog located in frmLoad.frm when
' File..Open URL is selected.
Private Sub openURL_Click()
  frmLoad.Show
End Sub


' *************************************************************


' Shows the typical 'Open' dialog box found in nearly
' every Windows program.
' The 'Open' dialog box is a part of the
' Microsoft Common Dialog Control.
Private Sub openLocal_Click()

  CommonDialog1.Flags = &H4 ' hide read only box
  CommonDialog1.filename = ""
  ' Register the XML file type.
  CommonDialog1.Filter = "XML Documents (*.xml)|*.xml|All files|*.*"
  CommonDialog1.ShowOpen

  ' Call loadURL to actually load and parse the XML document.
  If (CommonDialog1.filename <> "") Then
    loadURL (CommonDialog1.filename)
  End If
End Sub


' *************************************************************


' Kills the DOMifier when the user selects File..Exit.
Private Sub exit_Click()
  Unload Main
End Sub


' *************************************************************


' Shows the entire tree display when the
' user selects Edit..Expand All.
Private Sub expandAll_Click()
  Dim count As Integer
  count = TreeView1.Nodes.count

  ' For each node in the TreeView, set the Expanded property to true.
  For Index = 1 To count
```

```
        TreeView1.Nodes.Item(Index).Expanded = True
    Next Index
End Sub


' **************************************************************


' Collapses the tree display down to the Document node when the
' user selects Edit..Collapse All.
Private Sub collapseAll_Click()
    Dim count As Integer
    count = TreeView1.Nodes.count

    ' For each node in the TreeView, set the Expanded property to false.
    For Index = 1 To count
        TreeView1.Nodes.Item(Index).Expanded = False
    Next Index
End Sub


' **************************************************************


' Displays the text version of the DOM tree to a message box
' when Tools..Show XML is selected.
Private Sub showXML_Click()
    If (isXMLloaded = True) Then
        MsgBox (xml.xml)
    Else
        MsgBox ("An XML document must be loaded first.")
    End If
End Sub


' **************************************************************


' Shows the About box when the user selects Help..AboutDOMifier.
Private Sub about_Click()
    frmAbout.Show
End Sub
```

Summary

As we have shown in this chapter, XML is not limited to browsers only. Standalone applications can also take advantage of the opportunities that XML brings. Full blown applications, such as word processors, databases, and multiplayer games, can use XML to share data.

Rapid Application Development (RAD) packages, such as Visual Basic or Delphi, have become increasingly popular tools for software development. XML can be integrated into these applications using the DOM, with the DOMifier as an example. As parsers become more stable and abundant, we will see increased XML usage in the applications that are used on a daily basis.

This chapter brings us to the end of the Document Object Model section. Chapters 5 and 7 are designed in a reference style to allow you to consult them during programming. These last three scenario chapters are designed to give you a feel of where the DOM fits in and to stimulate ideas of where you can use it. Now, we move on to the displaying XML by covering the XML Stylesheet Language (XSL).

PART THREE

Presenting XSL—The XML Stylesheet Language

CHAPTER 11

XSL Overview

After reading the first two parts of this book, you should be comfortable with XML at a conceptual level and have developed a feel for how to begin writing code around XML applications. We focused a lot on how to define your XML content models and manipulate the data contained therein. Now we turn our attention to the second (and more human) part of presenting XML information to users. In this part of the book, we discuss one particular technology that we believe will become the dominant method for presenting XML information over the Internet: *XML Stylesheet Language* (XSL). This chapter is an overview of XSL and the general support that is currently available. We also tell you why we believe so much in XSL. We don't go too deeply into technical issues; this chapter should help you understand some of the roles that XSL can play in XML applications and decide whether you should invest in developing expertise in XSL.

Presenting Data—The Need to "See" Information

So far we have presented you with an in-depth look at creating XML documents and have reviewed in some detail how to manipulate the data contained in your XML documents from a programmer's perspective. We talked extensively about how XML redefines the concept of the document by separating content from format. In this part of the book, we illustrate how useful this concept is and show you how to do it.

Management and marketing majors will tell you that "perception is reality." *Perception* is most ostensibly created through *presentation*. As much as engineers dislike the idea (hey, we're purists!), people respond more to presentation than to content (think lawyers and advertisements). Let's face it, 99.9 percent of all Internet users are still interested in viewing information for themselves, even if they want to translate that information into different formats (tables, fields, databases, memos, reports, and so on) for further processing. Despite all the revolutions that XML has and will continue to bring, it's not going to change fundamental human nature. So, we do the next best thing: We deal with it.

"Dealing with It" the Traditional Way

Engineers and technical professionals agree that few tasks are more frustrating than putting together a report. Although writing the actual content of the report and putting it into a logical format doesn't take too long, putting it all together—applying fancy fonts to different sections, inserting pictures, adding captions, and laying the document out—takes up far more time than it should. This is primarily due to WYSIWYG (What You See Is What You Get) processors. When you use a WYSIWYG processor, you are virtually forced to simultaneously format while writing content. Misspelled words are underlined in red, and poorly phrased grammar is underlined in green. (Yes, you can turn these features off, but most of us are too lazy.) The result is that you don't focus on doing one thing at a time; instead, you are focusing on everything at once. Toss in a picture and then you need to add in a page break to make sure the next section starts on a separate page. And just when you think you're done, you give it to a colleague who identifies several places where changes need to be made, there isn't enough information, or there's too much information. Now, you have to go back and make changes in the content, which repaginates your entire document, forcing you to go back and format the document all over again.

Can you see a vicious cycle developing here?

Dealing with It the XML Way

We are the first to admit that we're bad at aesthetics and formatting. Sometimes it's a wonder that we wear matching socks (we do have occasional lapses there too). But for better or worse, we're pretty good at working with technology, understanding concepts, and turning them into meaningful applications. Our publishers, on the other hand, are great at formatting and experts in publishing. Each of us possesses a unique skill set that, when exercised individually, is good, but when combined together becomes great. By working together, we have put together a book that has meaningful content and is presented in a reader-friendly way.

When writing this book, we identified (or tagged) portions of the text with different "styles": some portions of the text are headings (with different hierarchy), some portions of text are body text, and so on. In doing so, we essentially marked up certain portions of text in our chapters so that our friends at Wiley Computer Publishing could apply different formatting styles to each section. They then decide which fonts to use and which formats (indenting, justification) and typestyles (bold, italics) to apply.

For us, as authors, this was a boon. We were able to work on our areas of expertise, while our publishers were able to focus on their areas of expertise.

How Would This Process Benefit from XML?

For starters, we had to use proprietary applications (word processors, drawing programs, painting tools, and so on) to encode and exchange information. Each of us had to purchase copies of those applications. Sometimes discrepancies arose while creating drawings, because our application didn't create output that was compatible with the publishing software. Though our problems were admittedly few (our publishers are pros) and were overcome pretty easily, the fact remains that the solution required proprietary intermediate data representations for exchanging information from one application to another. Proprietary formats are expensive—you need to have proprietary applications to render those formats, licensing costs, and time. The problem lies in the scalability of such solutions.

Not all organizations have the resources to buy enough licenses so that every user has proprietary software to render information. That's why businesses want to put their information online so that they can use virtually free applications, such as browsers, to exchange information both internally and externally. When you use XML, you realize that advantage.

How Would This Process Benefit from XSL?

If our manuscript had been written in XML according to our publisher's DTD, our publisher could have had several corresponding XSL stylesheets. These stylesheets would have immediately translate the manuscript into a print format and, if so desired, into a Web format. One stylesheet could be used to automatically generate a table of contents, another to generate limited versions for sending to reviewers. The key thing is that once the data was entered in XML, XSL could be used to format or translate the information into virtually any number of other media, immediately and efficiently. In addition, the publisher would not have to pay any overhead licensing for the use of the standard. It doesn't matter how big an organization is, cutting costs is a *good* thing.

XSL FAQ

Before we get into the big-picture aspects of XSL, let's go over some basic questions and concerns, and bring everyone up to speed.

What Are Stylesheet Languages and Why Are They Useful?

Stylesheets are templates that describe how to present documents. Stylesheets enable documents to be presented in a variety of different output media, such as monitors, paper, speech, music, or in a device-independent format. They have many advantages over independent, individually styled documents, including the ability to:

- Reuse data
- Provide a standardized style of presentation
- Transform the source document to multiple output formats
- Customize presentation for individual preferences

Stylesheet languages can be either *declarative* or *procedural* (that is, they can either dictate or hard code presentation, or describe "what to do in case of..." rules). Above all else, they allow authors to create content independent of presentation semantics.

What Is XSL?

XSL is the Extensible Markup Language Stylesheet Language. It is an XML application that has a fixed set of tags (vocabulary) used to define presentation templates (stylesheets), which can be used both to manipulate XML data and to describe formatting information contained in XML documents.

What Does XSL Do?

Short answer: XSL provides a language for creating stylesheets (also known as *templates*) that describe how XML documents should be rendered.

Longer answer: XSL is a very powerful, yet easy to use, syntax that facilitates the manipulation and display of information contained in XML documents. The display of information is not limited to screen representation; that is, the output could be to paper or some other medium. It has two essential functions:

- To provide an easy to use syntax for basic transformations and manipulations of XML documents
- To provide an XML lexicon for describing formatting semantics

To give you an idea of what was going on in the minds of the folks at the W3C while they were designing XSL, we've listed the nonnormative design principles against which the XSL recommendation is being prepared in Chapter 12.

How Do XSL Stylesheets Fit into an XML System?

From a systems perspective, XSL stylesheets do two things:

- Transform XML documents into other XML-based formats (for example, HTML, Rich Text Format)
- Provide a mechanism for manipulating (for example, sorting, searching, branching, adding, removing) XML documents, including providing an escape hatch to other languages such as ECMA or JavaScript for performing calculations)

Let's talk about these a little more.

Transforming XML Documents into Other XML-Based Formats

Look at Figure 11.1.

Stylesheets can be used to transform XML documents into something else—virtually any other XML application. In Figure 11.1, we show three possible stylesheets that can convert the same XML document into three different formats. For the sake of simplicity, we show each conversion stylesheet as a separate piece, though there is no binding reason why this has to be true. It is possible to write a single stylesheet that does everything at once (though admittedly, that takes away from an object-oriented approach).

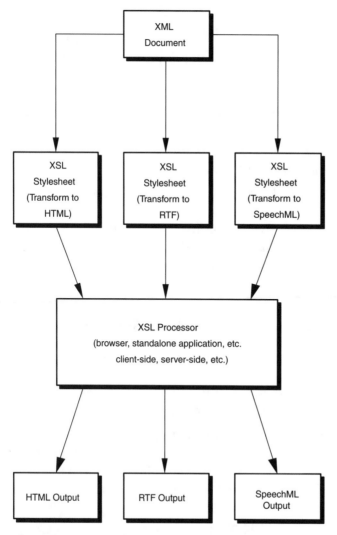

Figure 11.1 XSL stylesheets in an XML system.

Application Scenario: The News Agency

Let's look at a hypothetical scenario. Suppose the XML document we started with was a news report submitted by a journalist working in a news agency.

Assume that the news agency has a well-developed system whereby journalists have to type only their story, incorporating only logical formatting (that is, tagging sections with heading, caption, main story, footnote tags) Given the right GUI, this tagging could be called applying styles. When the story gets passed to the distribution group, the distribution group has several XSL stylesheets to format the logically marked-up XML report. By applying different stylesheets to the same data, the distribution group can immediately post a page up onto the Web using the XSL-HTML conversion stylesheet. They can also print the story out on paper using the XSL-RTF conversion stylesheet. In addition, the story can be broadcast over the company's Webcasting or radio station by using the SpeechML conversion stylesheet. Because all of these conversions are automated, they happen virtually instantaneously and simultaneously. Immediately after the report is submitted, it is broadcast around the world to millions of viewers or listeners on multiple media.

Figure 11.2 summarizes this hypothetical system to illustrate where XSL fits in.

Manipulating XML Information

XSL is more than a format converter. XML allows you to perform a fair amount of manipulation on the information contained in an XML document. Think of your XSL stylesheet as a gardener with a hedge trimmer and your XML document as a very leafy tree or shrub. You can take a big mangy shrub and prune it into virtually anything you want.

We go into more detail on exactly what we mean by this in the next section. For now, we simply list a few of the many uses of XSL in manipulating your XML documents:

- Display XML documents directly in your browser
- Perform rudimentary searches in your XML document (for example, list all items that cost under $50)

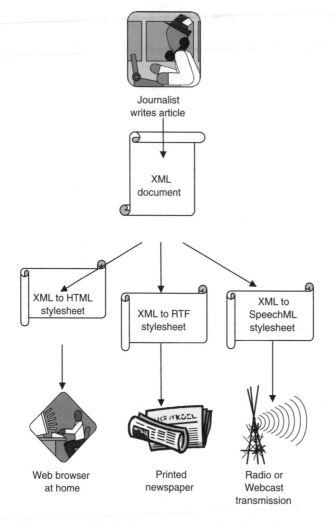

Figure 11.2 XSL in the News Agency hypothetical scenario.

- Prune XML documents (that is, if the structure is first_name, last_name, telephone, address, you can turn it into first_name, last_name, telephone only)

- Add information to XML documents (for example, adding address information/filling in form information)

- Sort XML documents (for example, rearrange all names alphabetically)

- Conditional formatting (for example, if the contents of an element are super fantastic, highlight it in bright red)

- Multiple combinations of all of the above

Is XSL a W3C Recommendation?

At the time of writing, XSL was in the *working draft* document stage at the World Wide Web Consortium. A working draft means that although the W3C doesn't endorse the standard (yet), that document contains specifications that have passed several layers of discussion among the members and is very likely to be along the lines along of the actual standard adopted. Historically, working drafts are good approximations of the final standard.

If XSL Is Not a Recommendation, Why Should It Be Supported?

Admittedly, it looks as though we're going out on a limb here recommending a technology that has not been completely specified yet. Though we're young and are risk takers, we don't gamble. In Chapter 3 when we talked about schemas and alternative approaches to creating DTDs, we said that we wouldn't talk about any other proposals that the W3C has received because, quite frankly, it was too early and too many proposals were under consideration.

In the case of XSL, it is the only proposal of its type under consideration by the W3C and is thus without competition. That such an XML application is necessary for XML itself to succeed is without question. Therefore, we are extremely confident that XSL will be approved soon. In fact, by the time this book hits the shelves, it is very likely that the XSL working draft will be superseded by an official XSL recommendation.

Why you should support XSL is really more of a business issue: Now is the time to get the competitive edge. XSL is a powerful technology that lets you take advantage of XML immediately and relatively easily. Wait, and your competitors will grab it before you.

Who Supports XSL?

Currently, the XSL working draft is supported in Microsoft's Internet Explorer 5. When we asked Netscape whether they would be supporting XSL in the next version of Navigator (slated for release later this year), Netscape said that it would depend on interest from users and the developer community. We're pretty sure that after using XSL in Internet Explorer 5, most developers are going to demand similar or better support from Netscape, if only to support interoperability. Besides, it's a standards-based recommendation (or will be) of XML, and Netscape is usually very good about supporting open standards.

Why Can't a Programming Language/the DOM Be Used to Manipulate XML Documents?

It can. However, XSL gives you a simple way to perform rudimentary manipulations and formatting. It also lets you escape into programming languages for performing more complex manipulations. XSL also has direct hooks into the DOM and lets you do all kinds of cool things as a result (check out Part Two of the book if you haven't already). Sure, you could reinvent the wheel and do everything from scratch—sometimes you end up with something better. Just ask yourself if the additional control and power is worth the additional effort.

Why Do You Believe in XSL So Much?

Beyond the obvious things like we're sure it's about to become an official recommendation and that it has current browser support, we believe in XSL because it simply makes sense to have an XML-based syntax for displaying and manipulating XML documents. Think about it: If XML is really as flexible as we keep saying it is, it should be able to work with itself. Just as we believe that DTDs are a lousy way of defining the structure of XML documents and should be replaced with XML-based syntax, we believe that XSL-type functionality should also be employed using XML-based syntax.

You could say it's a philosophical thing, but more than that, it's a practical thing too. It just makes more intuitive sense, and intuitive things are easier to work with than nonintuitive things.

XSL versus Other Stylesheet Syntax

We should mention that other stylesheet syntaxes exist for displaying XML information, for which the W3C has already presented official recommendations. Certainly, the biggest candidate among these is Cascading Stylesheets Level 2 (CSS2). Another stylesheet mechanism for working with XML is the Document Style and Semantics Specification Language (DSSSL).

Let's compare them:

XSL versus CSS2

Cascading Stylesheets Level 2 was officially recommended by the W3C in May 1998. It succeeds CSS1, which was released in 1996 and was slated to be the next hottest technology after HTML itself. CSS1 was used primarily for formatting (styling) information stored in HTML documents, with the hope being that it would reduce Web authoring and site maintenance. CSS1 never really became as wildly popular as it was hoped.

CSS2 builds up on everything that CSS1 did (all CSS1 stylesheets are CSS2 compliant) and more. While CSS1 was primarily concerned with styling HTML documents for display in browsers, CSS2 supports the translation of data in both HTML and XML documents into multiple media-specific stylesheets (for example, for translations into visual browsers, aural browsers, and Braille devices).

Admittedly, it sounds pretty exciting; however, to us, CSS isn't very exciting, primarily because XSL lets you do all this and more. In CSS, the formatting object tree is essentially the same tree as the source tree. In other words, CSS is an *as-is* formatter of XML documents. You can't do much with the information except push it out onto the screen in a fancy format. You can do some selective presentation of information, but not very easily and not without escaping to JavaScript or JScript. In our opinion, CSS doesn't give you the true benefit of the XML approach.

In Chapters 1 and 2, we spoke about how XML allows a document to be broken into three separate parts: content, structure, and formatting. In order to realize the full benefit of XML, you should be able to easily play with all of these parts of a document separately. That is, you should be able to change the content of document, rearrange the structure of your document, and be able to play with the formatting of your XML document, preferably using the same set of tools (in this case, stylesheet language).

XSL gives you the ability to change the structure of your XML document. CSS, on the other hand, is concerned primarily with presenting information in a structure-dependent fashion. For instance, using CSS2, it is not easy to change the order in which a name (consisting of a first name and a last name) is displayed. Nor can you replace the content of your document (for example, if you wanted to insert thumbs-up icon instead of text that says "thumbs up" in a document containing a movie review).

Table 11.1 compares the features of XSL with those of CSS2.

Table 11.1 Comparing XSL Stylesheet Features with CSS2 Stylesheets

FEATURE	XSL	CSS	DESCRIPTION
Used with HTML	No	Yes	XSL can be used to convert XML information into HTML and HTML/CSS but doesn't directly work with existing HTML documents (unless they are well formed, in which case they are also XML documents). CSS, on the other hand, can be used to style existing HTML information.
Allows "escape" to programming language for more power	Yes	Yes	Both XSL and CSS have built-in mechanisms for "escaping" into ECMA script.
XML-based syntax	Yes	No	XSL stylesheets are written in XML syntax. CSS are written in non-XML grammar.
Display XML information	Yes	Yes	Both XSL and CSS can used to display information contained in XML documents in a variety of different output specific formats.
Common Internet browser support	Partial	Yes	Both Microsoft's Internet Explorer 5 and Netscape's Navigator Explorer 5 and Netscape's Navigator 4.5 fully support CSS2. XSL has extensive support in Internet Explorer 5 but support from Netscape has not been implemented to date. We expect the next version of Netscape's Navigator to support XSL.
Transformation of XML document structure	Yes	No	XSL allows manipulation of the XML tree to create a new tree that is different from the original.

Table 11.1 *(Continued)*

FEATURE	XSL	CSS	DESCRIPTION
Transformation of XML document structure (continued)	Yes	No	In other words, you can reorder the structure of the information contained in the original document. CSS syntax doesn't provide this functionality. You can achieve it by escaping into JavaScript or JScript, but it requires more work.
Transformation of XML document content	Yes	No	XSL gives you the ability to change the actual content of your XML document. For example, you can replace the contents of an element from text with a picture or other text.
Manipulation of XML data (searching, sorting, filtering)	Yes	No	XSL stylesheets give you the ability to perform fundamental data manipulation that CSS2 sheets don't unless you program the same features in by escaping to a programming language.

XSL versus DSSSL

Unlike XSL and CSS, the Document Style and Semantics Specification Language (DSSSL) is not a W3C recommendation. It is a standard that comes from the International Standards Organization (ISO) and has been around almost as long as SGML. In fact, its purpose is to format and manipulate SGML documents. We mentioned in Chapter 1 that XML is a subset of SGML; ipso facto DSSSL can be used to format XML information. Just as XML's role model is SGML, XSL's role model is SGML.

As with other standards of the SGML genre, it DSSSL is extremely powerful and, of course, pretty complicated. Again, it's like swatting a fly with a bazooka. More often than not, you won't need that much power, and the overhead is something we'd rather not deal with. Besides, DSSSL stylesheets are written in a language called Scheme, which is derived from

Table 11.2   Comparing XSL Stylesheets with DSSSL Stylesheets

XSL	DSSSL
Able to transform and format XML documents.	Able to transform and format all SGML documents (including HTML and XML).
Fairly powerful/feature rich. Allows "escapes" to programming languages for additional power.	Very powerful. Allows (and expects) you to specify everything.
Relatively easy to use.	Complicated to use.
Browser support available.	Not supported in common browsers.

LISP. LISP was one of the first tools for implementing AI and was great for its time, but it's a little old now. Table 11.2 summarizes DSSSL versus XSL as XML formatting and manipulation languages.

When all is said and done, XSL remains the only XML-based syntax for transforming and formatting XML documents. It is powerful and, at the same time, fairly easy to use. We show you how in the next few chapters.

XSL and HTML

XSL is about formatting and rearranging XML documents. For the format to be rendered, however, the XML content needs to be translated or transformed into another format that has an available rendering application. Although XSL and other stylesheets are supposed to be independent of their output formats, the reality is that some formats are more important than others. Conversions to formats like Braille or RTF (rich text format) are important, but the most important output format from a business perspective is the one that has become the most popular display format over the past decade: HTML. In this book, we focus mostly on how XSL is used to transform XML into HTML.

Applying XSL: Client-Side XSL, Server-Side XSL, or Both?

XSL can be applied at the server side, at the client side, or both. Let's talk a bit about each model.

Client-Side XSL Model

This model takes advantage of XML and XSL. If your client is using an XSL and XML-enabled browser, you're lucky because you can send both the XML source document and the XSL stylesheet to the client and have the client's otherwise underutilized processor render both. The client can then perform several layers of processing on their side, completely independent of your server. Figure 11.3 illustrates this process.

Another great benefit of this model is that clients can use their own XSL stylesheets (supplied by a third party or based on their own user preferences) to render the XML data. In doing so, your server is completely oblivious and therefore untaxed.

Server-Side XSL Model

As attractive as the client-side model is, the reality is that, at least in the short run, the vast majority of Web users are not XML/XSL empowered. For now, you may want to keep the stylesheet and the XML source document on the server side and let your XML-HTML (or other format) conversion happen there. Then you can send the HTML document to the client. Admittedly, this model is similar to current client/server models. However, you are able to reap the benefits of using open standards discussed in Chapter 2.

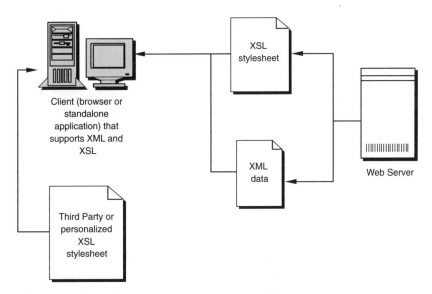

Figure 11.3 Client-side XSL model. Let the client perform rendering.

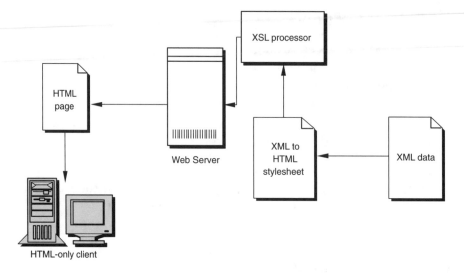

Figure 11.4 Server-side XSL model. XML-HTML conversion happens at server using XSL stylesheet. HTML document is sent to client.

Figure 11.4 illustrates the server-side XSL model.

Although it is possible that the average size of each exchange between client and server for the server-side XSL model is smaller than the size of exchanges between those of the client-side XSL model, the frequency of exchanges between the client and the server is likely to be much higher. This is because every time the user (client) wants a different view of the source data, the server has to generate an HTML page and send that to the client. The net result is that your server is tasked much more in this model.

Hybrid Model—Applying XSL to Both the Server Side and Client Side

The hybrid model is where XSL will be used most often in the future. The idea is to apply XSL at both the server side and the client side. Figure 11.5 illustrates this model.

Typically, this is useful when you are dealing with very large XML files. If you assume that the database in which the XML document is generated supplies a large answer to a client's query, it may not be in either the client's or the server's best interest to provide the complete result. Accordingly, the XML document could be trimmed at the server's side using an XSL stylesheet and then have the resultant XML document and another stylesheet sent to the client's side where the client can perform further data manipulation. This is useful with the results from a data-

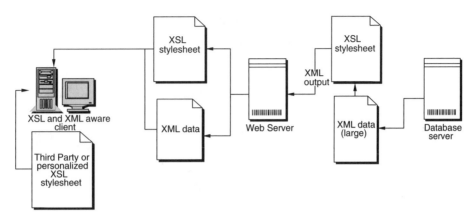

Figure 11.5 Applying XSL at both ends.

base query (for example, the contact information of all the people who live in Wyoming). The server-side XSL stylesheet could be used to truncate the XML document to only the first thousand names and then send that result to the client. The client could then use one or several XSL stylesheets to sort through the information at his or her end, and to perhaps create mailing labels. The possibilities are endless.

Summary

In this chapter, we presented an overview of XSL and how it can be deployed across an XML system. We've provided you with some example applications to help you visualize where XSL can fit in your system. Here are some thoughts we'd like you to take away from this chapter:

- Information stored in XML documents need to be displayed at some point.
- The nature of XML documents is such that they are uniquely suited to a stylesheet approach for formatting.
- XSL provides a powerful, yet simple, syntax that allows you both to manipulate XML source data and to specify its output format.
- XSL is not the only way of presenting information contained in XML documents. CSS and DSSSL are other ways of presenting XML data. XSL combines the best of both worlds.
- XSL is a standards-based application of XML. No one company owns it. In using it, you gain all the advantages of an open standards development environment.

- XSL is a flexible technology in that it can be used to support clients who are XSL aware as well as those clients who are using older technologies.

We believe very strongly in XSL. We think it's a great technology and can see it being used in thousands of applications yet to come. We hope we've been able to convince you to give it more than a passing glance and to consider adding it into your XML repertoire. In the next few chapters, we start talking technically again and take a closer look at how you can work with XSL to create XML-based solutions.

CHAPTER 12

XSL Syntax

I n this chapter, we review the basics of XSL syntax and present you many code examples to help you perform simple XML tree manipulation and HTML transformation. All of the code in this chapter has been tested in Internet Explorer 5, and we've tried to refrain from using any of Microsoft's custom XML and XSL extensions. You may want to treat this section as a reference section while working with XSL examples later on in this chapter and in Chapter 15.

XSL Design Principles

Before we embark on exploring the syntax of XSL, we think it's important to recognize why XSL exists and what functionality it was designed to perform. Therefore, what follows is the design principles the W3C adhered to while designing XSL (reproduced from the December 18, 1998, XSL Working Draft). Our interpretations are listed below each:

XSL should support browsing, printing, and interactive editing and design tools. General computer users (you, me, mom and pop, sis and bro) should be able to take advantage of XSL's functionality.

Therefore, the general syntax had to be designed such that tool vendors could easily design interfaces around it to provide simple access to nonprogrammers as well as folks like us who want more control. Think in terms of designing an application like Microsoft FrontPage or Netscape Composer.

XSL should be capable of specifying presentations for traditional and Web environments.   Regardless of whether you have access to the Web, XSL functionality should be useful to you. That is, if you're using a PC running windows, a workstation running Unix, or a Mac running OS 8, you should be able to render XSL documents both offline and online.

XSL should support interaction with structured information as well as the presentation of it. XSL should support all kinds of structured information, including both data and documents.   We've combined both of these design principles. Essentially, XSL should be able to work with XML documents such that it can interpret and manipulate their structure and contents and such that it can format the information contained in XML documents. Whether the contents are numerical or textual, XSL should provide levels of support so users can manipulate data to extract information.

XSL should support both visual and nonvisual presentations.   XSL should be able to transform XML information into other XML presentation formats, for example HTML, SpeechML, and Rich Text Format.

XSL should be a declarative language.   XSL instructions should be explicit, that is, every instruction tells the processor *what* to do. This is in contrast to *procedural* languages that tell a processor *how* to perform tasks.

XSL should be optimized to provide simple specifications for common formatting tasks and not preclude more sophisticated formatting tasks.   XSL should be easy to use so that you can easily do simple formatting (apply fonts, change typefaces, change alignments) but not limit you only to that. For example, you should be able to do advanced formatting tricks such as applying predefined styles and adding headers or footers.

XSL should provide an extensibility mechanism.   XSL is, in essence, a scripting language. No scripting language provides comprehensive coverage of every user's needs. Therefore, XSL needs to be able to provide an escape hatch to allow advanced users (programmers) to make use of programming language features like variables, looping, and calculations. XSL incorporates the standardized version of JavaScript called ECMA (European Computer Manufacturer's Association) Script. ECMA Script combines Microsoft's JScript and Netscape's JavaScript with server-side extensions from Borland.

The number of optional features in XSL should be kept to a minimum. To keep things simple, XSL syntax shouldn't have too many knobs to turn in order to make things work. This is a continuation of the KISS (keep it short and simple) philosophy.

XSL should provide the formatting functionality of at least DSSSL and CSS. In the last chapter, we discussed how XSL relates to DSSSL and CSS. Take a look at the "XSL versus DSSSL" and "XSL versus CSS" sections in Chapter 11 for a more detailed discussion of this principle.

XSL should leverage other recommendations and standards. Essentially, XSL should work with other W3C recommended applications and standards. That is, XSL should be able to transform XML documents into any of the W3C application languages, such as HTML and RTF, with relative ease.

XSL should be expressed in XML syntax. This is self-explanatory. We go over the actual syntax later in this chapter.

XSL stylesheets should be human readable and reasonably clear. This is a natural follow on from the XML standard design principle: If XSL is going to be an XML application, it has to meet the same design criteria. As you see in this chapter, XSL stylesheets are easy to write and to view.

Terseness in XSL markup is of minimal importance. Rather than save on finger (typing) effort, XSL markup is supposed to save on brain effort. Say farewell to function names like printf and say hello to names like xsl:value-of.

XSL Architecture

As we've mentioned repeatedly, XSL stylesheets are XML documents. The tag names used in XSL are all members of the xsl namespace. XSL stylesheets consist of *construction rules* that declaratively define the conversion of an XML source tree into a new XML document that is expressed in a hierarchy of formatting objects called *flow objects*. Flow objects are a carry over from digital typesetting formats that describe exactly how a document should be printed (that is, where and how text should wrap, the physical placement of characters, when a line should break). Examples of flow objects in the typesetting world include pages, paragraphs, tables, table rows, and table columns. As you can probably gather from the last enumeration of examples, HTML tags also have roots in the digital typesetting environment where its flow objects include <body>, <p>, <table>, <tr>, and <td>. From this, you can also tell that flow objects can nest themselves (for example, putting table rows inside table tags, which in turn can be nested within the <body> tag).

XSL defines a vocabulary of flow objects that all XSL stylesheets can use. These flow objects have *characteristics* that provide exact control over how the flow object works. These characteristics work in a fashion similar to the way HTML flow objects are controlled; that is, through attribute tweaking (think <table *align = "center"*>).

In addition to the core vocabulary of flow objects that XSL uses for all output formats, XSL also includes a set of flow objects that is specifically used for outputting HTML. Most of the examples in this chapter use these flow objects just because they are the easiest to render (everyone has an HTML browser, but not everyone has a SpeechML browser—yet).

XSL Models of Usage

XSL stylesheets are used in two generic ways depending on the nature of the XML document for which they are targeted. They are template-driven and data-driven models. Let's take a look at what each of these models entails.

Template-Driven Model

If the XML data source consists of repetitive structures that require similar transformation or formatting, then the *template-driven model* is used. This model would be used when representing relational data (that is, table-based data). An example would be an XML contact data set where a repetitive structure (contact, name, address, telephone) is used for representing information. You could think in terms of applying XSL as a mail merge utility in this case, for formatting mail labels for printing from a contact database.

Data-Driven Model

If the XML data source consists of irregular data, then a *data-driven model* is used. By irregular we mean nonrepetitive; for example, a document structure. Think of a letter consisting of various sections such as to, from, date, greeting, introduction, body, conclusion, and signature. Each section is generally used only once and may need to be treated separately for proper formatting. In the data-driven model, template fragments are defined and used to treat each section separately. The XSL processor combines the results of all the template fragments and spits out a complete resultant tree.

As you would expect, you can mix and match these models. For example, you could perform an actual mail merge where the contents of the letter are treated on a data-driven model and the "to" section is treated as a template driven model.

XSL Basics

A few XSL basics are common to all XSL stylesheets.

XSL Stylesheets Are XML Documents

By default, they all begin with the XML declaration:

```
<?xml version = "1.0" ?>
```

XSL Stylesheets Are Self-Declarative

All XSL stylesheets declare themselves to be stylesheets; all XSL tags utilize the concept of namespaces described in Chapter 3, whereby every tag is preceded by the namespace declaration, xsl:. When creating an XSL stylesheet, generally, the first line that follows the XML declaration is the stylesheet declaration that includes the XSL namespace declaration:

```
<xsl:stylesheet xmlns:xsl="http://www.w3.org/TR/WD-xsl">
```

Remember, that because this is an XML document, the xsl:stylesheet tag must be closed at the end of the document. This means that the last line of your stylesheet generally is as follows:

```
</xsl:stylesheet>
```

We are big believers in the inductive method of learning as opposed to the deductive method of learning. We feel it is easier to learn by looking at what someone has done and then experimenting with it yourself. Therefore, throughout the rest of this chapter, we go through example applications of the XSL syntax. We close the chapter with a reference section on the important XSL tags available for you to use.

XSL by Example: Creating and Populating an HTML Template

Enough of theory! Let's get our hands dirty and create our first XML to HTML conversion stylesheet. We begin with the following data set, which we use for most of our examples in this chapter:

```
<?xml version = "1.0" ?>
<!-- Define XSL Stylesheet to be used with current XML Document -->
<?xml-stylesheet type="text/xsl" href="restaurant.xsl"?>

<RESTAURANTS>
    <RESTAURANT FOOD_GENRE="Chinese">
        <NAME>Yin Yang</NAME>
        <FOOD_RATING>4</FOOD_RATING>
        <AMBIANCE_RATING>2</AMBIANCE_RATING>
        <AVERAGE_MEAL_COST>$6</AVERAGE_MEAL_COST>
        <REVIEW>Great food, but better to order take out
                than to eat in.</REVIEW>
    </RESTAURANT>
    <RESTAURANT FOOD_GENRE="Italian">
        <NAME>Little Italy</NAME>
        <FOOD_RATING>3</FOOD_RATING>
        <AMBIANCE_RATING>4</AMBIANCE_RATING>
        <AVERAGE_MEAL_COST>$8</AVERAGE_MEAL_COST>
        <REVIEW>Romantic setting, great place to go with a
                date.</REVIEW>
    </RESTAURANT>
    <RESTAURANT FOOD_GENRE="Chinese">
        <NAME>Lee Tang</NAME>
        <FOOD_RATING>4</FOOD_RATING>
        <AMBIANCE_RATING>5</AMBIANCE_RATING>
        <AVERAGE_MEAL_COST>$9</AVERAGE_MEAL_COST>
        <REVIEW>Excellent food and a wonderful decor. Great place
                for a business lunch.</REVIEW>
    </RESTAURANT>
    <RESTAURANT FOOD_GENRE="Seafood">
        <NAME>Pirate's Lair</NAME>
```

```
        <FOOD_RATING>2</FOOD_RATING>
        <AMBIANCE_RATING>1</AMBIANCE_RATING>
        <AVERAGE_MEAL_COST>$7</AVERAGE_MEAL_COST>
        <REVIEW>Bad food and even worse decor. Never go
                here unless you want an upset stomach.</REVIEW>
    </RESTAURANT>
    <RESTAURANT FOOD_GENRE="Pizza">
        <NAME>Howie's Pizzeria</NAME>
        <FOOD_RATING>3</FOOD_RATING>
        <AMBIANCE_RATING>4</AMBIANCE_RATING>
        <AVERAGE_MEAL_COST>$7</AVERAGE_MEAL_COST>
        <REVIEW>Great place to get together with friends. They
                also sport the hottest wings in town.</REVIEW>
    </RESTAURANT>
</RESTAURANTS>
```

For now, imagine that we want to display our restaurant's review data set as an HTML page. In this case, the data is obviously repetitive and lends itself to a template-driven model approach. While we are getting ahead of ourselves, let's take a look at what the corresponding XSL stylesheet would look like.

```
<?xml version='1.0'?>
<!--XML Declaration -->


<xsl:stylesheet xmlns:xsl="http://www.w3.org/TR/WD-xsl">
<!--declaration that the document is a stylesheet and that it
    is associated with the xsl: namespace -->

  <xsl:template match="/">
<!--Apply template to everything starting from the root node-->

    <HTML>
      <BODY>
<!-- Create a HTML document by inserting standard HTML tags
     all HTML tags are well formed and in UPPERCASE -->

        <TABLE BORDER="2">
<!--Set up header row -->
          <TR
            <TD><b>Restaurant</b></TD>
            <TD><b>Food Genre</b></TD>
            <TD><b>Food (max 5)</b></TD>
            <TD><b>Ambiance (max 5)</b></TD>
            <TD><b>Average Cost per Meal</b></TD>
            <TD><b>Review</b></TD>
          </TR>

        <xsl:for-each select="RESTAURANTS/RESTAURANT">
```

```
<!--set up a loop where for each occurence of the pattern defined
    in the "select", do the following -->
            <TR>
              <TD><xsl:value-of select="NAME"/></TD>
<!--"value-of" pulls the value of the contents specified in the
    "select" attribute -->

              <TD><xsl:value-of select="@FOOD_GENRE"/></TD>
<!--use the @ symbol to pull values of attributes -->

              <TD><xsl:value-of select="FOOD_RATING"/></TD>
              <TD><xsl:value-of select="AMBIANCE_RATING"/></TD>
              <TD><xsl:value-of select="AVERAGE_MEAL_COST"/></TD>
              <TD><xsl:value-of select="REVIEW"/></TD>
            </TR>
        </xsl:for-each>
<!-- close for-each loop -->

        </TABLE>
      </BODY>
    </HTML>
  </xsl:template>
<!-- close template tag -->

</xsl:stylesheet>
<!-- close stylesheet tag-->
```

Figure 12.1 shows what the XML document looks like when rendered in Internet Explorer 5.

We've added comments in our stylesheet to let you know what's going on. Let's talk a bit about what we've just done:

- We associated the XSL stylesheet with the XML source document.

- In the stylesheet, we used an xsl:template tag to declare what the stylesheet portion was supposed to do. We further specified that the template would work off of the root element (/) of the XML document by tweaking the match attribute's value.

- We created an HTML template by inserting standard HTML tags and based it on a tabular format. We could just as easily have used other HTML tags to create a more visually appealing format.

- We used the xsl:for-each tag to set up a for loop that iterates an action each time an event occurs. The event is specified by occurrences of the value of the select attribute.

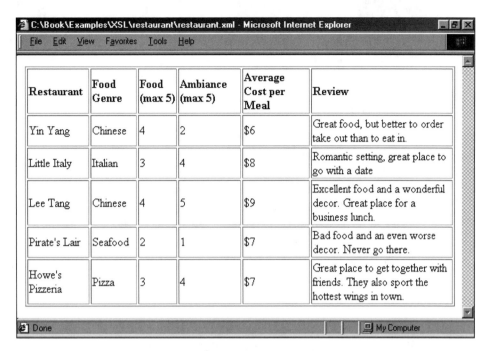

Figure 12.1   The Restaurant XML file after being transformed by the XSL stylesheet.

- During each iteration, we used the xsl:value-of tag to insert the value of a node of the source tree into the HTML document. The location of the node is specified in the value of the select attribute.

- Within the select attribute, a *pattern* is defined for locating a node. We look at patterns in more detail in the next chapter.

Also important to note is how we explicitly restructured the source XML tree. In the original XML document, the FOOD_GENRE attribute comes before the NAME of the restaurant. In our example, we arbitrarily chose to put the NAME before the GENRE. In addition, should we have chosen to, we could have left out any information by not specifying it. (To see how this works, erase a line or two containing the xsl:value-of tag and see what is displayed.)

Also, the output of the stylesheet—the well formed HTML—is sent to the browser directly without the creation of an intermediate HTML file. If you were executing XSL on the server side, you'd want the output written to a file which, in turn, gets sent to the client (see Chapter 15 for details).

If you spend a little time playing with the above example and using the XSL tags we've used, you'll soon realize that churning XML data into HTML is pretty easy.

A Note on Outputting Well Formed HTML

This is important. The output of our XSL stylesheet is, in all cases, an XML document. In this case, the tag names that we chose to write in our template defined our output to be HTML. It could just as easily have been an arbitrary set of tag names, in which case the document would not have been rendered as an HTML document by the output file. Whenever you output your XML as HTML, the HTML *must* be well formed. For a detailed description of what we mean by *well formed*, skim through Chapter 3. Briefly, though, this means:

- Closing all open tags
- Using same the case for opening and closing tags
- Putting attribute values in quotes
- Nesting all tags under a single root HTML element

In addition, if you are going to use any scripting (JScript or JavaScript) in your HTML, make sure that you insert it within a <SCRIPT> element as you normally would encase it in a CDATA section (see Chapter 3) to avoid any parsing errors.

A Note on Scalability

Just for fun, try increasing the size of the XML source document by adding in extra restaurant elements. (Don't worry about content, just try copying and pasting.) Note how the same stylesheet can be used irrespective of how many data elements you have. Now imagine the code for the same page in HTML and make some rough comparisons in your head. You will probably agree that sending the same formatted HTML file would take far longer than sending the raw data accompanied with the stylesheet. To prove it, here's the HTML file that would generate the same output as the above XML+XSL stylesheet.

```
<HTML>
  <BODY>
    <TABLE BORDER="1">
```

```
<!--Set up header row -->
    <TR>
      <TD><b>Restaurant</b></TD>
      <TD><b>Food Genre</b></TD>
      <TD><b>Food (max 5)</b></TD>
      <TD><b>Ambiance (max 5)</b></TD>
      <TD><b>Average Cost per Meal</b></TD>
      <TD><b>Review</b></TD>
    </TR>
    <TR>
      <TD>Yin Yang</TD>
      <TD>Chinese</TD>
      <TD>4</TD>
      <TD>2</TD>
      <TD>$6</TD>
      <TD>Great food, but better to order take out than to eat
          in.</TD>
    </TR>
    <TR>
      <TD>Little Italy</TD>
      <TD>Italian</TD>
      <TD>3</TD>
      <TD>4</TD>
      <TD>$8</TD>
      <TD>Romantic setting, great place to go with a date.</TD>
    </TR>
    <TR>
      <TD>Lee Tang</TD>
      <TD>Chinese</TD>
      <TD>4</TD>
      <TD>5</TD>
      <TD>$9</TD>
      <TD>Excellent food and a wonderful decor. Great place for
          a business lunch.</TD>
    </TR>
    <TR>
      <TD>Pirate's Lair</TD>
      <TD>Seafood</TD>
      <TD>2</TD>
      <TD>1</TD>
      <TD>$7</TD>
      <TD>Bad food and an even worse decor. Never go there.</TD>
    </TR>
    <TR>
      <TD>Howe's Pizzeria</TD>
      <TD>Pizza</TD>
      <TD>3</TD>
      <TD>4</TD>
      <TD>$7</TD>
      <TD>Great place to get together with friends. They also
          sport the hottest wings in town.</TD>
```

```
        </TR>
      </TABLE>
    </BODY>
  </HTML>
```

Granted, this doesn't look very big. Now imagine the same HTML code to represent 30 restaurants. Then imagine it for a hundred. Then imagine the same with more complicated formatting (more parameter descriptions). Then think about the file size. The XSL file size would stay the same. Gets you thinking, doesn't it?

Sorting with XSL

Suppose that now, instead of just outputting the XML into HTML verbatim, our objective is to list our restaurants in descending order of their FOOD_RATING. In the case of a tie, the next order of sorting would be descending order of AMBIANCE_RATING. By listing it this way, we're looking for the restaurant with the best quality of food and the best ambiance.

We still work with only two files. On the companion CD-ROM, you will find the examples listed as srt_restaurant.xml and srt_restaurant.xsl. The XML source document (srt_restaurant.xml) is almost exactly the same as the restaurant.xml. The only difference is that the new file's first two lines look like this:

```
<?xml version = "1.0" ?>
<?xml-stylesheet type="text/xsl" href="srt_restaurant.xsl"?>
```

We've done this to link the source XML file with the right XSL stylesheet.

Here's what the stylesheet (srt_restaurant.xsl) looks like:

```
<?xml version='1.0'?>
<!--XML Declaration -->

<xsl:stylesheet xmlns:xsl="http://www.w3.org/TR/WD-xsl">
<!--declaration that the document is a stylesheet and that it
    is associated with the xsl: namespace -->

  <xsl:template match="/">
<!--Apply template to everything starting from the root node-->
```

```
<HTML>
   <BODY>
     <TABLE BORDER="1">
<!--Set up header row -->
        <TR>
          <TD><b>Restaurant</b></TD>
          <TD><b>Food Genre</b></TD>
          <TD><b>Food (max 5)</b></TD>
          <TD><b>Ambiance (max 5)</b></TD>
          <TD><b>Average Cost per Meal</b></TD>
          <TD><b>Review</b></TD>
        </TR>

        <xsl:for-each select="RESTAURANTS/RESTAURANT"
                     order-by="-FOOD_RATING; -AMBIANCE_RATING">
<!--set up a loop that iterates for every match of the pattern
    defined in the "select" attribute. These instances are then
    sorted in ascending order (minus sign) of FOOD_RATING. Second
    order sorting is done on the basis of the AMBIANCE Rating-->

        <TR>
          <TD><xsl:value-of select="NAME"/></TD>
<!--"value-of" pulls the value of the contents specified in the
    "select" attribute -->

          <TD><xsl:value-of select="@FOOD_GENRE"/></TD>
<!--use the @ symbol to pull values of attributes -->

          <TD><xsl:value-of select="FOOD_RATING"/></TD>
          <TD><xsl:value-of select="AMBIANCE_RATING"/></TD>
          <TD><xsl:value-of select="AVERAGE_MEAL_COST"/></TD>
          <TD><xsl:value-of select="REVIEW"/></TD>
        </TR>
      </xsl:for-each>
<!-- close for-each loop -->

     </TABLE>
   </BODY>
  </HTML>

 </xsl:template>
<!-- close template tag -->

</xsl:stylesheet>
<!-- close stylesheet tag-->
```

Figure 12.2 shows the result of the above stylesheet in Internet Explorer 5.

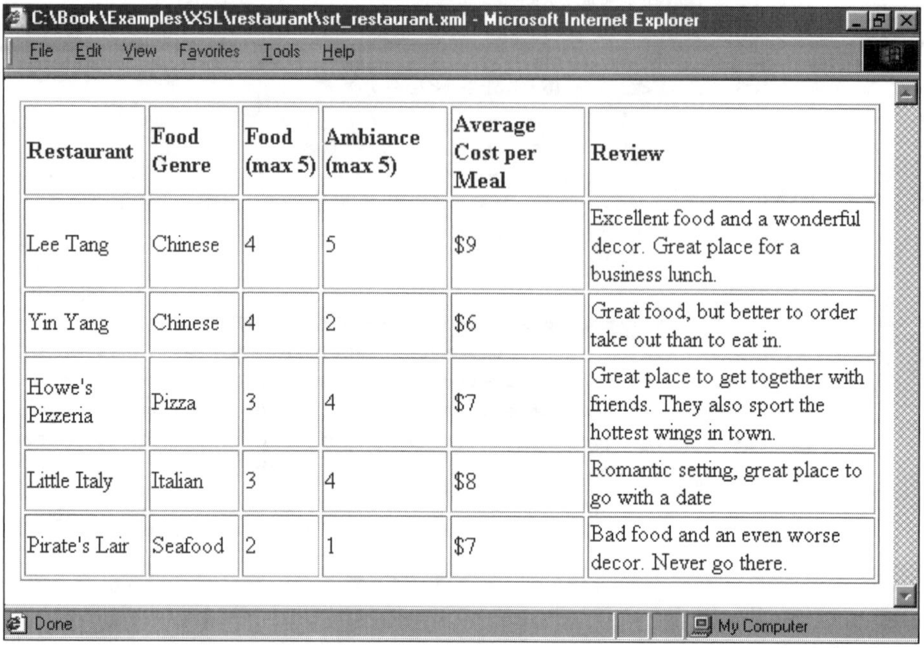

Restaurant	Food Genre	Food (max 5)	Ambiance (max 5)	Average Cost per Meal	Review
Lee Tang	Chinese	4	5	$9	Excellent food and a wonderful decor. Great place for a business lunch.
Yin Yang	Chinese	4	2	$6	Great food, but better to order take out than to eat in.
Howe's Pizzeria	Pizza	3	4	$7	Great place to get together with friends. They also sport the hottest wings in town.
Little Italy	Italian	3	4	$8	Romantic setting, great place to go with a date
Pirate's Lair	Seafood	2	1	$7	Bad food and an even worse decor. Never go there.

Figure 12.2 Restaurant example with sorting.

Though virtually everything is the same in this example, the important thing to note is the usage of the xsl:order-by attribute. You probably can imagine using the xsl:order-by attribute for virtually all your template driven stylesheets. It is important to note that the xsl:order-by attribute is an older attribute name that has been rendered obsolete by the current W3C working draft. The W3C working draft suggests using an xsl:sort element, which seems more intuitive. Microsoft has said that they plan to adopt the new syntax in future releases. However, because of the obvious use of this feature, we would suggest that you not hold your breath waiting. If, by the time you get to writing code, Internet Explorer 5 has a postrelease update, use the xsl:sort tag.

A few notes about the sorting that is going on:

- Because the current data types that can be specified by DTDs is limited to character data only, all sorting is done on the basis of *string values* and not numerical values. So for instance, "01" has a different value than "1". Once an official method of datatyping is recommended (for example, schemas) numerical comparisons should happen automatically or be made on the basis of additional attribute syntax.

- The order of sorting (ascending or descending) is specified by pre-fixing the sorting node (element or attribute) with a polarity sign—a plus sign (+) means order by ascending and a negative sign (-) means order by descending value. The plus sign is optional, as it is the default value.

Conditional XSL Stylesheets

You knew this was coming. For XSL to be really useful, you would expect to have the ability to perform conditional transformations based on the occurrence of certain characteristics, for example, the value of an element or attribute. XSL delivers. Let's illustrate how to create conditional stylesheets.

For this example, let's assume our mission is to represent the genre of each restaurant with a picture instead of boring text. Certainly, we could hard code it in, but it is much more flexible if we let XSL perform some conditional formatting for us.

For this example, the filenames on the companion CD-ROM are cnd_restaurant.xml and cnd_restaurant.xsl. The XML file again is exactly the same except for the association of the stylesheet. That is, our first two lines look like this:

```
<?xml version = "1.0" ?>
<?xml-stylesheet type="text/xsl" href="cnd_restaurant.xsl"?>
```

Everything else remains the same in the XML document.

Our XSL Stylesheet looks like this:

```
<?xml version='1.0'?>
<!--XML Declaration -->

<xsl:stylesheet xmlns:xsl="http://www.w3.org/TR/WD-xsl">
<!--declaration that the document is a stylesheet and that it
    is associated with the xsl: namespace -->

  <xsl:template match="/">
<!--Apply template to everything starting from the root node-->

    <HTML>
```

```
        <BODY>
          <TABLE BORDER="1">
<!--Set up header row -->
            <TR>
              <TD><b>Restaurant</b></TD>
              <TD><b>Food Genre</b></TD>
              <TD><b>Food (max 5)</b></TD>
              <TD><b>Ambiance (max 5)</b></TD>
              <TD><b>Average Cost per Meal</b></TD>
              <TD><b>Review</b></TD>
            </TR>

            <xsl:for-each select="RESTAURANTS/RESTAURANT"
                    order-by="AVERAGE_MEAL_COST">
<!--set up a "for loop" and order the results in ascending order
    of the average meal's cost-->

            <TR>
              <TD><xsl:value-of select="NAME"/></TD>
<!--"value-of" pulls the value of the contents specified in the
    "select" attribute -->

            <TD>
              <xsl:if test="@FOOD_GENRE[.='Chinese']">
                  <IMG SRC="china_flag.jpg" BORDER ="1"/>
              </xsl:if>
<!--conditional insertion of image based on the value of the
    FOOD_GENRE attribute-->

              <xsl:if test="@FOOD_GENRE[.='Italian']">
                  <IMG SRC="italy_flag.jpg" BORDER ="1"/>
              </xsl:if>
<!--conditional insertion of image based on the value of the
    FOOD_GENRE attribute-->

              <xsl:if test="@FOOD_GENRE[.='Pizza']">
                  <IMG SRC="pizza.jpg" BORDER ="1"/>
              </xsl:if>
<!--conditional insertion of image based on the value of the
    FOOD_GENRE attribute-->

              <xsl:if test="@FOOD_GENRE[.='Seafood']">
                  <IMG SRC="seafood.jpg" BORDER ="1"/>
              </xsl:if>
<!--conditional insertion of image based on the value of the
    FOOD_GENRE attribute-->

              <xsl:if test="@FOOD_GENRE[.!='Pizza' and ...!='Chinese'
                          and .!='Italian' and ...!='Seafood']">
                <B>N/A</B>
              </xsl:if>
```

```
<!--here we've explicitly defined what the other tests do NOT test
    for and put in directions on what to do when none of the previous
    conditions are met -->

              </TD>
<!--use the @ symbol to pull values of attributes -->

              <TD><xsl:value-of select="FOOD_RATING"/></TD>
              <TD><xsl:value-of select="AMBIANCE_RATING"/></TD>
              <TD><xsl:value-of select="AVERAGE_MEAL_COST"/></TD>
              <TD><xsl:value-of select="REVIEW"/></TD>
            </TR>
          </xsl:for-each>
<!-- close for-each loop -->

        </TABLE>
      </BODY>
    </HTML>
  </xsl:template>
<!-- close template tag -->

</xsl:stylesheet>
<!-- close stylesheet tag-->
```

Figure 12.3 shows our XSL document rendered in Internet Explorer 5.

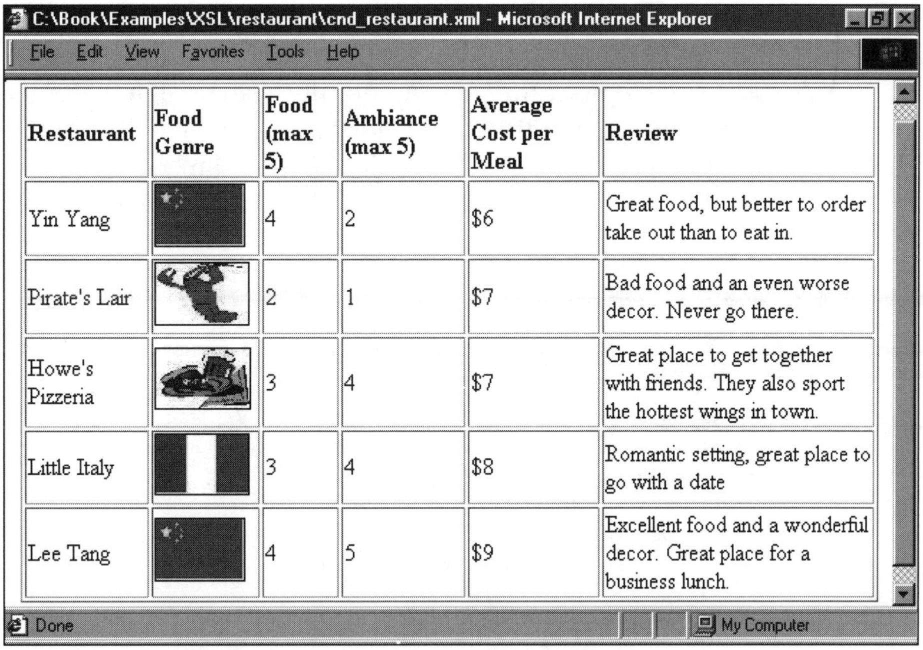

Restaurant	Food Genre	Food (max 5)	Ambiance (max 5)	Average Cost per Meal	Review
Yin Yang		4	2	$6	Great food, but better to order take out than to eat in.
Pirate's Lair		2	1	$7	Bad food and an even worse decor. Never go there.
Howe's Pizzeria		3	4	$7	Great place to get together with friends. They also sport the hottest wings in town.
Little Italy		3	4	$8	Romantic setting, great place to go with a date
Lee Tang		4	5	$9	Excellent food and a wonderful decor. Great place for a business lunch.

Figure 12.3 Results of applying a conditional stylesheet.

Let's talk about the important things we've done in this example:

- We used the order-by attribute to sort the restaurants in ascending order of the average cost of a meal.

- We used the xsl:if element to introduce conditional statements. The actual test against which the condition is checked is specified using the test attribute.

- We performed several checks (multiple xsl:if case statements) during each xsl:for loop iteration based on the values of a particular attribute.

- In this example, we knew exactly which conditions existed and had a case statement for each. However, if there were a case not handled (that is, a FOOD_GENRE attribute value such as Cajun) we would end up not inserting anything, as there is no default (else) case representation. We got around this limitation in a very crude way by inserting a case statement that essentially reiterated all previous cases and said if none of the previous tests are met, insert text saying N/A.

Another way of performing conditional statements is to use the xsl:choose element, which relies on a series of xsl:when elements used to define conditioning tests. The xsl:choose element also has an xsl:otherwise element that acts a default (else) switch statement when previous xsl:when conditions are not satisfied. If we wanted to use this syntax, our above stylesheet would be the same, except we would replace the contents between the <TD> element for FOOD_GENRE with:

```
<xsl:choose>
<!--begin xsl:choose conditions-->

    <xsl:when test="@FOOD_GENRE[.='Chinese']">
        <IMG SRC="china_flag.jpg" BORDER ="1"/>
    </xsl:when>
<!--each xsl:when case statement has the same "test" attribute
    and syntax as the xsl:if-->

    <xsl:when test="@FOOD_GENRE[.='Italian']">
        <IMG SRC="italy_flag.jpg" BORDER ="1"/>
    </xsl:when>

    <xsl:when test="@FOOD_GENRE[.='Pizza']">
```

```
        <IMG SRC="pizza.jpg" BORDER ="1"/>
    </xsl:when>

    <xsl:when test="@FOOD_GENRE[.='Seafood']">
        <IMG SRC="seafood.jpg" BORDER ="1"/>
    </xsl:when>

    <xsl:otherwise>
        <B>N/A</B>
    </xsl:otherwise>
<!--if none of the cases are met, perform this function -->

</xsl:choose>
<!--close xsl:choose conditions-->
```

The output of this stylesheet is exactly the same as the output in Figure 12.3.

Applying XSL to Irregular Data—The Data-Driven Model

Our above examples all worked well because our data was very simple and regular in its structure and we could treat it with a single template with ease. However, when our data is irregular or consists of different sections of repeating data, as in the following case, a little more involved approach is required.

For kicks, we decided to make a data set containing our author biographies. (Granted we're regular guys, but even our data can be irregular—besides, let it never be said that this book was written by faceless authors.) The names of the file on the companion CD-ROM are author.xml and author.xsl. The data file looks like this:

```
<?xml version = "1.0" ?>
<?xml-stylesheet type="text/xsl" href="authors.xsl"?>
<ABOUT_AUTHORS>
   <HEADING>
      <BOOK_TITLE>Applied XML</BOOK_TITLE>
      <ABOUT_CAPTION>The Authors</ABOUT_CAPTION>
   </HEADING>
   <AUTHOR>
      <NAME>Alex Ceponkus</NAME>
      <PICTURE>alex.jpg</PICTURE>
      <BIO>
         <SCHOOL_NAME>The University of Toronto</SCHOOL_NAME>
         <WEB_SITE>http://www.utoronto.ca/uoft.html</WEB_SITE>
```

```
            <DEPARTMENT>Division of Engineering Science</DEPARTMENT>
            <SPECIALIZATION>Computer Engineering</SPECIALIZATION>
            <OTHER_INTERESTS>In his spare time, Alex enjoys playing
                            basketball, and dreaming of &quot;what
                            comes next.&quot;
            </OTHER_INTERESTS>
         </BIO>
      </AUTHOR>
      <AUTHOR>
         <NAME>Faraz Hoodbhoy</NAME>
         <PICTURE>faraz.jpg</PICTURE>
         <BIO>
            <SCHOOL_NAME>Rensselaer Polytechnic Institute</SCHOOL_NAME>
            <WEB_SITE>http://www.rpi.edu/index.html</WEB_SITE>
            <DEPARTMENT>Department of Decision Sciences and Engineering
                       Systems</DEPARTMENT>
            <SPECIALIZATION/>
            <OTHER_INTERESTS>Faraz enjoys playing squash, cricket, and
                            trying to take over the world.
            </OTHER_INTERESTS>
         </BIO>
      </AUTHOR>
      <CLOSING>Applied XML -- The definitive toolkit for programming with
               XML
      </CLOSING>
   </ABOUT_AUTHORS>
```

As you can tell, this data set is fairly irregular. Sure, we could treat the entire document as a one-time replication and apply a single template to it, but that would entail a less object-oriented approach, which is bad for many reasons (scalability, ease of debugging, readability, to name a few). A better stylesheet would enable us to treat sections of our document with different templates.

The stylesheet we created for displaying this information looks like this:

```
<?xml version="1.0"?>
<xsl:stylesheet xmlns:xsl="http://www.w3.org/TR/WD-xsl">
  <xsl:template match="/">
<!--this template is applied to the root element-->
    <HTML>
      <HEAD>
        <TITLE>
           <xsl:value-of select="ABOUT_AUTHORS/HEADING/BOOK_TITLE"/>
        </TITLE>
      </HEAD>
      <BODY>
        <xsl:apply-templates select="ABOUT_AUTHORS"/>
```

```
<!--insert the results of another template identified by the value of
    the "select" attribute-->

    </BODY>
    <xsl:apply-templates select="ABOUT_AUTHORS/CLOSING"/>
<!--insert the results of another template identified by the value of
    the "select" attribute-->

    </HTML>
  </xsl:template>
<!--closes out main template-->

  <xsl:template match="ABOUT_AUTHORS">
<!--This template creates a table and begins populating it -->

    <TABLE BORDER="1">
      <CAPTION ALIGN="top">
        <FONT SIZE="6">
          <xsl:value-of select="./HEADING/BOOK_TITLE"/>
          -
          <xsl:value-of select="./HEADING/ABOUT_CAPTION"/>
        </FONT>
      </CAPTION>
      <xsl:apply-templates select="AUTHOR"/>
<!--this is a call to another template that is used to populate
    the table -->

    </TABLE>
  </xsl:template>
<!-- close the template that creates the table -->

  <xsl:template match="ABOUT_AUTHORS/AUTHOR">
<!--this template is responsible for further formatting and population
    of the table-->
    <TR>
      <TD COLSPAN="3">
        <FONT SIZE="5">
          <xsl:value-of select="./NAME"/>
        </FONT>
      </TD>
    </TR>
    <TR>
      <TD>
        <IMG><xsl:attribute name="SRC">
<!-- new tag! the xsl:attribute tag appends an attribute to
    whatever element it is embedded in. the "name" attribute is used
    to name it. The value of the new element is filled in the
    same way an element's value is entered -->

          <xsl:value-of select="./PICTURE"/>
```

```
                    </xsl:attribute>
                </IMG>
            </TD>
            <TD VALIGN="top">
                <xsl:apply-templates select="BIO"/>
<!-- this TD element is a little complex, so to keep things simple,
     we are handling it in another template -->


            </TD>
        </TR>
    </xsl:template>
<!-- once this template has run its course, our table is completely
     populated -->


    <xsl:template match="ABOUT_AUTHORS/AUTHOR/BIO">
<!--this template populates the contents of our last TD element in our
    table-->


                <xsl:value-of select="../NAME"/>
<!--the value of the "NAME" element is not in the current scope of
    this template. The "../" in the select attribute value allows
    us to use elements that are not in the scope of the template -->

            is a student at

            <A><xsl:attribute name="HREF">
                <xsl:value-of select="./WEB_SITE"/>
              </xsl:attribute>
            <xsl:value-of select="./SCHOOL_NAME"/>
            </A>

            in the
            <xsl:value-of select="./DEPARTMENT"/>


        <xsl:choose>
<!-- since we cannot predict whether an "author" element will have
     a "SPECIALIZATION" tag in it or not, we deal with it
     conditionally, in this case using an "xsl:choose" element -->

                <xsl:when test="./SPECIALIZATION[. !='']">
                  specializing in
                    <xsl:value-of select="./SPECIALIZATION"/>
                 .
                </xsl:when>
                <xsl:otherwise>.</xsl:otherwise>
            </xsl:choose>

        <P><I>
            <xsl:value-of select="./OTHER_INTERESTS"/>
        </I></P>
    </xsl:template>
```

```
<!-- close the template that populates the author biography
     cell-->

  <xsl:template match ="ABOUT_AUTHORS/CLOSING">
<!--this template writes the last line of the page-->

    <P ALIGN="center"><B><I><xsl:value-of select ="."/></I></B></P>
  </xsl:template>
</xsl:stylesheet>
```

To synch with our previous examples, Figure 12.4 shows our rendered XML document.

Admittedly, this example is a little more interesting. Let's talk about what is going on:

Figure 12.4 Applying XSL to irregular data.

- Most visibly, this stylesheet uses several templates to get the job done. We chose to create several templates to break up styling into manageable chunks.

- When declaring and defining each template, we entered a pattern in the match attribute to define its scope (area where it is valid). See Chapter 13 for more details on defining patterns in XSL.

- Just as you can call functions within functions in programming languages, XSL lets you use templates within templates using the xsl:apply-templates element. To specify which template to use, you need to refer to it by specifying its scope in the select attribute.

- We used the xsl-attributes element to append an attribute to an element. The name attribute lets us specify the name of the attribute, which in this case we knew to be SRC. The value of the attribute is entered by giving the xsl:attributes element a value that, in this case, we pulled from the data. This is the only way to enter in data-dependent attribute values into an HTML template.

- In the ABOUT_AUTHORS/AUTHOR/BIO template, we performed a combination of several of our previous examples: some conditional formatting using the xsl:choose element, some attribute insertions using the xsl:attribute element, and some simple data spewing using the xsl:value-of element.

- We were able to refer to elements that were not in the initial scoping of the template by varying the pattern in the select attribute of the xsl:value-of element. See Chapter 13 for more details on pattern matching.

XSL Syntax Reference

Now that we've introduced a rough idea of how to create and play with XSL stylesheets, let's go over some of the available syntax and it's usage. This section is intended to read like a reference section, so you may want to just skim over it and familiarize yourself with some of the available XSL elements and attributes and their usage. Also, it's useful to keep by your side while looking for a particular function.

All XSL syntax is expressed as XML and comes under the xsl: namespace, therefore, each XSL element is preceded with the xsl: namespace prefix. The attributes inherit the namespace prefix of the element and don't need to be preceded by the xsl: namespace prefix. The namespace is invoked in the stylesheet's declaration. See Chapter 3 for more discussion on namespace conventions.

For each XSL element and method described below, we've given a brief description of what the XSL processor interprets it as and listed the attributes that apply to each. Most elements have already been exemplified in the preceding code examples. In the following discussion, symbols in italics are not actual syntax values but are placeholders that are described later in the text.

XSL Elements

XSL defines a limited set of XML elements under the XSL namespace which XSL processors interpret as functions. Table 12.1 lists these XSL elements and briefly describes their purposes.

xsl:stylesheet

This section introduces the xsl:stylesheet element's syntax and describes its usage.

Syntax

```
<xsl:stylesheet default-space = "preseve"
                indent-result = "yes"
                language = "scripting-language"
                result-ns = "output namespace" >
```

Also, the XML namespace attribute is included in this element to establish a link with the XSL schema/DTD:

```
<xsl:stylesheet xmlns:xsl="http://www.w3.org/TR/WD-xsl">
```

Description

The xsl:stylesheet element is used once for every XSL stylesheet and is the root node of every stylesheet. It informs the XSL processor that the document is an XSL stylesheet and houses all templates.

Table 12.1 XSL Element Names

XSL ELEMENT	DESCRIPTION
xsl:stylesheet	Used as the root node of a spreadsheet and houses the set of templates that is applied to the XML source tree to generate the output tree.
xsl:template	Used to define a series of transformations or formatting procedures that are to be applied to a particular pattern.
xsl:apply-templates	Used to invoke previously declared templates. Templates are identified by the nearest value of their match attribute.
xsl:comment	Inserts a comment in the output XML.
xsl:pi	Inserts a processing instruction in the output.
xsl:element	Inserts an XML element with a specified name in the output.
xsl:attribute	Creates an attribute with a particular name and appends that element and its value to its parent output element.
xsl:value-of	Inserts the string value of a specified node.
xsl:for-each	Creates a for loop through which the same template can be applied to several target nodes. Target nodes are specified by a pattern.
xsl:if	Provides a way of performing simple if/then conditional functions.
xsl:choose	Provides a way of providing multiple conditional testing using xsl:when and xsl:otherwise.
xsl:when	Similar to an xsl:if but is a child of the xsl:choose element.
xsl:otherwise	A default case action in case previous xsl:when conditions are not met.
xsl:copy	Copies its contents values to the output.

Parent Elements

It has no parent elements as it is the root node of the XSL stylesheet.

Child Elements

```
xsl:script, xsl:template, xsl:include, xsl:import
```

Attributes

default-space. This attribute tells the processor whether to preserve white space. It is optionally specified (the default is to ignore white space) and takes on the value of preserve and strip, which do exactly what they mean with white space. Internet Explorer 5 supports only the default value and ignores this attribute.

indent-result. This attribute tells the processor whether to add in extra white space while formatting the output XML document for pretty printing purposes. It has no data value per se. It takes on the values of yes and no. Internet Explorer 5 only supports the yes value, which is also the default.

language. This attribute specifies the scripting language to be used (if any).

result-ns. This attribute specifies the default namespace prefix of the output elements. Internet Explorer 5 does not support this feature (though it should!).

xsl:template

This section introduces the xsl:template element's syntax and describes its usage.

Syntax

```
<xsl:template language="language-name"
              match="context" >
```

Description

The xsl:template element is used to create a template in which formatting and transforming actions are specified. Every stylesheet contains at least one and possibly many templates (no limit is defined). A template does not need to generate a complete XML document nor even elements under a single (root) node.

Parent Elements

```
xsl:stylsheets, xsl:apply-templates
```

Child Elements

```
xsl:apply-templates, xsl:value-of, xsl:element, xsl:attribute,
xsl:comment, xsl:pi, xsl:choose, xsl:for-each, xsl:if, xsl:copy
```

Also, all output XML (for example, well formed HTML) are allowable children of the xsl:template element.

Attributes

language. This attribute is used to specify the scripting language that will be used. The default is ECMA (JavaScript/Jscript—see Chapter 11 for more details on ECMA). It is an optionally included tag.

Match. This attribute defines the node-context of the template, that is, where the template should be applied in the document. In a sense, this defines the scope of the template. It is *strongly* recommended to include a value for this attribute as the default value, "node() | / | @*" specifies a match to *all* nodes, not just the root. See Chapter 13 for more details on pattern matching.

xsl:apply-templates

This section introduces the xsl:apply-templates element's syntax and describes its usage.

Syntax

```
<xsl:apply-templates select = "context"
                     order-by = "sorting criteria">
```

Description

The xsl:apply-templates element invokes the application of other xsl:template elements. The particular xsl:template to be applied is defined by the value of the select attribute. The xsl:apply-templates process is recursively applied on children of the source element. There is no limit on how many times you can use it in your stylesheet.

Parent Elements

```
xsl:template, xsl:element, xsl:attribute, xsl:comment, xsl:pi,
xsl:copy, xsl:for-each, xsl:if, xsl:otherwise, xsl:when
```

Also, output elements (for example, well formed HTML) can be parent elements of the xsl:apply-templates element.

Child Elements

```
xsl:template
```

Attributes

select. This attribute is used to specify which xsl:template to use. It looks for the xsl:template whose match value is closest to its select attribute's value. The context defined matches all node types except attributes. The default value is "node()", that is, the current node inherited from its parent.

order-by. This attribute is used to specify the sorting order of the results of running the specified template. The sort criterion is defined by XSL patterns (see Chapter 13 for detailed description of XSL patterns). To further specify secondary and tertiary sorting criteria in case of equal first-criteria results (for example, order two authors of the same last name, Smith and Smith, by their first name), use XSL patterns separated by semicolons. Ascending order is specified by a "+" and descending by a "-" sign. The default is ascending.

NOTE The order-by attribute is obsolete and belongs to a previous W3C working draft. The new draft calls for the use of an xsl:sort element. However, as it is implemented in Internet Explorer 5's release version, the order-by attribute is what works.

xsl:comment

This section introduces the xsl:comment element's syntax and describes its usage.

Syntax

```
<xsl:comment>
```

Description

The xsl:comment element is used for outputting a comment. It can be used any number of times. As expected, the output is delimited between the open comment syntax, '<!--" and close comment syntax "-->".

Parent Elements

```
xsl:template, xsl:copy, xsl:element, xsl:for-each, xsl:if,
xsl:when, xsl:otherwise
```

The xsl:comment element can also be a child of any XML output (for example, well formed HTML).

Child Elements

```
xsl:apply-templates, xsl:value-of, xsl:choose, xsl:copy,
xsl:for-each, xsl:if
```

Attributes

None.

xsl:pi

This section introduces the xsl:pi element's syntax and describes its usage.

Syntax

```
<xsl:pi name="processing_instruction_name">
```

Description

The xsl:pi element outputs a processing instruction in the output XML. The output, as expected is delimited between "<?" and "?>". It can occur any number of times.

Parent Elements

```
xsl:template, xsl:copy, xsl:element, xsl:for-each, xsl:if,
xsl:otherwise, xsl:when
```

The xsl:pi element can also be a child of any XML output (for example, well formed HTML).

Child Elements

```
xsl:apply-templates, xsl:choose, xsl:copy, xsl:for-each,
xsl:if, xsl:value-of
```

Attribute

name. This attribute gives the name of the PI.

xsl:element

This section introduces the xsl:element element's syntax and describes its usage.

Syntax

```
<xsl:element name="element-name">
```

Description

The xsl:element creates an element in the output XML with the name specified in the attribute. It can be used any number of times.

Parent Elements

```
xsl:template, xsl:copy, xsl:element, xsl:for-each,
xsl:if, xsl:otherwise, xsl:when
```

The xsl:element element can also be a child of any XML output (for example, well formed HTML).

Child Elements

```
xsl:apply-templates, xsl:element, xsl:attribute, xsl:comment, xsl:pi,
xsl:choose, xsl:when, xsl:copy, xsl:for-each, xsl:if, xsl:value-of
```

Also, all xsl:element elements can be parents of all other XML output (for example, well formed HTML).

Attributes

name. This attribute assigns the name of the element to be output.

xsl:attribute

This section introduces the xsl:attribute element's syntax and describes its usage.

Syntax

```
<xsl:attribute name="attribute-name">
```

Description

The xsl:attribute element creates a named attribute and appends it to the element in which it is embedded (for example, outputting an SRC attribute in a <IMG> element). The value of the xsl:attribute element becomes the value of the output attribute. It can be used any number of times.

Parent Elements

```
xsl:template, xsl:element, xsl:for-each, xsl:if, xsl:when,
xsl:otherwise, xsl:copy
```

Also, the xsl:attribute element can be a child of any output XML elements (for example, well formed HTML).

Child Elements

```
xsl:apply-templates, xsl:value-of, xsl:copy, xsl:choose,
xsl:for-each, xsl:if,
```

Attribute

name. This attribute assigns the name of the attribute to be output.

xsl:value-of

This section introduces the xsl:value-of element's syntax and describes its usage.

Syntax

```
<xsl:value-of select="XSL pattern">
```

Description

The xsl:value-of attribute is used to insert the string/text value of the node indicated by the pattern. It can be used any number of times.

Parent Elements

```
xsl:element, xsl:attribute, xsl:comment, xsl:pi, xsl:for-each,
xsl:if, xsl:when, xsl:otherwise, xsl:template, xsl:copy
```

The xsl:value-of element can also be a child of any XML output (for example, putting the value of an XML node into an HTML element). It can occur any number of times.

Child Elements

The xsl:value-of element has no children.

Attribute

select. This attribute defines the XSL pattern whose value is to be entered in the current context. The default value is "."—the value of the current node. XSL pattern syntax is discussed in the next chapter.

xsl:for-each

This section introduces the xsl:for-each element's syntax and describes its usage.

Syntax

```
<xsl:for-each select="XSL pattern"
              order-by="sorting_criteria">
```

Description

The xsl:for-each element sets up a "for loop" in which the same template is applied against multiple nodes. It can be used any number of times.

Parent Elements

```
xsl:template,xsl:element, xsl:attribute, xsl:comment, xsl:pi,
xsl:copy, xsl:for-each, xsl:if, xsl:when, xsl:otherwise,
```

The xsl:for-each element can also be a child of any XML output (for example, applying an XSL template within in an HTML element).

Child Elements

```
xsl:apply-templates, xsl:element, xsl:attribute, xsl:comment, xsl:pi,
xsl:copy, xsl:choose, xsl:for-each, xsl:if, xsl:value-of
```

The xsl:for-each element can also be a parent of all other XML output (for example, well formed HTML).

Attributes

select. This attribute specifies the XSL pattern value that is to be run through the current template. The default value is ".", which is the current node inherited from its parent.

order-by. This attribute is used to specify the sorting order of the results of running the specified template. The sort criterion is defined by XSL patterns (see Chapter 13 for detailed description of XSL patterns). To further specify secondary and tertiary sorting criteria in case of equal first-criteria results (for example, order two authors of the same last name, Smith and Smith, by their first name), use XSL patterns separated by semicolons. Ascending order is specified by a "+" and descending by a "-" sign. The default is ascending.

NOTE

The order-by attribute is obsolete and belongs to a previous W3C working draft. The new recommendation calls for the use of an xsl:sort element. However, as it is implemented in Internet Explorer 5's release version, the order-by attribute is what works.

xsl:if

This section introduces the xsl:if element's syntax and describes its usage.

Syntax

```
<xsl:if test="condition">
```

Description

The xsl:if element allows the simple conditional application of a template. It can be used any number of times in a stylesheet.

Parent Elements

```
xsl:attribute, xsl:comment, xsl:copy, xsl:element, xsl:for-each,
xsl:if, xsl:otherwise, xsl:pi, xsl:template, xsl:when, output elements
```

The xsl:if element can also be a child of any XML output (for example, putting the value of an XML node into an HTML element).

Child Elements

```
xsl:apply-templates, xsl:element, xsl:attribute, xsl:comment, xsl:pi,
xsl:copy, xsl:for-each, xsl:if, xsl:choose, xsl:value-of
```

The xsl:if element can also be the parent of output XML (for example, well formed HTML).

Attributes

test. This attribute sets the condition for the source data to meet in order for the action (contents of the xsl:if element) to be met. We talk about the syntax of the test attribute in greater detail in Chapter 13. Generally it involves comparing (performing a logical/Boolean operation) an XSL pattern against a value. When only a pattern is entered, the default check is to perform a logical TRUE/FALSE test, that is, if the pattern exists, then the contents of the xsl:if element are executed.

xsl:choose

This section introduces the xsl:choose element's syntax and describes its usage.

Syntax

```
<xsl:choose>
```

Description

The xsl:choose element provides a way of performing multiple conditional testing by using the xsl:when and xsl:otherwise elements. It can occur any number of times in a stylesheet.

Parent Elements

```
xsl:template, xsl:element, xsl:attribute, xsl:comment, xsl:pi, xsl:copy,
xsl:for-each, xsl:if, xsl:when, xsl:otherwise
```

The xsl:choose element can also be a child of any XML output (for example, putting the value of an XML node into an HTML element).

Child Elements

```
xsl:when, xsl:otherwise
```

Attributes

This element has no attributes.

xsl:when

This section introduces the xsl:when element's syntax and describes its usage.

Syntax

```
<xsl:when test="condition">
```

Description

The xsl:when element helps provide multiple conditional testing when working with xsl:choose and xsl:otherwise elements. It can occur any number of times in a stylesheet.

Parent Elements

```
xsl:choose
```

Child Elements

```
xsl:apply-templates, xsl:element, xsl:attribute, xsl:comment, xsl:pi,
xsl:copy, xsl:choose, xsl:for-each, xsl:if, xsl:value-of
```

The xsl:when element can also be the parent of output XML (for example, well formed HTML).

Attribute

test. This attribute provides the trigger/switch for executing the contents of the xsl:when element. The syntax of the condition is the same as that of the xsl:if element's test attribute.

xsl:otherwise

This section introduces the xsl:otherwise element's syntax and describes its usage.

Syntax

```
<xsl:otherwise>
```

Description

The xsl:otherwise element acts like an "else" case statement and becomes the default action of the xsl:choose element. It can occur any number of times in a stylesheet.

Parent Elements

```
xsl:choose
```

Child Elements

```
xsl:apply-templates, xsl:element, xsl:attribute, xsl:comment, xsl:pi,
xsl:copy, xsl:choose, xsl:for-each, xsl:if, xsl:value-of
```

The xsl:otherwise element can also be the parent of output XML (for example, well formed HTML).

Attributes

Since this element is triggered by inaction of it preceding xsl:when sibling elements, no attribute is defined as a trigger for it.

xsl:copy

This section introduces the xsl:copy element's syntax and describes its usage.

Syntax

```
<xsl:copy>
```

Description

The xsl:copy element is used to copy the contents of the target node to the output. It can occur any number of times in a stylesheet.

Parent Elements

```
xsl:template, xsl:element, xsl:attribute, xsl:comment, xsl:pi, xsl:copy,
xsl:for-each, xsl:if, xsl:when, xsl:otherwise
```

The xsl:copy element can also be a child of any XML output (for example, putting the value of an XML node into an HTML element).

Child Elements

```
xsl:apply-templates, xsl:element, xsl:attribute, xsl:comment, xsl:pi,
xsl:copy, xsl:for-each, xsl:if, xsl:choose, xsl:value-of
```

Attributes

This element has no attributes.

Summary

We hope that after going through this chapter, you have enough details to start creating your own XSL stylesheets. The examples we presented in this chapter, though crude and rudimentary, have, we hope, given you some affinity for creating your own stylesheets. Once you start working with stylesheets, you will find yourself having more fun than you should trying to come up with ways of using XSL. In the next chapter, we talk about something that we've hinted on and on about in this chapter: creating XSL patterns to help get the most out of your data. That's important stuff, so we've separated it from this chapter, though it really is a basic building block.

What we've gone through in this chapter was, more or less, simple stuff. The beauty of XSL is that is doesn't get much harder than this, as we'll show in "Putting It All Together" in Chapter 15. The next two chapters are again basic chapters that are intended to help you familiarize yourself with the tools that XSL provides.

Querying XML with XSL

In Chapter 2, we talked about how XML documents are at heart databases with hierarchical structure. As with any database, there is a natural need for performing queries on XML data to extract useful information. XSL gives you a reasonably simple and powerful syntax for generating queries on XML data through the use of *patterns*. In Chapter 12, we skimmed over the existence of patterns but didn't go into detail about them. In this chapter, we focus on pattern syntax and spend some time showing example code to demonstrate how to generate pattern queries. As in the previous chapter, these examples currently only work with Internet Explorer 5, and you can find both the source (.XML) and stylesheet (.XSL) files on the accompanying CD-ROM.

XSL Patterns

In Chapter 12, we referred to XSL patterns. Now we take an in-depth look at them! XSL patterns provide a simple, yet flexible and powerful query language for identifying nodes in XML trees. Patterns are based on the node's type, value, name, and/or the relationship of the node to other nodes in the XML document.

By definition, an XSL pattern is "a string which selects a set of nodes in source document" (XSL Working Draft, December 1998).

Patterns are quite an area of specialization and interest in the XML world. The W3C is currently considering a proposal regarding the XQL or XML Query Language. Though this too is not in a recommendation stage, it includes a very useful set of expansions to the current pattern syntax. Internet Explorer 5 supports most of these extensions, and, though we are not trying to push one company's technology over another's, these extensions make sense to us, so we listed some of them.

XSL patterns are expressed in a fashion similar to the way URLs are expressed across an hierarchical file system (HFS) or a network file system (NFS). This makes the syntax intuitive to anyone who's navigated any file system by typing keystrokes. For instance, anyone who's typed in a URL to navigate a file system knows how to use syntax such as

```
cd c:/my_disk/my_directory
```

to change the current directory to c:/my_disk/my_directory. Under the URL method of navigation, each file has a unique name and can be identified using the same syntax. For instance, to execute a file called my_file .exe located on the C hard drive in my_folder directory, you'd type:

```
c:\my_disk\my_folder\my_file.exe
```

to uniquely identify and execute the file my_file.

Let's say you have an XML file that looks like this:

```
<REPORTS>
   <REPORT1>
      <INTRODUCTION>This is my report</INTRODUCTION>
      <BODY>My report is very short</BODY>
      <CONCLUSION>The end.</CONCLUSION>
   </REPORT1>
   <REPORT2>
      <INTRODUCTION>This is the second report</INTRODUCTION>
      <BODY>This is also very short</BODY>
      <CONCLUSION>The end.</CONCLUSION>
   </REPORT2>
</REPORTS>
```

The XSL pattern that you would use to identify the INTRODUCTION element of REPORT1 would be:

```
/REPORTS/REPORT1/INTRODUCTION
```

While the XSL pattern syntax is similar, there are some notable differences. In the above case, it just so happened that the INTRODUCTION

Table 13.1 Comparing XSL Patterns with File System (URL) Syntax

FILE SYSTEMS (URLS)	XSL PATTERNS
Hierarchical structure of directories and files.	Hierarchical structure defined by elements, attributes, and other XML nodes present in an XML document.
Each file can be uniquely identified by virtue of its position and filename; that is, files at the same level cannot have the same name.	Elements at the same level can have the same name (for example, you could have many contacts). XSL patterns return a complete list of all elements that match the search criteria.
URLs are evaluated relative to a fixed point in the hierarchy, also known as the current directory.	XSL patterns are evaluated relative to a particular node known as the context of the query.

element of REPORT1 was uniquely identified by its position. However, that doesn't necessarily have to be true. Generally, nodes don't have unique names in an XML document. If your document looks like this:

```
<CONTACTS>
    <CONTACT TYPE="friend">
        <NAME>Joon August</NAME>
        <PHONE_NUMBER>(413)343-12343</PHONE_NUMBER>
    </CONTACT>
    <CONTACT TYPE="business">
        <NAME>Sally May</NAME>
        <PHONE_NUMBER>(921)324-51543</PHONE_NUMBER>
    </CONTACT>
    <CONTACT TYPE="friend">
        <NAME>Kyle Aaron</NAME>
        <PHONE_NUMBER>(815)537-1286</PHONE_NUMBER>
    </CONTACT>
</CONTACTS>
```

each contact, though unique, would be unidentifiable in the traditional URL syntax. Table 13.1 compares analogous features of XSL patterns and file system (URL) syntax.

Basic Pattern Syntax

Pattern syntax is extremely important in XSL for generating queries. XSL patterns are supported in XSL and in the Document Object Model (see Part Two of this book). Though most of this is intuitive, it's important that you have a reference to guide yourself against while working with XML documents. We start out with some simple examples, but keep in mind that you can mix and match as appropriate.

XSL Patterns Are Declarative

XSL pattern syntax is declarative, that is, it explicitly tells the syntax processor what to find as opposed to being procedural (that is, telling it *how* to find). So for example, the pattern

```
cans/soup_can
```

means find the soup_can elements that are in the cans elements.

Again, though this syntax is similar to a URI (file system) syntax in that the forward slash operator "/" is used to describe a hierarchy, in XSL, patterns specifies a navigation path through the nodes of the XML source tree.

Context

Each XSL pattern query occurs within a particular *context*. A context in XML is similar to a context in normal speech. The *Merriam Webster Dictionary* defines context as "the interrelated conditions in which something exists or occurs." When someone takes remarks "out of context," they no longer mean the same thing. Therefore when remarks are taken in context, they make more sense. Context, in the XSL pattern sense, means a particular level within the XML tree hierarchy. That level can encompass several nodes that may or may not have the same direct parent. Take a look at Figure 13.1, which illustrates what we mean by context.

If it helps, you could think of a pattern as a scope. The context defines the node against which pattern matching occurs.

XSL pattern queries are extremely flexible; you can retrieve information from a source tree using a particular context and perform further pattern matches on the results that you receive. Let's say you search for all books in a bookstore about a particular subject. Once you have those results, you can perform further sifting of those results based on finer details (perhaps some sort of a specialization). The point is that you don't have to go back and begin the query all over again. That gives you a lot of flexibility. Sure, if you *want* to perform a single-shot top-down query, you can, but with XSL, you have the ability to essentially walk the entire

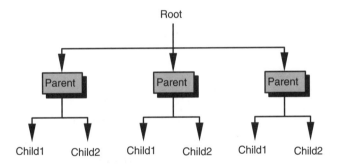

Context = all "Parent" elements

Syntax: Root/Parent

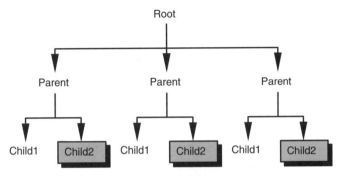

Context = all "Child2" elements of all "Parent" elements

Syntax: Root/Parent/Child2

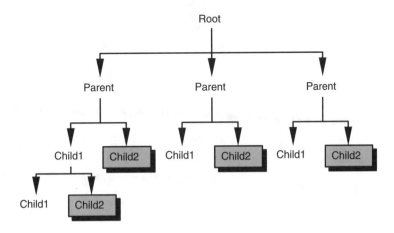

Context = all "Child2" elements under Root

Syntax: Root//Child2

Figure 13.1 Context of patterns.

tree through logical operations as opposed to explicitly programming it in. The best part is that the performance is very impressive. Tree hierarchies are traditionally very efficient from a processing perspective.

Pattern Operators and Special Syntax

Like any syntax, patterns have operators and special terms that serve a useful purpose. While most of the pattern operators are intuitive, in the interest of thoroughness, we want to mention them at least once. Table 13.2 summarizes the pattern operators, and the remaining text provides example code and details on each operator.

Child Operator

To start a query from the root node's context, a pattern should be started with a forward slash /. Therefore, if you wanted all elements occurring under the root node, your pattern would simply be:

```
/
```

Table 13.2   Pattern Operators and Special Syntax

OPERATOR	NAME	DESCRIPTION
/	Child Operator	Used by itself, it specifies a pattern of finding all children of the root element. Used to define the hierarchy of the pattern. Every match specified to the left of the slash is collected.
*	Wildcard	Used with both elements and attributes. By itself, it returns all elements regardless of their name from the current node. It provides single depth searching only.
//	Recursive Descent	Recursively drills down from a specified node (specified on the right side) regardless of position in the tree.
@	Attribute Operator	Used to specify an attribute.
:	Namespace Operator	Used to separate elements based on their namespace.
[]	Filter Operator	Applies a filter.
[]	Index Operator	Used for locating specific elements based on their index value.

For example, the following finds all customer elements immediately under the root element:

```
/customer
```

If you want to go deeper into a node, use another child operator. If a node's name is library and that has child elements called book, then

```
library/book
```

returns all books that belong to the library element.

If you are already in a particular context (library) and want to drill down further within the same context, use a period "." with a forward slash "/" to go one level deeper.

```
./
```

Equivalently, you could ignore that and just put the following:

```
book
```

If you know the structure of your data, you can walk down the nodes yourself:

```
country/state/city
```

Wildcard

If you wanted all the children of a particular element, say all elements that belong to a state element (for example, cities, towns, villages), you could use the wildcard operator "*" to indicate your interest in all elements, regardless of their name. Here's what the pattern looks like:

```
country/state/*
```

For the previous example to work, we assume that country elements have state elements. What if a country element (like Canada, which has provinces) doesn't have states? In that case, if you wanted to list all cities of all countries, you could use the wildcard operator "*" like so:

```
country/*/city
```

This example finds all city elements of all child elements of country elements.

Recursive Descent

Continuing with our hypothetical geography structure, the following syntax means something different from the last:

```
//city
```

This means find all city elements located anywhere in the current document, regardless of the depth of their position in the tree; that is, if the source includes elements such as independent territories as well, their city elements are also be included in the result. It recursively goes down every available path from its current context and collects nodes as it goes along. In the above case, the context would be the root node.

Namespace Operator

If your document uses elements with namespace prefixes, you should include the namespace prefix while creating the pattern. If you have a root element called lot that has car elements coming from different namespaces (say mnfg1:, mnfg2:, etc.) then to find all cars in the lot elements coming from the mnfg2: namespace, your pattern could be:

```
lot/mnfg2:car
```

If you wanted to get a collection of all elements belonging to a particular namespace (say mnfg1:):

```
//mnfg1:*
```

However, you can't find all car elements in a source tree that has a namespace per se. That is,

```
//*:car
```

will generate an error.

Attributes

Attributes are represented by an "@" symbol. Here's how you would make a pattern to find all the attributes of a car element:

```
car/@*
```

Similarly, to find the align attributes of table elements:

```
table/@align
```

The namespace operator works with attributes as well. To find all attributes under a myns namespace, your pattern would be:

```
myns:@*
```

Filters

Filters are used to further qualify the pattern to get finer results. We go into more details on filters and filter patterns in the next section. For now, let us just say that filters are represented within square brackets, "[]".

Filters and Filter Patterns

Filters do exactly what they sound like: They provide you with a way to sift through results of your pattern and give you a more refined search. They are probably the most important part of XSL patterns in that this is where your data mining logic can be implemented.

Filters works by defining a pattern within your pattern, that is, your patterns take on this general structure:

```
pattern[filter_pattern]
```

The filter pattern is applied to every element returned by the regular pattern and returns a Boolean TRUE if there are any matches and a Boolean FALSE if there are no matches. If you are familiar to SQL syntax, filters are analogous to the WHERE clause.

Filters patterns are evaluated with respect to the context that they inherit from the normal pattern. So for instance, the filter

```
restaurant[review]
```

means that for every restaurant element found, return only those that have a review element with them.

Filters also let you sift through elements and attributes based on their values. To find only those restaurants elements that have a review element whose value is Excellent:

```
restaurant[review="Excellent"]
```

You can also use filters with attribute values, for example:

```
restaurant[@genre="Mexican"]
```

You can also have multiple filtering criteria, such as: Find all restaurant elements that have a review element and genre attribute whose value is Mexican:

```
Restaurant[review= "Excellent"][@genre= "Mexican"]
```

Filtering can happen at all levels of the pattern. For instance:

```
books[@subject=   "Archeology"]/author[first_name=   "Indiana"]
[last_name= "Jones"]
```

returns all author elements that (in order of processing):

Are members of "book" elements *that have*

- a "subject" attribute *whose value*
  - is "Archeology"

and of the author elements, each *must have*

- a first_name element, *whose value*
  - is "Indiana" *and*
- a last_name element *whose value*
  - is "Jones"

Empty filters are not allowed, for instance:

```
library[]
```

is an error.

any and all Keywords

When a filter that compares the values of elements is applied to more than one child element, only the first matching child is used for comparison. To get around this, you can use the any and all keywords. For example, if you're looking for a shoe element with a color element whose value is white, you'd use:

```
shoes/shoe[color= "white"]
```

This pattern looks through each shoe element and if the first color element (assuming that each shoe can have several color elements) has a value of white, the shoe is returned. This means that if a shoe has a color element whose value is white but that color element is listed after the first one, then the entire shoe will be ignored. Figure 13.2 shows what we mean.

To get around this, you can use the any keyword to examine all color elements of each shoe. If any of those elements has a value of white, the shoe is returned. Here's the syntax:

```
shoes/shoe[$any$ color= "white"]
```

The all keyword also lets you look at all color elements, but it only returns the shoe element if all of the color elements have a value of

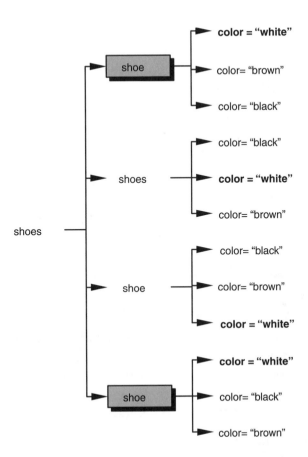

Figure 13.2   By default, filters look at only the first matching element's value.

white. If the shoe comes in more colors than white, the shoe is not returned. You could also think of the all keyword as a purity check. Here's how you'd use it in our shoes example:

```
shoes/shoe[$all$ color= "white"]
```

XSL Patterns Describe Collections

In URIs, paths describe individual files. In XSL patterns, they define collections of nodes.

So, while

```
pictures/alex.jpg
```

identifies the unique file alex.jpg, when writing a pattern,

```
pictures/picture
```

would identify a *collection* of picture elements.

Collections Retain Their Order

The element collections that are returned by a pattern maintain their document order, hierarchy, and identity to the extent that they are already defined. However, when a pattern looks for attributes, that doesn't remain true because attributes, by definition, are unordered.

When you define a pattern asking for all elements of a particular name (say all car elements), the resulting elements have the same name, that is, car (as opposed to being called cars or result). Also, by definition, a collection does not have root element per se, unless only one element is returned.

Indexing Collection Results

XSL patterns assign zero-based index numbers (that is, numbers that start from zero, go to n-1, where n is the total number of elements returned in the collection) to the collection results so you can easily find a particular node within a collection of nodes. The index numbers assigned to each element are relative to the parent.

For example, if you wanted to find the first person who volunteered from a list of volunteers, your pattern would look like this:

```
list/volunteer[0]
```

Indexing works with filters as well. If you wanted the *second* volunteer whose training attribute's value is two years, your pattern would look like this:

```
list/volunteer[@training ='2'][1]
```

To find the last element of a collection, you would use the end() method. To find the last volunteer in the list, your pattern would look like this:

```
list/volunteer[end()]
```

Boolean Operators, Comparison Operators, and Set Expressions

When comparing element and attribute values in the previous filter patterns, we only showed the equal operator. For filter patterns to be really effective, you need to have the ability to perform classical logical operations such as Boolean operations and comparisons. The XSL pattern syntax specification is currently in flux as there is a move to merge the XSL syntax with the XQL syntax.

Table 13.3 lists these operators as they currently work in Internet Explorer 5.

Table 13.3   Boolean Operators, Comparison Operators, and Set Expressions

OPERATOR (SYNTAX)	ALTERNATIVE SYNTAX	NAME	REMARKS
and	and	Logical AND operator	Performs a logical AND operation.
or	or	Logical OR operator	Performs a logical OR operation.
not()	not	Logical NOT operator	Negates the expression (inverter).
=	eq	Equality	Checks the value of nodes specified in the pattern for equality against a given value.
!=	ne	Not equal	Returns values that are not equal to the check specified. *Continues*

Table 13.3 Boolean Operators, Comparison Operators, and Set Expressions *(Continued)*

OPERATOR (SYNTAX)	ALTERNATIVE SYNTAX	NAME	REMARKS
	ieq	Case-insensitive equality	Performs a case-insensitive equality check.
	ine	Case-insensitive inequality check	Analog to ieq operator.
<	lt	Less than	Checks if the value of the node specified is less than a given value. The comparison is made on a case-sensitive, string value basis.
>	gt	Greater than	Checks if the value of the node specified is greater than a given value. The comparison is made on a case-sensitive, string value basis.
	ilt	Case-insensitive less than	Performs a case-insensitive literal string comparison on pattern-specified node values against a filter-specified value and returns values that are less than the filter-specified value.
	igt	Case-insensitive greater than	Performs a case-insensitive literal string comparison on pattern-specified node values against a filter-specified value and returns values that are greater than the filter-specified value.
<=	le	Less than or equal to	Returns values that are less than or equal to the filter-specified pattern. This check is case sensitive.
>=	ge	Greater than or equal	Returns values that are greater than or equal to the filter-specified pattern. This check is case sensitive.
	ile	Case insensitive less than or equal to	Returns a case-insensitive check.
	ige	Case insensitive greater than or equal to	Returns a case-insensitive check.

Table 13.3 *(Continued)*

OPERATOR (SYNTAX)	ALTERNATIVE SYNTAX	NAME	REMARKS
	all	ALL operator	This is a set operation that returns a TRUE value if the filter-specified conditions are met by all occurrences of the pattern.
	any	ANY operator	This is a set operation that returns a TRUE value if the filter-specified conditions are met by any occurrences of the pattern.
|		Union	Another set operator. This returns the union of two sets of nodes.

Examples

Most of these operators are intuitive, but here are some examples to help clarify things:

Boolean Operations

The Boolean Operators supported in XSL perform logical operations. You can use them with one another and with grouping parentheses to create very sophisticated filters and patterns to extract information from data.

The *and* operator performs a logical AND operation that explicitly states that both conditions must be met in order for a result to be returned. For example, to find all restaurant elements that have *both* a genre attribute and a Food_Rating element your pattern would look like this:

```
restaurants/restaurant[@genre and Food_Rating]
```

The *or* operator performs a logical operation, that is, if one of the conditions is met, the node in the results of the pattern are returned. For example, if we switched the above statement to

```
restaurants/restaurant[@genre or Food_Rating]
```

we'd get back all restaurant elements that have at either an attribute of type genre or an element of type Food_Rating or both.

The *not* operator negates the value of the filter expression and returns the complement of it. If you want all restaurant elements that do not have a Food_Rating element, here's your pattern:

```
Restaurant[not(@genre)]
```

Of course, these can be coupled as well. For instance, to find all restaurant elements that have *either* a genre attribute or a Food_Rating element and an Ambience_Rating element whose value is 4, your pattern would be:

```
restaurant[(@genre or food_rating) and (Ambiance_Rating = '4')]
```

Here we've used parentheses to show grouping of elements. We talk about grouping later in the precedence section of this chapter.

Comparison Operators

More often than not, you will be using comparisons in your filter patterns to specify the trigger for your filter. Comparison operators look at the value of the target nodes and then perform their operation. Note: Since currently no XML-based datatyping recommendation is available, all comparisons are made on string values. Internet Explorer 5 has its own set of methods for performing comparisons based on numerical values but we don't recommend using them until the W3C makes a formal recommendation. Yes, this is a big limitation and causes a lot problems, but you can think of ways around it through script. In addition, if you'd like, you could use Microsoft's own set of XSL elements like the xsl:eval to help assist you, but since those aren't W3C compliant per se, we can't openly advocate using them. Besides, string comparisons do have many uses.

The comparison operator we've already used a lot is the *equal to* operator, which looks at a target node's value and compares it with the value provided in the filter pattern. For example,

```
employees[last_name = "Smith"]
```

finds all employee elements that have a last_name element whose value is Smith.

The *inequality* operator, "!=" returns those nodes whose value is not equal to the value specified in the filter pattern. In this case,

```
employees[last_name != "Smith"]
```

finds all employee elements whose last_name element values are not Smith.

The *less than* and *greater than* operators perform the tests you expect them to, so

```
restaurant[average_cost < "50"]
```

returns all restaurant elements whose value is less than 50.

Internet Explorer also supports the syntax proposed in the XQL proposal, where the $operator$ syntax is used. Looking at the values in Table 13.2, the equivalent would be:

```
restaurant[average_cost $le$ "50"]
```

The previous operands perform case-sensitive comparisons, which in our opinion is a little harsh. If you want to perform case-insensitive comparisons, you can use the $ioperator$ syntax as listed in Table 13.3. For example, if you wanted to find all people elements whose last_name element's value is Le Marca the following pattern would suit your purposes:

```
people[last_name $ieq$ "le marca"]
```

Using the "=" or eq operator with the above value specified would not result in a match.

Set Operators

The set operators, any and all, work exactly as we described earlier in this chapter so we won't spend any more time on them. The "|" operator lets you perform a union operation, that is, retrieve several collections at a time.

If you wanted to retrieve all book and periodical elements from a library element, you would use the following pattern:

```
library/book | library/periodical
```

Equivalently, you could use:

```
library/(book | periodical)
```

If you wanted to find all the book and periodical elements in a library whose author element's value is Hoodbhoy, you could use:

```
library/(book | periodical)[author = "Hoodbhoy"]
```

Precedence

Now that we've gone over most of the available syntax for creating patterns and filter patterns, we can talk a bit about the precedence rules XSL employs while evaluating patterns. Precedence rules do exactly what they sound like: they define the order in which operations occur. Table 13.4 summarizes the precedence rules in descending order (highest precedence first).

If you're looking for samples, the precedence rules have been in effect throughout all our previous examples in this chapter.

XSL Pattern Methods

Throughout the above discussion, we've shied away from talking about XSL pattern methods to keep things simple. Now things get a little more

Table 13.4   Precedence Rules in Patterns

OPERATOR SYNTAX	OPERATOR NAME	DESCRIPTION
()	Grouping	Performs group actions before moving onto next operation.
[]	Filters	Filters are performed on the results of a pattern.
/, //	Child and recursive descent	
any, and	Set operators	
=, !=, $operands$, $ioperands$	Comparisons	Comparisons are performed on the string values of the nodes returned in the pattern. $ioperands$ are case insensitive.
|	Union	Allows you to collect the results of two or more patterns.
not()	Boolean NOT	Performs a logical negation. Similar to a logical inverter.
and	Boolean AND	Performs a logical AND.
or	Boolean OR	Performs a logical OR.

interesting. We won't go into a lot of details in this section, as the missing data-typing specification from the W3C makes it difficult to create working examples. Some of these methods are applied by default, and we showed a few explicit applications of the methods (such as the *index* method) in the previous pattern syntax examples.

A method, by definition, is the processing that an object performs in object-oriented technology. XSL pattern methods are applied by appending the following syntax to the end of a pattern's context (that is, an element or an attribute):

```
context!method_name()
```

All XSL pattern method names are case sensitive and return case-sensitive results.

XSL pattern methods fall into two general categories based on their behaviors: *information methods* and *collection methods*. Let's discuss each of these independently.

Information Pattern Methods

Information methods return information about the collection of nodes returned from the context. *Information* refers to the node's type, name, value, and text. We list the available methods in Table 13.5 and include a brief description of each method.

Here are a few examples of how to use these methods:

To find all book elements in a bookstore, use:

```
bookstore/*[()nodeName= "book"]
```

Note that this is equivalent to:

```
bookstore/book
```

Similarly, to find all book elements whose author element value is Hoodbhoy:

```
book[author!value()="Hoodbhoy"]
```

This is equivalent to:

```
book[author="Hoodbhoy"]
```

Table 13.5 XSL Information Pattern Methods

METHOD NAME	DESCRIPTION
nodeName	This method returns the tag name of the node, including its namespace prefix. Useful when you want to trace the origin of a value.
nodeType	This method returns a number that indicates the type of node (for example, element, attribute). See the chapters on the DOM methods and properties for details on which numbers mean what.
index	This method returns the zero-based index number of the node relative to its parent.
end	This method returns the last element (relative to the parent node) in a collection.
number	This method casts string values to number formats so that they can be used with mathematical operations.
value	This returns the typed value of an element or attribute. When data types are not used, it returns the string value of the element or attribute (the default method for comparisons in filter patterns).
date	This method casts string values to date format. Not particularly helpful until datatypes are completely specified.

Finally, an example where the method is not redundant:

```
restaurants/restaurant[index() $le$ 1]
```

This returns the first two restaurant elements.

Collection Pattern Method

Collection methods return collections of nodes of a particular type, for instance, all elements. We've gone over a few of these in our previous examples. Table 13.6 lists all of them.

Summary

In this chapter, we spent a lot of time discussing how to make patterns and pattern filters. Patterns are important because they give you an easy way of querying your data and extracting information from it (information by definition is processed data). The query language pro-

Table 13.6 XSL Collection Pattern Methods

METHOD NAME	DESCRIPTION
text	This method returns a collection of all nodes in the current context that represent text strings, including CDATA sections.
textNode	This method returns a collection of all text nodes in the current context.
pi	This method returns a collection of all processing instructions found in the current context.
element	This method returns all elements occurring in the pattern specified context. This feature is normally performed by the * character as discussed above.
attribute	Similar to the element method. This returns a collection of all attributes occurring in the current context. The equivalent syntax is @*.
comment	This method returns a collection of all comments occurring in the current context.
cdata	This method returns a collection of all the CDATA nodes occurring in the current context.

vided through XSL pattern syntax is extremely flexible, easy to use, and allows you to create sophisticated queries that help you extract almost any information from XML source documents.

As you've read through this chapter, you've probably asked yourself why we bothered being so explicit. After all, most of this stuff seems to be at the no-brainer level. You're right, it is simple. However, pattern matching is really important, and we don't want you to get stuck without having the right set of syntax at your fingertips. That's why we listed everything out in detail.

In the next chapter, we talk about the basics of XSL formatting objects and give you a sneak peak at what XSL will look like in the near future. In Chapter 15, we walk you through some examples of how you can use pull of these concepts together in a real-world system.

XSL Formatting Model

In this chapter, we briefly touch upon the W3C's working draft on formatting in XSL. Currently, these issues have not been implemented so you won't find a lot of code here. We already discussed where XSL is. Now we focus on helping you see which way XSL is headed so that you can begin to strategically plan ahead.

Where Is XSL Going?

As we mentioned in Chapter 11, XSL has two primary objectives:

1. To provide an easy to use syntax for basic transformations and manipulations of XML documents.
2. To provide an XML lexicon for describing formatting semantics.

In Chapters 12 and 13, we focused mostly on the first objective. We left the formatting up to HTML. In the short run (and perhaps long run), that is how XSL is deployed most actively—to transform XML data and then output that information in HTML.

But the second part, providing a lexicon for describing formatting semantics, has really been left untouched. What do we mean by "a lexicon for describing formatting semantics"? Well, just as HTML provides a set of elements with allowable attributes that are used to tweak the display of a page on a screen, XSL presents a vocabulary of tags that allow you to completely describe aspects of formatting for all visual output media.

Doesn't HTML Do the Same Thing?

The answer is no. HTML provides a set of tools that is useful for screen display but doesn't translate very well to other media, for example, paper printing. If you've ever printed a Web page you know what we mean. What looks good on your screen doesn't necessarily look as good on paper. Screen formats are very different from paper formats. Similarly, formatting for moving video is different from formatting for static video. Each output medium has its own unique set of formatting semantics and that becomes a real problem for anyone whose job it is to present information.

In many ways, we've already been trying to tackle this problem. For the past several years, the printing industry has made use of proprietary formatting information from Tex and LaTex to PostScript and Rich Text Format (RTF). At the high end of publishing, these technologies have been fairly impressive and have made tremendous inroads. However, the tools needed to work with them are expensive and are normally very specialized. You won't find many of them on a desktop PC, nor are they well known for their user friendliness. In addition, the problems associated with translation from one format to another persist.

XML provides a universal format for representing our information. XSL is an attempt at a universal syntax for manipulating the information contained in XML documents and for formatting that information in a device-independent way. The latter part means that by using XSL, you should be able to create stylesheets that work with all output media. For now, the focus is performing rudimentary transformations of XML data using XSL but the universal formatting aspect of it has neither been completely specified nor implemented.

If There Are XML-Based Output Formats, Would Translating XML Using XSL Fit the Bill?

The answer to that is yes, but you're still getting diminishing returns on your use of technology. Customizing for each output format, like HTML or RTF, requires much redundant work, including defining a paragraph, word wrapping, line-feeds, and hyphenation. While all of this is processor (parser) specific, it doesn't mean that you won't be affected as a presenter. What you expect to see when a line breaks should be constant for every output format; the reality is that it isn't.

XSL sets out to create a number of formatting objects that encode instructions to the formatting processor. For instance, when you translate XML to HTML, the HTML output serves as a series of instructions to the HTML parser on how to render your data. The HTML formatter in turn interprets the instructions it gets and constructs a structured arrangement of spaces and display objects (like text and pictures) that create the formatted output. When you translate XML to RTF, though, the formatting rules and syntax are different (for example, you need to take into account page breaks and paper size), and you have to go through the same process all over again.

Here's what it boils down to: XML gives us the ability to universally interpret data so we can perform further processing. In addition to providing a data manipulation semantic, we'd like XSL to provide a common syntax for describing formatting objects that specialized processors can share and interpret accordingly. As a result, information once formatted using XSL would be directly translatable to your monitor, home printer, and printing presses as well.

Formatting in the XSL Working Draft

XSL applies formatting rules the same way it applying translation and manipulation rules: through templates.

The Formatting section in the current XSL working draft describes a general model of spaces and areas as well as how they interrelate with one another. It does so by specifying the semantics of the formatting objects and their properties, but it doesn't specify the individual flow objects. This means that it defines a core set of methods and properties for formatting that any output formatting processor should provide, but it doesn't describe the actual algorithmic approach that each object needs to employ. For instance, it specifies that there should be a line-break method that has several properties but it doesn't tell you, as a processor designer, how to implement the result.

The formatting model in XSL is the reflection of many different formatting initiatives. It borrows liberally from the Cascading Stylesheets (CSS) and from the Document Style and Semantics Specification Language (DSSSL). The idea is to take the best of all worlds to create a comprehensive conceptual model called the W3C Common Formatting Model and to provide a syntax that can be expressed in XML. The name given to that syntax is XSL.

The XSL Formatting Model

The XSL model as it currently is being discussed, is based on a system of rectangular *areas* and *spaces*. Areas reserve space and hold content. Spaces reserve space between, after, or before areas and don't hold content. As you'd imagine, they are used primarily for making adjustments to the layout. These are very flexible entities and allow for overlapping, individual and relative coordinate systems, and a host of formatting properties, depending on the object that creates them.

XSL has a huge array of formatting objects and properties. To show you what we mean by huge, we've listed the key components proposed in the XSL working draft in a series of tables later in this chapter. The level of detail at which each object is defined by properties is incredible. To our minds, that level of control—though very powerful—is XSL's biggest weakness. Complexity is bad, but often it is necessary.

To give you an idea of how fine the details get, the rectangular areas defined in the XSL formatting model come in four flavors: area containers, block areas, line areas, and inline areas. Each of these have several common features including margins, borders, and padding. If you're familiar with CSS, you probably recognize this syntax as similar to that of a CSS box.

- A *border* is an open box surrounding the content of the area that the rectangle holds. The border is configured by its color and the thickness of each of its four sides. The thickness of each side is specified by a range of minimum, optimum, and maximum values.

- The *padding* of a rectangular area is the space between the inside of the border and the content of the area. It is specified by its thickness in each of the four directions of the rectangle.

- A *margin* is used to determine the open space reserved between the outside of the border of the rectangular area and those of other rectangular areas. It is specified by its thickness in each of the four directions of the rectangle.

If this level of detail is too easy, you will be happy to know that these are only the tip of the iceberg.

Table 14.1 XSL Formatting Objects List

OBJECT	
fo:basic-page-sequence	fo:inline-sequence
fo:block	fo:link-end-locator
fo:character	fo:list-block
fo:display-graphic	fo:list-item
fo:display-link	fo:list-item-body
fo:display-rule	fo:list-item-label
fo:display-sequence	fo:page-number
fo:inline-graphic	fo:queue
fo:inline-link	fo:simple-page-master
fo:inline-rule	

XSL Formatting Objects

XSL defines a fairly huge vocabulary of formatting objects. These formatting objects do not come under the xsl: namespace, rather they have their own dedicated namespace, which has the prefix fo: assigned to it. This set of objects is worthy of a book in itself, however, Table 14.1 lists these objects.

We don't go into more detail, but to help illustrate our point that the XSL format semantics go into enormous detail and offer you an incredible degree of flexibility, in Table 14.2 we've listed the names of properties that are associated with the formatting objects listed in Table 14.1.

Table 14.2 XSL Formatting Object Properties

PROPERTIES	
asis-truncate-indicator	body-writing-mode
asis-wrap-indent	border-color-after
asis-wrap-indicator	border-color-before
background-attachment	border-color-bottom
background-color	border-color-end
background-image	border-color-left
background-position	border-color-right
background-repeat	border-color-start
body-overflow	border-color-top
	Continues

Table 14.2 XSL Formatting Object Properties *(Continued)*

PROPERTIES	
border-width-after	footer-separation
border-width-before	footer-size
border-width-bottom	footer-writing-mode
border-width-end	glyph-alignment-mode
border-width-left	glyph-id
border-width-right	header-overflow
border-width-start	header-separation
border-width-top	header-size
break-after	header-writing-mode
break-before	height
character	href
color	hyphenate
contents-alignment	hyphenation-char
contents-rotation	hyphenation-keep
destination	hyphenation-ladder-count
end-indent	hyphenation-push-char-count
end-side-overflow	hyphenation-remain-char-count
end-side-separation	id
end-side-size	ignore-record-end
end-side-writing-mode	image
escapement-space-end	inhibit-line-breaks
escapement-space-start	input-whitespace-treatment
expand-tabs	keep
first-page-master	keep-with-next
font-family	keep-with-previous
font-size	kern
font-size-adjust	kern-mode
font-stretch	language
font-style	left
font-variant	length
font-weight	letter-spacing
footer-overflow	letter-spacing-limit

Table 14.2 *(Continued)*

PROPERTIES	
ligature	page-writing-mode
line-height	position-point
line-height option	provisional-distance-between-starts
line-offset	provisional-label-separation
line-spacing-precedence	queue-name
line-thickness	repeating-even-page-master
margin-end	repeating-odd-page-master
margin-start	scale-graphic
max-height	score-spaces
max-width	show-content
merge-link-end-indicators	space-after
min-leading	space-before
min-post-line-spacing	space-between-list-rows
min-pre-line-spacing	space-end
orientation	space-start
orphans	start-indent
overflow	start-side-overflow
padding-after	start-side-separation
padding-before	start-side-size
padding-bottom	start-side-writing-mode
padding-end	system-font
padding-left	text-align
padding-right	text-align-last
padding-start	text-indent
padding-top	text-shadow
page-height	vertical-align
page-margin-bottom	widows
page-margin-left	width
page-margin-right	word-spacing
page-margin-top	word-spacing-limit
page-master-name	wrap-option
page-width	writing-mode

Summary

Why did we go through this chapter and spend time talking about something that hasn't even been implemented yet? The reason is simple: We don't want to mislead you about XSL. Many parts of XSL have not yet been decided and venturing into it now may not be the best option for you.

XSL as it currently stands can still perform an impressive array of features—features that are critical to the success of XML. However, we would be lying if we said that it represents a complete solution in and of itself. Though XSL currently meets the requirement of enabling the transformation of XML to other XML formats, particularly HTML, until its formatting semantics are completely defined and implemented, XML won't have the primary tool it needs to truly realize its potential of separating content from formatting. Until that happens, you cannot create documents that are easily rendered across both online and print media.

This doesn't mean you should lose hope. We're right at the beginning of a revolution, and every day the support for XML grows by leaps and bounds. "Fortune favors the brave" aside, that XSL will be realized in a very big way is something that we believe is a rational conclusion.

Besides, the fact remains that the majority of your target audience is the online community. That being true, XSL, as is, provides you with several nifty solutions already. In our next chapter, we look at how you can deploy these solutions.

Putting It All Together

Now that we have covered the details about writing stylesheets, it's time to see how to use XSL in your site solution. In a nutshell, XSL is used to convert your XML to a presentation medium, such as HTML, PDF, or any other document format. In this chapter, we use HTML as the presentation medium so the browser can display information to the user. Getting XSL to work involves varying degrees of complexity, depending on your situation. We present several site designs that use XSL and explain under which circumstances each one would be used. Finally, we develop some working scenarios to show all the details of designing a site that uses XSL. Throughout this chapter, we focus less on XSL stylesheet design and more on how to use XSL for your Web site.

Site Designs

Here is a list of different systems that use XSL, in the order of increasing complexity:

- **The no-brainer design.** Figure 15.1 shows the system for using a single XSL stylesheet with a browser that supports XSL. It's obvious that the system designer has little to do; a browser such as Internet Explorer 5 takes care of applying the XSL when the XML comes in. Note that the XSL originally comes from the server, but appears to

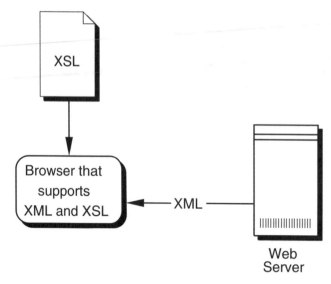

Figure 15.1 Using XSL with a browser that supports XSL.

be on the client side. After the initial download of the stylesheet, it is cached on the local machine, making it available for subsequent XML transactions. This design is practical in many intranet scenarios, when the system designer knows which browser is being used internally. Unfortunately, for most Internet sites, this scenario is not practical, since you cannot assume that every browser supports XSL. In an ideal world, every browser would support every technology, and we could get away with such designs.

- **Generating HTML from XSL on the server.** Figure 15.2 shows how the server can be used to apply the XSL stylesheet to the XML on the server and then send the resulting HTML to the browser. This scenario is the complete opposite from the previous scenario. We are throwing out all the advantages of XML and going back to the old model of the Web—the data and the presentation are sent up together in the form of HTML. This design is necessary for browsers that cannot render XSL with XML. Unfortunately, we don't take advantage of XML and XSL for the browsers that support it. Just to refresh, using XML and XSL reduces the amount of traffic over the pipe. The XSL stylesheet (presentation) needs to be transferred only the first time. Subsequent requests on the same site require only the XML (data) to be transferred. In HTML, the presentation and the data are sent down for each request.

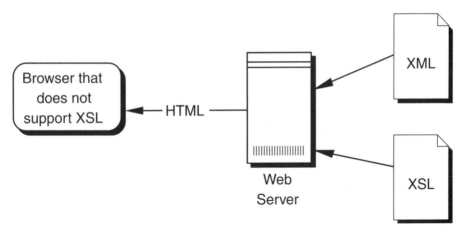

Figure 15.2 Using XSL from a browser that does not support XSL.

- **XSL and client side script.**   Figure 15.3 shows how we can extend the first scenario by supporting multiple XSL stylesheets. Script on the client is used to select the necessary stylesheet,

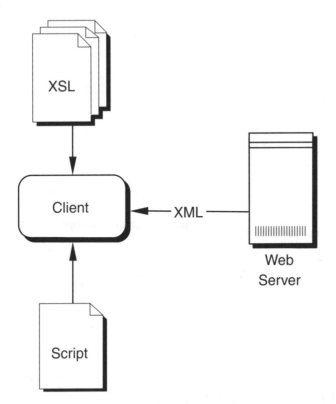

Figure 15.3 Using multiple stylesheets from Internet Explorer 5.

depending on what the user wants to see. The script initially travels to the Web page with an HTML page and then begins interacting with the server using XML. For example, an online investment site sends stock quotes to the browser so the user can track stocks. The server sends the price of a stock for each day in the past year in the form of XML. Now the client has a lot of information. We can use XSL to look at it in different ways. We allow the user to select between three display views—a graph of the performance of the stock for the last week, month, or year—using a stylesheet for each of these three options. The stylesheet applied to the XML is dependent upon which option the user chooses. The user can flip from one display to the other. The only bottleneck is the processing power of the local machine. The speed is increased tremendously because round-trips to the server aren't necessary. Later in this chapter, we demonstrate how to use the transformNode(...) facility to achieve these results.

A Typical XSL Design

Now that we have seen the different ways of using XSL for your Web site, it's time to look for a solution that works for you. As with most Web sites, the type of browser from which requests come is not guaranteed. Fortunately, you can check for the type of browser making the request and tailor the response for that browser. In fact, sending back browser-specific pages has become quite common. Because the DHTML behavior in Navigator and Internet Explorer differs, many site designers have been constructing two sites to accommodate the differences.

Figure 15.4 shows the overall data flow of a typical XSL system.

According to this figure, it looks like a lot of magic is happening inside the Web server. Let's list exactly what the Web server responsibilities are:

1. We need to check what type of browser is making the request. This can easily be achieved through Perl, C, ASP, or Java Servlet programs. We know ahead of time which browsers support XSL. (At the time this book was written, Internet Explorer 5 was the only browser that supported XSL.)

2. We get the necessary data from the database server. For the moment, we assume that the database server produces XML and not some other form of native data. Also, any kind of database logic is left to the database server.

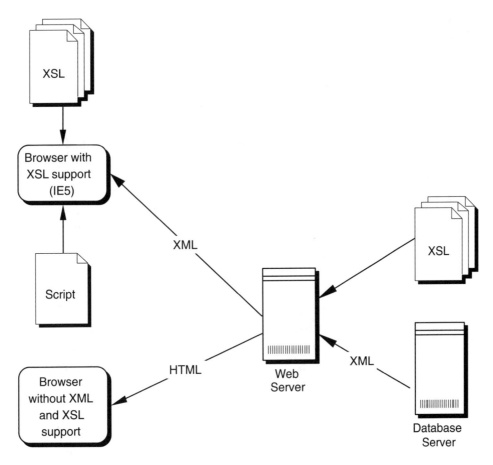

Figure 15.4 Typical XSL system.

3. If the browser supports XSL, send the XML as is to the browser.

4. Otherwise, apply the necessary XSL stylesheet to the XML and then send back the resulting HTML.

It seems like the Web server's job is pretty straightforward as long as the database server produces XML. We know that many database servers out there don't produce XML. The database server in Figure 15.4 is a catchall for the actual data; that is, the database logic to assemble the necessary data and the component necessary for converting the data to XML. Chapter 8 shows how to accomplish this task using ASP scripts on the Web server. Depending on your situation, some database server tasks, such as the conversion of the native data to XML, can be done on the Web server.

XSL on the Client

XML documents can be used in conjunction with more than one stylesheet. By using different stylesheets, you can create different views of your data. With the MSXML parser, you can apply a stylesheet to your XML by using the transformNode(...) method. Chapter 7 outlines the details of this method and presents a simple example. Let's briefly go over this method and present a typical scenario that would be used on a Web site.

Here is the general syntax for transformNode:

```
var result;
result = xmldocument.transformNode( xslstylesheet.documentElement );
```

This line of code applies the stylesheet xslstylesheet to the document xmldocument and stores the outcome as a string into result. Both xmldocument and xslstylesheet are document nodes. In other words, they are names associated to the ID attribute on a data island. Our example uses data islands to hold the stylesheets. Note that the XML contained in xmldocument and xslstylesheet is not modified, but is read to produce result.

The following scenario displays a page that allows the user to select a view of the incoming XML data. When the user selects a view, the script is used to apply an XSL stylesheet to the XML and then display the result to the user. We isolate the key concepts in this scenario by leaving the data transfer complexities out. We download the same piece of static XML from the server. Chapters 8 and 9 show how to build the XML transfer link between the client and the server. Also, we made the XSL stylesheets simple in this example so we don't get bogged in the presentation details and instead can focus on getting this system to work.

We use three data islands for this scenario: bookXML, OverviewXSL, and CommentsXSL. The first one holds the XML data, while the other two contain the stylesheets. The actual XML and XSL files used in this scenario are irrelevant. The following code can be used with your own XML and XSL documents to tailor this application to your interests. By using the SRC attribute on the XSL data islands, we ensure that the XSL stylesheets are downloaded with the script.

Figure 15.5 shows a shot of the scenario by displaying the Comments view.

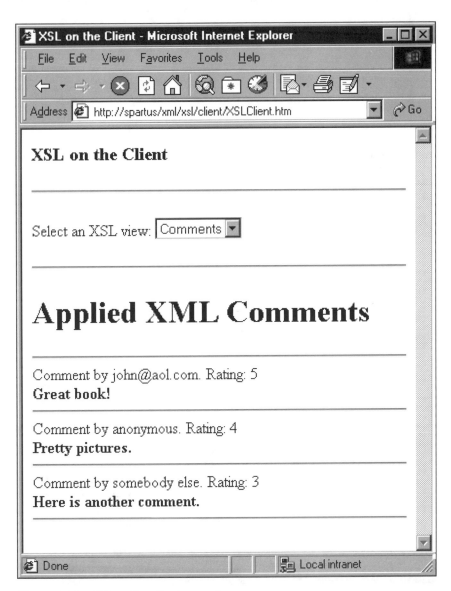

Figure 15.5 XSL on the client scenario.

```
<HTML>
<HEAD>
<TITLE>XSL on the Client</TITLE>
</HEAD>
<BODY ONLOAD="init()">

<H3>XSL on the Client</H3>
<HR>
<P>Select an XSL view:
  <SELECT NAME="XSLSelect" SIZE="1" onchange="select()">
```

```
      <OPTION VALUE="Overview">Overview</OPTION>
      <OPTION VALUE="Comments">Comments</OPTION>
   </SELECT>
</P>
<HR>
<DIV ID="displayDiv"></DIV>

<SCRIPT LANGUAGE="javascript">

   // init takes of tasks that need to be performed the first time
   // the page is loaded.
   function init() {

      // Turn off asynchronous downloading (see Chapter 7).
      bookXML.async = false;

      // Load the XML document from the server.
      // In reality, some form of query would be done to the
      // server that would dynamically produce your XML data.
      bookXML.load("book.xml");

      // Call select to initially display something to the screen.
      select();
   }

   // select is called when a user asks for a different view
   // the XML document.
   function select() {

      // index is index of the selected item (first item is 1, ....)
      var index = XSLSelect.selectedIndex;

      // selection is the string value pointed to by index. (ex: ⏎
      // Overview)
      var selection = XSLSelect.options(index).text;

      // Append 'XSL' to the end of the selection string.
      // This step is needed because of our naming convention
      // of the dataislands: (ex: 'Overview' becomes 'OverviewXSL').
      xslString = selection + "XSL";

      // Use the eval(..) function to convert the string into
      // actual code. The string 'OverviewXSL' becomes
      // the DOM Document node OverviewXSL as referred to by
      // the ID attribute on the data island.
      var stylesheet = eval(xslString);

      // Here is the key step where we apply the stylesheet.
      var result = bookXML.transformNode(stylesheet.documentElement);

      // Now we show the result by using a HTML DIV element.
```

```
        displayDiv.innerHTML = result;
    }

</SCRIPT>

<XML ID="bookXML"></XML>
<XML ID="OverviewXSL" SRC="overview.xsl"></XML>
<XML ID="CommentsXSL" SRC="comments.xsl"></XML>

</BODY>
</HTML>
```

This is the XML document that provides the necessary data:

```
<book orderid="A2344" salesrank="1">
  <name>Applied XML</name>
  <authors>
    <author>Alex Ceponkus</author>
    <author>Faraz Hoodbhoy</author>
  </authors>
  <distributor>A&amp;F Books</distributor>
  <description>Description goes here</description>
  <comments num="3">
    <comment author="john@aol.com" rating="5">Great book!</comment>
    <comment author="anonymous" rating="4">Pretty pictures.</comment>
    <comment author="somebody else" rating="3">Here is another ⏎
comment.</comment>
  </comments>
  <info>
    <pagenum>400</pagenum>
    <isbn>1234567890</isbn>
    <publisher>John Wiley &amp; Sons Inc.</publisher>
    <illustrated>yes</illustrated>
    <date year="1999" month="06" />
    <edition>1st</edition>
  </info>
</book>
```

Here are the stylesheets. The first one is comments.xsl.

```
<xsl:stylesheet xmlns:xsl="http://www.w3.org/TR/WD-xsl" ⏎
xmlns:fo="http://www.w3.org/TR/WD-xsl/FO" >
  <xsl:template match="/">
    <H1><xsl:value-of select="/book/name"/> Comments</H1> <HR/>
    <xsl:for-each select="//comments/comment">
      Comment by <xsl:value-of select="@author"/>.
      Rating: <xsl:value-of select="@rating"/> <BR/>
      <SPAN STYLE="font-weight:bold"><xsl:value-of select="."/></SPAN>
      <HR/>
```

```
      </xsl:for-each>
    </xsl:template>
  </xsl:stylesheet>
```

And here is overview.xsl.

```
<xsl:stylesheet xmlns:xsl="http://www.w3.org/TR/WD-xsl" ⏎
xmlns:fo="http://www.w3.org/TR/WD-xsl/FO" >
  <xsl:template match="/">
    <H1><xsl:value-of select="//name"/></H1>
    <P><xsl:value-of select="/book/info/edition" /> edition<BR/>
    pages: <xsl:value-of select="/book/info/pagenum" /> <BR/>
    isbn: <xsl:value-of select="/book/info/isbn" /> <BR/>
    illustrated: <xsl:value-of select="/book/info/illustrated" />
    </P>
    <HR/>
    <P><H3>Description</H3>
    <xsl:value-of select="/book/description" />
    </P>
  </xsl:template>
</xsl:stylesheet>
```

XSL on the Server

XSL can also be used on the server by using a mechanism similar to the one we just presented. In fact, if you are going to do your Web site authoring in XML and XSL, then you need to use XSL on the server. Not all browsers currently support XML and XSL, so you need to produce HTML on the server and send that up to the client. For the scenario in this section, we design an ASP script that sends up HTML or XML with XSL, depending on your browser. A quick glance at Figures 15.6 and 15.7 yields a similar page—the Netscape page is in HTML whereas the Internet Explorer 5 page is XML with XSL. Both browsers accessed the same script, but different pages were returned. By checking the source from the browsers, you can see that one is HTML while the other is XML. You can perform this check by running the scenario from the CD-ROM.

The first obstacle for our upcoming scenario is determining which browser made the request. Common Gateway Interface (CGI) defines a number of environment variables that provide information about a request from the browser. One of these is HTTP_USER_AGENT, which identifies the browser, version, and operating system. This variable is accessed easily from a variety of languages:

- From ASP: browser = Request.ServerVariables("HTTP_USER_AGENT")
- From Perl: $browser = "$ENV{'HTTP_USER_AGENT'}";
- From C: char *browser = getenv("HTTP_USER_AGENT");

In each of the above cases, the string browser contains a copy of the HTTP_USER_AGENT environment variable. Here are eight examples of this variable that are commonly seen:

```
Mozilla/4.0 (compatible; MSIE 5.0; Windows NT)
Mozilla/4.5 [en] (WinNT; I)
Mozilla/4.0 (compatible; MSIE 4.01; Windows 98)
Mozilla/4.04 [en] (Win95; I ;Nav)
Mozilla/4.5 (Macintosh; I; PPC)
Lotus-Notes/4.5 ( Solaris 2.0 Unix )
Mozilla/4.0 (compatible; MSIE 4.5; Mac_PowerPC)
Mozilla/4.08 [en] (X11; I; Linux 2.0.36 i686)
```

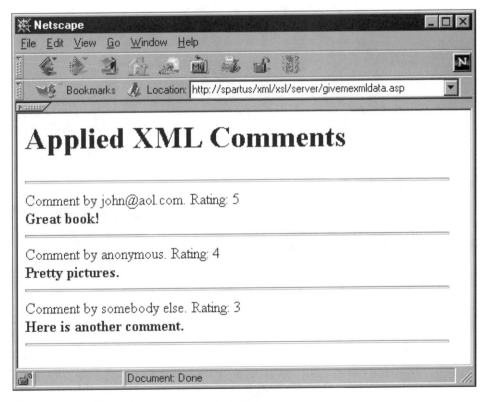

Figure 15.6 XSL on the server scenario in Netscape.

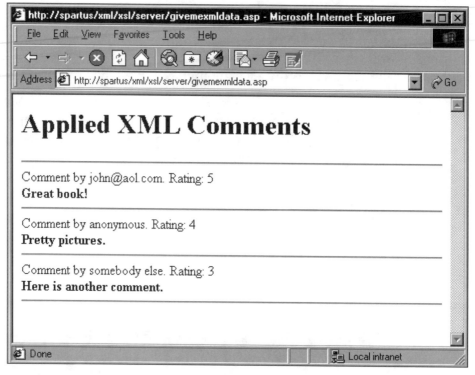

Figure 15.7 XSL on the server scenario in Internet Explorer 5.

As you can see, the format changes quite a bit from browser to browser. For the purposes of this scenario, our job is simplified because we only need to check if the browser was Internet Explorer 5 (the only browser that currently supports XSL). The code that we soon take a look at checks the string after the first semicolon and compares it to Microsoft Internet Explorer 5.

Next, we need to look at how to associate an XSL stylesheet with an XML document. This task is accomplished by adding the following line to the top of your XML document:

```
<?xml-stylesheet type="text/xsl" href="comments.xsl" ?>
```

In our case, comments.xsl is the name of the stylesheet applied in our example. The XML and XSL used in this scenario are the same as the XSL on the client scenario, so we save some trees by not printing them again. Make sure that you put the xml-stylesheet processing instruction after <?xml version="1.0" ?>; otherwise, you run into trouble with the parser.

In many cases, we can assume that the XML document is already associated with a stylesheet. This assumption breaks down when you are tapping into an XML stream or when your XML can take on different views. In these situations, we need to dynamically associate a stylesheet with the XML document. As we show in the code for this scenario, the DOM can be used to create a ProcessingInstruction (PI) node that you can then insert into the tree. Inserting the PI node before the root element (documentElement) ensures that you don't insert it before the <?xml version="1.0" ?> processing instruction. To make things even more complicated, depending on the application, your XML might already have a stylesheet associated with it. In that case, you need to do some extra checking and delete the old association.

Now it's time to look at some code. The comments explain the details.

```
<%
' Global variable declarations
' Modify XMLDOC and XSLDOC here to use this script for your
' own application.
Dim XMLDOC, XSLDOC
XMLDOC = "http://spartus/xml/xsl/server/book.xml"
XSLDOC = "http://spartus/xml/xsl/server/comments.xsl"
%>


<%
' isXSLBrowser() returns either True or False indicating whether
' the request was made from a browser that supports XSL.
Function isXSLBrowser()

  Dim browser, details

    ' browser is a text string that holds of the name of the browser.
    ' HTTP_USER_AGENT is one of the environment variables that is
    ' set when using CGI.
    browser = Request.ServerVariables("HTTP_USER_AGENT")

    ' The Split function is used to parse the browser string.
    details = Split(browser,"; ",3,1)

    ' Do some bounds checking of the resulting array.
    if ( UBound(details) < 1 ) then
      isXSLBrowser = False
      exit function
    end if

    ' Currently, only IE5 and IE5 Beta 2 support XSL.
    if ((details(1) = "MSIE 5.0b2") OR (details(1) = "MSIE 5.0")) then
      isXSLBrowser = True
      exit function
    end if
```

```
      isXSLBrowser = False

End Function
%>

<%
' ASP SCRIPT EXECUTION STARTS HERE.

Response.Expires = 0

' Load the XML document that is to be displayed. This load
' could also come dynamically from a database server.
Set xml = Server.CreateObject("microsoft.xmldom")
xml.async = false
xml.load( XMLDOC )

' Check if the browser supports XSL by using the isXSLBrowser
' function.
if (isXSLBrowser = True) then

   ' Browser supports XSL.
   Response.ContentType = "text/xml"

   ' At this point, we need to associate an XSL stylesheet
   ' with the xml. In other words, we need to add
   ' <?xml-stylesheet type="text/xsl" href="comments.xsl" ?>
   ' to the top of the XML document.

   ' The next lines create a ProcessingInstruction node and
   ' insert it into the appropriate location in the tree.
   set pi = xml.createProcessingInstruction("xml-stylesheet", _
   "type='text/xsl' href='" + XSLDOC + "'")

   set tempnode = xml.insertBefore (pi, xml.documentElement)

   ' Use xml.xml to convert the tree to text format and
   ' send it to the browser.
%>

<%=xml.xml%>

<%
else
   Dim html

   ' Browser does NOT support XSL.
   Response.ContentType = "text/html"

   ' We already have the XML document, so now let's get the XSL
```

```
' stylesheet for this document.
Set xsl = Server.CreateObject("microsoft.xmldom")
xsl.async = false
xsl.load( XSLDOC )

' Use the transformNode(...) function to apply the XSL stylesheet
' to the XML document and put the text string result into the
' variable html.
html = xml.transformNode(xsl.documentElement)

' Send the resulting HTML to the browser.
%>

<%=html%>

<%
end if
%>
```

Using XSL To Manage Web Sites

The two scenarios just presented can be combined to provide some more sophisticated XSL usage. On the server, we can offer multiple XSL stylesheets and decide which one to apply, depending on the browser that made the request. In the DHTML world, Netscape and Microsoft both shipped different versions of DHTML, causing serious headaches for site designers. Many Web sites have multiple versions to cater to both these browsers.. A side usage for XSL can be to manage the different sites by making a stylesheet for each one. Text-only and no-frames sites can also be managed as separate stylesheets. When a browser makes a request, the server checks which browser made the request, applies the appropriate stylesheet to the common XML data and returns HTML. In fact, for browsers such as Internet Explorer 5, the raw XML and XSL can be sent to where the client does the processing. Figure 15.8 shows the data flow of the XSL-based, Web site version management system.

Summary

This chapter demonstrates how XSL can be used within your Web site. Creative use of XSL technology can provide great benefits to your system, as we've seen in Chapter 11. XSL allows your site to be managed in a clean and controlled manner. Higher-level design tools, when they become available (hint, hint to all you entrepreneurs looking for a busi-

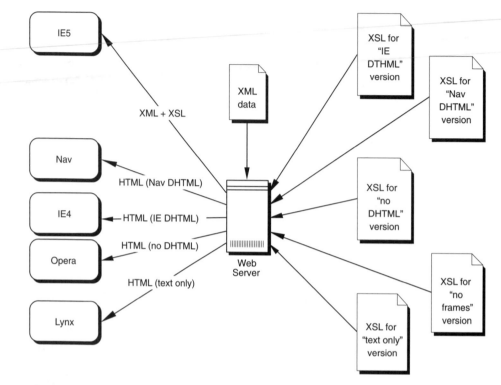

Figure 15.8 Using XSL to manage sites.

ness opportunity) will allow XSL stylesheets to be created in a visual manner, simplifying the process. The technology itself can then be easily deployed as shown throughout this chapter.

Throughout this part of the book, we've focused on providing the details you need to use XSL as a conduit to achieving all the benefits of XML. Although we've focused mostly on Microsoft Internet Explorer as a vehicle for using XSL, it is important that we reiterate that this is NOT because we are endorsing Microsoft above Netscape or any other browser. However, Internet Explorer 5 is currently the only browser that supports XSL. As we've shown, it is possible to use XSL with clients that are not XSL or XML aware (albeit with diminishing returns).

For XML to succeed, a standards-based, easy-to-use transformation language such as XSL is necessary because it makes life easier for programmers, developers, and Web site maintainers. Its inherent flexibility and simplicity is the key to its success—that and the fact that no one company owns it.

Finally, we believe that now is the time to get on the XSL bandwagon. For tool vendors, it means a nearly virgin marketplace where exponential growth can be realized over the next few years. For developers it provides a simple, powerful, and scalable toolset for working with XML data. In our minds, XSL will be the most visible technology that will facilitate XML's adoption in organizations. XSL provides you with the means to realize the benefits that XML promises.

DOM Definitions for Script

This appendix contains the W3C DOM Level 1 Core object definitions for ECMA Script. These definitions are useful for programmers familiar with the DOM methods and properties described in Chapter 5, because only the parameter and return types are shown. These definitions are included with the W3C DOM Level 1 specification, which can be found in its entirety on the CD-ROM or at http://www.w3.org/TR/REC-DOM-Level-1/. Also, the entire W3C copyright notice can be found on the CD-ROM.

Copyright Notice

Status of DOM Level 1 Specification

This document has been reviewed by W3C members and other interested parties and has been endorsed by the Director as a W3C Recommendation. It is a stable document and may be used as reference material or cited as a normative reference from another document. W3C's role in making the Recommendation is to draw attention to the specification and to promote its widespread deployment. This enhances the functionality and interoperability of the Web.

The authors of this document are the DOM Working Group members. Different chapters may have different editors.

Comments on this document should be sent to the public mailing list www-dom@w3.org.

A list of current W3C Recommendations and other technical documents can be found at http://www.w3.org/TR.

Script Language Binding

Following are descriptions of script language binding for the DOM objects.

Object Node

The Node object has the following properties:

- nodeName. This property is of type String.
- nodeValue. This property is of type String.
- nodeType. This property is of type Short.
- parentNode. This property is of type Node.
- childNodes. This property is of type NodeList.
- firstChild. This property is of type Node.
- lastChild. This property is of type Node.
- previousSibling. This property is of type Node.
- nextSibling. This property is of type Node.

- attributes. This property is of type NamedNodeMap.
- ownerDocument. This property is of type Document.

The Node object has the following methods:

- insertBefore(newChild, refChild). This method returns a Node. The newChild parameter is of type Node. The refChild parameter is of type Node.
- replaceChild(newChild, oldChild). This method returns a Node. The newChild parameter is of type Node. The oldChild parameter is of type Node.
- removeChild(oldChild). This method returns a Node. The oldChild parameter is of type Node.
- appendChild(newChild). This method returns a Node. The newChild parameter is of type Node.
- hasChildNodes().This method returns a boolean.
- cloneNode(deep). This method returns a Node. The deep parameter is of type boolean.

Object Document

Document has all the properties and methods of Node as well as the properties and methods defined below.

The Document object has the following properties:

- doctype. This property is of type DocumentType.
- implementation. This property is of type DOMImplementation.
- documentElement. This property is of type Element.

The Document object has the following methods:

- createElement(tagName). This method returns a Element. The tagName parameter is of type DOMString.
- createDocumentFragment().This method returns a DocumentFragment.

- createTextNode(data). This method returns a Text. The data parameter is of type DOMString.
- createComment(data). This method returns a Comment. The data parameter is of type DOMString.
- createCDATASection(data). This method returns a CDATASection. The data parameter is of type DOMString.
- createProcessingInstruction(target, data). This method returns a ProcessingInstruction. The target parameter is of type DOMString. The data parameter is of type DOMString.
- createAttribute(name). This method returns an Attr. The name parameter is of type DOMString.
- createEntityReference(name). This method returns an EntityReference. The name parameter is of type DOMString.
- getElementsByTagName(tagname). This method returns a NodeList. The tagname parameter is of type DOMString.

Object Element

Element has all the properties and methods of Node as well as the properties and methods defined below.

The Element object has the following property:

- tagName. This property is of type String.

The Element object has the following methods:

- getAttribute(name). This method returns a DOMString. The name parameter is of type DOMString.
- setAttribute(name, value). This method returns a void. The name parameter is of type DOMString. The value parameter is of type DOMString.
- removeAttribute(name). This method returns a void. The name parameter is of type DOMString.
- getAttributeNode(name). This method returns an Attr. The name parameter is of type DOMString.
- setAttributeNode(newAttr). This method returns an Attr. The newAttr parameter is of type Attr.

- removeAttributeNode(oldAttr). This method returns an Attr. The oldAttr parameter is of type Attr.
- getElementsByTagName(name). This method returns a NodeList. The name parameter is of type DOMString.
- normalize().This method returns a void.

Object Attr

Attr has all the properties and methods of Node as well as the properties and methods defined below.

The Attr object has the following properties:

- name. This property is of type String.
- specified. This property is of type boolean.
- value. This property is of type String.

Object NodeList

The NodeList object has the following property:

- length. This property is of type int.

The NodeList object has the following method:

- item(index). This method returns a Node. The index parameter is of type unsigned long.

Object NamedNodeMap

The NamedNodeMap object has the following property:

- length. This property is of type int.

The NamedNodeMap object has the following methods:

- getNamedItem(name). This method returns a Node. The name parameter is of type DOMString.
- setNamedItem(arg). This method returns a Node. The arg parameter is of type Node.

- removeNamedItem(name). This method returns a Node. The name parameter is of type DOMString.
- item(index). This method returns a Node. The index parameter is of type unsigned long.

Object CharacterData

CharacterData has all the properties and methods of Node as well as the properties and methods defined below.

The CharacterData object has the following properties:

- data. This property is of type String.
- length. This property is of type int.

The CharacterData object has the following methods:

- substringData(offset, count). This method returns a DOMString. The offset parameter is of type unsigned long. The count parameter is of type unsigned long.
- appendData(arg). This method returns a void. The arg parameter is of type DOMString.
- insertData(offset, arg). This method returns a void. The offset parameter is of type unsigned long. The arg parameter is of type DOMString.
- deleteData(offset, count). This method returns a void. The offset parameter is of type unsigned long. The count parameter is of type unsigned long.
- replaceData(offset, count, arg). This method returns a void. The offset parameter is of type unsigned long. The count parameter is of type unsigned long. The arg parameter is of type DOMString.

Object Text

Text has all the properties and methods of CharacterData as well as the properties and methods defined below.

The Text object has the following method:

- splitText(offset). This method returns a Text. The offset parameter is of type unsigned long.

Object Comment

Comment has all the properties and methods of CharacterData. It does not have any methods or properties of its own.

Object CDATASection

CDATASection has all the properties and methods of Text. It does not have any methods or properties of its own.

Object DocumentType

DocumentType has all the properties and methods of Node as well as the properties and methods defined below.

The DocumentType object has the following properties:

- name. This property is of type String.
- entities. This property is of type NamedNodeMap.
- notations. This property is of type NamedNodeMap.

Object Notation

Notation has all the properties and methods of Node as well as the properties and methods defined below.

The Notation object has the following properties:

- publicId. This property is of type String.
- systemId. This property is of type String.

Object Entity

Entity has all the properties and methods of Node as well as the properties and methods defined below.

The Entity object has the following properties:

- publicId. This property is of type String.
- systemId. This property is of type String.
- notationName. This property is of type String.

Object EntityReference

EntityReference has all the properties and methods of Node. It does not have any methods or properties of its own.

Object ProcessingInstruction

ProcessingInstruction has all the properties and methods of Node as well as the properties and methods defined below.

The ProcessingInstruction object has the following properties:

- target. This property is of type String.
- data. This property is of type String.

Object DOMException

DOMException does not have any methods or properties of its own.

Object ExceptionCode

ExceptionCode does not have any methods or properties of its own.

Object DOMImplementation

The DOMImplementation object has the following method:

- hasFeature(feature, version). This method returns a boolean. The feature parameter is of type DOMString. The version parameter is of type DOMString.

Object DocumentFragment

DocumentFragment has all the properties and methods of Node. It does not have any methods or properties of its own.

DOM Definitions for Java

T his appendix contains the W3C DOM Level 1 Core object definitions for Java. These definitions are useful for programmers familiar with the DOM methods and properties described in Chapter 5, because only the parameter and return types are shown. The Java definitions are different than the script definitions in Appendix A, which have been the focus of this book. Script is different in that is uses only methods and not properties. Properties in languages such as Java are static; therefore, the DOM implementation could not perform calculations or lookup when returning values to the programmer. As a solution, all the properties are changed into methods by appending a *get* or *put* to the property. Included on the CD-ROM are the interfaces in Java files for those who would like to implement the DOM themselves. The definitions in this appendix are included with the W3C DOM Level 1 specification, which can be found in its entirety on the CD-ROM or at http://www.w3.org/TR/REC-DOM-Level-1/. Also, the entire W3C copyright notice can be found on the CD-ROM.

Copyright Notice

The original document can be located at: http://www.w3.org/TR/REC-DOM-Level-1/java-language-binding.html.

Status of DOM Level 1 Specification

This document has been reviewed by W3C members and other interested parties and has been endorsed by the director as a W3C Recommendation. It is a stable document and may be used as reference material or cited as a normative reference from another document. W3C's role in making the Recommendation is to draw attention to the specification and to promote its widespread deployment. This enhances the functionality and interoperability of the Web.

The authors of this document are the DOM Working Group members. Different chapters may have different editors.

Comments on this document should be sent to the public mailing list www-dom@w3.org.

A list of current W3C Recommendations and other technical documents can be found at http://www.w3.org/TR.

Java Language Binding

```
public abstract class DOMException extends RuntimeException {
  public DOMException(short code, String message) {
    super(message);
    this.code = code;
  }

  public short   code;
  // ExceptionCode
  public static final short    INDEX_SIZE_ERR      = 1;
  public static final short    DOMSTRING_SIZE_ERR   = 2;
  public static final short    HIERARCHY_REQUEST_ERR = 3;
  public static final short    WRONG_DOCUMENT_ERR   = 4;
  public static final short    INVALID_CHARACTER_ERR = 5;
  public static final short    NO_DATA_ALLOWED_ERR  = 6;
  public static final short    NO_MODIFICATION_ALLOWED_ERR = 7;
  public static final short    NOT_FOUND_ERR       = 8;
  public static final short    NOT_SUPPORTED_ERR   = 9;
```

```
        public static final short              INUSE_ATTRIBUTE_ERR   = 10;


}

// ExceptionCode
public static final short              INDEX_SIZE_ERR        = 1;
public static final short              DOMSTRING_SIZE_ERR    = 2;
public static final short              HIERARCHY_REQUEST_ERR = 3;
public static final short              WRONG_DOCUMENT_ERR    = 4;
public static final short              INVALID_CHARACTER_ERR = 5;
public static final short              NO_DATA_ALLOWED_ERR   = 6;
public static final short              NO_MODIFICATION_ALLOWED_ERR = 7;
public static final short              NOT_FOUND_ERR         = 8;
public static final short              NOT_SUPPORTED_ERR     = 9;
public static final short              INUSE_ATTRIBUTE_ERR   = 10;


}

public interface DOMImplementation {
  public boolean                hasFeature(String feature,
                                    String version);

}

public interface DocumentFragment extends Node {
}

public interface Document extends Node {
  public DocumentType      getDoctype();
  public DOMImplementation  getImplementation();
  public Element           getDocumentElement();
  public Element           createElement(String tagName)
                                    throws DOMException;
  public DocumentFragment   createDocumentFragment();
  public Text              createTextNode(String data);
  public Comment           createComment(String data);
  public CDATASection      createCDATASection(String data)
                                        throws DOMException;
  public ProcessingInstruction createProcessingInstruction(String target,
                                                    String data)
                                                    throws
DOMException;
  public Attr              createAttribute(String name)
                                        throws DOMException;
  public EntityReference    createEntityReference(String name)
                                            throws DOMException;
  public NodeList          getElementsByTagName(String tagname);
}

public interface Node {
  // NodeType
  public static final short              ELEMENT_NODE          = 1;
  public static final short              ATTRIBUTE_NODE        = 2;
```

```
    public static final short        TEXT_NODE           = 3;
    public static final short        CDATA_SECTION_NODE  = 4;
    public static final short        ENTITY_REFERENCE_NODE = 5;
    public static final short        ENTITY_NODE         = 6;
    public static final short        PROCESSING_INSTRUCTION_NODE = 7;
    public static final short        COMMENT_NODE        = 8;
    public static final short        DOCUMENT_NODE       = 9;
    public static final short        DOCUMENT_TYPE_NODE  = 10;
    public static final short        DOCUMENT_FRAGMENT_NODE = 11;
    public static final short        NOTATION_NODE       = 12;

    public String            getNodeName();
    public String            getNodeValue()
                                            throws DOMException;
    public void              setNodeValue(String nodeValue)
                                            throws DOMException;
    public short             getNodeType();
    public Node              getParentNode();
    public NodeList          getChildNodes();
    public Node              getFirstChild();
    public Node              getLastChild();
    public Node              getPreviousSibling();
    public Node              getNextSibling();
    public NamedNodeMap      getAttributes();
    public Document          getOwnerDocument();
    public Node              insertBefore(Node newChild,
                                    Node refChild)
                                    throws DOMException;
    public Node              replaceChild(Node newChild,
                                    Node oldChild)
                                    throws DOMException;
    public Node              removeChild(Node oldChild)
                                        throws DOMException;
    public Node              appendChild(Node newChild)
                                        throws DOMException;
    public boolean           hasChildNodes();
    public Node              cloneNode(boolean deep);
}

public interface NodeList {
    public Node              item(int index);
    public int               getLength();
}

public interface NamedNodeMap {
    public Node              getNamedItem(String name);
    public Node              setNamedItem(Node arg)
                                        throws DOMException;
    public Node              removeNamedItem(String name)
                                            throws DOMException;
    public Node              item(int index);
    public int               getLength();
```

```
    }

    public interface CharacterData extends Node {
      public String           getData()
                                    throws DOMException;
      public void             setData(String data)
                                    throws DOMException;
      public int              getLength();
      public String           substringData(int offset,
                                            int count)
                                            throws DOMException;
      public void             appendData(String arg)
                                        throws DOMException;
      public void             insertData(int offset,
                                        String arg)
                                        throws DOMException;
      public void             deleteData(int offset,
                                        int count)
                                        throws DOMException;
      public void             replaceData(int offset,
                                         int count,
                                         String arg)
                                         throws DOMException;
    }

    public interface Attr extends Node {
      public String           getName();
      public boolean          getSpecified();
      public String           getValue();
      public void             setValue(String value);
    }

    public interface Element extends Node {
      public String           getTagName();
      public String           getAttribute(String name);
      public void             setAttribute(String name,
                                          String value)
                                          throws DOMException;
      public void             removeAttribute(String name)
                                            throws DOMException;
      public Attr             getAttributeNode(String name);
      public Attr             setAttributeNode(Attr newAttr)
                                            throws DOMException;
      public Attr             removeAttributeNode(Attr oldAttr)
                                               throws DOMException;
      public NodeList         getElementsByTagName(String name);
      public void             normalize();
    }

    public interface Text extends CharacterData {
      public Text             splitText(int offset)
                                      throws DOMException;
```

```
}

public interface Comment extends CharacterData {
}

public interface CDATASection extends Text {
}

public interface DocumentType extends Node {
  public String              getName();
  public NamedNodeMap        getEntities();
  public NamedNodeMap        getNotations();
}

public interface Notation extends Node {
  public String              getPublicId();
  public String              getSystemId();
}

public interface Entity extends Node {
  public String              getPublicId();
  public String              getSystemId();
  public String              getNotationName();
}

public interface EntityReference extends Node {
}

public interface ProcessingInstruction extends Node {
  public String              getTarget();
  public String              getData();
  public void                setData(String data)
                                     throws DOMException;
}
```

DOM IDL Definitions

T his appendix contains the W3C DOM Level 1 Core IDL definitions. These definitions are useful for programmers who work with C/C++ and are already familiar with the material covered in Chapter 5. These definitions are included with the W3C DOM Level 1 specification, which can be found in its entirety on the CD-ROM or at http://www .w3.org/TR/REC-DOM-Level-1/. Also, the entire W3C copyright notice can be found on the CD-ROM.

Copyright Notice

The original document can be located at: http://www.w3.org/TR/ REC-DOM-Level-1/idl-definitions.html.

Copyright © 1995–1999 World Wide Web Consortium <http://www.w3 .org>, (Massachusetts Institute of Technology <http://www.lcs.mit .edu>, Institut National de Recherche en Informatique et en Automa- tique <http://www.inria.fr>, Keio University <http://www.keio.ac .jp>). All Rights Reserved. <http://www.w3.org/Consortium/Legal/>.

Status of DOM Level 1 Specification

This document has been reviewed by W3C members and other interested parties and has been endorsed by the director as a W3C Recommendation. It is a stable document and may be used as reference material or cited as a normative reference from another document. W3C's role in making the Recommendation is to draw attention to the specification and to promote its widespread deployment. This enhances the functionality and interoperability of the Web.

The authors of this document are the DOM Working Group members. Different chapters may have different editors.

Comments on this document should be sent to the public mailing list www-dom@w3.org.

A list of current W3C Recommendations and other technical documents can be found at http://www.w3.org/TR.

DOM IDL Definitions

```
exception DOMException {
  unsigned short   code;
};

// ExceptionCode
const unsigned short    INDEX_SIZE_ERR     = 1;
const unsigned short    DOMSTRING_SIZE_ERR = 2;
const unsigned short    HIERARCHY_REQUEST_ERR = 3;
const unsigned short    WRONG_DOCUMENT_ERR = 4;
const unsigned short    INVALID_CHARACTER_ERR = 5;
const unsigned short    NO_DATA_ALLOWED_ERR = 6;
const unsigned short    NO_MODIFICATION_ALLOWED_ERR = 7;
const unsigned short    NOT_FOUND_ERR      = 8;
const unsigned short    NOT_SUPPORTED_ERR  = 9;
const unsigned short    INUSE_ATTRIBUTE_ERR = 10;

// ExceptionCode
const unsigned short    INDEX_SIZE_ERR     = 1;
const unsigned short    DOMSTRING_SIZE_ERR = 2;
const unsigned short    HIERARCHY_REQUEST_ERR = 3;
const unsigned short    WRONG_DOCUMENT_ERR = 4;
const unsigned short    INVALID_CHARACTER_ERR = 5;
const unsigned short    NO_DATA_ALLOWED_ERR = 6;
const unsigned short    NO_MODIFICATION_ALLOWED_ERR = 7;
```

```
const unsigned short       NOT_FOUND_ERR       = 8;
const unsigned short       NOT_SUPPORTED_ERR   = 9;
const unsigned short       INUSE_ATTRIBUTE_ERR = 10;

interface DOMImplementation {
  boolean                       hasFeature(in DOMString feature,
                                           in DOMString version);
};

interface DocumentFragment : Node {
};

interface Document : Node {
  readonly attribute  DocumentType         doctype;
  readonly attribute  DOMImplementation    implementation;
  readonly attribute  Element              documentElement;
  Element                       createElement(in DOMString tagName)
                                           raises(DOMException);
  DocumentFragment              createDocumentFragment();
  Text                          createTextNode(in DOMString data);
  Comment                       createComment(in DOMString data);
  CDATASection                  createCDATASection(in DOMString data)
                                           raises(DOMException);
  ProcessingInstruction createProcessingInstruction(in DOMString target,
                                            in DOMString data)
                                           raises(DOMException);
  Attr                          createAttribute(in DOMString name)
                                           raises(DOMException);
  EntityReference               createEntityReference(in DOMString name)
                                           raises(DOMException);
  NodeList                      getElementsByTagName(in DOMString tagname);
};

interface Node {
  // NodeType
  const unsigned short       ELEMENT_NODE        = 1;
  const unsigned short       ATTRIBUTE_NODE      = 2;
  const unsigned short       TEXT_NODE           = 3;
  const unsigned short       CDATA_SECTION_NODE = 4;
  const unsigned short       ENTITY_REFERENCE_NODE = 5;
  const unsigned short       ENTITY_NODE         = 6;
  const unsigned short       PROCESSING_INSTRUCTION_NODE = 7;
  const unsigned short       COMMENT_NODE        = 8;
  const unsigned short       DOCUMENT_NODE       = 9;
  const unsigned short       DOCUMENT_TYPE_NODE = 10;
  const unsigned short       DOCUMENT_FRAGMENT_NODE = 11;
  const unsigned short       NOTATION_NODE       = 12;

  readonly attribute  DOMString             nodeName;
            attribute  DOMString             nodeValue;
                                // raises(DOMException) on setting
```

```
                                            // raises(DOMException) on retrieval
  readonly attribute  unsigned short        nodeType;
  readonly attribute  Node                  parentNode;
  readonly attribute  NodeList              childNodes;
  readonly attribute  Node                  firstChild;
  readonly attribute  Node                  lastChild;
  readonly attribute  Node                  previousSibling;
  readonly attribute  Node                  nextSibling;
  readonly attribute  NamedNodeMap          attributes;
  readonly attribute  Document              ownerDocument;
  Node                insertBefore(in Node newChild,
                                   in Node refChild)
                                   raises(DOMException);
  Node                replaceChild(in Node newChild,
                                   in Node oldChild)
                                   raises(DOMException);
  Node                removeChild(in Node oldChild)
                                   raises(DOMException);
  Node                appendChild(in Node newChild)
                                   raises(DOMException);
  boolean             hasChildNodes();
  Node                cloneNode(in boolean deep);
};

interface NodeList {
  Node                item(in unsigned long index);
  readonly attribute  unsigned long         length;
};

interface NamedNodeMap {
  Node                getNamedItem(in DOMString name);
  Node                setNamedItem(in Node arg)
                                   raises(DOMException);
  Node                removeNamedItem(in DOMString name)
                                   raises(DOMException);
  Node                item(in unsigned long index);
  readonly attribute  unsigned long         length;
};

interface CharacterData : Node {
          attribute  DOMString              data;
                                // raises(DOMException) on setting
                                // raises(DOMException) on retrieval
  readonly attribute  unsigned long         length;
  DOMString           substringData(in unsigned long offset,
                                    in unsigned long count)
                                    raises(DOMException);
  void                appendData(in DOMString arg)
                                   raises(DOMException);
  void                insertData(in unsigned long offset,
                                 in DOMString arg)
```

```
                                               raises(DOMException);
  void                       deleteData(in unsigned long offset,
                                         in unsigned long count)
                                         raises(DOMException);
  void                       replaceData(in unsigned long offset,
                                          in unsigned long count,
                                          in DOMString arg)
                                          raises(DOMException);
};

interface Attr : Node {
  readonly attribute  DOMString           name;
  readonly attribute  boolean             specified;
          attribute  DOMString           value;
};

interface Element : Node {
  readonly attribute  DOMString           tagName;
  DOMString                  getAttribute(in DOMString name);
  void                       setAttribute(in DOMString name,
                                           in DOMString value)
                                           raises(DOMException);
  void                       removeAttribute(in DOMString name)
                                              raises(DOMException);
  Attr                       getAttributeNode(in DOMString name);
  Attr                       setAttributeNode(in Attr newAttr)
                                              raises(DOMException);
  Attr                       removeAttributeNode(in Attr oldAttr)
                                                 raises(DOMException);
  NodeList                   getElementsByTagName(in DOMString name);
  void                       normalize();
};

interface Text : CharacterData {
  Text                       splitText(in unsigned long offset)
                                       raises(DOMException);
};

interface Comment : CharacterData {
};

interface CDATASection : Text {
};

interface DocumentType : Node {
  readonly attribute  DOMString           name;
  readonly attribute  NamedNodeMap        entities;
  readonly attribute  NamedNodeMap        notations;
};
```

```
interface Notation : Node {
  readonly attribute  DOMString              publicId;
  readonly attribute  DOMString              systemId;
};

interface Entity : Node {
  readonly attribute  DOMString              publicId;
  readonly attribute  DOMString              systemId;
  readonly attribute  DOMString              notationName;
};

interface EntityReference : Node {
};

interface ProcessingInstruction : Node {
  readonly attribute  DOMString              target;
           attribute  DOMString              data;
                                             // raises(DOMException) on setting
};
```

Glossary

API (Application Programmer Interface) — An interface that programmers can use when using an object without needing to understand the underlying implementation of that object.

ASP (Active Server Pages) — Server-side scripting for IIS and PWS.

Attribute — Small descriptive bits of information used for further describing elements.

Casting — Converting an object into another, but retaining its contents when possible.

CDF (Channel Definition Format) — An application of XML that enables push technology on the Web. For example, Internet Explorer uses CDF to provide Active Channels.

CGI (Common Gateway Interface) — A standard for communication between the server and the client.

COM (Component Object Model) — Microsoft's component software model. See www.microsoft.com/com.

CORBA (Common Object Request Broker Architecture) — See www.omg.com.

CSS (Cascading Style Sheets) — A stylesheet mechanism that was introduced for HTML page design and is now being used for XML page design. See www.w3.org/Style/CSS/.

DCD (Document Content Description) — A proposed replacement for DTD. See www.w3.org/TR/NOTE-dcd.

DCOM (Distributed Component Object Model) — Microsoft's technology for creating standard components that will work in a distributed environment. See www.microsoft.com/dcom.

DHTML (Dynamic HTML) — DHTML technology exposes an HTML page through an object model that can be manipulated from script.

DOM (Document Object Model) — The object model for XML. See Chapter 4 and www.w3.org/DOM/.

DSSSL (Document Style and Semantics Specification Language) — The analog to XSL in the SGML world.

DTD (Document Type Definition) — See www.w3.org/XML/.

ECMA Script — A cross between JScript and JavaScript that utilizes server-side extensions from Borland.

Element — The most basic unit of information in XML documents. Elements hold information as well as defining structure by virtue of their position in a document.

HTML (Hypertext Markup Language) — See www.w3.org/MarkUp/.

ID — Unique identifiers of an element expressed as an attribute value. Similar to Primary keys on database fields. See www.w3.org/XML/.

IDL (Interface Definition Language) — Language to describe methods and properties that are available through a given object. See www.w3.org/XML/.

IDREF — Pointer to an ID. See www.w3.org/XML/.

IIS — Internet Information Server for Windows NT.

Java — Object-oriented language that provides an standard environment for program execution on various computing platforms. See http://java.sun.com.

Meta-Tag — An HTML tag that is used to contain certain information about the document that is not displayed but is exposed to search engines. It is intended to provide a way of categorizing HTML documents.

Namespaces — A solution to naming clashes in XML constructs. See www.w3 .org/TR/REC-xml-names/.

NMTOKEN — String type attributes that do not allow any white space in their values. See www.w3.org/XML/.

NOTATION — A type of attribute that is used to specify an external helper program that should be used for reading/processing the contents of an element. Used when an element contains nontextual (perhaps binary) data. See www.w3.org/XML/.

Persisting — Convert from object form to text form. Also known as "saving to the disk."

PWS — Personal Web Server for Windows 95/98.

RDF (Resource Description Framework) — A layer that sits on top of XML and defines semantics to organize data. See www.w3.org/TR/REC-rdf-syntax/.

Recursive — A routine that employs recursion.

Recursion — The ability of a routine or subroutine to call itself. Useful for performing repetitive processes.

SAX — Simple API for XML. See www.megginson.com/SAX/index.html.

Schema — Similar in functionality to a DTD but expressed in XML syntax. See www.w3.org/XML/.

SGML (Standard Generalized Markup Language) — An ISO standard for defining a format for describing information in text documents. HTML and XML are subsets of SGML.

URI (Uniform Resource Identifier) — The generic set of all names/addresses that are short strings that refer to resources. See www.w3.org/Addressing/URL/URI_Overview.html.

URL (Uniform Resource Locator) — The set of URI schemes that have explicit instructions on how to access the resource on the Internet.

URN (Uniform Resource Name) — An URI that has an institutional commitment to persistence, availability, and so on. See www.w3.org/Addressing/URL/URI_URN.html.

W3C (World Wide Web Consortium) — Consortium of companies that oversees the development and deployment of Web standards. See www.w3.org/.

XML (Extensible Markup Language) — A data transport language that is similar to HTML in construct, but allows user-definable tag sets. See www.w3.org/XML/.

XML-DATA — A proposed replacement for DTD. See www.w3.org/TR/1998/NOTE-XML-data/.

XPointer (XML Pointer Language) — Constructs that allow linking between XML documents. See www.w3.org/TR/WD-xptr.

XSL (XML Stylesheet Language) — Stylesheet language that provides a presentation view for XML data. See www.w3.org/Style/XSL/.

References

Related W3C Specifications

- Extensible Markup Language (XML). www.textuality.com/sgml-erb/WD-xml.html
- Document Object Model Level 1 (DOM). www.w3.org/TR/WD-DOM/
- XML Stylesheet Language (XSL). www.w3.org/TR/WD-xsl

Java XML Parsers

- Datachannel XML parser. http://xdev.datachannel.com
- IBM Alphaworks XML parser. alphaworks.ibm.com/tech/xm14j
- Sun XML Parser. http://developer.java.sun.com/developer/earlyAccess/xml/index.html

Other XML Resources

- Microsoft's XML support. http://msdn.microsoft.com/xml/
- IBM's XML support. www.ibm.com/xml/
- xml-dev. A list for W3C XML Developers. www.lists.ic.ac.uk/hypermail/xml-dev/
- XML.COM. A Web site that tracks events in the XML community. www.xml.com

What's on the CD-ROM

The companion CD-ROM contains all the examples and scenarios found in this book. We have also included tools that will be useful for your XML projects.

- **Microsoft Internet Explorer 5.** Microsoft Internet Explorer 5 provides support for XML on several levels. First, the Microsoft XML parser (MSXML) is an integral component of Internet Explorer 5. Since MSXML is a COM object it can be used from various languages (for example, Visual C++, Visual Basic and Visual J++). Second, the XML Stylesheet language (XSL) is supported. Also, Internet Explorer 5 allows XML files to be viewed directly by the user through a default stylesheet.

- **XML Spy.** XML Spy is a Windows-based editor for XML files. XML Spy is a useful tool when working with XML files to alleviate tag clutter.

- **Link to Netscape's Gecko.** This product is currently being developed through the Mozilla open source initiative and offers a preview of the future of Netscape's Navigator.

We've also included two parsers to give you the opportunity to experiment with Java-based XML parsers:

- **IBM XML Parser for Java**
- **DataChannel XJParser**

There's also a link to Sun's XML Parser for Java.

We've also included links to the following specifications from the W3C:

- Extensible Markup Language 1.0 (XML)
- Document Object Model, Levels 1 and 2 (DOM)
- XML Stylesheet Language (XSL)
- Namespace in XML
- Mathematical Markup Language (MathML)
- Synchronized Multimedia Integration Language (SMIL)

Using the CD-ROM

This CD-ROM was implemented with XML and XSL technology to speed the design time. Using the XML2HTML, an HTML version was auto-generated to support non-XSL-capable browsers. The two versions of the site are identical, making all software and information accessible from either site.

To access the information and software on this CD-ROM, follow these simple steps:

1. Start Windows on your computer.
2. Place the CD-ROM into your CD-ROM drive.
3. From Program Manager, Select File, Run, and type **X:\index.html** (where **X** is the correct letter of your CD-ROM drive).
4. Those that have XSL-capable Web browsers, such as Microsoft's Internet Explorer 5, can use the XML version of the index at **X:\index.xml**.

User Assistance and Information

The software accompanying this book is being provided as is without warranty or support of any kind. Should you require basic installation assistance, or if your media is defective, please call our product support number at (212) 850-6194 weekdays between 9 A.M. and 4 P.M. Eastern Standard Time. Or we can be reached via e-mail at: **wprtusw@wiley.com**.

To place additional orders or to request information about other Wiley products, please call (800) 879-4539.

CUSTOMER NOTE: IF THIS BOOK IS ACCOMPANIED BY SOFTWARE, PLEASE READ THE FOLLOWING BEFORE OPENING THE PACKAGE.

This software contains files to help you utilize the models described in the accompanying book. By opening the package, you are agreeing to be bound by the following agreement:

This software product is protected by copyright and all rights are reserved by the author, John Wiley & Sons, Inc., or their licensors. You are licensed to use this software as described in the software and the accompanying book. Copying the software for any other purpose may be a violation of the U.S. Copyright Law.

This software product is sold as is without warranty of any kind, either express or implied, including but not limited to the implied warranty of merchantability and fitness for a particular purpose. Neither Wiley nor its dealers or distributors assumes any liability for any alleged or actual damages arising from the use of or the inability to use this software. (Some states do not allow the exclusion of implied warranties, so the exclusion may not apply to you.)

IBM® XML for Java ™ © Copyright IBM Corp. 1991, 1999. All Rights Reserved.

Using XML Parser for Java™ means you accept the license terms contained on the CD-ROM.

Licensed materials: IBM® XML Parser for Java ™.

IBM is a trademark of IBM Corp. in the U.S. and/or other countries. Java and all Java-based trademarks and logos are trademarks or registered trademarks of Sun Microsystems, Inc. in the U.S. and other countries.

XML Spy © 1999 Icon Informations-Systeme GmBH

XJParser has been co-developed by Microsoft and DataChannel

Microsoft ® Internet Explorer 5 © Copyright Microsoft Corporation. 1997-99. All rights reserved.

Microsoft is a registered trademark of Microsoft Corporation in the United States and other countries.

This program was reproduced by John Wiley & Sons, Inc. under a special agreement with Microsoft Corporation. For this reason, John Wiley & Sons, Inc. is responsible for the product warranty and for support. If your CD-ROM is defective, please return it to John Wiley & Sons, Inc., which will arrange for its replacement. PLEASE DO NOT RETURN IT TO MICROSOFT CORPORATION. Any product support will be provided, if at all, by John Wiley & Sons, Inc. PLEASE DO NOT CONTACT MICROSOFT CORPORATION FOR PRODUCT SUPPORT. End users of this Microsoft program shall not be considered "registered owners" of a Microsoft product and therefore shall not be eligible for upgrades, promotions or other benefits available to "registered owners" of Microsoft products.

To use this CD-ROM, your system must meet the following requirements:

Platform/Processor/Operating System: To install all of the third-party software included on this CD-ROM, users will need a 100% IBM-compatible machine with a Pentium processor or better, running Windows 95/98/NT. The DataChannel XJ Parser and IBM XML Parser for Java are also available for Unix platforms.

RAM: 16MB RAM recommended.

Hard Drive Space: Refer to the specific third-party software readme files for hard drive space requirements.

Peripherals: CD-ROM drive; Internet browser installed to navigate the CD-ROM.